Female Personalities in th
and Sunna

GW01494022

This book investigates the manner in which the Qur'an and *sunna* depict female personalities in their narrative literature.

Providing a comprehensive study of all the female personalities mentioned in the Qur'an, the book is selective in the personalities of the *sunna*, examining the three prominent women of *ahl al-bayt*; Khadīja, Fāṭima, and Zaynab. Analysing the major sources of Imāmī Shī'ī Islam, including the exegetical compilations of the eminent Shī'ī religious authorities of the classical and modern periods, as well as the authoritative books of Shī'ī traditions, this book finds that the varieties of female personalities are portrayed as human beings on different stages of the spiritual spectrum. They display feminine qualities, which are often viewed positively and are sometimes commendable traits for men, at least as far as the spiritual domain is concerned. The theory, particularly regarding women's humanity, is then tested against the depiction of womanhood in the *ḥadīth* literature, with special emphasis on *Nahj al-Balāgha*.

Contributing a fresh perspective on classical materials, this book will be of interest to students and scholars of Islamic Studies, Women's Studies and Shī'ī Studies.

Dr Rawand Osman received a BA in History from the American University of Beirut, and an MA and PhD in Islamic Studies from the University of Edinburgh and the University of Birmingham, respectively. Her research interests include textual analysis of Islamic scripture with emphasis on Shi'i sources, women's history, and feminist theology and hermeneutics.

Routledge Persian and Shi'i Studies Series
Series editor: Andrew J. Newman
University of Edinburgh

Editorial Board: Dr Robert Gleave, Department of Religious Studies, University of Bristol; Dr Marco Salati, Faculty of Oriental Studies, University of Venice, Italy; Dr Kazuo Morimoto, Institute of Oriental Culture, University of Tokyo, Japan; Dr Maria Szuppe, CNRS, Paris, France; Mr Rasul Ja'fariyan, Library of Iranian and Islamic History, Qum, Iran; Dr Mansur Sefatgul, Department of History, University of Tehran, Iran.

1 **The Twelver Shi'a as a Muslim Minority in India**
Pulpit of Tears
Toby M. Howarth

2 **Female Personalities in the Qur'an and Sunna**
Examining the Major Sources of Imami Shi'i Islam
Rawand Osman

Female Personalities in the Qur'an and Sunna

Examining the Major Sources of Imami Shi'i Islam

Rawand Osman

Routledge
Taylor & Francis Group
LONDON AND NEW YORK

First published 2015 by Routledge

2 Park Square, Milton Park, Abingdon, Oxfordshire OX14 4RN
52 Vanderbilt Avenue, New York, NY 10017

Routledge is an imprint of the Taylor & Francis Group, an informa business

First issued in paperback 2019

British Library Cataloguing in Publication Data
A catalogue record for this book is available from the British Library

Library of Congress Cataloging in Publication Data
Osman, Rawand.
Female personalities in the Qur'an and Sunna : examining the major sources of Imami Shi'i Islam / Rawand Osman.
pages cm. -- (Routledge persian and shi'i studies)
Includes bibliographical references and index.
1. Women in the Qur'an. 2. Women in the Hadith. 3. Women--Religious aspects--Islam. 4. Shi'ah--Doctrines--History. I. Title.
BP173.4.O76 2014
297.1'2283054--dc 3
2013049200

ISBN: 978-0-415-83938-9 (hbk)
ISBN: 978-0-367-86805-5 (pbk)

Typeset in Times New Roman
by Taylor & Francis Books

To Imam al-Zaman

Contents

Acknowledgments ix

Introduction **1**

1 Woman in creation **15**

Introduction 15

The creation of the human duality in the Qur'an and exegesis 16

The creation of Eve in the ḥadīth *22*

The universal meanings of the story of creation 29

Reassessing the symbols: Adam and al-arḥām *32*

Conclusions 36

2 Female personalities in the Qur'an **43**

Introduction 43

The wives of the prophets Noah and Lot 45

The wives of the prophet Abraham 47

Zulaykha 51

The women in the life of the prophet Moses 60

The Queen of Sheba 66

Mary 72

The wives of the prophet Muhammad and other Muslim women 83

*The women of paradise (*al-Ḥūr al-ʿĪn*) 89*

Summary and conclusions 91

3 Female personalities in the *sunna* **105**

Introduction 105

Khadīja al-Kubrā *107*

Fāṭima al-Zahrā' *108*

Zaynab al-ʿAqīla *128*

Summary and conclusions 136

4 Female personality in the *ḥadīth* **152**
Introduction 152
Woman as evil and necessary 155
Women as deficient in faith, fortune, and intellect 157
Women as flowers to be secluded 165
Woman's jihād *towards her husband 167*
Women-friendly traditions in the "Four Books" 171
Conclusions 172

Conclusion **181**

Bibliography 185
Index 197

Acknowledgments

I am indebted to Professor David Thomas, Professor of Christianity and Islam at the University of Birmingham, for supervising this research when it was a PhD thesis, for helping me organise my thoughts and refine my presentation, and for his overall graciousness. I am grateful to Dr Andrew Newman, Dr Salwa el-Awa, Dr Haifaa Jawad and Professor Haleh Afshar for their advice and guidance. Professor Farah Musa, Dean at the Islamic University in Beirut, provided me with easy access to much of the primary sources, and was always willing to offer his valuable opinion.

I owe an ocean of debt to my parents, Wafa' and Zoulfikar, "who are the origin of any good that is in me, and who cannot be fairly recompensed". My siblings, Zanoubia, Nardine, and Muhammad Hussein have also been generous friends. Last but not least, I am obliged to my husband Pejman Khosrokiani, and to his sister Faranak, without whose love and support this book might have never seen the light of day.

All mistakes and shortcomings of this work are entirely my own responsibility.

Introduction

This book is a study of the representation of female personalities in the Qur'an and *sunna* (Prophet's example) in the authoritative sources of Imāmī Shī'ī Islam. It is comprehensive in discussing all the female persons mentioned in the Qur'an, and it is selective in the personalities of the *sunna* to the three major women of *ahl al-bayt* (the Prophet's holy family). Therefore, what is meant by "female personalities" are those women who are presented as examples in the Qur'an, and role-models in the *sunna* of the Prophet, but not all women who accompanied him. The theme of *jihād al-nafs* (the soul's efforts/struggle) will be traced throughout, and it will be observed that under this title, two specific features of "spiritual motherhood" and earthly/political *jihād* (pursuit/struggle) will be recurrent themes in the depiction of those personalities. The study is based on the sources of Shī'ī Islam, because the second part of it deals with the women of *ahl al-bayt* in particular. Fāṭima's position, in the Shī'ī tradition, as an impeccable female and spiritual mother will confirm some observations made about the representation of Mary in the Qur'an. Moreover, the women of *ahl al-bayt*, particularly the ones discussed here, represent from the Shī'ī point of view, exemplary women's *jihād* in its various forms. Both the spiritual *jihād* epitomised by Mary and Fāṭima, and the political *jihād* of Pharaoh's wife, expounded upon by the female personalities of *ahl al-bayt*, are twin elements of the representation of female personalities in the Islamic Shī'ī tradition. The use of only the major sources which are considered authentic by the tradition itself, serves to provide an intellectual discussion of the personalities, rather than delve into the images of these women in the more popular literature, which is outside the scope of this study.

The field of "Islamic feminism" comprises scholars who might not necessarily define themselves as such, and it includes religious Muslims, secular Muslims, and non-Muslims.[1] The term "Islamic feminism" is sometimes seen as problematic,[2] although the incompatibility of feminism with an old religion, philosophy, or even language is by no means restricted to Islam. Some Muslim women propagating women's rights in Islam are not comfortable with the term feminism,[3] conservative Muslims deem feminism, sometimes understandably, a tool of foreign aggression,[4] and some secularists find that Islam is not compatible with feminism and describe "Islamic feminism" as an oxymoron.[5] Indeed feminism in general, is a contested term. Among secular feminists are some who are utterly dismissive of the possibilities for liberation that Islam may offer, but these are often dogmatic in their definition of feminism.[6] Ziba Mir-Hosseini rightly contends that Islamic feminist interpretations have produced practical gains because they were purely Islamic.[7] Moreover, the spiritual dimension as a need for many women is not always taken into account, but Islamic feminist endeavours, on the whole, appear to be a genuine search to find more justice within the religion, thus strengthening women's bond with the source of revelation. Therefore, the Islamic feminist project is not only legitimate but necessary: "For Muslims, Islam is both a religion and a culture – a source of spiritual ideas and social norms. To be interested in Islam is, for Muslim women, to seek an engaged understanding of beliefs that affect one's entire way of life."[8]

The "quest for equality" or defining Islamic feminism as the attempt "to sever patriarchy from Islamic ideals and sacred texts"[9] is far-fetched. One remembers Amina Wadud's stance, after having exerted her efforts in rereading the Qur'an in a woman-friendly fashion, that the text can only take us so far.[10] Today, what is asked of Islam by western nations is to adhere to their understanding of human rights as unequivocal equality before the law.[11] These however neglect that Islamic law, while acknowledging the equality in worth and dignity among all human beings, is far more concerned with the principle of justice than it is with a superficial equality. *'Adl* (justice) comes immediately after *tawḥīd* (roughly translated as "monotheism") in Islamic ideals.[12]

Commenting on men's greater financial responsibilities in the Qur'an, which are often incorrectly read as male excellence, Maysam al-Faruqi accurately points out that, "it is a system in which the inequitable division of biological tasks have been straightened out".[13] However, it is also clear that in patriarchal systems in general, male authority derives from male responsibility.[14] It might well be that in the Islamic worldview, a certain degree of male responsibility/authority is considered just, and this idea is not exclusive to Muslims or to organised religions.[15] In the context of the "equal but different" argument, perhaps "equity feminism"[16] is the type that is most compatible with the Qur'anic vision of women's rights. In this regard, Qudsia Mirza has asked some very pertinent questions about Islamic feminism's emphasis on sameness rather than difference in the scriptures. She argues that the idea of sexual difference has almost become immaterial, that equality has been used as a "levelling up" of the status of women, whereas orthodox interpretations of difference are perceived as having been the cause of women's subjugation. She explains that questions regarding when and to what extent scriptural difference is acceptable have not yet been addressed, nor have the cases when more rights are given to women than to men.[17]

The question of the status of women in Islam is primarily a legal problem, but has been discussed in two main spheres, the legal and the mystical. Feminists' rereading of Islamic law and their debate with the clerics has shifted "the focus of *fiqh* away from women as sexual beings to women as social beings".[18] This caused a major change in perspective on the question of women in Islam.[19] Another feminist-informed contribution to *fiqh* has been a historical attempt at pointing out the distinction between the imagined lives of Muslim women as they are perceived by the jurists, and the reality of women's experiences.[20] It has also been explained that the discourses of the jurists are based on the ideal example of the forebears, but that the ideal itself is a construct of succeeding generations, which represents the image that modern women are supposed to live by.[21] In fact:

> the past is axial for both Islamist and feminist perspectives, in that both recognise that it is this moment that has determined the Muslim ethico-moral code that must be reconstituted in the present ... it is also from this decisive moment of genesis that all future interpretations of Islam must commence. What divides them is the contrasting vision each possesses of the substantive content of that ethically correct past, resulting in the feminist quest for an authentic genealogy of women's legal and cultural rights in Islam.[22]

The mystical approach to understand the spiritual status of women in Islam tends to rely on the Sufi paradigm, and is valuable in offering the spiritual perspective which provides an image of equality between men and women in Islam, where the feminine is valued and seen as complementary to the masculine, and even exceeds the masculine in being a better manifestation of divine compassion.[23] Moreover, many women were traditionally accepted in Sufi circles as teachers and saints.[24] However, this trend is not without its problems. Sufi writings tend to equate, at least symbolically, women with the lower world, and men with the higher realm. The *nafs* (human soul) is seen as woman, because it is worldly and because it is receptive of God's creativity and light.[25] However, the Qur'an says, "O human being! Thou art labouring unto thy Lord laboriously, and thou shalt encounter Him" [84: 6], thereby portraying a highly active soul, and a receptive God in this instance. When the individual soul struggles to seek God, they describe it as "manly".[26]

Since the early 1980s, a third trend other than the legal and mystical, had been developing, and that is rereading the primary sources of Qur'an and *ḥadīth* from women's perspective, and developing new methods in order to yield new results. This approach culminated in Amina Wadud's *Qur'an and Woman*. Wadud confirms that her method is the traditional one of interpreting the Qur'an based on itself, but she extends five particular terms to her method. These are that she understands each verse in its historical-social context, in the context of similar topics in the Qur'an, similar linguistic usages in the Qur'an, in light of overriding Qur'anic principles, and within the larger Qur'anic worldview.[27] Her contention is that if the Qur'an is universal then its meanings cannot be limited to any one cultural perspective, even if it were the culture of the Prophet's community.[28] Asma Barlas furthers Wadud's analysis of the patriarchal enterprise of exegesis by focusing on the interaction between text, interpreter, and context.[29] She also argues that the Qur'an undermines the rule of the fathers, by not allowing either God or the prophets to be represented as male or as fathers. Analysing the stories of the prophets in the Qur'an, particularly Abraham and Muhammad, she finds that patriarchies historically provided the core resistance to the divine message.[30] Therefore, Barlas successfully widens the scope of information relevant to the topic. One problematic with the two scholars is a lack of any systematic analysis or comparative study of the traditional commentaries on the Qur'an.[31] That is why Shuruq Naguib criticises the construction by some modernists, including feminists, of the division between tradition as oppressor and Qur'an as liberator, and perceptively invites a Muslim feminist hermeneutic that "liberates itself from the limitations of a counter-position".[32] While she concurs with Wadud and Barlas' viewpoint that the oblivion to the unity of the Qur'an's message was the result of the "atomistic" (verse by verse, as opposed to "holistic") interpretations, she then suggests that "atomism" may be "re-evaluated in terms of a conscious choice not to subdue the text to a (masculinist) [*sic*] quest for a totalizing order of reading".[33]

It has to be mentioned, however, that Wadud's method is not very different from the traditional one in principle, although it diverges from it in its application and findings. Muḥammad Mahdī Shams al-Dīn (d.1421/2001) – late chief of the Supreme Islamic Shīʿī Council in Lebanon – has written four volumes on Islamic laws for women.[34] He explains a major problem in Islamic law, particularly as regards reading the *ḥadīth*, by discussing the oft repeated Qur'anic term of *ʿurf* (reputable custom). He says that jurists agree that *ʿurf* is an authority to be considered in the law making process; however, he himself distinguishes between two kinds of *ʿurf*, one juristic and another interpretive. On the first one, he says referral to *ʿurf* is only needed when the scripture is silent on an issue. When consulted, this *ʿurf* ought not to be limited to the customs of the prophetic era but of the jurists' era as well, as long as it accommodates the religious principles, and unless these new customs are "unislamic". On the second one, he explains that the *ʿurf* of the times when any given religious text was produced must be known in order to interpret the text adequately; otherwise the text cannot be binding. He says when the jurists mix the two kinds of *ʿurf*, so that customs of the Prophet or Imams' eras are made binding at all times, the law making process becomes deadened.[35] This idiosyncrasy ought to be kept in mind while reading texts such as *ḥadīth* especially, which are a product of a pre-modern period and vary significantly from our worldview.

Feminist-informed research on *sunna* in the English language, has been less than that on the Qur'an. Fatima Mernissi may be credited with highlighting the roles of early Muslim women in their "feminist" streak and their debate with revelation, which is an era that is of utmost importance to Muslims in general. Mernissi, however, focuses on the person of the Prophet rather than the text. She assumes the temporality of particular verses without her argument being grounded in the Qur'an or *ḥadīth*, thus she fails to solve the dichotomy between the egalitarian verses and the hierarchical ones.[36] Another study which has found relevance in the female personalities of yore is Barbara Stowasser's *Women in the Qur'an, Traditions, and Interpretation*, which is a systematic study of women in Muslim sacred history.[37] Stowasser emphasises the historicity of changing interpretations, and explains the link between "religious ideas" and "social reality".[38] In treating her subject matter of women in Islam, she does not settle the argument but presents different sides of it for discussion.[39]

While the title and chapter headings of this book might seem similar to Stowasser's, this present study differs from hers in three ways. First, only the major/authoritative religious sources will be consulted here, which is unlike Stowasser who used *tafsīr*, *ḥadīth*, and even hagiography, a factor which added significantly to her thesis regarding the historical context of meaning. This is an ahistorical study, neither the female personalities of the Qur'an and *sunna* nor the primary texts that represent them are meant to be analysed from a historical perspective. The similarities and especially the differences between the various commentaries used here will be pointed out clearly, however, this is done in order to provide the various understandings of a Qur'anic verse, in hope of reaching a normative meaning, which is different from Stowasser's aims. Second, while Stowasser does not attempt to formulate any conclusions about the personalities of the women, this book does follow the theme of *jihād al-nafs* in the women of the Qur'an and *sunna*, and further emphasises two dimensions within that broad title, which are the themes of "spiritual motherhood" and of the lesser *jihād*, or earthly and political pursuit. Third, while Stowasser divides her book into two main parts, the first being on the women in the Qur'an, and the second on the wives of the Prophet, this book places the wives of the Prophet among the women in the Qur'an, and contains a second part which is on the women of the *sunna* as a separate category which focuses on *ahl al-bayt*. Again, the aim of this division is to attempt to reach a normative understanding by finding whether the depiction of women in the *sunna* of the Prophet's family conforms with the Qur'anic picture, and how it might differ from it.

Furthermore, the women of *ahl al-bayt* have been largely neglected in western research, despite their tremendous influence. Fāṭima, the Prophet's daughter and mother of the Shī'ī Imams, is a prominent figure in early Islam, and yet she has not been given much attention. Therefore, there is a need to go to the sources that discuss Fāṭima thoroughly. Fāṭima's daughter, Zaynab, is similarly a very potent revolutionary symbol for Shī'i women today. Most pertinently, the women of *ahl al-bayt*, it will be argued, do confirm the conclusions made on the female personalities in the Qur'an. Fāṭima's example as spiritual mother confirms some of the observations made about Mary, and therefore helps create a hypothesis about the tradition's potential views on spirituality and motherhood. Moreover, as it will be argued that religio-political *jihād* in the Qur'an is set by the example of Pharaoh's wife, but this is confined to a single statement. It is the religio-political *jihād* of the women of *ahl al-bayt* that helps explain the Qur'anic symbol of Pharaoh's wife as an example to all believers.

It may be argued that 'Ā'isha, one of the Prophet's wives, is also an important role model from the women of the Islamic era. However, she faced the fourth Caliph 'Alī in battle, in the first Muslim civil war, and is said to have been standing on shaky ground due to her vague demands for reform.[40] More importantly, despite 'Ā'isha's outspokenness and standing in society, her political experience has arguably been cause for further restrictions on women's public roles.[41] Sunni sources, in which 'Ā'isha is revered, exhibit a mixed response about her political example. There are discussions about her motivations, whether they were honourable or dishonourable, whether she felt regret or just remorse about her defeat, and most pertinently, there is a warning against women's involvement in politics.[42] Denise Spellberg argues that Khadīja and her daughter Fāṭima's limited biographies made it easier to project on them an image of motherhood and purity which would fit Islamic ideals much more than that of the controversial 'Ā'isha. Spellperg finds that the Sunni comparison of Fāṭima and 'Ā'isha with the Qur'anic Mary assumes very different symbolic interpretations for each, but that they link Fāṭima to Khadīja more than with Mary, in order to identify her as daughter rather than mother, and that is for political reasons.[43]

The Shī'ī view of the women of *ahl al-bayt* encourages the legitimisation of women's public action. Moreover, only the Prophet's wife Khadīja and then her daughter Fāṭima bore the Prophet's descendants, which makes the projection of the image of motherhood unto them come easily. Therefore, the book will show that both themes emphasised in the female personalities of the Qur'an, motherhood and *jihād*, are traced and expanded in the examples of the women of *ahl al-bayt*. In this way, this book attempts to shape a unified theory regarding the possibilities that the Shī'ī tradition holds with respect to its views on women and their responsibilities.

One of the premises of this book is based on what Sachiko Murata proposes regarding the law projecting an image of a masculine God, while the mystics project a more feminine God.[44] If that is so, then continuing to look at Islamic law for the study of the status of women in Islam will inevitably be limited because the very subject matter favours and depends on a patriarchal worldview. The conclusions on male supremacy then would hardly be surprising. Therefore, perhaps the narrative literature on the examples of living women in the Qur'an and *sunna* would yield different results. Then, if there is spiritual equality between men and women in Islam, as it is widely held, then should there not be female prophets and Imams? This point is often brought up by the male establishment as a sign of male excellence but has not yet been answered. Moreover, if the female personalities in the Qur'an and *sunna* are portrayed as human and as examples for men and women, what is the scope of their equality, and is there nothing about them that is particularly feminine? If there is, then this might shed light on the issue of difference, but from outside the legal framework. Furthermore, assuming there is a female particularity, does this belittle women or may it be said that those feminine characteristics are suggested as recommendable traits to be found in men as well? Finally, in view of Shams al-Dīn's assertion that an understanding of the Qur'anic depiction of these women as strong and fully human would change the premises of *fiqh* (the human interpretation of Islamic law, as opposed to *sharī'a*, the divine law itself), the findings of this work on the female personalities will need to be applied to the *ḥadīth* literature, which is a major contributor and decisive factor in making *fiqh*. Crucial for the wider relevance of the topic of this book, a study of the Qur'anic vision about its female personalities may enlighten juristic arguments by revealing dimensions and particularities not previously taken into account.[45]

Even though the research, as the title indicates, is informed and supported by the major sources of Shī'ī Islam, the theory that is proposed here has not been articulated within the tradition, and the findings are new for two reasons. First, as was mentioned above, the traditional approach is usually atomistic (verse by verse), whereas the approach here is thematic because it asks one question out of the whole body of scripture: how are female personalities presented in authoritative Islamic texts? Or, put differently, what do the female personalities contribute to the Qur'an and *sunna* narratives? While the thematic approach might not be traditional, it is not foreign to the tradition either. Some traditional religious scholars have encouraged the thematic approach based on the saying of Imam 'Alī, "This is the Qur'an, so make it speak (*dhālika al-Qur'ānu fa-stanṭiqūh*)".[46] Therefore, modern questions and concerns must be asked, and the Qur'an given an opportunity to answer. This brings us to the second issue about why the theory proposed in this book has not been formulated as such by the Shī'ī tradition, and that is because in this case the traditional texts, and the questions posed on them are read here with a mind that is aware of feminist theology in general, and Islamic feminist discourse in particular. Considering that some elements of women's subjugation are repeated across cultures, an otherwise uninformed mind might miss the opportunity to identify and assess patterns of male dominance when they exist within the Islamic tradition. Similarly, the mind of a male theologian might not emphasise or connect seemingly unrelated themes relating to women's experience. Therefore, this book tries to make as much use as possible of the Islamic feminist or feminist-informed discussions on any given topic. Yet, the substance is ultimately based on the "authorities" of Shī'ī Islam, whether they are exegetes or compilers of *ḥadīth*, because these are considered the very sources of Islamic knowledge.

It has to be mentioned that there is a lot of puritanical language within this book. This is perhaps inevitable when the main theme is about *jihād al-nafs*. This does not mean to portray such an attitude on the Islamic religion as a whole, because material rights, including monetary and sexual rights for men and women, are amply discussed in Islamic texts. Yet, the very nature of the subject matter at hand is theological. Mary's obedience for instance, is meant to be towards God's will not towards any man. In another example, it will be seen that Zulaykha's soul evolved from a purely lustful one to a loving one, which is not to be understood as a condemnation of human nature as such, but a celebration of the human soul that realises its higher potential. One hopes that this nuance could be kept in mind throughout.

The research relies on four main hermeneutical principles, which belong to traditional Islamic methodology anyway. First, the Qur'an interprets itself, and since the Qur'an is in Arabic, this will include some semantic analysis. Second, the *sunna* (Prophetic example) is the context of the Qur'an. Third, *ḥadīth* (reported words of the Prophet or Imam) explains the Qur'an. Fourth, suspect *ḥadīths* are applied to the Qur'an and *sunna* for verification.

In reading the Qur'an, the approach adopted here is comparative, analytical, and semantic. It is a systematic study based on five major exegetical compilations. Those are chosen because they represent various time periods, as well as different exegetical methods. Moreover, their authors have come to be viewed as authorities of Shīʿī scholarship and exegesis. First, is the exegesis of ʿAlī Ibn Ibrāhīm al-Qummī (d. after 307/919), one of the main Shīʿī traditionists of the pre-Buyid period. His father Ibrāhīm Ibn Hāshim is said to have been acquainted with the eighth Imam ʿAlī Ibn Mūsā al-Riḍā (d.202/818), migrated from the city of Kūfa to Qum, and spread Kufan traditions in the Iranian city. ʿAlī Ibn Ibrāhīm himself was a contemporary of the eleventh Imam al-Ḥasan al-ʿAskarī (d.260/873). His *Tafsīr* is seemingly the only one of his collections that has reached us, and also one of the earliest commentaries available to us. It is supposed that his book contains some fragments of a Qur'an commentary by the fifth Imam Muḥammad al-Bāqir (d. c. 119/737). Unlike some of his contemporaries such as the exegeses of Furāt al-Kūfī and al-ʿAyyāshī, Qummī does not only list Imāmī traditions, but includes his own reasoning. His book, however, has been abridged several times. Qummī was also a teacher of the traditionist Kulaynī (see the following on *ḥadīth* books).[47] Second is the exegesis of Muḥammad Ibn al-Ḥasan al-Ṭūsī's (d. 459 or 460/1066–7), also known as "*Shaykh al-Ṭā'ifa*" for his lasting influence on the Imāmī tradition. In completing the work of his teachers, "he succeeded in endowing Imāmī law with a structure and a scope of activity practically independent of the figure of the Imām".[48] He is the compiler of two of the four authoritative books of Shīʿī traditions. His exegesis, *al-Tibyān*, is rationalist, and includes the opinions of the people of his day, in addition to some traditions and semantic analysis, with Ṭūsī giving his opinion in the end. Third, al-Faḍl Ibn al-Ḥasan al-Ṭabrisī (d. c. 565/1169–70) was a prominent jurist, although it does not seem that he left any written work of *fiqh*.[49] His exegesis *Majmaʿ al-Bayān* is primarily linguistic, even though it includes traditions and the opinions of the scholars of his day. Fourth, ʿAbd ʿAlī Ibn Jumuʿa al-ʿArūsī al-Ḥuwayzī's (d. 1112/1700) exegesis, *Nūr al-Thaqalayn*, is widely respected for attempting to include all the traditions available to the author in his day; however, this also means that he includes traditions without much regard for their degree of authenticity.[50] Yet, he indicates that his aim in including this is for research purposes,[51] and he indeed shows in his book awareness of the inconsistencies and difficulties with this genre. Finally, Muḥammad Ḥusayn Ṭabāṭabā'ī (d.1402/1981), one of the most prominent thinkers in contemporary Shī'ī Islam,[52] is the author of an exegesis that is considered by many Shī'ī scholars to be the best commentary on the Qur'an yet. *Al-Mīzān fī Tafsīr al-Qur'ān* is a twenty-volume analytical commentary. In it Ṭabāṭabā'ī debates with classical opinions as well as modern ones. He relies heavily on interpreting the Qur'an by the Qur'an, and tends to use traditions as a secondary source, and is almost indifferent to them when they seem to be irrelevant or contradictory to the Qur'anic text. His analysis often includes extensive reflections on philosophy, various fields of the social and empirical sciences, history, tradition, and even comparative religion.

After an overview of these commentaries, they will be compared with each other especially where there are apparent differences, and will be analysed in light of contemporary writings on any given topic, including feminist and feminist-informed ones. When needed, some semantic analysis will be elaborated here to stress certain elements in the Qur'anic language and message. Moreover, where the exegetes' "atomistic" interpretation might be lacking, their comments on other relevant verses will be brought into the analysis. Since *ḥadīth* explains the Qur'an, the relevant authentic ones will have to enter the discussion at times. *Sunna* as the context of the Qur'an will not always be relevant. The female personalities in the stories of the past prophets, for example, will not be grounded in any biographical context. The section on the Prophet's wives in the Qur'an, however, needs some knowledge of context because the Qur'an itself refers to this.

In discussing the female personalities of the *sunna* of *ahl al-bayt*, the main reference will be the authoritative traditions. While these personalities are not discussed for their historical relevance as such, some of the history books which are generally agreed upon by Muslims as reliable will be needed to set the context and relevance of the actions and contributions of these women. The aim, however, will be to discover the depiction of these women in Shī'ī piety, as well as to read closely the women's own reported speeches.

Throughout this book, what is known as the "Four Books" of *ḥadīth* which are considered authoritative to the Shī'a will be the main references on traditions. The first is Muḥammad Ibn Ya'qūb al-Kulaynī's (d.328–9/939–41) "*al-Kāfī*".[53] His compilation is divided into a book on *uṣūl*, another on *furū'*, and a volume of miscellaneous traditions entitled *al-Rawḍa*. It is reported that he spent twenty years compiling these traditions. It seems that Kulaynī had a modest reputation during his life, but that his book was highly praised by subsequent scholars, particularly Ṭūsī, which gained it popularity.[54] The second is Qummī's son Muḥammad Ibn 'Alī Ibn Bābawayh al-Ṣadūq's (d.381/991) *Man lā yaḥḍuruhū al-faqīh*.[55] Not much is known about Ṣadūq, but that he was a pillar among Shī'ī traditionists, and he has several surviving works in that regard. The other two of the four books are by Shaykh al-Ṭā'ifa al-Ṭūsī, *al-Istibṣār* and *Tahdhīb al-aḥkām*.[56]

Therefore, this is a close analysis of the authoritative religious texts. Considering the differences between the Qur'an and *ḥadīth* in the Islamic tradition and in line with the four hermeneutical principles above, the reading of the Qur'an will be "interpretation-oriented", whereas the reading of *ḥadīth* will be "text-oriented".[57] Reading the Qur'an will rely on a comparative and analytical approach towards *tafsīr* (Qur'anic exegesis) along with some semantic analysis. Reading the *ḥadīth* will go behind the text and pose questions on context. The historical context of *ḥadīth* will not be investigated as such, but it will be shown how questions on context might alter the meanings of traditions. In dealing with both the Qur'an and *ḥadīth*, the textual context will prove valuable.

The first chapter is on Eve, and therefore more broadly, on woman in creation; with emphasis on woman and man as having derived from a single soul and hence their shared status as potential vicegerents. These two issues have been discussed already by Amina Wadud and Asma Barlas, but they did not include much of the available *tafsīr* nor *ḥadīth* on the subject. The chapter will highlight Amina Wadud's three key words in the primary verse on the subject [4: 1], and add to them the vital feminine term, *al-arḥām*. This vital feminine symbol was always dealt with extensively by traditional exegetes.

The second chapter is on the rest of the female personalities in the Qur'an, Eve's daughters as it were. The theme of *jihād al-nafs* will be traced throughout, in addition to the theme of earthly *jihād*. Verses [66: 10–12] will be the guiding group of verses here, as they emphasise women as negative as well as positive examples, thereby portraying them as simply human. Moreover, the positive examples of Mary and the wife of Pharaoh will be analysed in specific reference to Mary's capacity as spiritual mother, and Āsiyā's worldly *jihād* which followed her spiritual one. The theme of *jihād al-nafs* will also extend to the prophet Muhammad's wives, although it will be argued that the model of seclusion they share with the women of paradise is exceptional either way.

The third chapter is on the female personalities of the *sunna*. It focuses in particular on the most prominent women of *ahl al-bayt*, Khadīja, Fāṭima, and Zaynab. It will be shown that these women are portrayed as having performed the religio-political *jihād* in three different ways. The theme of "spiritual motherhood" will be revisited with Fāṭima. An analysis of these personalities will attempt to highlight the empowering roles that these women represent, in addition to some restrictions and limitations imposed on them by the Shī'ī tradition.

The fourth and final chapter is on female personality in the *ḥadīth* literature. The singular form "personality" denotes the portrayal of a monolithic female personality according to the *ḥadīth*, which is opposed to the varieties in the representation of the personalities in the Qur'an and *sunna*. Here, the hypothesis of the previous chapters regarding women's full personhood, intelligence and faith, will be tested against the *ḥadīth*. This chapter in no way finalises the feminist-informed debate with *ḥadīth* but aims to put it within the larger perspective of the themes discussed in the narrative literature.

A note on translations, technical terms, and transliterations: Arberry's translation of the Qur'an is adopted here as the standard translation, although in a few instances some modifications have been made, such as where he translates *al-insān* as "man", it has been corrected as the "human being", or where he translates *azwāj* as "wives", it has been more adequately rendered "spouses". In paraphrasing the Qur'an Pickthall's translation has been consulted, and on very few occasions when a phrase from Arberry's was substituted by Pickthall's, this has been noted in a footnote. Translations of *ḥadīth* and the sermons of the women of *ahl al-bayt* are all this author's, unless otherwise noted. Technical Arabic terms have been translated between brackets upon their first use. Biblical names have been retained in English, but Arabic proper names have been transliterated according to the system of the *Islamic Journal of Middle Eastern Studies.* Only five Arabic words were not transliterated due to their consistent use, and to their becoming a part of the English language anyway. Those are: Qur'an, Muhammad, Mecca, Medina, and Imam. The Arabic definitive particle "*al*" has been omitted for convenience, except when it is a part of a larger name. In the footnotes, a date after an ancient name indicates nothing more than the edition of the text that has been used.

Notes

1 Badran, M. (2002) "Islamic feminism: what's in a name?" *al-Ahram Weekly* [online]. 17–23 January. Available from: http://weekly.ahram.org.eg/2002/569/cu1.htm [Accessed 20.02.2014].
2 For some useful discussions, refer to: Moghadam, V.M. (2002) "Islamic feminism and its discontents: towards a resolution of the debate". *Journal of Women in Culture and Society*, 27 (4): 1135–71. Mir-Hosseini, Z. (2006) "Muslim women's quest for equality: between Islamic law and feminism". *Critical Inquiry*, 32: 629–45.
3 Badran (2002).
4 On feminism and orientalism, refer to: Ahmed, L. (1992) *Women and gender in Islam: historical roots of a modern debate.* New Haven and London: Yale University Press. Abu Lughud, L. (2002) "Do Muslim women really need saving? Anthropological reflections on cultural relativism and its others". *American Anthropologist*, 104 (3): 783–90. Mirza, Q. (2002) "Islamic feminism, possibilities and limitations". In Strawson, J. (ed.) *Law after Ground Zero.* London: Cavendish, pp. 108–12. For a reproduction of orientalist discourse, refer to: Moghissi, H. (1999) *Feminism and Islamic fundamentalism: the limits of post-modern analysis.* London: Zed Books.
5 Moghadam (2002, p. 1150).
6 Moghadam (2002, pp. 1148–56, including fn. 27).
7 Mirza (2002, p. 118). On Muslim women's gains from an Islamic feminist discourse, outside of academia, refer to: Mir-Hosseini, Z. (2000) *Islam and gender: the religious debate in contemporary Iran.* London and New York: I. B. Tauris. Doorn-Harder, P.V. (2006) *Women shaping Islam: Indonesian women reading the Qur'an.* Urbana and Chicago: University of Illinois Press.
8 Sharify-Funk, M. (2008) *Encountering the transnational: women, Islam and the politics of interpretation.* Aldershot: Ashgate, p. 23.
9 Mir-Hosseini (2006, p. 645).

10 Wadud, A. (2006) *Inside the gender Jihad: women's reform in Islam*. Oxford: Oneworld Publications, pp. 190–200.
11 For example: Mayer, A.E. (1999) *Islam and human rights: tradition and politics*. 3rd edn. Boulder: University of Pennsylvania Westview Press, pp. 83–130.
12 al-Raḍī, al-Sharīf, Muḥammad Ibn al-Ḥusayn (n.d.c) *Nahj al-balāgha*. 4 volumes. Beirut: Dār al-Ma'rifa, vol. 4, p. 108.
13 Faruqi, M.J. (2000) "Women's self-identity in the Qur'an and Islamic law". In Webb, G. (ed.) *Windows of faith: Muslim women scholar-activists in North America*. New York: Syracuse University Press, p. 81.
14 Kandiyoti, D. (1991) "Islam and patriarchy: a comparative perspective". In Keddie, N.R. and Baron, B. (eds) *Women in Middle Eastern history: shifting boundaries in sex and gender*. New Haven and London: Yale University Press, pp. 34–5.
15 Refer to the discussion on "the inevitability of patriarchy" with Steven Goldberg, in: Leacock, E. (1981) *Myths of male dominance: collected articles on women cross-culturally*. New York: Monthly Review Press, pp. 264–80.
16 The term coined by the American philosopher/scholar Christina Hoff Summers: London, S. (n.d.) "The future of feminism: an interview with Christina Hoff Summers". Available from: www.scottlondon.com/interviews/sommers.html [Accessed 20.02.2014].
17 Mirza (2002, pp. 118–19).
18 Mir-Hosseini, Z. (1996) "Stretching the limits: a feminist reading of the Shari'a in post-Khomeini Iran". In Yamani, M. (ed.) *Feminism and Islam: legal and literary perspectives*. London: Ithaca, p. 316.
19 Mir-Hosseini (1996, p. 316).
20 For example, Sonbol, A. (2001) "Rethinking women and Islam". In Haddad, Y.Y. and Esposito, J.L. (eds) *Daughters of Abraham: feminist thought in Judaism, Christianity, and Islam*. Florida: University Press of Florida, pp. 111–16, reclaims Muslim women's history and convincingly shows that the rights enjoyed by some Muslim women in the pre-modern period, especially in reference to women's labour, actually exceeded the rights given to them by the emerging patriarchal nation states.
21 Sonbol (2001, p. 117).
22 Mirza, Q. (2000) "Islamic feminism and the exemplary past". In Richardson, J. and Sandland, R. (eds) *Feminist perspectives on law and theory*. London: Cavendish, p. 191.
23 Murata, S. (1992) *The Tao of Islam: a sourcebook on gender relationships in Islamic thought*. Albany: State University of New York Press, pp. 191–3. Schimmel, A. (1997) *My soul is a woman: the feminine in Islam*. New York: Continuum, pp. 21–3. Jawad, H. (2009) "Islamic spirituality and the feminine dimension". In Howie, G. and Jobling, J. (eds) *Women and the divine: touching transcendence*. New York: Palgrave Macmillan, pp. 194–201.
24 Jawad (2009, pp. 196–9).
25 Schimmel (1997, pp. 20 and 22–3).
26 Schimmel (1997, p. 20). Murata (1992, pp. 266–9). Murata indeed observes that receptivity is also a divine attribute, but does not challenge the association of woman with the world (Murata, 1992, pp. 206–11). Moreover, she explains that there is a relativity in Sufi thought, whereby receptivity of the soul is right when it is towards God and wrong in the face of appetite, similarly, activity of the soul is blameworthy towards God (does this contradict the Qur'anic verse above?), but commendable when mastering the appetite (Murata, 1992, pp. 316–17). In the final analysis, however, the woman is always likened to the soul and the man to intellect, with a theological necessity of the former to be dominated by the latter (Murata, 1992, pp. 317–18).

27 Wadud-Muhsin, A. (1994) *Qur'an and woman*. Kuala Lumpur: Penerbit Fajar Bakti, p. 5.
28 Wadud-Muhsin (1994, p. 6).
29 Sharify-Funk (2008, p. 56). Barlas, A. (2002) *Believing women in Islam: unreading patriarchal interpretations of the Qur'an*. Austin: University of Texas Press, ch. 2 and 3.
30 Barlas (2002, ch. 4).
31 Jawad on Wadud, Jawad, H. (2003) "Muslim feminism: a case study of Amina Wadud's Qur'an and woman". *Islamic Studies*, 42 (1): 124.
32 Naguib, S. (2010) "Horizons and limitations of Muslim feminist hermeneutics: reflections on the menstruation verse". In Anderson, P.S. (ed.) *New topics in feminist philosophy of religion, feminist philosophy collection*. Dordrecht: Springer Press, p. 47.
33 Naguib (2010, pp. 45, and 47–8).
34 Shams al-Dīn, Muḥammad Mahdī (1994) *al-Sitr wa al-naẓar*. 2nd edn. Beirut: al-Mu'assasa al-Duwaliyya li al-Dirāsat wa al-Nashr. Shams al-Dīn, Muḥammad Mahdī (1995) *Ahliyyat al-mar'a li tawalli al-sulṭa*. Beirut: al-Mu'assasa al-Duwaliyya li al-Dirāsāt wa al-Nashr. Shams al-Dīn, Muḥammad Mahdī (1996a) *Ḥaqq al-'amal li al-mar'a*. Beirut: al-Mu'assasa al-Duwaliyya li al-Dirāsāt wa al-Nashr. Shams al-Dīn, Muḥammad Mahdī (1996b) *Ḥuqūq al-zawjiyya*. Beirut: al-Mu'assasa al-Duwaliyya li al-Dirāsāt wa al-Nashr.
35 Shams al-Dīn (1994, pp. 40–4). That the Islamic juristic process is dead and only its tenets have survived is also the opinion of Abou El Fadl, Kh. (2003) *Speaking in God's name: Islamic law, authority and women*. Oxford: Oneworld, p. 171.
36 Scott, R.M. (2009) "A contextual approach to women's rights in the Qur'an: readings of 4:34". *The Muslim World*, 99: 68–69. Mernissi, F. (1991) *The veil and the male elite: a feminist interpretation of women's rights in Islam*. Reading, MA: Addison-Wesley. Translated by M.J. Lakeland, ch. 7 and 8.
37 Stowasser, B. (1994) *Women in the Qur'an, traditions, and interpretation*. New York: Oxford University Press.
38 Mir, M. (1998) Book reviews. *Journal of Islamic Studies*, 9 (1): 63.
39 Mir (1998, p. 64).
40 Peterson, E.L. (1964) *'Ali and Mu'awiya in early Arabic tradition*. Copenhagen: Ejnar Munksgaard, p. 10.
41 Spellberg, D.A. (1991) "Political action and public example: 'A'isha and the battle of the camel". In Keddie, N.R. and Baron, B. (eds) *Women in Middle Eastern history: shifting boundaries in sex and gender*. New Haven and London: Yale University Press, p. 54, where the author debates with Nabia Abbott's view. Also refer to: Mernissi (1991, ch. 3 and 4).
42 Spellberg (1991, pp. 49–54). Spellberg, D.A. (1994) *Politics, gender, and the Islamic past: the legacy of 'A'isha bint Abi Bakr*. New York: Columbia University Press, ch. 4. A modern and understanding view of 'Ā'isha's role in the war finds that it was an unfortunate misunderstanding at best, and the war remains a regrettable event in any case: Ziyāda, A.A.M. (2001) *Dawr al-mar'a al-siyāsī fī 'ahd al-nabī wa al-khulafā' al-rāshidīn: wa bihā taḥqīq tārīkhī wa fiqhī wa tashrī'ī li fahm dawr al-sayyidah 'Ā'isha fī aḥdāth al-fitna*. Cairo: Dar al-Salam, pp. 328–444.
43 Spellberg (1994, pp. 156–78).
44 Murata (2002, pp. 8–10).
45 Shams al-Dīn (1994, pp. 26–40).
46 al-Sadr, Muhammad Baqir (1991) *Trends of history in the Qur'an*. London: al-Khoei Foundation, lecture 3. al-Raḍī (n.d.c, vol. 2, p. 54).
47 Amir-Moezzi, M.A. "'Alī b. Ibrāhīm al-Qummī". *Encyclopaedia of Islam, THREE*. Edited by Gudrun Kramer, Denis Matringe, John Nawas, and Everett Rowson. Brill online, 2014 [Accessed 20.02.2014].

48 Amir-Moezzi, M.A. "al-Ṭūsī". *Encyclopaedia of Islam, second edition.* Edited by P. Bearman, Th. Bianquis, C.E. Bosworth, E. van Donzel, and W.P. Heinrichs. Brill online, 2014 [Accessed 20.02.2014].

49 Kohlberg, E. "al-Ṭabrisī". *Encyclopaedia of Islam, second edition.* Edited by P. Bearman, Th. Bianquis, C.E. Bosworth, E. van Donzel, and W.P. Heinrichs. Brill online, 2014 [Accessed 20.02.2014].

50 Lawson, B.T. (1993) "Akhbari Shi'i approaches to tafsir". In Hawting, G. and Shareef, A.-K.A. (eds.) *Approaches to the Qur'an.* London: Routledge, pp. 178–80.

51 al-Ḥuwayzī, 'Abd 'Alī Ibn Jumu'a al-'Arūsī (1412h) *Nūr al-thaqalayn.* 4th edn. 5 volumes. Qum: Mu'assasat Isma'ilyan, vol. 1, p. 2.

52 For a series of books that presents Ṭabāṭabā'ī's views in English, refer to: Tabataba'i, M.H. (1980) *A Shi'ite anthology.* London: Muhammadi Trust of Great Britain & Northern Ireland. Translated by William C. Chittick, with an Introduction by Seyyed Hossein Nasr. Tabataba'i, M.H. (1987) *The Qur'an in Islam: its impact and influence on the life of Muslims.* London: Zahra. Edited and translated by Seyyed Hossein Nasr. Tabataba'i, M.H. (1979) *Shi'ite Islam.* 2nd edition. New York: State University of New York Press. Edited and translated by Seyyed Hossein Nasr.

53 al-Kulaynī, Muḥammad Ibn Ya'qūb (1388h) *al-Kāfī.* 3rd edn. 8 volumes. Dar al-Kutub al-Islamiyya.

54 Madelung, W. "al-Kulaynī (or al-Kulīnī), Abū Dja'far Muḥammad". *Encyclopaedia of Islam, second edition.* Edited by P. Bearman, Th. Bianquis, C.E. Bosworth, E. van Donzel, and W.P. Heinrichs. Brill online, 2014 [Accessed 20.02.2014].

55 al-Ṣadūq, Muḥammad Ibn 'Alī Ibn Bābawayh (1404ha) *Man lā yaḥḍuruhū al-faqī h.* 2nd edn. 4 volumes. Qum: Jami'at al-Mudarrisin.

56 al-Ṭūsī, Muḥammad Ibn Ḥasan (1390ha) *al-Istibṣār.* 4th edn. 4 volumes. Tehran: Dar al-Kutub al-Islamiyya. al-Ṭūsi, Muḥammad Ibn Ḥasan (1390hb) *Tahdhīb al-aḥkām.* 10 volumes. Tehran: Dar al-Kutub al-Islamiyya.

57 The two terms here are borrowed from: Roald, A.S. (1998) "Feminist reinterpretation of Islamic sources: Muslim feminist theology in the light of the Christian tradition of feminist thought". In Ask, K. & Tjomsland, M. (eds) *Women and Islamization: contemporary dimensions of discourse on gender relations.* Oxford: Berg, pp. 40–1.

1 Woman in creation

Introduction

The opening verse of the Qur'anic chapter of *al-Nisā'* (The Women) is key in the story of woman's creation, because it speaks of the creation of the single soul, the creation of its mate, and then the rest of humanity's existence on earth. The latter part of this opening verse stresses that human beings should show piety towards God, and towards "the wombs". Therefore, it is an adequate starting point to define certain fundamental concepts, such as the Qur'anic view of what it means to be human, as well as the origin of the first woman, because the full personhood of women may be described as the ultimate feminist quest.

Most feminists of the three monotheistic traditions find the creation of woman from man to be highly problematic and indicative of a primordial sexism, which is at the core of views that degrade woman.[1] Some of the earliest feminists wrote, "all political parties and religious denominations have alike taught that woman was made after man, of man, and for man, an inferior being, subject to man. Creeds, codes, scriptures and statutes, are all based on that idea".[2] A contemporary radical feminist theologian describes the story of Eve's creation from Adam as "not only a hoax, but a typical instance of what I call 'reversal' of biological and historical fact ... the female is *more* active (in the production of the child) – a fact which patriarchal ideology simply reversed" [emphasis in original].[3] Of course, there is also the point of view that, read with the proper understanding of language, and within the broader context, the scriptures' narration of the story of creation reveals strong egalitarian principles.[4] A contemporary Muslim feminist says:

> I regard the issue of woman's creation as more important, philosophically and theologically, than any other. If man and woman have been created equal by God, who is believed to be the ultimate arbiter of value, then they cannot become unequal, essentially, at a subsequent time. Hence their obvious inequality in the patriarchal world is in contravention of God's plan. On the other hand, if man and woman have been created unequal by God, then they cannot become equal, essentially, at a

> subsequent time. Hence any attempt to equalize them is contrary to God's intent.[5]

For these reasons, the story of Eve is unique among all the female personalities in the Qur'an. Eve herself is not a dominant character in the story, but the wider implications of her creation need to be examined in order to find some clues regarding the Qur'anic views on the sameness and difference between men and women.

The verse governing this chapter is the opening of *Sūrat al-Nisā'*. Amina Wadud has examined this verse [4: 1] and identified three key words in this regard: *min*, *nafs*, and *zawj*.[6] This chapter seeks to build on her findings by engaging with the *tafsīr* and *ḥadīth*. Eve's creation will be discussed, with emphasis on whether she was created from Adam, for Adam, and after Adam. Some Shī'ī traditions which support an egalitarian view on the manner of Eve's creation will be put forth, and it will be argued that attempts to reconcile opposing traditions sometimes result in diminishing the potential for liberation from the idea of Eve as lesser than a whole human being. Moreover, it will be shown that there is another key word in the verse, namely, *al-arḥām*, which was not identified as such by Wadud but is taken very seriously by the exegetes, and which would have serious implications for the story of creation and the concept of vicegerency. The universal themes of the story of creation will be discussed in order to gain a better understanding of *jihād al-nafs* that is central to the overall thesis.

The creation of the human duality in the Qur'an and exegesis

The opening verse of *Sūrat al-Nisā'* states:

> Humankind, fear/reverence your Lord (*yā ayyuha al-nās ittaqū rabbakum*), who created you of a single soul (*al-ladhī khalaqakum min nafsin wāḥida*), and from it created its mate (*wa khalaqa minhā zawjahā*), and from the pair of them scattered abroad many men and women (*wa baththa minhumā rijālan kathīran wa nisā'an*); and fear/reverence God by whom you demand one of another (*wa-ttaqu-llāha-lladhī tasā'aluna bihī*), and the wombs (*wa-l-arḥām*); surely God ever watches over you (*inna-llāha kāna 'alaykum raqībā*).
>
> [4: 1]

Creation in exegesis

Abū al-Naṣr Muḥammad Ibn Mas'ūd Ibn Muḥammad al-'Ayyāshī[7] (d.320/932), author of one of the earliest books of Shī'ī exegesis, relies entirely on the narration of *ḥadīth* for his interpretation. For this verse, he narrates three groups of traditions. The first is about the origin of Adam and Eve, the second is concerning their children and how they procreated, but this is not very relevant to the present discussion on the Qur'anic view of womanhood, and the third is about the meaning of the wombs in this verse. He reports two traditions that Eve was created from Adam's lower rib, and one in which the sixth Shī'ī Imam al-Bāqir criticises the rib story for theological reasons, and explains that Eve was created from the same material as Adam. Ḥuwayzī, whose exegesis is also based on *ḥadīth*, reports traditions that are in the same vein, but there are many more traditions in Ḥuwayzī's exegesis than there is in 'Ayyāshī's,[8] which is perhaps due to it being produced much later in time.

'Ayyāshī does not comment on the contradictions between stories of Eve's creation,[9] but Ḥuwayzī does mention that traditions about the rib are weak.[10]

Qummī explains that the first soul in the verse is a reference to Adam, and its mate is a reference to Eve who was created from his bottom rib, albeit without any justification for his claims. Ṭusī explains that the single soul is a reference to Adam and Eve its mate, according to the exegetes. He continues that they claim that she was created from one of Adam's ribs, whereas Imam al-Bāqir had said that she was created from the same clay as Adam. Then however, he narrates one prophetic tradition which likens woman to a crooked rib (more on this below), before repeating the tradition that claims she was created from the same clay.[11]

Ṭabāṭabā'ī is mostly concerned with the universal implications of the creation of humanity from a single soul. He begins by observing that the original single soul is meant as a reminder that humanity is one, and therefore one ought to show reverence to God and to the wombs by abiding by God's just laws:

> The verse invites people to show reverence to God in their affairs, because they are all united in their humanity, without any difference between the man and the woman, the young and the old, the weak and the strong, so that the man does not oppress the woman, and the old among them the young … this makes evident the wittiness of the verse being addressed to human beings and not to the believers in particular, as well as attaching reverence to their Lord without mentioning the name of Allah.[12]

He then explains that the word *nafs*, here translated as "soul", also denotes sameness or identity. Thus the human *nafs* is the human identity which includes the soul and the body in this material world, and the soul alone in the beyond. In this particular verse, he continues, it appears that the single soul is a reference to Adam, and its mate is his wife, and both are the parents of humanity. He refuses the interpretation of some exegetes whom, he tells us, consider that the single soul and its mate are the human male and female in general. He says that such a reading would imply that the meaning of the verse is that human beings are similar in that they all descend from a human male and female, which is the idea expressed in another Qur'anic verse, "O humankind, We have created you from a male and female, and appointed you races and tribes, that you may know one another. Surely the noblest among you in the sight of God is the most god-fearing of you" [49: 13]. Ṭabāṭabā'ī says that while the latter verse unifies human beings in their belonging to the human kind, as they all originate from a human male and a human female, the verse from *al-Nisā'* unifies human beings in their essential truth, and that "in spite of their multiplicity, men and women have been derived from a common origin".[13]

As for the creation of the mate (*zawj*), Ṭabāṭabā'ī finds it to mean that its mate, or consort, was created of its same nature. His understanding is based on the meaning of the term *zawj* in several Qur'anic verses which he quotes, among them, "And of His signs is that He created for you, of yourselves, spouses, that you might repose in them, and He has set between you love and mercy" [30: 21], and "God has appointed for you of yourselves spouses, and He has appointed for you of your spouses sons and grandsons" [16: 72].

Ṭabāṭabā'ī further states that what is mentioned in some exegeses regarding the mate originating from that soul and being created from a part of it, based on some narrations that say Eve was created from Adam's rib, has no proof in this verse.[14]

As for the phrase, "and from the pair of them (God) scattered abroad many men and women", it means that all human beings have descended from this original pair, and from no one else. In fact, this important idea inclines Ṭabāṭabā'ī to the interpretation that Adam and Eve's children married one another because there was no one else available at the time, and he maintains that this is not problematic because the law prohibiting incest would have came to pass afterwards.[15]

For the exegetes, unlike modern reformists, it is the latter part of the verse that is controversial. Concerning the phrase, "and fear/reverence God by whom you demand one of another, and the wombs; surely God ever watches over you", 'Ayyāshī reports a number of traditions on the wombs in this verse; these are, that God ordained maintaining the ties of kinship, literally "connecting the wombs/kin" (*ṣilat al-arḥām*), that God has given the wombs a grand status by placing them next to him in this verse, and even a tradition that the primordial womb is connected to God's "throne".[16]

This status of "the wombs" being next to God in the verse, and given its mystical standing in the *ḥadīth*, was difficult to explain by the exegetes. Qummī understands the second part of the verse to mean that the fear/reverence for God (*taqwa*), is what humankind will be asked about on judgement day, as they will be asked about the wombs (*al-arḥām*), whether they had maintained the bonds of kinship. Therefore, to him, *al-arḥām* is annexed not to the command to revere God (*ittaqū*), but to the questioning (*tasā'aluna*) which he understands to be the one that will occur on judgement day.[17]

Ṭusī seems particularly concerned with the latter part of the verse and how it fits into the general aim. He reads that phrase to mean, fear/reverence God by whom you demand your rights, and fear/reverence the wombs meaning fear untying the bonds of kinship. Ṭusī observes here that that the verse is admonishing people to care particularly for children, women, and the weak in society by reminding them that they are all from a single soul.[18]

Ṭabāṭabā'ī, like Ṭūsī, takes on a thorough grammatical study to understand the place of the wombs in this sentence, and he considers several readings which would give different meanings. He concludes, as does Ṭūsī, that the meaning therein is an admonishment to fear/revere God and the wombs.[19] He makes a point that his interpretation is the most appropriate both grammatically as well as theologically, and that his understanding is akin to another Qur'anic verse which admonishes fear and reverence to something other than God, "And fear/revere a day wherein you shall be returned to God" [2: 281]. He understands the second statement of reverence to the wombs as a particularity of reverence to God.[20]

Finally, he points out that God as watcher, in the final phrase, is not the same as God the protector. Rather, he is a watcher and a guide of people's actions. There is an implicit warning in the command to fear God the watcher and revere him. Thus, this verse is a fitting beginning for a chapter that will deal mostly with legal issues and inter-human relationships.[21]

One important feature of this verse is the gradualness in creation; first the one, then the two, and finally the many. The second step of duality is neglected in interpretation. The exegetes seem to focus more on the single soul and its universal implications, rather than the duality and its gender implications.

To further clarify the Qur'anic view of the human *nafs*, as it pertains to the themes of common humanity and of *jihād al-nafs*, in addition to the words that explain the derivation of the dual from the one, expounding on the three key words *nafs wāḥida*, *minhā*, and *zawjahā* would be in order. The emphasis on *al-arḥām* will come later.

Nafs wāḥida

In language, the *nafs* is the reality of someone or something (as in our saying "itself"); it is also defined as the spirit (*rūḥ*),[22] but some linguists have maintained that it is the seat of the mind, but not the spirit.[23] *Nafs* is also the generator of breath (*nafas*);[24] the term may mean blood,[25] and it might occur in reference to the body.[26]

Ṭabāṭabā'ī explains that the *nafs* is the combination of flesh and spirit together, which forms the reality of the individual in the physical world, and it is the spirit alone in the *barzakh*,[27] which is the place where the soul resides between death and resurrection.[28] He finds that some Qur'anic verses imply that the *nafs* is the whole of the individual in the physical world,[29] while others imply that it is the human being separate from his or her body.[30] Ṭabāṭabā'ī deduces that the *nafs* is essentially the spirit, just like the human is essentially his spirit. However, in the beginning of its existence the *nafs* is the body, the spirit then springs from it like a fruit from a tree, and upon death it becomes an entity separate from the body. He further contends that verses [23: 12–14] give a visible image of the creation of flesh as a starting point, followed by the introduction of the spirit which renders the human complete.[31]

The Qur'an avoids giving a sexual identity to the *nafs wāḥida*,[32] it rather uses this theme of the creation of humankind from a single soul as a sign of God's power.[33]

Crucial for the concept of *jihād al-nafs*, the human *nafs* according to the Qur'an naturally combines a pious element and a deviate element, and therefore each *nafs* has to make a choice about which of the two roads it will take, "By the soul (*nafs*), and That which shaped it and inspired it to lewdness and god-fearing! Prosperous is he who purifies it, and failed has he who seduces it" [91: 7–10]. Ultimately, the Qur'an reminds that the *nafs* is related to God, and those who forget God subsequently forget themselves, "Be not as those who forgot God, and so He caused them to forget their souls (*anfusahum*); those – they are the ungodly" [59: 19].

Minhā

The meaning of "*min*" as a particle is a major issue in Arabic grammar. There is a lengthy discussion on this, indicating that "*min*" could be used for negation, similar to the word "any", or for denoting a part of a whole, for denoting a kind, for a beginning of something in space or time, as in "from" here or "from" now. It could also be an added particle, and it could be used in the sense of "instead of".[34]

In the context of the phrase in the main verse, "and from it (*minhā*) created its mate", the meanings of "*min*" may be narrowed down to either a part of a whole (*tabʿīḍ*) or part of a kind (*jins*).

Ṭabrisī, in his linguistic exegesis, supports the view that this term could imply either meanings; that Eve was created from Adam or that she was created of his kind. He supports the latter view however, with a Qur'anic verse which has almost identical words, "God has appointed for you of yourselves spouses (*wa jaʿala lakum min anfusikum azwājan*), and He has appointed for you of your spouses sons and grandsons" [16: 72]. Telling spouses that they were created from each other means from the same kind not from a part.[35] This is the same as Ṭabāṭabāʾī's view discussed above.

In fact, several classical and renowned Shīʿī Muslim scholars supported the view that God created the mate of the same kind as the original *nafs*, based on a comparison with other Qur'anic verses.[36] These say that the Prophet is from the people, obviously meaning from their kind, "Now there has come to you a Messenger from among yourselves (*min anfusikum*)" [9: 128], and "Truly God was gracious to the believers when He raised up among them a Messenger from themselves (*min anfusihim*)" [3: 164]. In this classical debate, the opposite point of view argued that if Eve were an equally original creation, then humankind would have been created from two souls not one, which is contrary to the Qur'an. However, the answer to that was that Adam was the beginning of creation in time.[37] Moreover, they argued that since God created Adam from clay, he was equally capable of creating Eve from clay as well, and the story of her creation from his rib becomes aimless.[38]

Since the traditions on this matter are contradictory, a deconstruction of those traditions in the next section will shed more light on the debate.

Zawjahā

In language, *zawj* is the opposite of single; it is whatever has a mate, in which case, each of the two would be referred to as a *zawj*.[39] The origin of the word *zawj* means "sort"[40] and it is a term given to any two things that are related to each other whether similarly or oppositely.[41] Imam al-Ḥasan had said that "the sky is a *zawj* and the earth is a *zawj*, winter is a *zawj* and summer is a *zawj*, night is a *zawj* and day is a *zawj*".[42] As a verb, it means to join and generate.[43]

The Qur'an tells us that everything has a *zawj*, "And of everything created We two kinds; haply you will remember" [51: 49]. The theme that duality is one of the signs of divinity is told often, including in reference to the human couple, and each member of the pair is described as splendid.[44] Moreover, dualities are described as derivatives of a common origin, "God created you of dust then of a little fluid, then He made you pairs" [35: 11], and "Have not the unbelievers then beheld that the heavens and the earth were a mass all sewn up, and then We unstitched them" [21: 30]. They are also continuously related to each other, "That is because God makes the night enter into day and makes the day to enter into the night" [22: 61].

One may then observe how differently God describes himself. The original human soul is described as *nafs wāḥida*. *Wāḥida* by definition implies a second (*thāniya*), whether the second is in material existence or in the realm of the intellect.[45] This is unlike the term *aḥad* which also means "one", and is one of the names of God [112: 1]. *Aḥad* is a singular which is always alone. Other than its use in numbers, such as "*aḥad 'ashar*", it is perhaps never used on its own except in the negative sense, such as "you are not as other (*las-tunna ka-aḥadin*) women" [33: 32]. *Aḥad* in this negative sense may be used for one and many, feminine and masculine.[46] *Aḥad* in the Qur'an is a name of God because *aḥad* cannot be divided and cannot be multiplied, unlike *wāḥid*.[47] Perhaps this meaning is also the reason why the term is generally used in the negative; in one word it negates all possibilities.[48]

Therefore, the original *nafs wāḥida* needed a second existentially. The use of *zawjahā*, that is "its mate" instead of "a mate" (*zawj*), could be taken to confirm Ṭabāṭabā'ī's point, that the mate already existed intellectually before it was materialised. Indeed, the gradual mode of creation, of the one, then the mate, and finally the multiplicity is repeated in the Qur'an [42: 11], and reveals that duality is fundamental and is the source of multiplicity, for "all the other numerical relationships grow out of duality", thus God's command to Noah, "Embark therein, of each kind two, male and female".[49] After the two were created (*khalaqa*), multiplicity ensued from both (*baththa minhumā*), therefore "procreation repeats creation".[50]

To shed some more light on the human *zawj* in particular, there is one instance in the Qur'an which seems to describe the wife/spouse as *sakan* (lodging, tranquillity, security, mercy, blessing, and humility),[51] "It is He who created you out of one living soul, and made of it its spouse that he might rest in her (*wa ja'ala minhā zawjahā li-yaskuna ilayhā*)" [7: 189]. Some understood this to be a reference to Adam and Eve,[52] but others saw that this is the human couple in general.[53] Here the wife is a source of tranquillity for the husband; he trusts her or relies upon her so as to become quiet in mind.[54] It is also the case that the merciful relationship between spouses is described as mutual in another verse, "And of His signs is that He created for you, of yourselves, spouses, that you might repose in them, and He has set between you love and mercy. Surely in that are signs for a people who consider" [30: 21].

The exegetes all insist that the creation of humanity from a single soul nullifies the apparent differences among people because the essence of all humans is one. The Qur'anic repeated references to the fundamentality of duality and the interdependence of its members show that the couple, at least in theory, are non-hierarchical.[55] The man and woman are each simultaneously a *nafs* and a *zawj*.[56]

The creation of Eve in the *ḥadīth*

It was mentioned above that when exegetes explain that the single soul is Adam and its mate is Eve, they do so on the authority of previous exegetes. Those whose interpretation does not rely solely on the *ḥadīth* seem to be inclined to the explanation that woman was created from the same clay as man. The difficulty as far as a feminist interpretation is concerned, is in two allegorical traditions that utilise the story of woman's creation from man to make claims about woman's inferiority and her limited social and economic space. The following is an analysis of those traditions, and the existing attempts to reconcile them. Following traditional methodology in authenticating *ḥadīth*, traditions which counter the Qur'an, sound reasoning, or irrefutable empirical evidence may be challenged.

The Imams' denial of the rib story

In *al-Kāfī*, the standard book of traditions for the Shī'a and one of the most authoritative "four books", there are eight traditions on Eve. Five of those are on issues that have to do with her and Adam and their descent to earth.[57] The other three traditions include one on Eve's creation from Adam, one on the metaphor that likens woman to a crooked rib, and one on an allegory inspired by the story of woman's creation from man, and its socio-economic consequences.

The story of Eve's creation from Adam's rib is told in *al-Kāfī* as part of the explanation of the verse, "And it is He who created of water a mortal, and made him kindred of blood and marriage; thy Lord is All-powerful" [25: 54]. It claims that kindred by blood (*nasab*) started with Eve's creation from Adam and, and kindred by marriage (*ṣihr*) began with her marriage to him.[58]

Interestingly, it is precisely on these grounds, the alleged marriage of Adam to a part of himself, that the Imams' harshly criticised such claims. In another one of the four reliable books, *Man Lā Yaḥḍuruhū al-Faqīh*, which is equally authoritative, there is a different account on the creation of Eve.

> Someone asked Abū 'Abdallāh (the sixth Imam al-Ṣādiq) peace be upon him about the creation of Eve, and told him that "some of our people are saying that God the Exalted and Magnificent created Eve from the lowest left rib of Adam". So he (the Imam) said, "Praise be to God who is high above what they say. Is, whoever is saying that, saying that God does not have the power to create for Adam a wife from other than his rib?! And he gives way to the speaker of calumny to say that Adam was mating with a part of himself, if she were from his rib. These people have no judgement, and God is the judge between us!" Then he, peace be upon him, said, "when God the blessed and exalted created Adam from clay and ordered the angels to prostrate themselves before him, he made him rest, then he innovated for him Eve and placed her on the alveolus between his hips, so that the woman may be a follower to the man … This is the story of Eve, prayers be upon her".[59]

Another tradition following this one in the same book simply states that "God created from the clay of the original *nafs* its mate".[60] A slightly more elaborate version of the latter is found in the exegesis of 'Ayyāshī, on the authority of the fifth Imam al-Bāqir, saying that they lie about the story of the rib, and that God held a piece of clay with his right hand – and both his hands are right – and created Adam from it, and with the remainder of the clay he created Eve.[61]

These traditions agree that Eve was created from the same substance as Adam, but in the most elaborate tradition, Eve was made to follow Adam nonetheless.

In the tradition from al-Ṣādiq, only partially cited above, there is a lot about Eve's marriage. When Adam asks her about her identity, she describes herself as "God's creature". Then Adam addresses God asking, "My Lord, what is this beautiful creature that is pleasant for me to be near to and look at?" God answers, "This is my worshipper Eve. Would you like her to be with you, to be amiable to you, converse with you, and obey your command?" Adam, of course, answers affirmatively. God then instructs him to ask him to betroth them, "For she is my worshipper and might also be a wife for your pleasure". The tradition continues, "God then cast lust into Adam and he had taught him before that knowledge of all things". When Adam asks God's permission to be betrothed, God accepts and asks him to teach her his religion, and then he marries them.[62] Twice Eve is described by God as his worshipper, and after God proposes the idea of marriage he explicitly states that one of her roles would be to obey Adam's command. It is as though after the marriage, pleasant company and obedience would be Eve's roles, whereas before it she was simply "God's creature" and "God's worshipper". Then, for what seems to be her dowry (*mahr*), God tells Adam to teach his bride the religion. The story is very much like a normal Muslim marriage whereby Adam is the suitor and God is the father. In this marriage, however, nobody asks Eve for her opinion. This tradition simultaneously idolises both the father and the husband, one as a god and the other as an ultimate being. They are in charge of her affairs and she obeys them both. There are, however, two clues which may be seen to shed light on some weaknesses in this tradition, or at least parts of it.

This tradition claims that God created Eve while Adam was resting, after the angels had prostrated to him. This gives the impression that he was resting in the Garden. If that were so, it would be contrary to the Qur'an where God tells them both to enter the Garden together, "And We said, Adam, dwell thou, and thy wife, in the Garden, and eat thereof easefully where you desire" [2: 35]. If this tradition suggests that Eve was introduced into the Garden after Adam, then it threatens the ancientness of Eve. As one author puts it, "the very concept of the female existence is being compromised and, perhaps, divorced from its Qur'anic roots as being equally primordial to that of the male existence".[63]

Then, the idea that lust was cast into Adam shortly after the creation of Eve and after the angels prostrated to him may be challenged not only on feminist grounds, but also on theological ones. It seems that the tradition tries to link the creation of woman with the creation of lust, as it links Adam to the possession of knowledge. This late introduction of lust into Adam, however, may threaten a fundamental element in the story of the angels' prostration to Adam, and that is that they did so knowing full well that his *nafs* has a baser side to it; indeed, they inquired about why they should prostrate to one who will do corruption in the earth [2: 30]. This tradition however implies that they had prostrated to him when he was given the knowledge, and only after their prostration was lust cast into him. Moreover, the Qur'an itself illustrates that awareness of man and woman's sexuality was introduced simultaneously, "and when they tasted the tree, their shameful parts revealed to them, so they took to stitching upon themselves leaves of the Garden" [7: 22, 20: 121].

This tradition begins with the promise of primordial equality, that both are of the same substance. However, it goes on to describe an Eve which is not at all equal to Adam. In the latter part of this tradition, Eve is not the same *nafs* as her husband, because she lacks knowledge, while he lacked lust before her. Eve was not given knowledge by God upon her creation, the knowledge to which the angels prostrated, but some amount of knowledge was given to her by her husband as a dowry. This tradition thus implies that Adam is the higher soul and Eve the lower. This is contrary to the Qur'anic description of each individual *nafs* as inspired to lewdness and piety [91: 7–10]. Moreover, here Eve is not a *zawj* but a follower. The tradition tells how she was created for him, to provide pleasant company and obey his orders, but it does not tell us how they completed each other as a *zawj* would. This is contrary to the Qur'anic idea of partnership between woman and man where the couple are meant to find love and mercy mutually [30: 21], where they are described as raiments for one another [2: 187], and "when each of you has been privily with the other" [4: 21].

Some feminists have considered the chronology of creation, that Eve was created after Adam in time, to be problematic. To be sure, the Islamic account of creation does imply a chronology in the creation of the first pair, at least through the word *thumma* ("then" created its mate) in [39: 6]. The Qur'an itself does not explicitly reveal the identity of the first soul or its mate, however the traditions unanimously portray Adam as the first soul and Eve as the mate who was created after him in time.

One author writes, "Time is one of the foundations of power; it is the first, and space comes afterward. The relationship of beings to power is closely wed to their relationship to time. Chronology determines the degree of power".[64] She continues, "The schema of pyramidal relationships not only embodies a hierarchization of duties characterized by an increasing distance from the divine being and a multiplication of intermediaries. It also reflects the time sequence of creation".[65] However another contemporary feminist-informed scholar correctly points out that in Islam the creator does not act in the beginning of time only, therefore time itself does not reflect any distance from the divine.[66] Moreover, it may be of relevance here that Adam was created after the angels, but it was they who prostrated themselves to him.

Note that the traditions seem to imply that Eve was created shortly after Adam, when they say that she was made with both God's hands and with the remainder of the clay. This is unlike the objection voiced above regarding Eve's creation while Adam was in the Garden. That objection was not strictly about chronology but about her exclusion from the beginning of the human journey marked by the entry into the Garden.

Attempts to reconcile or analogise the traditions

Ibn Bābawayh al-Ṣadūq in an attempt to reconcile the contradictory traditions, regarding whether Eve was created from the rib of Adam, or from the same clay as Adam, suggests that perhaps Eve was created from the clay of Adam's rib.[67] Muḥammad Bāqir al-Majlisī (d.1110–11/1698–9), an expert bibliographer and an influential and authoritative religious figure in the Safavid era,[68] suggests two possibilities. One is that the narrations about Eve's origin from the rib were pronounced out of 'pious dissimulation' (*taqiyya*), and the second possibility he borrows from Ṣadūq, that she was created from the clay of his rib.[69]

It is unclear how the clay of the rib is perceived by the respected scholars to be any different from the rib itself. This compromise also does not explain why the Imams were so harsh in their criticism of the rib story. This reconciliation actually continues to say that Eve was made from Adam's rib, the clay of his rib, and it does not really answer the criticisms of the Imams who argued that God does not need the rib to make Eve, and that if Adam's wife was made from his rib, or any part of him for that matter, then that leads to the grave consequence of saying that Adam mated with a part of himself.

Muḥsin Fayḍ al-Kāshānī (d.1091/1680),[70] a philosophical mystic whose exegesis is so inclined, takes the allegorical route saying that the story that Eve was created from Adam's left rib hints that the woman's sensuality is stronger than that of the man's, while the man is more inclined to the spiritual realm. Kāshānī explains that the right represents the spiritual world and the left the physical world, and adds that the Imams' denial of the rib story is a denial of its literal meaning but not of its allegorical one.[71]

There are two problems with this however. The first is that there is no proof that women are more sensual and men more spiritual. In the story of Adam and Eve in the Qur'an, the couple's awareness of their own sexuality was introduced simultaneously after they ate of the forbidden tree.

There are some traditions that speak of the greatness of female desire and pleasure. For example, a tradition from Imam 'Alī states:

> God created desire/pleasure (*shahwa*) of ten parts, and made nine parts in women and only one part in men. Had God not put in them (the women) as much bashfulness (*ḥayā'*) as he did desire/pleasure, each man would have had nine wives (the compiler notes that last phrase must have been changed because the meaning demands that what was meant was that "each woman would have had nine husbands").[72]

That an equal amount of modesty is naturally placed in women to create a balance contradicts Kāshānī's point that women are highly sensual, at the expense of their spirituality.

Moreover, one may further consider the Qur'anic verses that admonish women to dress modestly as a measure of protection from "those in whose hearts there is sickness" [33: 59–60] in reference to the hypocrites, thereby giving a rather pessimistic view of a potentially destructive element in male sexuality. This may be taken to contradict Kāshānī's contention that men are more spiritual.

Furthermore, Kāshānī understands the tradition's claim that Eve was created from the lowest left rib, to align women with the left and men with the right. This gendered alignment is unsubstantiated considering the general use of the symbols of right and left in the Qur'an:

> Have We not appointed to him (the human) two eyes, and a tongue, and two lips, and guided him on the two highways? Yet he has not assaulted

> the obstacle; and what shall teach thee what is the obstacle? The freeing of a slave, or giving food upon a day of hunger to an orphan, near of kin, or a needy person in misery; then that he become of those who believe and counsel each other to be steadfast, and counsel each other to be merciful. Those are the Companions of the Right Hand. And those who disbelieve in Our signs, they are the Companions of the Left Hand; over them is a Fire covered down.
>
> [90: 8–20]

Here again, in its description of the human *nafs*, the Qur'an refers to the two available paths for every human being, the right and the left, and it explains in detail that these are choices that are based on deeds, faith, and mutual counsel, never on gender.

Finally, Kāshānī's understanding assumes that the Imams' denial of the tradition is of its literal and historical meanings only, but he continues to use it as a valid metaphor. However, when the Imams objected they did not allude to any valid metaphor in the story they were rejecting, instead, they gave an alternative story altogether. It seems absurd to maintain that the same story the Imams repeatedly denied and criticised may be understood as a purposeful story nonetheless, for it is the thought that is much more powerful and with everlasting effects than the historical authenticity. Indeed, the rib story has been rejected by some modern editors of the *ḥadīth* compilations.[73]

It may be said that having shown that the rib story is most probably inauthentic, it logically follows that traditions derived from it must be inauthentic as well. However, in defence of those traditions it may also be said that they are valued metaphors, even if they do not bespeak woman's creation from man as such.

The rib metaphor

In a *ḥadīth* attributed to the Prophet, "Woman is a similitude of a crooked rib; if you keep it as it is you will benefit (and in another version 'you will take pleasure in it'), and if you straighten it you will break it".[74] The woman's "crookedness" here seems to refer to her alleged bent morality; as the variant of this tradition says that when Abraham complained to God about Sarah's manners, God inspired in him that idiom, and added that he should be patient with her.[75]

An Islamic feminist perspective has found this tradition to be misogynistic because it portrays woman as "irremediably crooked", whereas the Qur'an describes humans as having been created *fī aḥsani taqwīm* (in the best form).[76] The Qur'anic verse quoted here continues, "We indeed created the human being in the fairest stature, then We restored him the lowest of the low, save those who believe, and do righteous deeds" [95: 4–6].[77] Again, the perfection of the human being and his collapse are not described in gendered terms.

Some modern Muslim authors have given this problematic tradition due thought. One finds that this tradition does not describe woman's creation but is a metaphor;[78] however, she does not address the value of the metaphor. Another one reads this tradition as God explaining to men that women are different from them and that woman's "crookedness" is a reference to her compassion, which is needed in raising children whereas intelligence is not needed, he finds. Then he continues that this crookedness is actually her straightest quality,[79] thus implicitly affirming that the description of woman as crooked is indeed derogatory. The problem with this interpretation is that it neglects the variant of this tradition which explains crookedness as ill manners and advises the man to be patient. Moreover, it fails to explain why this issue is understood to be in reference to compassion; it associates love with crookedness and pretends that there is nothing derogatory about the term. This neglects that in the Qur'an, the image of the righteous path is repeatedly described as a straight path, "Guide us in the straight path" [1: 6], and "Surely my Lord is on a straight path" [11: 56]. In fact, such interpretations[80] seem to imply that the tradition does not really mean to say "crooked", and they perpetuate the negative implications of the tradition instead of solving them, when really, there is something quite hopeless about the tone of the tradition itself.

Women's zeal is towards men

Another tradition that is inspired by the Qur'anic phrase "from it created its mate" is expressed in Imam al-Ṣādiq's reported words, "God created Adam from water and clay, and the son of Adam's zeal is for water and clay. He created Eve from Adam and women's zeal is for men, so safeguard them (the women) in the houses".[81] The first contention here is that the son of Adam's zeal is for water and earth, presumably meaning work in the land, and the second is that women's zeal is for men, and that they need to be safeguarded because of it.

However, women's connection to agricultural work in particular is remarkable. There is a widely held theory that women discovered gardening and agriculture as an extension of their gathering activities.[82] Today, women play the primary role in agriculture around the world, and many feel ethically committed to the land.[83]

Concerning the second part of the tradition, the editor's footnote explains that what is meant with houses here, is the husband. Therefore, it is not incarceration as such that is recommended, but to make women safe through marriage, so that their endeavours towards men would not lead them astray.

Interestingly, the tradition preceding this one in the compilation admonishes girls to marry as soon as they reach puberty "otherwise they might not be protected against corruption, because they are human (*li'anna-hunna bashar*)".[84] This tradition is similar to the one from Imam al-Ṣādiq in that it is saying that women should marry to be safeguarded. However, it is different in that it does not imply that this advice is exclusive to women, rather that women are human, so that if we know this to be true about men, then it is also true about women. One may further argue that there are ample observations from life which would indicate men's zeal towards women, and need not be expounded upon here.

Therefore, there is some empirical evidence to disprove both claims of this tradition. Women's connection with the land is documented, and the fervour the couple have for each other is mutual, and by virtue of their being a pair (*zawj*), not because one was made from the other.

While the concept of Eve's making from man's rib has not much weight in Qur'anic exegeses, the *ḥadīth* literature does make use of the story allegorically. The best way to sum up this debate is with the observation that, "while borrowing from Jewish and Christian sources may have been officially rejected, assumptions about these materials continued to influence early Islamic written interpretations".[85] The problem with these traditions is that they systematically reduce woman to a place that is less than her full humanity, a matter that needs to be contested further through the lens of the concept of vicegerency.

The universal meanings of the story of creation

The main theme derived from the Qur'anic account of the story of creation, after that of the unity of origin, is what it means to be a vicegerent (*khalīfa*) for God on earth; a birthright for men and women. The first couple's experience in their descent to earth, the concept of vicegerency, and its requisite of knowledge are some of the most pertinent themes in the story of creation.

In the Qur'anic accounts of the events in the Garden, Adam and Eve are mentioned together, in the Arabic dual form, throughout their journey from being introduced into the Garden, and warned by God not to eat of the forbidden tree [2: 35, 7: 19], to being warned of Satan and then tempted by him [2: 36, 7: 20–2], and both eating of the tree and becoming conscious of their genitals [7: 22, 20: 121], until finally they are both sent to the earth with Satan who continues to be the enemy of both [2: 36, 7: 24, and 20: 123]. Moreover, both Adam and Eve quickly confess to God that they have wronged themselves and they seek God's mercy and forgiveness [7: 23], and both are parents of humanity and are made examples for their children [7: 27]. All this strongly suggests "female ethical responsibility and freedom".[86]

The fall as such happens simultaneously to both, and in the same manner; suddenly their private parts (*saw'ātihimā*) that were already there became revealed to them, but now they were aware of them as shameful; "the sense of shame was not awakened in man until after his first transgression".[87] Then the couple started stitching some of the leaves of the Garden over themselves in order to cover themselves. The very same passage continues to describe three kinds of garments that have been bestowed on humans, those which cover the shameful parts, the splendid vesture such as feathers, and the garment of piety, which is best [7: 26]. The next verse warns humans not to be deceived by Satan as he caused their two parents to be expelled from the

Garden, by taking off their garment in order to show them their shameful parts [7: 27]. Therefore, the garment of god-fearing covers the shameful aspects of the soul as clothes cover the shameful parts of the body, and Satan had taken Adam and Eve's raiment of piety in order to manifest to them their shame. Each human is in the happiness of paradise, until he is seduced to remove his god-fearing.[88]

In one passage, however, these events are spoken interchangeably between the singular grammatical form addressed to Adam, and the double addressed to the couple [20: 115–23].[89] Ṭabāṭabā'ī's analysis of this passage points out that Adam was singled out here because of the prophetic covenant.[90]

However, the more crucial events in which Adam appears to be singled out are in the description of his creation, the purpose of which seems to be being taught "the names" [2: 31–3], and therefore leading to the angels' prostration to him [2: 34, 7: 11–12, 15: 28–33, and 38: 71–6]. However, these passages and the commentaries around them reveal that Adam in the prostration episode is meant as a symbol for humanity. When the angels were informed of God's plan to put a vicegerent on earth, they instantly knew that what is meant is a human community/society, which will necessarily produce corruption and bloodshed [2: 30].[91] So when they question why that creature who will do corruption there and shed blood, will be God's vicegerent on earth, even while they, the angels, praise and worship God all the time, God answers that He knows what they do not know [2: 30]. Then right after that in verse [2: 31], the Qur'an says that God taught Adam "the names, all of them", and it goes on to describe how God showed the angels that Adam has been given more knowledge than they were, thus answering their question [2: 31–3].[92]

That this vicegerency is the domain of all human beings is shown in several Qur'anic verses, "Then We appointed you viceroys (*khalā'if*) in the earth after them, that We might behold how you would do" [10: 14], "and appoints you to be successors (*khulafā'*) in the earth" [27: 62]. Thus, according to Ṭabāṭabā'ī, the meaning of teaching the names is that knowledge has been deposited in all human beings without exclusivity. If a human being were guided to tread the righteous path, then knowledge, and with it vicegerency, would be transformed from a potentiality to an actuality.[93]

Thus to Ṭabāṭabā'ī, the prostration of the angels was to the status of vicegerency represented by Adam, as he sees is evident in the Qur'anic verse, "We created you (plural), then We shaped you (plural), then We said to the angels: 'Bow yourselves to Adam'" [7: 11], which moves from the creation of the plurality of human beings to the prostration to Adam alone. That, to him, is also evident in the verses [38: 77–83] in which Satan threatens to tempt all human beings right after he refuses to prostrate to Adam. The prostration was for the status of vicegerency; otherwise Satan need not have sworn to lead all humans astray, if his objection was to the prostration to Adam alone.[94] This, however, does not imply, as some have suggested, that Adam is not a person but a kind, because the Qur'an calls humans "the children of Adam", hence Adam is certainly a person.[95] The angels, however, did not prostrate to the person of Adam but to what he represents, much in the same manner that the Ka'ba is made the direction in which worship is held, due to its representation of divinity.[96]

One understands from the story of creation that the human condition is unique:

> There are two fundamental differences between human beings and all other creatures ... The second fundamental difference is that other creatures have fixed courses from which they never swerve, courses defined by the limited qualities that they manifest. In contrast, human beings have no fixed nature since they manifest the whole ... They must undergo a process whereby they become what they are to be.[97]

As Ṭabāṭabā'ī pointed out, the actuality of becoming God's vicegerent is the outcome of human beings' guidance and their walking towards righteousness. The human being was created to be the vicegerent of God on earth, but due to the arduousness of this task and the nature of the human soul, vicegerency comes at a price, as the Qur'an explains:

> We offered the trust to the heavens and the earth and the mountains, but they refused to carry it and were afraid of it; and the human carried it. Surely he is sinful, very foolish. That God may chastise the hypocrites, men and women alike, and the idolaters, men and women alike; and that God may turn again unto the believers, men and women alike. God is All-forgiving, All-compassionate.
>
> [33: 72–3]

Therefore, vicegerency is particular to humans, and it is the domain of all human beings, men and women. Moreover, in the story of the angels' prostration, it was Adam's knowledge of the names that convinced the angels to prostrate themselves. Thus, it may be said that the knowledge is a prerequisite for vicegerency.

The possibilities for knowledge are always available in the world, and Adam's vicegerency was intended for all human beings, for as a tradition teaches, "The knowledge that was brought down to earth with Adam was not taken back, for knowledge does not disappear with its bearer, and it is inherited".[98]

The number of traditions that stress the necessity of learning and knowledge is vast. The view that all Muslims should gain knowledge goes far beyond being a mere right, and is in fact a religious duty, as the Prophet said, "The quest for knowledge is a duty incumbent upon every Muslim, indeed God loves the passionate seekers of knowledge".[99]

The traditions further explain the conduits of knowledge. Even though no knowledge is bad, some is irrelevant, for not any kind of education qualifies as being the knowledge these traditions refer to. It is reported from the Prophet, "that knowledge is of three kinds, a sign of clear meaning (*āya muḥkama*), a just religious duty (*farīḍa ʿādila*), or a living (prophetic) tradition (*sunna qāʾima*), and anything other than those is a blessing".[100] Qur'anic verses are called *ayas*, and "signs/portents" are also found "in the earth", "in the horizons", and "in your souls/selves" [41: 53, and 51: 20–1]. That is why Murata observes:

> When the Koran commands people to see all things as God's signs, it is encouraging them to make use of a particular type of mental process that is not oriented towards objects, things, or data. On the contrary, the Koran tells us that we must perceive things not so much for what they are in themselves but for what they tell us about something beyond themselves.[101]

A tradition from Imam ʿAlī further explains the value of the intellect and its relationship with prophecy and Imamate, which are vicegerency exemplified: "God has given human beings two proofs, one is external and the other internal, the external proofs are the messengers, prophets, and Imams peace be upon them, and the internal proofs are the intellects."[102]

Acquiring knowledge and living accordingly are always coupled in the traditions which repeatedly tell that the final judgement is based primarily on one's intellect (*ʿaql*).[103]

These traditions and others show that learning and expanding the mind are matters of urgency for they are related to the hereafter. The idea that gaining knowledge is not merely allowed for women but considered their religious duty, is of the utmost importance because this is the means for them to be vicegerents for God on earth and therefore manifest their full personhood. Adam and Eve are both shown to have been accountable for their mistakes and carried the burden of responsibility. The story of Adam teaches that vicegerency is fulfilled through knowledge, and both vicegerency and knowledge are accessible to males and females and there is no gender based distinction in this regard. Adam was only a symbol for that status, yet he is a male symbol.

Reassessing the symbols: Adam and *al-arḥām*

The status of vicegerency and its prerequisite of knowledge have been shown to be universal, although expressed through the symbol of Adam. The second part of the governing verse from *Sūrat al-Nisāʾ* has not yet been thoroughly analysed. This is a very important though overlooked phrase, and it clarifies that compassion is linked to vicegerency, and in expressing this particular quality, the Qur'an utilises the uniquely feminine symbol of the womb.

What remains problematic, particularly for a feminist-informed reading, is that a man would represent humanity as the prototype being, as the one who was given knowledge and before whom the angels prostrated. A contemporary reformist Christian feminist articulates the problem (although she talks about the representation of Christ, but the similarities in this context are obvious):

> The male alone is the normative or generic sex of the human species; only the male represents the fullness of human nature, whereas woman is defective physically, morally, and mentally. It follows that the incarnation of the *Logos* of God into a male is not a historical accident but an ontological necessity. Just as Christ [read: Adam] has to be incarnated in a male, so only can the male represent Christ [read: Adam].[104]

Adam's vicegerency however is a burden, and the vicegerent may abuse his status, as the angels were sure that the human vicegerent will fill the earth with corruption and bloodshed [2: 30]. The Qur'an once asks, "If you were given the command,[105] would you then haply work corruption in the land, and break your bonds of kin (*wa tuqaṭṭiʿū arḥāmakum*)?" [47: 22], thereby linking corruption and the exploitation of status on earth, with breaking the bonds of kinship, or *al-arḥām*.

The second segment of the governing verse [4: 1] reads, "And fear/reverence God by whom you demand one of another, and the wombs; surely God ever watches over you". Literally, the *raḥm* (womb) is the uterus of the female, and among the Arabs it is a metaphor for close kinship[106] because kin come out of the same womb,[107] and when pronounced *ruḥm*, it means compassion.[108]

The exegetes discussed above did in fact pay close attention to this *taqwa* (fear/reverence) for "the wombs", and despite their concern for this verse, they generally found that the meaning of "fear/reverence God and the wombs" is the grammatically stronger one, as it is also the meaning available in the traditions.[109] For instance, Imam al-Ṣādiq interprets this part of the verse, exclaiming, "It is (a reference to) the wombs of people which he ordained connection with and gave it a high status; can you not see that he (God) has made it of himself (*jaʿalahā minhu*)".[110]

The "connection" referred to in this tradition comes from the Arabic phrase *ṣilat al-raḥm*, which literally means "connection of the womb", but the actual meaning of which may be translated as maintaining the bonds of kinship, or as "regard/consideration for kinship".[111] Therefore, it is filial piety and much more. The various traditions that utilise the terms *ṣilat al-raḥm* or simply *al-arḥām* (the wombs) give three meanings for the term. One meaning refers to connection with and consideration for kin, the other refers to the wombs as flesh, the last refers to "the wombs" as a single mysterious entity that is connected to God, and also named after one of his most prominent names, *al-Raḥmān*.

One tradition gives the meaning of consideration for kin, "Connect with your kin even with a greeting".[112] Another tradition says that "Consideration for kin is the fastest way to gain rewards for good deeds".[113]

The second meaning of flesh may be seen in traditions that value touch as a way to calm an angry person. A part of a larger tradition, which will be fully discussed in the third meaning below, suggests, "Any man of you who feels anger towards his kin, let him come closer to him, for if the 'womb' was touched by a 'womb' it settles/rests".[114] This gives the term "womb" the meaning of flesh. Indeed, Ṭabāṭabā'ī says that the womb is the material unity between individuals of the family, and he says that this has physical and spiritual effects that are undeniable.[115]

As for the third meaning of the wombs as an entity with a divinely ordained status, a couple of traditions are of special significance. Imam 'Alī explains in an authenticated tradition:

> The one of you gets angry and would not become calm until he is entered into hell. Any man of you who feels anger towards his kin let him come closer to him, for if the "womb" was touched by a "womb" it settles/rests. It (the womb) is connected to the Throne (God's throne), it strikes it like metal that reverberates, and it calls, "Oh God! Connect whoever connects me and disconnect whoever disconnects me" ... and any man who gets angry while standing, should stay sitting on the earth in his gush, for that gets rid of Satan's abomination.[116]

The "Throne of God" in the traditions could mean the whole creation, and it could mean knowledge.[117] It has been established in several exegeses that many traditions explain or imply that the Throne represents knowledge that was given to the prophets.[118] Ṭabāṭabā'ī explains that the Throne in the Qur'an and *ḥadīth* is the place of comprehensive knowledge of events. It is the stage in existence where different events, causes, and effects gather. The womb puts the chain of events in action in the sense that it is connected to the spirit motivator of the chains. This is similar to the position of the king where all the different problems of the kingdom gather, and who, with one command, orders a chain of active powers in the kingdom to act. Therefore, the womb, which is like the spirit that connects kin, is connected to the Throne, when it is abused and oppressed, it takes refuge in and seeks justice from that which she is connected to. This causes the whole Throne to reverberate. The image of the womb complaining to the Throne is the image of a metallic body being struck, upon one strike the whole body would make a sound and reverberate.[119] This, Ṭabāṭabā'ī says, explains the tradition in which the womb calls on to God to connect with himself whoever connects her,[120] and this is also the meaning of other traditions that confirm that consideration for kin prolongs one's life, and disconnection from kin disconnects life.[121]

According to Ṭabāṭabā'ī, the Islamic vision is that the human soul is naturally inclined towards compassion and away from anger. This, he says, is evident in several traditions that discuss anger.[122] Moreover, Ṭabāṭabā'ī says that the Islamic view is that God is constantly driving the universe towards good goals,[123] and therefore whoever disconnect themselves from their kin are actually fighting God's essence, and this is why God would fix the problem either by rehabilitating them or by eliminating them with death.[124]

Murata writes, "The Throne marks the demarcation line between the unseen and the visible worlds, or the World of Command and the World of Creation".[125] Ibn 'Arabī explains this more clearly in his interpretation of the verse in question, he says that the wombs are disconnected with the lack of love, and he says that this leads to isolation, detachment, and disconnection from God. He explains that the womb to the visible world is similar to the connection with God in the invisible world. Therefore maintaining unity in the physical connection is similar to unifying God, and one who cannot maintain physical unity would not be able to attain spiritual unity.[126]

Another tradition on the third meaning of "the womb" as an entity is a widely reported *ḥadīth qudsī* where God addresses the womb saying, "I am *al-Raḥmān* and you are *al-raḥm*, I derived your name from my name, so whoever connects you I will connect and whoever disconnects you I will disconnect".[127] In this tradition, the creator links one of his most prominent names, which means the all-compassionate, to this entity that is the womb. Moreover, it has been shown that the divine name *al-Raḥmān* is unlike the other names of God. While the other names signify one aspect of the divine, and may be used as an attribute of someone other than the divine, *al-Raḥmān* designates "God himself", and cannot designate anyone or anything other than him.[128] Thus, the honour bestowed upon the womb is not only by being placed next to God in reverence, but also through his choice of that particular one of his names to give to her.

Since the story of Adam and Eve aims to teach that humanity is literally one family, then consideration for kin and unity between individuals may extend to the whole race, or even to the earth itself which is the material source of the human kind [71: 17]. It has been observed that one of the main themes of the story of creation is its suggestion regarding human beings' "affinity with the earth, and our responsibility towards it and dependence on it".[129]

The three meanings of *al-arḥām* may thus come together. The consideration for kin may extend to all of the earth and its children because of the material bond among them. Moreover this connection with and consideration for kin as a whole may be suitably placed right next to reverence towards God in importance. One may further argue that this theme, which may be summarised as showing compassion to living things in order to gain God's mercy and be connected with him, is tightly knit with the theme of vicegerency. It was shown above that vicegerency is only a test that might cause either the elevation of people or their depression. Causing corruption and bloodshed does not represent the true status of vicegerency; rather, it is the abuse of that status. In fact, as mentioned above, the Qur'an clearly criticises humans who, after being made vicegerents on the earth, would cut their bonds of kinship (*tuqaṭṭi'ū arḥāmakum*) [47: 22]. Thus, the mention of the wombs next to God in this very verse that speaks of the creation of the first couple and the rest of humanity is very befitting.

This reading then gives a place for the feminine in the divine plan. If Adam represents the original being, woman represents the unity of humans and the very material of compassion.

In any case, it has to be remembered that this is an analysis of symbols, not a contention that men are Adam and women their wombs. The symbols do not pertain to individual men and women in the world; surely one may think of innumerous counter-examples, nor should people be constrained to these symbols but, "the woman and the man must be demythologized".[130] Vicegerency is not complete without both the elements of knowledge and compassion, and each true vicegerent needs to fulfil both. Yet this investigation into the symbols is important, not only to demonstrate that the feminine is equally essential and linked to the divine in the Qur'an, but also to restore a balance between the feminine and the masculine symbols in this key verse on the story of creation.[131]

Conclusions

This chapter discussed the opening verse of *Sūrat al-Nisā'*, which has two main components. The first speaks of the creation of the single soul, followed by its mate, and then the scattering of a multitude of men and women. The second speaks of reverence for God and for "the wombs".

Regarding the first segment, it was argued that men and women are each a *nafs* and *zawj*. There is an emphasis in verse [4: 1] and its exegesis that the verse is a reminder that people come from one soul and therefore that they should be merciful towards each other. The Qur'anic description of Eve's creation *min* Adam accepts both possibilities, that she was created from a part of him or from the same material as him. Her creation has contradictory stories in the traditions, one specifies Eve's origin from Adam, but others utterly refute that story on theological grounds and promote the idea that she was created from the same material as he. The allegorical traditions that make use of the rib story or that she is part of him undermine her humanity. On the contrary, the theme of human vicegerency portrays woman as an equally full person. She is capable of knowledge and invited to pursue it in order to achieve her potential. In the story of the angels' prostration, Adam is a symbol for the totality of the human race and their carrying the knowledge. Yet, this status will necessarily bring corruption with it, and a part of the vicegerent's guidance is that he reveres "the wombs". With this powerful feminine symbol and its connection to the Throne in the traditions, the balance in vicegerency, and in its masculine and feminine dimensions, is restored.

Eve is certainly a *nafs* that took accountability for removing her garment of god-fearing and reverence, thus descending into the earthly life. The story of Eve's daughters as told in the Qur'an and later in the *sunna*, is a story of how these women lived their vicegrency, and how some of them attempted to hold tight to their piety through their earthly and spiritual pursuits. The question whether the other terms of *zawj* and *raḥm* play a role in the portrayal of the female *nafs* will be pursued throughout.

Notes

1 For example, refer to: Bronner, L.L. (1994) *From Eve to Esther: Rabbinic reconstructions of Biblical women*. Louisville: Westminster John Knox Press, pp. 22–36. Lloyd, G. (1990) "Augustine and Aquinas". In Loades, A. (ed.) *Feminist theology:*

a reader. London: SPCK, pp. 90–7. Cantor, A. (1983) "The Lilith question". In Heschel, S. (ed.) *On being a Jewish feminist: a reader*. New York: Schocken Books, pp. 40–50.

2 Stanton, E.C. and the Revising Committee (1974) *The woman's Bible*. Seattle: Coalition Task Force on Women and Religion, p. 7.

3 Daly, M. (1975) *The church and the second sex*. New York: Harper & Row, pp. 22–3.

4 For example, refer to: Bird, P. (1974) "Images of women in the old testament". In Ruether, R.R. (ed.) *Religion and sexism: images of woman in the Jewish and Christian traditions*. New York: Simon & Schuster, pp. 41–77; Wadud-Muhsin, A. (1994) *Qur'an and woman*. Kuala Lumpur: Penerbit Fajar Bakti, pp. 15–28; Barazangi, N.H. (2004) *Woman's identity and the Qur'an: a new reading*. Florida: University Press of Florida, pp. 37–51.

5 Hassan, R. (n.d.) *Equal before Allah? Woman-man equality in the Islamic tradition* [online]. Available from: www.wluml.org/node/253 [Accessed 20.02.2014], pp. 6–7.

6 Wadud-Muhsin (1994, pp. 16–26), where she also considers the word *'āya* a key term, although it does not occur in this particular verse, therefore will be excluded here.

7 Lewis, B. "al-ʿAyyashī", *Encyclopaedia of Islam, second edition*. Edited by: P. Bearman, Th. Bianquis, C.E. Bosworth, E. Van Donzel, and W.P. Heinrichs. Brill online, 2014 [Accessed 20.02.2014].

8 One "new" tradition is about the origin of the name of Eve or *Ḥawwā'*, a name which does not occur in the Qur'an, and even on the origin of the Arabic words for "woman" and "women", all implying that woman was derived from man, perhaps an effort to give credence to the theory of her creation from a part of the man (al-Ḥuwayzī, 'Abd 'Alī Ibn Jumuʿa al-ʿArūsī (1412h) *Nūr al-thaqalayn*. 4th edn. 5 volumes. Qum: Mu'assasat Isma'ilyan, vol. 1, pp. 429–30). Here he contends that *Ḥawwā'* comes from *ḥayy* (a living being), that *mar'a* comes from *mar'*, and that *nisā'* comes from *'anas* because Adam found no amiability except in her. However, according to the lexicons, the root of the word *ḥ-y-ā* means life, and could also indicate rain and fertility. *Ḥayy* may also mean a clan, or even a woman's genitalia and reproductive system. *Ḥawwā,'* however, is composed from another root, *ḥ-w-ā*. In this case also there is a variety of meanings, among them is a black green colour which in Arab culture indicates extreme lushness, or an empty space that gathers or embraces things, such as the woman's uterus, or it could mean a man who has snakes (Ibn Manẓūr, Muḥammad Ibn Mukarram (1405h) *Lisān al-'Arab*. 15 volumes. Qum: Nashr Adab al-Ḥawza, pp. 206–8, 211, 214–15, 220, and vol. 12, p. 209). There is also one tradition which attributes most legal issues that are particular for women, to woman's origin in creation. It states that Eve was made from Adam and that is why divorce is in the hands of men, that she was made from a part of him which is why she is worth half the man in blood money, that she was made from inside him, which explains why women need to be hidden under their veils, that she was created from his left rib rather than his right explains why she inherits less than him and why her testimony is worth less than his (Ḥuwayzī, 1412h, vol. 1, p. 434). This narration is peculiar because its inner reasoning is not at all clear, but it does not occur anywhere else in other exegeses or in the major *ḥadīth* collections. Interestingly however, the alternative story of Eve's creation from the original clay, where it was one tradition in 'Ayyāshī's, here there is a variety of them attributed to three different Imams, 'Alī, al-Bāqir, and al-Ṣādiq, which still criticise the story of woman's creation from the rib and maintain that Eve was created from the same clay as Adam (Ḥuwayzī, 1412h, vol. 1, p. 429–31, 434).

9 al-ʿAyyāshī, Muḥammad Ibn Masʿūd (n.d.) *Tafsīr al-Qur'ān*. 2 volumes. Tehran: al-Maktaba al-'Ilmiyya al-Islāmiyya, vol. 1, pp. 215–17.

10 Ḥuwayzī (1412h, vol. 4, p. 476).
11 al-Ṭūsī, Muḥammad Ibn Ḥasan (1409h) *al-Tibyān fī tafsīr al-Qur'ān*. 10 volumes. Qum: Maktab al-I'lām al-Islamī, vol. 3, pp. 99–101.
12 al-Ṭabāṭabā'ī, Muḥammad Ḥusayn (1402h) *al-Mīzān fī tafsīr al-Qur'ān*. 20 volumes. Qum: Mu'assasat al-Nashr al-Islami, vol. 4, pp. 134–5.
13 Ṭabāṭabā'ī (1402h, vol. 4, pp. 135–6).
14 Ṭabāṭabā'ī (1402h, vol. 4, p. 136).
15 Ṭabāṭabā'ī (1402h, vol. 4, pp. 136–7), whereas 'Ayyāshī, for example, finds that some of their children married angels, and some others married from the *jinn* ('Ayyāshī, n.d., vol. 1, p. 216).
16 'Ayyāshī (n.d., vol. 1, pp. 215–17).
17 al-Qummī, 'Alī Ibn Ibrāhīm (1404h) *Tafsīr al-Qur'ān*. 3rd edn. 2 volumes. Qum: Mu'assasat Dār al-Kitāb, vol. 1, p. 130. Note that this is different from reading *al-arḥāmi* as added to *bihi*, which would then mean that humans demand of one another with respect to God, and to the wombs – a reading that Ṭabāṭabā'ī considers but rejects.
18 Ṭūsī (1409h, vol. 3, pp. 98–9).
19 Ṭabāṭabā'ī (1402h, vol. 4, pp. 137–8).
20 Ṭabāṭabā'ī (1402h, vol. 4, pp. 138–9).
21 Ṭabāṭabā'ī (1402h, vol. 4, pp. 139, 134).
22 al-Fayrūz Ābādī, Muḥammad Ibn Ya'qūb (n.d.) *al-Qāmūs al-muḥīṭ*. 4 volumes. Cairo: Muḥammad 'Abd al-Ḥamīd, vol. 2, p. 255. al-Iṣfahānī, al-Rāghib, al-Ḥusayn Ibn Mufaddal (1404h) *al-Mufradāt fī gharīb al-Qur'ān*. Tehran: Daftar Nashr al-Kitāb, p. 501.
23 Ibn Manẓūr (1405h, vol. 6, pp. 233–4), where he explains that those who reject that *nafs* is *rūḥ*, do so partly based on [39: 42].
24 Iṣfahānī (1404h, p. 501). Ibn Manẓūr (1405h, vol. 6, pp. 234–5).
25 Fayrūz Ābādī (n.d., vol. 2, p. 255). Ibn Manẓūr (1405h, vol. 6, pp. 234–5).
26 Ibn Manẓūr (1405h, vol. 6, pp. 234–5).
27 Ṭabāṭabā'ī (1402h, vol. 4, p. 135).
28 Ṭabāṭabā'ī (1402h, vol. 1, p. 349).
29 Such as [2: 233] and [31: 34].
30 Such as [21: 47] and [2: 48].
31 Ṭabāṭabā'ī (1402h, vol. 1, pp. 351–2).
32 Wadud-Muhsin (1994, p. 20).
33 al-Ṭabrisī, Faḍl Ibn Ḥasan (1415h) *Majma' al-Bayān*. 10 volumes. Beirut: Mu'assasat al-A'lamī, vol. 3, p. 8, and vol. 8, p. 92. Also refer to [6: 98], [31: 28], and [39: 6].
34 Ibn 'Aqīl, Bahā' al-Dīn al-Hamdānī (n.d.) *Sharḥ Ibn 'Aqīl li alfiyyat Ibn Mālik*. 2 volumes, vol. 2, pp. 15–19.
35 Ṭabrisī (1418h, vol. 1, p. 729). It is noteworthy that Wadud-Muhsin finds the creation of the mate in another verse [39: 6] to be expressed by use of the term *ja'ala* instead of *khalaqa* (used for both the *nafs* and its *zawj* in this verse [4: 1]) problematic, because *ja'ala* is "to create something from another thing", which she finds gives min the meaning of a part of a whole (Wadud-Muhsin, 1994, pp. 18–19). However, *Lisān al-'Arab* states that while *ja'ala* means "to make", *khalaqa* "to create" is another one of its meanings (Ibn Manẓūr, 1405h, vol. 11, pp. 110–11). The difference is that *ja'ala* can also mean "to change something from its previous state" (Ṭabrisī, 1415h, vol. 1, p. 146). This need not have any particular significance for Eve, because Adam too was made from clay, a mixture of earth and water, not from nothing. The Qur'an explains, "and of water (We) fashioned (*ja'alnā*) every living thing" [21: 30].
36 One such opinion is expressed by: al-Raḍī, al-Sharīf, Muḥammad Ibn al-Ḥusayn (n.d.b) *Ḥaqā'iq al-ta'wīl fī mutashābah al-tanzīl*. Beirut: Dār al-Muhājir, pp. 308–9,

and that is the same opinion as Abū Muslim al-Iṣfahānī, in: al-Majlisī, Muḥammad Bāqir (1403h) *Biḥār al-anwār*. 110 volumes. Beirut: Mu'assasat al-Wafā', vol. 11, p. 222.

37 In which case the first use of "min" in the verse (created you from a single soul) would take the meaning of "from", in the sense of beginning in time.
38 Majlisī (1403h, vol. 11, p. 222).
39 Ibn Manẓūr (1405h, vol. 2, p. 291). Iṣfahānī (1404h, pp. 215–16).
40 Ibn Manẓūr (1405h, vol. 2, p. 292).
41 Ibn Manẓūr (1405h, vol. 2, p. 292). Iṣfahānī (1404h, pp. 215–16).
42 Ibn Manẓūr (1405h, vol. 2, pp. 291–2).
43 Fayrūz Ābādī (n.d., vol. 1, pp. 192–3).
44 For example: [10: 6], [22: 5], [30: 21–5], [36: 36], [43: 12], [50: 7], [53: 45].
45 Ṭabāṭabā'ī (1402h, vol. 20, p. 387).
46 Ibn Manẓūr (1405h, vol. 3, p. 70).
47 Ṭabrisī (1415h, vol. 10, pp. 485–6).
48 Ṭabrisī (1415h, vol. 10, p. 486).
49 Murata, S. (1992) *The Tao of Islam: a sourcebook on gender relationships in Islamic thought*. Albany: State University of New York Press, p. 58.
50 Bouhdiba, A. (1998) *Sexuality in Islam*. London: Saqi Books, p. 8.
51 Lane, E.W. (n.d.) *Arabic-English lexicon* [online]. Available from: www.studyquran.co.uk/PRLonline.htm [Accessed 20.02.2014].
52 Ṭūsī (1409h, vol. 5, pp. 52–5), where he says that the rest of the verse and the following one refer to the human couple in general.
53 Ṭabāṭabā'ī (1402h, vol. 8, p. 375), due to the following verse, which speak of humans who associate others with God, which could not be referring to Adam and Eve.
54 Lane (n.d.): *s-k-n*.
55 Murata (1992, p. 58) points out, "There can be no absolutes when the two sides depend on each other."
56 Barlas, A. (2002) *Believing women in Islam: unreading patriarchal interpretations of the Qur'an*. Austin: University of Texas Press, p. 103, argues, in line with Murata, that man and woman "each manifest the whole". Also refer to: Wadud-Muhsin (1994, pp. 22–3).
57 al-Kulaynī, Muḥammad Ibn Ya'qūb (1388h) *al-Kāfī*. 3rd edn. 8 volumes. Tehran: Dār al-Kutub al-Islāmiyya, vol. 4, pp. 190–2, 196, vol. 6, pp. 393–4, 514, vol. 8, p. 233, which include topics such as the pilgrimage, the Ka'ba, the prohibition of alcohol, the use of perfume, and the extraordinary physical length of those first humans.
58 Kulaynī (1388h, vol. 5, p. 442).
59 al-Ṣadūq, Muḥammad Ibn 'Alī Ibn Bābawayh (1404ha) *Man la yaḥḍuruhū al-faqīh*. 2nd edn. 4 volumes. Qum: Jāmi'at al-Mudarrisīn, vol. 3, pp. 379–80.
60 Ṣadūq (1404ha, vol. 3, p. 380).
61 'Ayyāshī (n.d., vol. 1, pp. 216–17).
62 Ṣadūq (1404ha, vol. 3, p. 380).
63 Barazangi (2004, p. 47).
64 Sabbah, F.A. (1984) *Woman in the Muslim unconscious*. New York: Pergamon Press. Translated by M.J. Lakeland, p. 73.
65 Sabbah (1984, p. 74).
66 Barlas (2002, pp. 50–3).
67 Ṣadūq (1404ha, vol. 3, p. 381).
68 On the life and contribution of this religious authority, refer to: Momen, M. (1985) *An introduction to Shi'i Islam*. New Haven: Yale University Press, pp. 114–15. Newman, A.J. (2006) *Safavid Iran: rebirth of a Persian empire*. London: I.B. Tauris, pp. 93f.

69 Majlisī (1403h, vol. 11, p. 116).
70 Newman (2006). Also refer to: Achena, M. "Fayḍ-i Kāshānī". *Encyclopaedia of Islam, second edition*. Edited by P. Bearman, Th. Bianquis, C.E. Bosworth, E. Van Donzel, and W.P. Heinrichs. Brill online, 2014 [Accessed 20.02.2014].
71 al-Kāshānī, Muḥsin Fayḍ (1416h) *al-Ṣāfī fī tafsīr kalām Allāh al-wāfī*. 2nd edn. 5 volumes. Tehran: Maktabat al-Ṣadr, vol. 1, p. 415.
72 Kulaynī (1388h, vol. 5, pp. 338–39, including fn. 3). The term *shahwa* seems to denote not only desire but physical pleasure as well, as in its other uses in: Kulaynī (1388h, vol. 3, pp. 47–8). Therefore, it might be that the tradition is not only talking about women's desire, but their capacity for intense pleasure anatomically.
73 Ṣadūq (1404ha, vol. 3, p. 381, and vol. 4, p. 326, and 328 footnotes).
74 Kulaynī (1388h, vol. 5, p. 513).
75 Kulaynī (1388h, vol. 5, p. 513). In Ṣadūq (1404ha, vol. 3, pp. 440–1), there is a curious incident here when the disciple asks the Imam about the source of this tradition, but the Imam confirms that it is from the Prophet. It is also noteworthy that the Umayyad poet Ḥājib bin Dhibyān uses in one of his verses the admonishment not to attempt to straighten the *ḍil'* (the word for 'rib' and anything with a bent shape) so as not to break it, although he does not extend the analogy to woman (Ibn Manẓūr, 1405h, vol. 8, p. 226).
76 Hassan (n.d., p. 6).
77 Also refer to [32: 7], "(God) who has created all things well".
78 'Ā'isha 'Abd al-Raḥmān, as quoted in Smith, J.I. and Haddad, Y.Y. (1982) "Eve: Islamic image of woman". In al-Hibri, A. (ed.) *Women and Islam*. Oxford: Pergamon, p. 141.
79 Sha'rāwī, as quoted in Stowasser, B. (1994) *Women in the Qur'an, traditions, and interpretation*. New York: Oxford University Press, p. 37.
80 I refer to such interpretations, in the plural, because they abound, even though only one has been paraphrased here. For example, refer to a reference to a spoken lecture by 'Amr Khāled, in: bint Muḥammad bin Fahd al-Rashīd, N. (1427h) *Shakhsiyyat al-mar'a fī al-qasas al-Qur'ānī: dirāsa adabiyya taḥlīliyya*. Dammam: Dār Ibn al-Jawzī, p. 154.
81 Kulaynī (1388h, vol. 5, p. 337).
82 For example, refer to: Stanley, A. (1995) *Mothers and daughters of invention: notes for a revised history of technology*. New Brunswick: Rutgers University Press, pp. 1–86.
83 For example, refer to the UN report "Women feed the world" (n.d.) [online]. Available from: www.fao.org/docrep/x0262e/x0262e16.htm [Accessed 20.02.2014], and: Jensen, J.M. (1991) *Promise to the land: essays on rural women*. Albuquerque: University of New Mexico Press.
84 Kulaynī (1388h, vol. 5, p. 337).
85 Spellberg, D.A. (1996) "Writing the unwritten life of the Islamic Eve: menstruation and the demonization of motherhood". *International Journal of Middle East Studies*, 28 (3): 305.
86 Stowasser (1994, p. 21).
87 Heidel, A. (1963) *The Babylonian genesis: the story of creation*. Chicago: Chicago University Press, p. 124.
88 Ṭabāṭabā'ī (1402h, vol. 8, pp. 69–71). Also, their private parts had to be hidden from them while they were connected to the realm of spirit and the angels, and Satan was insistent on showing these to them, because that would guarantee their descent to the earthly realm (Ṭabāṭabā'ī, 1402h, vol. 1, pp. 126–7). To Qummī, Ḥuwayzī, and Kāshānī the garment of piety is *'afāf* – loosely translated as restraint (Qummī, 1404h, vol. 1, p. 226; Kāshānī, 1416h, vol. 2, p. 187), but Ḥuwayzī adds, in view of a sermon by Imam 'Alī, that the garment of piety is also *jihād* (Ḥuwayzī, 1412h, vol. 2, pp. 15–16, and vol. 5, p. 30). Ṭabrisī similarly

finds that it is *ḥayā'* – or shyness and "good deeds" (Ṭabrisī, 1415h, vol. 4, p. 236).
89 Wadud-Muhsin (1994, p. 25) points out that Adam is singled out in these verses due to a particular point being made in this passage, which is a comparison between what she describes as Adam's forgetfulness as a prophet and Muhammad's forgetfulness as a prophet.
90 Ṭabāṭabā'ī (1402h, vol. 14, pp. 220–1) argues against what has been suggested, that the singularity of Adam in the phrase "so that thou art unprosperous" [20: 117] means that work in the world is the domain of man. He refuses this understanding of gender roles in this verse because Adam is singled out in most verses of that passage, even in places where Eve would have been included, such as, "It is assuredly given to thee neither to hunger therein, nor to go naked" [20: 118].
91 Ṭabāṭabā'ī (1402h, vol. 1, p. 115).
92 Ṭabāṭabā'ī (1402h, vol. 1, pp. 115–16, p. 120, pp. 133–4, and pp. 148–9).
93 Ṭabāṭabā'ī (1402h, vol. 1, p. 116).
94 Ṭabāṭabā'ī (1402h, vol. 8, pp. 20–1).
95 Ṭabāṭabā'ī (1402h, vol. 4, pp. 142–3).
96 Ṭabāṭabā'ī (1402h, vol. 8, p. 20).
97 Murata (1992, p. 43). For a brief analysis of vicegerency as anti-patriarchal and the domain of all humans, refer to: Barlas (2002, pp. 106–8).
98 Kulaynī (1388h, vol. 1, p. 222).
99 Kulaynī (1388h, vol. 1, pp. 30–1).
100 Kulaynī (1388h, vol. 1, p. 32).
101 Murata (1992, p. 24).
102 Kulaynī (1388h, vol. 1, p. 16).
103 Kulaynī (1388h, vol. 1, pp. 12–33).
104 Ruether, R.R. (1989) *Sexism and God-talk: towards a feminist theology*. London: SCM Press Ltd, p. 126. Here, it would be useful to insist that the male form is not specially related to the divine. Traditions refute the idea that "God created man in his image". Al-Bāqir answers this saying, "The image is new, it is created, God chose it over the other images and added it to himself, just like he added the Ka'ba to himself and the Spirit to himself" (Kulaynī, 1388h, vol. 1, p. 134). Also refer to: al-Ṣadūq, Muḥammad Ibn 'Alī Ibn Bābawayh (1404hb) *'Uyūn akhbār al-Riḍā*. 2 volumes. Beirut: Mu'assasat al-A'lamī li al-Matbū'āt, vol. 2, p. 110.
105 This particular segment of the verse is from Pickthall, M.M. (2002) *The meaning of the glorious Qur'an: text and explanatory translation*. Maryland: Amana Publications. Revised edition – because it seems more accurate than J. Arberry's (1955) *The Koran interpreted*. London: Allen & Unwin – "if you were turned away" in the context of the passage.
106 Ibn Manẓūr (1405h, vol. 12, p. 230).
107 Iṣfahānī (1404h, p. 191).
108 Ibn Manẓūr (1405h, vol. 12, pp. 232–3).
109 Ṭūsī (1409h, vol. 3, pp. 97–100); Ṭabrisī (1415h, vol. 3, p. 6); Ṭabāṭabā'ī (1402h, vol. 4, pp. 137–8 and 147).
110 Kulaynī (1388h, vol. 2, p. 150).
111 Translation from: al-Raḍī, Sh. (1996) *Peak of eloquence*. 7th edn. New York: Tahrike Tarsile Qur'an. Translated by Y.T. Jibouri, p. 591, 620, 621, etc.
112 Kulaynī (1388h, vol. 2, p. 155).
113 Kulaynī (1388h, vol. 2, p. 152).
114 'Ayyāshī (n.d., vol. 1, p. 217).
115 Ṭabāṭabā'ī (1402h, vol. 4, p. 148).
116 Kulaynī (1388h, vol. 2, p. 151). 'Ayyāshī (n.d., vol. 1, p. 217).
117 Kulaynī (1388h, vol. 1, pp. 127–8).

118 For example, refer to: Kāshānī (1416h, vol. 1, p. 283), and Ṭabāṭabā'ī (1402h, vol. 1, p. 124, and vol. 2, p. 341, and vol. 8, pp. 163–7).
119 Ṭabāṭabā'ī (1402h, vol. 4, pp. 149–50).
120 Kulaynī (1388h, vol. 2, pp. 151–6).
121 Kulaynī (1388h, vol. 2, p. 152).
122 Ṭabāṭabā'ī (1402h, vol. 4, p. 149).
123 Ṭabāṭabā'ī (1402h, vol. 2) discusses this extensively.
124 Ṭabāṭabā'ī (1402h, vol. 4, p. 150). He continues here that this reality is not felt by humans today because of the extreme medication of the human body, which no longer perceives the subtle pains.
125 Murata (1992, p. 219).
126 Ibn 'Arabī, Muḥammad Ibn 'Alī (n.d.) *Tafsīr al-Qur'ān*. Also available from: www.altafsir.com/Tafasir.asp?tMadhNo=3&tTafsirNo=33&tSoraNo=4&tAyahNo=1&tDisplay=yes&UserProfile=0 [Accessed 18.07.2011] – in his *tafsir* of this verse [4: 1].
127 al-Ṣadūq, Muḥammad Ibn 'Alī Ibn Bābawayh (1379h) *Ma'ānī al-akhbār*. Qum: Intisharāt Islāmī, p. 302. Ṭabrisī (1415h, vol. 3, p. 9).
128 Jomier, J. (2001) "The divine name 'al-Raḥmān' in the Qur'an". In Rippin, A. (ed.) *The Qur'an: style and contents*. Aldershot: Ashgate, pp. 198–9.
129 Abdel Haleem, M. (1999) *Understanding the Qur'an: themes and style*. London: Tauris, p. 134. Symbolic links between the earth and the mother are ample in the Qur'an, such as in: Sells, M. (1999) *Approaching the Qur'an: the early revelations*. 2nd edn. Oregon: White Cloud Press Sells, pp. 213–16. As well as in traditions, such as the Prophet's saying, "Wipe yourselves with the earth for it is compassionate towards you as a woman to her children": al-Raḍī, al-Sharīf, Muḥammad Ibn al-Ḥusayn (n.d.a) *al-Majāzāt al-nabawiyya*. Qum: Baṣīratī, p. 269.
130 McLaughlin, E.C. (1974) "Equality of souls, inequality of sexes: woman in medieval theology". In Ruether, R.R. (ed.) *Religion and sexism: images of women in the Jewish and Christian traditions*. New York: Simon & Schuster, p. 257.
131 Murata sees a different but interesting balance in the symbols of creation when she says, "Being is yang, and the divine knowledge is yin" (Murata, 1992, p. 67).

2 Female personalities in the Qur'an

Introduction

As the previous chapter was devoted to the story of Eve, this chapter will continue the discussion on female personalities of the Qur'anic narratives, which include the stories of the past prophets, the time of Muhammad, and a small section at the end will be on the women of paradise.

The narratives of the prophets (*qiṣaṣ al-anbiyā'*) comprise a major part of the Qur'anic message, about one-seventh of the book.[1] Most of the prophets mentioned in the Qur'an are Biblical, but some are old Arabian prophets. The Islamic versions of their stories diverge from the Biblical ones in minor or major details. One of the main themes of the Qur'anic narratives is that prophets have had the same basic message, which is the oneness of the creator, even though their experiences differed as well as a part of their message such as the religious law. The Qur'an instructs people to accept all the prophets and messengers and not distinguish between them [2: 136, 2: 285, 3: 84], even though it also states that God did cause some of them to excel over others and granted varying degrees to his messengers [2: 253]. The term *Islam* and being *Muslim*, is employed everywhere in the Qur'an, including in the narratives of the past, as the original and natural religion of all creation. Therefore, the "Islam" of previous prophets is not to be confused with Islam as the religious doctrine brought by Muhammad.

While each story has its own morals, there are some general aims for the *Qaṣaṣ*. The Qur'an itself explains that the narratives are told to make firm the prophet Muhammad's heart [11: 120], whereby remembering the experiences of his predecessors would make him stand firm in his own prophetic career. The stories are also a reminder for believers [11: 120], and a lesson for people of understanding [12: 111].

It should be noted that the tales of the prophets or *Qiṣaṣ al-Anbiyā'* as a popular genre of "Islamic mythological literature" was a product of medieval storytellers, and the demands of their societies, which was frowned upon by Islamic theologians.[2] These started with the Qur'an and its exegeses, but in their form and content went beyond the narrow Qur'anic framework.[3]

This study, however, is removed from that popular genre and concerned only with the Qur'an and its exegeses, and with authentic traditions where they are available. The following is a study of each one of the female characters in the Qur'anic narratives of the prophets. Due to the wide variety in their personalities and circumstances, each character in this chapter will be discussed individually and analysed according to her own contribution to the larger story and to the Qur'an. Special emphasis will be laid on aspects of these women's humanity, particularly regarding their faith, intellects, and fortunes, which are characteristics normally portrayed in the traditions to be lacking in women.

In the previous chapter, it was shown that the Qur'an sees humanity as having emanated from a single soul, the nature of which encompasses both misconduct and piety. It was argued that Eve is a *nafs* in her own right, rather than being a part of a whole. In this chapter, the notion of woman as an independent human *nafs* will be elaborated. The women of the *qaṣaṣ* will be examined to see whether the Qur'an portrays them as particularly feminine, or whether they provide examples of a universal human *nafs*, or whether they combine feminine with universal qualities.

In his article "Qur'anic Concepts of Human Psyche", Absar Ahmad argues that the human soul in the Qur'anic view point is not merely a psychological entity but one that has God-consciousness in its depth, and that is because humanity emerged in creation primarily in the transcendental dimension of existence. God-consciousness and self-consciousness are therefore intertwined. He explains that the three kinds of *nafs* that are referred to in the Qur'an are to the majority of scholars three dimensions or stages of the human soul. He further elaborates that *al-nafs al-ammāra bi-s-sū'* [12: 53], the commanding soul is the appetitive soul. He understands *al-nafs al-lawwāma* [75: 2], the blaming soul to be the seat of reason, because it is through thoughts that people issue moral judgements. Finally, he explains that *al-nafs al-muṭma'inna* [89: 27] is the pacified soul where both emotions and thoughts have calmed, and this is the seat of the heart which is the spiritual core of the human being.[4]

The women examined here may be seen to fall into one or other of these categories. For example, the wives of Noah and Lot are commanding souls which did not progress and were doomed to punishment in the hereafter. The soul of Potiphar's wife was also a commanding soul, but this one finally progressed and issued moral judgements blaming herself and commending Joseph. The mother of Moses seems to have had an inner struggle but finally God pacified her heart so that she had complete trust in what he inspired in her. The Queen of Sheba is a blaming soul who, due to her intelligence, was able to see the harm that she had been doing to herself. Mary is seen by some Sufis as the prototype pacified soul,[5] for from before her birth, through her early childhood and into her later experiences, she remained disconnected from people and concerned only with God and worship. Other female personalities also fall within these categories and thus portray a spiritual struggle, or what the Prophet called *jihād al-nafs*,[6] which is however mixed with active earthly struggle. This will be most clearly seen in Hagar and Pharaoh's wife. That is in the form of worldly pursuit that was divinely acknowledged in the case of Hagar, and a spiritual *jihād* followed by a political one in the story of Āsiyā and Pharaoh. The wives of the prophet Muhammad are described as exceptional women, and pertaining to their status is the theme that a human in a place of responsibility has a heavier burden of struggle.

It should be mentioned that with the exception of Mary, women in the Qur'an are not referred to using their proper names. It has often been suggested that this follows Arabic mannerisms which demonstrate respect for women,[7] although this proposition has been discredited.[8] It has also been suggested that, as a rule, only prophets are mentioned by name in the Qur'an.[9] This however is not true, since Abraham's father Azar, a disbeliever, is mentioned by name [6: 74]. Pharaoh's minister is identified as Hāmān [28: 38, 40: 24, 36], and a wealthy Israelite on Pharaoh's side as Qārūn [40: 24]. Zayd, the adopted son of the Prophet, is also named [33: 37]. On the other hand, one Qur'anic character which tradition identifies as the prophet al-Khiḍr is never mentioned by name, rather as "one of Our servants unto whom We had given mercy from Us, and We had taught him knowledge proceeding from Us" [18: 65]. The reasoning, if there is any, behind naming an individual or not, is not clear and that is why this issue will be left at that.

The wives of the prophets Noah and Lot

"God has struck a similitude for the unbelievers – the wife of Noah, and the wife of Lot; for they were under two of Our righteous servants, but they betrayed them, so they availed them nothing whatsoever against God; so it was said, 'Enter, you two, the Fire with those who enter'" [66: 10].

This verse is from *Sūrat al-Taḥrīm*, which deals with "female rebellion in a prophet's household and its punishment".[10] That is because, as will be shown below, the chapter starts with the issue that one of the prophet Muhammad's wives betrayed a secret and conspired against him with another wife. Towards the end of the chapter, this verse on the wives of Noah and Lot occur, followed by two other verses that give as examples to the believers, the wife of Pharaoh, and Mary [66: 11–12]. Exegetes find that these verses are given as admonishments to two of the prophet Muhammad's wives who were discussed in the beginning of *Sūrat al-Taḥrīm*, and were the occasion of revelation.[11] However, Ṭūsī adds to this that the aim of this group of verses is to show that every person shall be judged according to their own actions. The wives of the two prophets were not saved despite their husbands' righteousness, but the wife of Pharaoh was saved despite her husband's wickedness.[12] Ṭabāṭabā'ī finds that even though the verses are addressing the Prophet's wives, the aim is universal whereby the verses give two examples for the disbelievers and believers respectively, saying that death comes as a result of infidelity and happiness as a result of faith. He notes that these examples are represented by women.[13]

The major reason that makes the wives of Noah and Lot examples for the disbelievers is their betrayal (*khānatāhumā*). The root of this word *khawn* indicates that a person is unfaithful to a trust that he was given,[14] and that a person did not abide by admonishments.[15] One lexicon adds that betrayal is a "betrayal of admonishment and betrayal of enduring love".[16] That seems very appropriate in this context, where Noah and Lot were prophets as well as husbands to their wives, therefore both their advice and their love were betrayed.[17]

Some have claimed that the betrayal was of an adulterous nature, based on the scene in which Noah pleads for the life of his son, but God reminds him that the son is not of his family, but that he is an unrighteous deed, after which Noah seeks forgiveness and mercy [11: 45–7]. This has been interpreted by some to mean that the boy was not his son but his wife's son.[18] However, this claim has been rejected categorically for its incompatibility with the Qur'anic account. The main reason given is that the Qur'anic story is teaching that when it comes to standing by truth, one ought not to give any preference to one's own blood relations, thus God's reminder to Noah that it is not his son but evil conduct.[19] Exegetes often add that no wife of a prophet has ever committed adultery.[20]

Traditions also confirm that the betrayal was in religion and in trust.[21] In the case of Noah's wife, her betrayal was accusing him of insanity, and in the case of Lot's wife, it was her alerting the Sodomites of his male guests.[22]

The Qur'an narrates that when Lot's people came to his house for the guests, he offered them his own daughters in marriage as a purer alternative if they were insistent on their deed, and to relieve the shame they caused him, but none was upright among them [11: 78, 15: 71]. Lot's wife, however, was on the side of the Sodomites, and therefore, as Noah's wife was left to drown, so also Lot was instructed to flee at night with his family, except for his wife who was made to lag behind [11: 81, 15: 60, 27: 57, 37: 135].

Lot's behaviour towards his daughters is problematic; they were offered in marriage by their father to the Sodomites, presumably without being consulted, and to people whom Lot himself strongly condemned as wanton and immature folk [7: 81, 11: 78]. Those daughters were among those who fled with Lot, and therefore one may assume that they were believing women. This makes Lot's behaviour uncharacteristic of a good father unless there is a hidden reason behind his offer.[23]

The wives of Noah and Lot are described here to have been "under" the two righteous men, which indicates that they were their wives.[24] This seems to be the apparent meaning of the expression, but it has also been argued that the element of their husbands' prophethood is another reason that the women were "under" their husbands.[25] Notice that, in the very next verse that speaks of the wife of Pharaoh as an example for the believers, she is not described as having been "under" Pharaoh, even though she was indeed his wife and subject to his tyranny.

Even though the verse speaks of two specific women, it gives them as examples to disbelievers in general (*mathalan li-l-ladhīna kafarū*), just as the verses that follow it also give two women as examples for the believers, men and women (*mathalan li-l-adhīna āmanū*). The gender of individuals is not as important as their conduct. The fact that precisely two women are named on either side creates a delicate balance between the good and the bad. Perhaps this verse addresses in particular the people who think they might have an advantage by being close to a prophet in one way or another. It says that if people betray the prophets and their message, then no intercession can avail them against God's judgement.

The wives of the prophet Abraham

The two wives of Abraham are barely mentioned in the Qur'an, most of what we know about Sarah and Hagar comes from the traditions. Sarah is mostly remembered for the miraculous birth of her son Isaac in her old age. Hagar is remembered for her contribution to the story of bringing life to Mecca, through her *sa'y* and the springing of the well of *zamzam*, a contribution that would ultimately lead to the birth of Islam. Some tensions are noted between the two women considering that the former was a wife and the latter a concubine of the same man. However, these tensions are not addressed in the Qur'an, and they are minimised in the traditions where both women are portrayed as pious individuals.

Sarah and Hagar

Sarah, the wife and cousin of Abraham, was wealthy and gave him her land and cattle from which he made a vast wealth.[26] Upon persecution and the people's rejection of his preaching, Abraham decided to leave his homeland with his believing wife Sarah, whereupon he made a prayer for God to grant him a good son, and God gave him the good tidings of a forbearing/meek boy [37: 83–101]. When they were later in Egypt, the king offered Sarah his "beautiful and sensible" slave girl, whom Abraham later bought from his wife and conjugated with, in hope that she might bring the barren couple a child, and she indeed brought Ishmael.[27] The Qur'anic passage [37: 102–13] is an account of the sacrifice that was about to be done on Abraham's son, followed by the good tidings of Isaac. Medieval scholars had debated whether the sacrificial boy was Ishmael or Isaac,[28] however, Shīʿī traditions and exegeses maintain that it was Ishmael, and that Isaac had not been born at the time.[29] This is relevant here because it means that Hagar will be considered the mother of the willing sacrificial boy.

Sarah is mentioned twice in the Qur'an. In the first instance, when she and Abraham were worried of their visitors' identity and intentions, then the guests informed them that they were angels sent to Lot's people. Upon that news the Qur'an describes Sarah as "*qā'ima fa-ḍaḥikat*" [11: 70–1]. She was standing and listening to the conversation, or perhaps standing and serving the guests.[30] Then *ḍaḥikat* primarily means that she laughed, another possible meaning for the word is that she menstruated.[31] If she "laughed", it was a sign of relief concerning the identity of the guests, but if she "menstruated", it was as a prerequisite for the tidings of Isaac that followed.[32] The primary meaning of laughter is considered secondary here because the reason for her laughter is claimed to be not very clear.[33] However, one lexicon adds that "*ḍaḥik*" may also indicate surprise, and finds that this best fits the context because Sarah expressed astonishment at two other instances in the Qur'an.[34]

Then, Sarah was given the good tidings of Isaac and, after him, his son Jacob. She expressed her surprise at the news because both she and her husband were in their old age, to which the angels replied, "What, dost thou marvel at God's command? The mercy of God and His blessings be upon you, O people of the House! Surely He is All-laudable, All-glorious" [11: 71–3]. Note that Sarah is addressed here as among the "people of the house" (*ahl al-bayt*), which is important for future discussions on Mary and Fāṭima who are also described as among *ahl al-bayt*. In the other occasion, upon hearing the tidings of a knowledgeable son, "came forward his wife, clamouring, and she smote her face, and said, 'An old woman, barren!'" [51: 29]. Some have said describing her behaviour that this is what women typically do when they are astonished.[35] This might well be the case, especially with eastern women, but perhaps another reason for the Qur'an vividly recounting her acts of astonishment, is to bring the reader's attention to the inconceivability of the event that was being foretold.[36]

Hagar is mentioned only once and very indirectly in the Qur'an. Apparently due to Sarah's jealousy of the slave girl after Ishmael's birth,[37] Abraham took Hagar and his son to the desert until they reached Mecca, and he called God, "Our Lord, I have made some of my seed (*min dhurriyyatī*) to dwell in a valley where is no sown land by Thy Holy House; Our Lord, let them perform the prayer, and make hearts of men yearn towards them, and provide them with fruits; haply they will be thankful" [14: 37]. While the translation of the term as seed and posterity are confined to descendants, the Arabic *dhurriyya* primarily means offspring but includes fathers and women,[38] in which case it could include Hagar with her child.

The reason for this migration being Sarah's jealousy has been mentioned scantily in the traditions. The Qur'an does not give a direct explicit reason for the relocation, however it does describe their prayers to make this a region of security and bestow fruits upon it. It also describes the building of the foundations of the Ka'ba by Abraham and Ishmael at the holy site, and recounts their prayers to God, to make of themselves and their seed a (spiritually) submissive/Muslim nation, to show them their rites and relent towards them, and to raise up in their nation's midst a Messenger from among themselves who would recite God's revelation, teach the scripture and wisdom, and make them pure [2: 125–9]. These words will prove to be most relevant to Hagar's contribution.

The theme of "female rivalry in a patriarchal household"[39] is evident in the traditions, though not in the Qur'an, but it is not given due thought because of the emphasis on the outcome rather than the cause of the tension between the women and the subsequent relocation of Hagar and her son.

Sa'y *and* zamzam

According to authentic traditions, when Abraham left Hagar and her son in the valley, she went to the hill of *al-Ṣafā* looking for help, and then she went to the hill of *al-Marwa* for the same reason. She kept going back and forth seven times and God made that a ritual. When she finally came back to her son, she found that water had gushed forth from beneath his feet.[40] The ritual that God prescribed is the *sa'y*, walking or running seven times between *al-Ṣafā* and *al-Marwa*, which is a requirement for any Muslim pilgrimage at Mecca [2: 158]. As for the water that came to them in the desert, it is the well of *zamzam*, so named because as soon as the water gushed out, Hagar gathered soil round it in order to contain it (*zammat-hu*). The traditions add, had she not done so it would have spilled.[41]

Perhaps, at first glance, this might seem to be a simple story of a mother looking for water in the desert to give her child. However, one is forced to dig deeper, because these very actions of Hagar, particularly the *sa'y* seven times but also drinking from *zamzam*, remain a token of the pilgrimage, one of the five pillars of Islam.

Sa'y means walking, running, working, or seeking.[42] It has been said that striving is the cause of sustenance.[43] This is one clear theme from Hagar's pursuit, and her finding water in the desert.

The Qur'an uses the term *sa'y* in reference to spiritual pursuit, "hasten to God's remembrance (*fa-s'aw ilā dhikr-i-llāh*)" [62: 9]. However, it describes people's efforts as being dispersed, "surely your striving is to diverse ends (*inna sa'yakum la-shattā*)" [92: 4]. Therefore, it reminds each human soul of its judgement based on what it had pursued, "and that the human shall have to his account only as he has laboured, and that his labouring shall surely be seen" [53: 39–40], and "upon the day when the human shall remember what he has striven" [79: 35].

Traditions mostly use the term *sa'y* in reference to the pilgrimage rite. The importance of *sa'y* is heightened in the traditions that describe it as God's favourite ritual because it is the humiliation of tyrants.[44]

Notice that from the traditions mentioned earlier, which state that Hagar kept going back and forth seven times and God made that a ritual, one understands that Hagar's actual *sa'y* preceded God's making the *sa'y* into ritual. This means that Hagar herself, running between the two hilltops, was unaware of any divine ritual that she was performing. She was simply a mother searching for water in the desert to quench her child's thirst. However, something in her actions made God look at her and make the *sa'y* his own.

The relevance of *sa'y* is pinned to another potent symbol in the story which is water, the product of *sa'y* and an element of utmost relevance for life. As the Qur'an puts it "and of water (We) fashioned every living thing" [21: 30].

Water is seen in the Qur'an as a sign of God's existence, unity and power. By bringing forth water, God provides food and drink for all his creatures, as well as physical, psychological and spiritual purification [77: 27, 80: 24–30, 8: 11, etc.].[45] The authentic traditions that describe the blessings of the water of *zamzam* specifically are numerous.[46]

Therefore, when God sent water to Hagar and Ishmael, he sent life to the barren valley of Mecca and in it was a promise of spiritual purification as well. One can see that from the point when Hagar started her pursuit, the prayers of Abraham with Ishmael discussed earlier, that God bestow security upon that region, give its people fruits, that God "show us our rites (*arinā manāsikanā*)", and raise a Messenger who would purify the people [2: 126–9], all started to be answered. Her *sa'y* became a major part of Muslims' rites, and the water of *zamzam*, which she sought and contained, was the answer for all their other prayers of life, and purification.

The conceptualisation of Hagar as a potent symbol for "a woman seeking reform in a patriarchal society"[47] seems to be an overstatement. The fact that her somewhat ordinary actions were seen by God to be fit for a ritual undertaking by all Muslims, men and women, means that her actions and significance are beyond gender.

Some have seen in Hagar a "female figure of sufferance", and have understood the message of her story as a message for women to be "persevering, hard working, simple, obedient, and with few expectations".[48] In the analysis above it has been shown that suffering in itself is not the legacy of Hagar, as it is not the legacy of her son. Rather, their suffering created a situation for them to leave a more glorious legacy; that patience, perseverance, and prayer are soon rewarded. When Abraham informed his son of his dream instructing him to kill him, and asked his opinion, Ishmael did not see himself a victim but submitted to the will of God and showed courage; he advised his father to do it and stated that he will, with God's permission, be patient [37: 102–3]. Similarly, Hagar accepted what was given to her and directed her energies at useful pursuits. If the gift of water is understood in modern times to be a modest expectation, it may be seen from the Qur'anic point of view as a symbol for all that can be given. Both her *sa'y*, and the product of her *sa'y* which is *zamzam*, became not only for her family, but for generations, a divine gift bestowed upon that land.

In the story of Hagar and the ritual that followed, there is an exemplification of the Islamic motif that work is worship. The role Hagar plays in the story of Abraham's planting a seed in the barren but holy place, is a very vigorous and influential role, both in its worldly and spiritual dimensions. Abraham planted his and Hagar's seed, he and his son prayed, but through her actions was the answer to much of their prayers. This makes her a partner in the making of this story/history. Thus, it rings true that her "near absence from scriptural commentary is not necessarily a signal of her insignificance; it may be quite the opposite".[49]

Sarah and Hagar are both mentioned rarely in the Qur'an. Sarah saw and conversed with the angels that visited her house, and she was addressed by them as a member of *ahl al-bayt*. She was also miraculously given a son and a grandson who were in a line of prophets from her descendants. Hagar's story connects the monotheism of Abraham with Muhammad's Islam. Through her actions the prayers of Abraham came true, and her legacy continues to form and renew Muslims' identity, through their imitation of her *sa'y* in that sacred space.[50]

Zulaykha

The story of Joseph, unlike the stories of other prophets, is narrated from beginning to end in a chronological order of his life. The beginning of *Sūrat Yūsuf* describes the story that will follow as "the best of narratives" (*aḥsan al-qaṣaṣ*) [12: 3].[51]

Some feminists were suspicious of this description especially due to the notion of the wiles of women expressed in the chapter, and asked whose best story is this story.[52] Some Sufis, however, suggest that it is so because this is a story about love.[53]

In this section on Zulaykha, the problem of the infamous statement on the wiles of women will be addressed in its context. The Sufi idea that this Qur'anic chapter, in which Zulaykha is one major character, is about love will be examined in the light of the Qur'an and traditions. Finally, the redemption of Zulaykha, or the lack of it, which is a textual problem among exegetes, will be analysed. This problem is particularly relevant because it expresses whether or not Zulaykha identified herself as the soul that bids evil and outgrew it.

The wiles of women

The story begins with Joseph's dream in which he saw eleven planets and the sun and moon prostrating unto him. His father advised him not to tell his brothers of his vision. His brothers had always been envious of Joseph so they threw him into a pit. Through a sequence of events he was sold into slavery to an Egyptian governor. When Joseph became mature and was given knowledge and wisdom, the wife of the governor, whom traditions name Zulaykha, seduced him but he refused her, at least partly due to loyalty towards the governor's hospitality, or towards God.[54] As he ran towards the door she chased him and caught him by the shirt so that his shirt got torn. At the door they found her husband, so she immediately accused Joseph of seducing her and encouraged her husband to imprison him or torture him. A witness from her family suggested that if his shirt was torn from the back then she is a liar and vice versa. At that point her husband said, "This is of your guile (feminine plural); surely your guile (feminine plural) is great" [12: 28]. He then asked Joseph not to mention the incident, and told his wife to seek forgiveness for her sin. Later, however, in spite of the signs of Joseph's innocence, the men of the town decide to imprison Joseph for a while because of the havoc he unintentionally created among the women of the town. Later, due to his unique ability to correctly interpret dreams, Joseph is freed and made governor, but not before clearing his name regarding the reasons of his imprisonment. In the end, he is reunited with his family who prostrate themselves before him. Thus the vision Joseph had as a child became realised, whereby the parents were represented by the sun and moon, and the eleven planets were his brothers.

While many exegetes focus on Zulaykha's and the women's guile as the main problem in the story, Sayyid Qutb finds that the enemy of Joseph was Egyptian *jāhilī* society ("the time of ignorance", before the prophetic message reaches a people), partly because of the spoiled women, but also the weak governor who put an innocent man in jail merely to avoid scandal.[55]

It may be added to Qutb's view, however, that the problem was not only of Egyptian society because Joseph's brothers were not *jāhilī* but sons of a monotheistic prophet, and yet they envied the love of their father Jacob for Joseph and their younger brother over the rest of them, "When they said, 'Surely Joseph and his brother are dearer to our father than we, though we are a band. Surely our father is in manifest error'" [12: 8]. Their logic is twisted, "they see their father's affection as a commodity, as merchandise to be shared out, and calculate that ten should receive more than two".[56] The Qur'an narrates the brothers' dialogue when they discuss what to do with the prophet, "Kill you Joseph, or cast him forth into some land, that your father's face may be free for you, and thereafter you may be a righteous people" [12: 9]. Notice the irony in their planning to be righteous right after killing their brother.[57] The brothers pressured and deceived their father into allowing Joseph to go out with them [12: 11–14], and then they threw him into a pit. The Qur'an narrates how after they had done their deed, they returned to their father "crying" about the loss of their brother [12: 16]. Had the Qur'an attributed those actions to a female character, most exegetes surely would not have spared the chance to point out that women really do have crocodile tears. Throughout the story, Joseph's brothers are portrayed to be mocking their father [12: 8, 85, 95][58] and towards the end falsely accusing Joseph of being a thief [12: 77].

Guile (*kayd*) is a common and repeated theme in this story. The term occurs in the beginning of the story when Jacob hears of Joseph's dream and advises his son not to mention the dream to his brothers lest they scheme against him (*fa yakīdū laka kaydan*) [12: 5]. The same term is also used later in the chapter when Joseph devises a plot, a contrivance taught to him by God, to plant the king's cup in his brother's sack in order to accuse his beloved brother of theft so that he may keep him with him (*kadhālika kidnā li Yūsuf*) [12: 76].

As for the wiles of women, "This is of your guile (feminine plural); surely your guile (feminine plural) is great (*inna kaydakunna 'aẓīm*)" [12: 28], Ṭūsi only points out that the governor attributed guile to his wife and excluded Joseph from it, and while he acknowledges that it is in the grammatically plural feminine, he does not comment on it.[59] Ṭabāṭabā'ī however considers women's guile to be in their ability to attract men and their hearts, thereby ridding them of their sound minds and controlling them.[60] It has sometimes been correctly pointed out that the verse need not carry much weight because it is spoken by the character of the governor of Egypt,[61] neither by a prophet as in the first use of the term *kayd* mentioned above, nor by the narrator of the Qur'an as in the last use of the term. Therefore, this attribution of guile to women by the governor may not necessarily carry in it the Qur'anic approval. Soon afterwards in the story, the governor himself plots against Joseph by putting him in jail despite the signs of Joseph's innocence, merely to avoid scandal [12: 35]. This renders his statement on the wiles of women hypocritical. Zulaykha attempted to seduce Joseph, but as far as scheming against him by putting him in prison for their own personal grudges, she and her husband were the same.

In addition to Zulaykha's wiles, there are those of her female friends. After the incident when the governor walked in on his wife chasing Joseph, the women in society started talking about Zulaykha seducing her slave boy against his will. They concluded that he had impassioned her and they deemed her to be in plain aberration. Ṭabāṭabā'ī claims that gossip is in the nature of women, so is their love of themselves and their envy towards others. His understanding is that those women were judgemental in order to console themselves, and their envy was because they had not seen Joseph's beauty.[62] This seems far-fetched because a simpler explanation would be that they really did consider what they heard of Zulaykha's actions as inappropriate for her status. Moreover, it is not at all clear why it would be assumed that the women were envious for not having seen Joseph. The story continues that Zulaykha heard of their slyness, so she invited them to her house and presented them with knives, presumably to cut fruits with. She then asked Joseph to enter their place of gathering. Upon seeing him the women started cutting their hands, presumably smitten with his beauty, they exalted him and declared that this was no man but a noble angel [12: 31]. Zulaykha thus proved her point, telling them this is the one you blamed me about, and she continued to threaten Joseph with prison if he did not submit to her will. The women then joined in the seduction, as is understood from Joseph's words afterwards asking God to shield him from their plots to seduce him. Some have seen the bleeding of the women to be a symbol for the display of female sexuality, albeit implicit, because it is the words of Joseph that "transform the scene from one of collective empathy by the women of the town for Zulaykha into a scene of collective seduction".[63]

One question put forth by some feminists asks, whose best story is this story? That point of view expresses scepticism about the possibility of appropriating the story as an "emancipatory narrative for female sexual liberation", because the story is male-centred and because female sexuality is described as an "uncontrollable threatening force that men have to be wary of, not seduced by".[64] Later, however, this idea was revisited, and it was seen that the theme of such tales of guile, in which women seduce men, actually reverses the traditional image of women as passive and subservient, and puts women "in control of the sexual scene".[65]

Indeed, due to this chapter's depiction of a powerful female sexuality, one tradition claims that the Imam declared that *Sūrat Yūsuf* should not be taught to women because it causes discord, whereas teaching them *Sūrat al-Nūr* is commendable because it contains admonishments.[66] It is very strange that some parts of the Qur'an should not be taught because the Qur'an, all of it, is supposed to be guidance to humankind; unless what is meant in the tradition is not to teach this to young girls. However, what this reveals is some difficulty the culture had in coming to terms with the image of Zulaykha as a married woman quite forcefully seducing a young man in her care.[67] The advice to teach *Sūrat al-Nūr* instead seems to say that Zulaykha's open sexuality is precisely the problem, because *Sūrat al-Nūr* begins with prescribing the punishments for the adulteress and adulterer.

It has been shown above that guile is one of the major themes in this story, and that it is not exclusive to the female characters. Towards the middle of the story it will be said that God does not guide the guile of betrayers [12: 52], thereby completing the theme of guile. The scenes of Zulaykha's passion and later the women's passion do exhibit the power of sexual energy. This energy is portrayed through female characters, although there seems to be an understanding for these women too. Zulaykha inviting the women to her house in a way gives her space to tell her side of the story, that it was not only due to a folly in herself but it was Joseph's sublime beauty that crazed her. The women of the town, who blamed Zulaykha when they first heard the news, seem to have lost their minds upon seeing Joseph. This group reaction reveals that Zulaykha was not the only one to react as such, which is exactly what Zulaykha sought to prove in that gathering, and she even pointed out to the women that this is what they blamed her for. Therefore, perhaps another important element in the scene is not to condemn female sexuality, but to hint that, having attracted all those women, Joseph's abstinence itself seems all the more majestic.

Islamic tradition often speaks of Joseph's beauty as exemplary, but Sufi exegesis observes that "this radiance emanated not from Joseph's external beauty, but from his inner qualities".[68] This issue of external beauty and internal beauty is linked to the story's differentiation between illusory love and true love.

Lover and beloved

A repeatedly narrated tradition says that when Joseph was in jail, one of the prison guards told him, "I love you", Joseph answered him, "do not love me; my aunt loved me and accused me of theft, and my father loved me so my brothers envied me and threw me in the pit, and the wife of the governor loved me so they jailed me".[69] This tradition should be kept in mind, because it seems to agree with the point of view that this story is about love, whether it is Joseph's perfect love for God or the unperfected and misdirected love of others.

When the women blamed Zulaykha they said that Joseph had inflamed her with love. The Qur'anic expression is (*qad shaghafahā ḥubban*) [12: 30]. In Arabic, *shaghaf* is literally the layer of fat that veils the heart, and normally when an illness reaches that layer the heart is inflicted beyond cure. This is precisely what the Arabs mean when they employ the term in reference to love.[70] Therefore, this suggests that Zulaykha's love was actually a sickness in her heart.

Ṭabāṭabā'ī contrasts Zulaykha's love for Joseph with Joseph's love for God. Her love to him was like a fire that consumed her heart. He was beautiful so her love to him was lustful, and she attempted to use her social status to subdue him. His heart, on the other hand, was filled with the love of God, due to what he saw of God's beautiful work and His support of every soul. Joseph was almost like a ghost, the only reality behind him was divine love that made him forget everything else including himself. This is the meaning of the Qur'an describing him saying, "He was one of Our sincere/devoted servants (*mukhlaṣīn*)" [12: 24]. His soul was purified and chosen by God for himself alone. She wanted to turn him away from himself to herself, but he did not want to turn to anyone other than God. Animal love and divine love, represented by these two characters in the story, were fighting the will of one another. That fight was also an inner fight inside Joseph's soul. God's word and divine love soon protected Joseph, however, and he abstained from entertaining the woman because he would not show disloyalty to his real owner and protector.[71]

Rashīd al-Dīn al-Maybūdī's (d.520/1126) Sufi interpretation, on the other hand, compares Zulaykha's love for Joseph with Jacob's love for his son. Zulaykha's love had no truth in it, and only later when she admitted her fault, did real love for Joseph dominate her heart. Maybūdī sees that this is in the nature of love, that in the beginning the lover shows bewilderment, and after habituation the lover shows stability. That, in his view, explains why Zulaykha did not cut her hands when the women who saw Joseph for the first time did.[72] In one of Maybūdī's several interpretations, Jacob's love is shown to have begun where Zulaykha's love ended, which is the point where love has complete control over the lover.[73] Remember that in the Qur'anic narrative, Jacob's crying and longing for Joseph caused his eyes to become blind, and in the end only Joseph's garment was able to restore his eyesight [12: 96].

Towards the end of the story, Joseph's dream is finally realised. When the family is reunited in Egypt, Joseph asked that his parents be brought onto the throne, and they prostrated before Joseph. Ṭabāṭabā'ī says, based on the Qur'anic description of them falling into prostration (*wa kharrū lahū sujjadan*), that when he entered into their gathering they were overcast with divine light that was shining through his beauty, and they just fell into prostration.[74]

While Ṭabāṭabā'ī sees Zulaykha as an outer representative of an inner animalistic reality within the soul, Maybūdī sees her as a lover in progress.

Zulaykha represents the appetitive soul, but it is difficult to concede to Ṭabāṭabā'ī's claims that she represents the lower soul even within Joseph himself. That is because the repeated Qur'anic expression that is being translated here as "she seduced him" is actually *rāwadat-hu 'an nafsih*, which literally means that she fought with him a battle of wills.[75] Even though Joseph sought God's support in those times, his will was evidently opposed to hers. As for Maybūdī's interpretation, it seems to be an exaggeration to compare Zulaykha's love to Jacob's. She was completely absorbed with her desires, and when she did not meet them she took revenge at the perceived cause of her misery. That is unlike Jacob who understood the real value of Joseph, and who suffered because of love but continued to show great forbearance. Yet, there is an element in the observation that both Jacob's and Zulaykha's love were directed towards Joseph, although they were each at a different stage of love. That becomes clearest when even Jacob the prophet prostrated before his son in the end, whereas Joseph's love was always directed towards God alone.

The tradition in which Joseph complains of people's "love" for him emphasises the theme of illusory love as opposed to divine love. The use of the word *shaghaf* in the Qur'an to describe Zulaykha's love is interesting. She did not see beyond Joseph's physical beauty, and she punished him because he did not satisfy her. She failed to see the paradox of her situation, that it was precisely the source of his beauty that made him refuse her. The prostration scene, however, again reveals that Joseph's beauty was magnificent, and that the women were not amiss when they compared him to a noble angel. It also points out that Zulaykha's love was not entirely unjustified, although it was untrue. Seeing Zulaykha as a symbol of the inner appetitive soul is problematic because it fixes her in that position, whereas seeing her as a lover in progress emphasises the possibility for growth even though she was misguided; but either identification is more closely related to her as an individual than as a woman. The difference between these two viewpoints, however, unfolds in the debate regarding the identity of the speaker of verses [12: 52–3], concerning the soul that bids evil.

The soul that incites to evil

During his time in prison, Joseph met two cell mates who eventually discovered Joseph's unique ability to interpret dreams correctly. Later, the king of Egypt had a complex dream which no one was able to explain, until one of the cell mates that had been freed suggested consulting Joseph. The Qur'anic passage reads:

> The king said, "Bring him to me!" And when the messenger came to him, he said, "Return unto thy lord, and ask of him, 'What of the women who cut their hands?' Surely my Lord has knowledge of their guile." [12: 50]. "What was your business, women," he said, "when you solicited Joseph?"

> "God save us!" they said. "We know no evil against him." The Governor's wife said, "Now the truth is at last discovered; I solicited him; he is a truthful man [12: 51]. That, so that he may know I betrayed him not secretly, and that God guides not the guile of the treacherous [12: 52]. Yet I claim not that my soul was innocent – surely the (human) soul incites to evil – except inasmuch as my Lord had mercy; truly my Lord is All-forgiving, All-compassionate" [12: 53]. The king said, "Bring him to me! I would attach him to my person".
>
> [12: 54]

These verses are particularly important for the purposes of this discussion because in them the women confess their faults, and this brings closure to the problem, as the king's statement ends Joseph's life of hardship. The statement on "the soul that incites to evil (*al-nafs al-ammara bi-s-sū'*)" is particularly meaningful not only because of its relevance to Islamic theology in general, but also because it seems to be the crux of the entire story of Zulaykha and Joseph.

There is a debate on the identity of the speaker of the two verses [12: 52–3]. Qummī, one of the earliest commentators, understands this to be a continuation of Zulaykha's speech, and does not give the matter further attention.[76] Classical exegetes understand the text to be possibly the speech of either one of them, that is, either Zulaykha or Joseph. If Joseph were the speaker, then the lack of betrayal mentioned is that he did not betray the governor with his wife. As for his saying that he does not exculpate himself, that is because he abstained from succumbing to temptation because of God's mercy, and therefore did not take credit for himself. The reference to the soul that incites to evil "except inasmuch as my Lord had mercy (*illā mā raḥima rabbī*)" is in this case understood to imply that this is the nature of the soul except until God bestows his mercy on the soul. In this case the exception is an exception not of certain souls as such, but an exception that occurs in time. In which case, he would have been saying that his soul incited to evil until God saved him. However, if the speech belongs to Zulaykha, then her claim that she did not betray Joseph secretly is a reference to the fact that she testified to Joseph's honesty in his absence, and she did not exculpate herself because in fact she did previously betray him by putting him in jail. In that case, the reference to the soul that incites to evil is simply a reference to the nature of the human soul in general, with the exception of a few souls, such as Joseph himself.[77] Most classical exegetes give priority to the speech belonging to Joseph, with the exception of Ṭūsī who considers, although without elaboration, that attributing the words to Joseph is problematic and that it is more likely to be a continuation of Zulaykha's speech.[78]

Ṭabāṭabā'ī considers the point of view that the two verses in question could be Zulaykha's speech a very inferior possibility. He gives three reasons for this. First, that attributing the words, "That (testimony), so that he may know I betrayed him not secretly" to her is not sensible, partly because if it were her speech she would have continued it with "and", not with "that". Also because if she were the speaker, it means that she testified just to take credit for her new-found honesty, not because of a desire on her part to reveal the truth. Moreover, she had betrayed him and her confession does not negate her betrayal. Second, the continuation, "so that he may know … and that God guides not the guile of the treacherous", has no meaning because Joseph already knows that. Third, there is a contradiction between her alleged claim that she did not betray him in secret, and the next statement that she does not exculpate herself. Moreover, Ṭabāṭabā'ī continues, the statement that, "surely the (human) soul incites to evil – except inasmuch as my Lord had mercy; truly my Lord is All-forgiving, All-compassionate", with all the monotheistic knowledge that is contained within it, is not fit to emanate from an idolatress who had been governed by whim.[79]

Ṭabāṭabā'ī's objections are not entirely convincing. To answer his first question, the use of "that (testimony)" rather than "and" need not signify a discontinuation in the speech and a shift in the speaker, but could be because she testified to the king to Joseph's personality, but then wished to add something that is other than her testimony. It is understandable that Zulaykha would sincerely testify to the truth, and wish that Joseph would know about it, and that is not necessarily incompatible. While the confession does not negate the betrayal, it is nonetheless a step in the right direction. This leads to the third question, that her claim that she did not betray him in secret is a contradiction to her saying that she does not exculpate herself. Rather, her testimony in Joseph's absence was truthful, even though she does not claim she had been innocent in the past. There is a valid point, however, in Ṭabā-ṭabā'ī's second objection, which is that there is no point in her reporting to Joseph "that God guides not the guile of the treacherous" because he already knows that. It could be, however, that through this testimony is her affirmation to the listeners, based on experience, that God indeed does not guide the evildoers, which is what Joseph had counselled her in the beginning [12: 23].

The point of view that the speech belongs to Joseph has its own problems and inconsistencies. There are two problems pertaining to [12: 52] and [12: 53] respectively. Joseph could have taken the first opportunity to leave the prison but he wished to clear his name first. Notice that he asked the king to inquire about the women who cut their hands, but did not mention Zulaykha, perhaps to refrain from scandalising the house of the governor,[80] who had previously asked Joseph to keep the issue to himself, which means that he knew of Joseph's innocence. Also, Joseph asked the king to inquire about the women who cut their hands, but the king asked the women why they seduced Joseph against his will. This might imply that people knew what the problem was really about. This is confirmed by the Qur'an, "Then it seemed good to them, after they had seen the signs, that they should imprison him for a while" [12: 35]. This verse is explained by a tradition that the signs were signs of his innocence through the witness, the shirt torn from the back, and her husband at the door having already heard some of what was happening.[81]

Ṭabāṭabā'ī himself, who claims that Joseph wished to prove to the governor that he did not betray him, actually adopts the explanation that the governor and others knew of Joseph's innocence when they jailed him.[82] In fact Ṭabāṭabā'ī commends earlier exegetes who gave nine verses which show that Joseph, Zulaykha, her husband, the women, the witness, God, and the devil all knew of Joseph's innocence.[83] However, he adds that Joseph's statement that he did not betray the governor is further proof.[84] The Qur'an, traditions, and exegeses clearly inform us that the governor was already aware of Joseph's innocence in the matter. It therefore seems unlikely that Joseph would request the women's testimony to the governor who put him in jail in spite of his knowledge of his innocence.

Another problematic point is Joseph affirming that he does not exculpate himself. The exegetes go to great lengths to show that Joseph neither encouraged the women to seduce him, nor did he contemplate the idea of engaging them. For example, on Joseph's feelings towards Zulaykha the Qur'an says, "For she desired him; and he would have desired her, but that he saw the proof of his Lord. So was it, that We might turn away from him evil and abomination; he was one of Our devoted servants" [12: 24]. The eighth Imam al-Riḍā clarifies that the statement is conditional, that had he not seen the proof of his lord, he would have desired her; however he was impeccable and did not incline towards sin.[85] Ṭabāṭabā'ī notices that the latter part of the verse says that God averted evil and abomination from Joseph, not that he averted Joseph from them, which means that Joseph was not inclined to them in the first place.[86] As for the other incident when Joseph was seduced by the women collectively, "He said, 'My Lord, prison is dearer to me than that they call me to; yet if Thou turnest not from me their guile, then I shall yearn towards them, and so become one of the ignorant'" [12: 33]. He preferred prison, which shows that he did not like what they asked of him, except for what his human nature dictated upon him.[87]

The question of Joseph as speaker of the words on the soul that incites to evil inevitably takes the discussion to the topic of the impeccability of the prophets, which is too vast a topic to discuss here. Suffice to say that Imam 'Alī considered this desire of Joseph, as well as other lapses told of the prophets in the Qur'an, to show God's wisdom, because He knows that the testimonials for the prophets are grand in the hearts of their people, and because He knows that some people worship their prophets as gods, and He wanted to show that perfection is unique to God.[88] This explains why the Qur'an tells of Joseph's dilemma and his invoking divine help upon every test that he encountered. However, the Imams also explain that the "proof of his lord" that made Joseph steadfast was exactly his prophethood and wisdom which disinclined him from committing transgressions and ugly behaviour.[89] It seems then, that in spite of this prophet's humanity, he did not commit a mistake of the sort that would lead him to declare that he does not exculpate himself.

The most problematic aspect of this is the timing of this statement, if it were uttered by Joseph. During the debate between the king and the women

Joseph was not present, and the Qur'anic passage shows that after all those statements were made, the king asked for Joseph to be brought to him. This is why those who say this is Joseph's speech maintain that it was a monologue made in his prison cell.[90] If Joseph asked the women to clear his name by confessing their deeds in public, it would not have been fair of him to proclaim his own lack of innocence in private. That would have been lacking in honesty and grace. Rather, one would expect a prophet who does not consider himself innocent to have made that statement in public, before the very assembly that was discussing his innocence. Perhaps he could have also used that opportunity to teach about "the soul that incites to evil".

The insistence that Zulaykha could not have said those words because she was an idolatress governed by whim, promotes the pessimistic impression that people are incapable of identifying with and learning the prophetic message. Considering that Qummī considered this to be Zulaykha's speech and Ṭūsī stated that there would be problems otherwise, in addition to what has been argued regarding the speech being Joseph's having more serious problems and inconsistencies than its being Zulaykha's, one finds that perhaps the real issue at stake is a deep-seated misogyny that does not wish to allow this woman her redemption. This is especially so considering that [12: 53] is the verse that speaks of *al-nafs al-ammara bi-s-sū'*, a basic idea in Islamic theology, and thus it would be difficult for some to accept that this teaching be done through the character of a wildly passionate woman.

It is interesting to add here that Jacob's statements to his sons, "No; but your souls beguiled you into something (*sawwalat lakum anfusukum*)" [12: 18, 83], reflect another verse on the soul that beguiles in reference to the Samaritan who convinced the Israelites to build and worship the golden calf, "So my soul prompted me (*sawwalat lī nafsī*)" [20: 96]. Perhaps these statements could remove the stigma of the lower soul being seen as feminine.

The focus on Zulaykha's character alone may lead to a narrow interpretation of her personality and role in the story. Joseph's brothers provide male examples of guile and of the lowest self. Jacob's love and longing, his forbearance, the loss and restoration of his eyesight, and finally his prostration to Joseph, in a way put Zulaykha's passion in a wider framework of love. Even the women of Egypt help put Zulaykha's experience in perspective. In the end all guile is defeated. Joseph's love for God seems to be the only absolute. The debate on whether or not Zulaykha identified herself as *al-nafs al-ammāra* is important, because if she didn't, then she is not very different from the wives of Noah and Lot, but if she did, then she offers a different example of *al-nafs al-ammāra* that evolves.

The women in the life of the prophet Moses

The four women mentioned in the Qur'an surrounding the prophet Moses all shaped his life before his prophethood began. His mother and sister, as well as the wife of Pharaoh, were responsible for saving his life and, knowingly or unknowingly, carrying God's plan forward by planting Moses in the house of Pharaoh. Moses' bride helped him when he was in refuge until he was ready to return to Egypt and free the Israelites. There are a couple of references that seem to point towards an elevated spirituality within Moses' mother, and there is also an emphasis on her experience as a mother through the focus on breastfeeding in her story. The wife of Pharaoh is given as an example for believing men and women, and the possible reasons for this will be investigated. Moses' bride has been seen by some modern authors as an example for women's proper behaviour in the public space.

Moses' mother and sister

Sūrat al-Qaṣaṣ begins by describing the oppression that Pharaoh had spread in the land, dividing the people and suppressing a group of them, killing the men and capturing the women. This is then followed by the divine promise that the oppressed will inherit the earth and become its leaders, and thus Pharaoh, his minister and their soldiers shall see from the believers that which they had feared [28: 4–6].

The story continues, "So We revealed to Moses' mother, 'Suckle him, then, when thou fearest for him, cast him into the sea, and do not fear, neither sorrow, for We shall return him to thee, and shall appoint him one of the Envoys'" [28: 7]. She did, and the child ended up in Pharaoh's house, "to be an enemy and a sorrow to them" [28: 8]. The wife of Pharaoh, whom the traditions name Āsiyā, told her husband that the child could be a consolation for them, and persuaded him not to kill him, perhaps he might benefit them or they may choose him as a son [28: 9]. The story continues, "On the morrow the heart of Moses' mother became empty, and she well-nigh disclosed him had We not strengthened her heart, that she might be among the believers" [28: 10]. The mother told her daughter, Moses' sister, to trace him. The girl watched him from a distance while they did not perceive [28: 11]. God made all the women that were brought to suckle Moses prohibited upon him by God, so his sister suggested to them a household that would rear him for them [28: 12]. That is how God restored Moses to his mother, "that she might be comforted and not sorrow, and that she might know that the promise of God is true; but most of them do not know" [28: 13].

Some have suggested that the mother of Moses was a prophet because of the inspiration that God had given her,[91] which is in Arabic the same word for revelation (*waḥy*) [28: 7]. This claim however is unsubstantial considering that the term *waḥy* has been used in the Qur'an in other contexts than prophetic revelation, in reference to the bees [16: 68] and to the earth [99: 5]. One lexicon finds that the term is used for a swift sign, an indication in some way through body language, the use of symbols or writing, and it is used in reference to divine revelation.[92] Another focuses on the meanings of writing, giving a message, and hidden speech.[93] She is, in any case, portrayed as a firm believer in God's promise. When she was inspired to throw the child into the river, God consoled her that the hardship will be relieved, "cast him into the sea, and do not *fear*, neither *sorrow*, for We shall return him to thee" [28: 7]. She believed this and acted on it. Soon afterwards, "the heart of Moses' mother became empty, and she well-nigh disclosed him had We not strengthened her heart, that she might be among the believers" [28: 10]. Exegetes differ in their understanding of the emptying of her heart. Some say it was empty of everything other than Moses, or that it was empty of the inspiration that was given her, or empty of sorrow due to her knowledge that Moses will be returned to her. They do agree, however, that the next statement means that she did not disclose him because God strengthened her heart.[94] Ṭabāṭabā'ī finds that the interpretation of her heart being empty of anything other than Moses does not fit in with the context. Rather, he accepts the latter interpretation and says that her heart became empty of fear and sorrow which are mentioned in a preceding verse. This then means that after the inspiration told her to cast him and neither fear nor sorrow, she put the child into the river, and were it not for that inspiration and subsequent emptying of her heart, she would not have been steadfast and would have come close to revealing the matter.[95]

One may observe that reference to these two psychological states of fear and sorrow is signifying. The people of paradise are described to have neither fear nor sorrow [7: 49, 43: 68]. This is also the state of the *awliyā'*, "Surely God's friends (*awliyā'*) – no fear shall be on them, neither shall they sorrow" [10: 62]. The translation of *awliyā'* includes such meanings as friends, ones that are near, patrons, and inheritors.[96]

In addition to the mentioning of her trust in God, the Qur'an also hints at her knowledge, which many people do not have, "that she might know that the promise of God is true; but most of them do not know" [28: 13].

Moses' refusal of the wet nurses was the means through which he was returned to his mother, "Now We had forbidden to him aforetime to be suckled by any foster-mother" [28: 12]. The word of forbiddance was the force by which God made Moses refuse the wet nurses that were brought to him, and the forbiddance here is existential, not judicial.[97] This interpretation means that there was no legal impediment that would have made his feeding from these women *ḥarām*, but it was a force that stopped Moses. Even though this issue worked as the means to return Moses, when his sister traced him and suggested to them her mother as a wet nurse, there seems to be another dimension here, which is an emphasis on the nurturing and emotional relationship between the mother and child through breastfeeding. The first word of the inspiration told Moses' mother to "suckle him" and then cast him (*wa awḥaynā ilā ummi Mūsā an 'arḍi'īhi*). He was later returned to his mother to be suckled "that she might be comforted".

One may add to this also, that Islamic law considers it hateful to allow a woman who is consuming prohibited foods, to suckle Muslim children. Moreover, the Imams recommended that people should consider the psychological state of the wet nurse, as well as her general character, because, they said, breast milk is contagious and affects the character of the child.[98]

Surely, the Qur'an describes the breastfeeding incident as a means for Moses' return to his mother, but there is also an insistence on suckling in the story. Considering the depiction of Moses' mother as a faithful and knowledgeable woman, in addition to the dominant view in the traditions that breast milk is contagious, one wonders whether prohibiting Moses from all the wet nurses had to do with the character of Moses' mother as the most suitable person to feed the future messenger.

The wife of Pharaoh

There is not much about Āsiyā in the story of Moses, other than the scene where she persuaded Pharaoh to keep the child and not kill him [28: 9].

She is however mentioned in one other place in the Qur'an were she is considered, together with Mary, as an example for the believers. That is because she said to God, "My Lord, build for me a house in Paradise, in Thy presence, and deliver me from Pharaoh and his work, and do Thou deliver me from the people of the evildoers" [66: 11]. Āsiyā, in these verses from *Sūrat al-Taḥrīm*, is put in direct contrast to the wives of Noah and Lot, who are examples for the disbelievers. Despite being married to prophets they did not heed advice but, on the contrary, mistreated and betrayed their husbands. Āsiyā was married to the ultimate tyrant, yet she was a believer who wished to be saved from her husband and his people, and prayed for a home in heaven. She asked God to deliver her from evil folk by keeping her faith strong.[99] Her words portray her goal in life, and they indicate that a true believer must have his words follow his heart so that the interior and exterior are one.[100]

It is interesting that her request that God build her a home in heaven, is similar in form only to Pharaoh's words, "Pharaoh said, 'Hāmān, build for me a tower, that haply so I may reach the cords, the cords of the heavens, and look upon Moses' God; for I think that he is a liar'" [40: 36–7]. While she asked God for a home near himself, Pharaoh asked Hāmān for a tower that he may go to the heaven and check if Moses' God really exists. These verses not only show Āsiyā's faith, but the contrast with the silliness of Pharaoh's words reveals a disparity in their understanding of Moses' message.

However, the Qur'anic choice of Āsiyā to be placed next to Mary as an example for the believers remains intriguing. In spite of being the wife of Pharaoh who is most rich and powerful, Āsiyā considered her husband and the elite around him evil, and she prayed for an abode of proximity to God. It has been suggested that it is this attitude of relinquishing the worldly wealth and power available to her that makes her a fine example for believers.[101] Others have seen in Āsiyā an example of a free mind and a liberated will.[102]

Perhaps the latter observation is particularly relevant considering that she is given in contrast to wives of prophets who betrayed their husbands. Āsiyā was married to Pharaoh, the Qur'anic symbol of the ultimate political and religious tyrant, and this necessarily brings politics into the analysis. As Ṭabāṭabā'ī noticed above, her words followed her heart, and therefore, it is possible that she sets an example for religio-political *jihād*. Āsiyā refused to submit to the highest political and religious power, and she withstood tyranny by being steadfast in her faith and prayer. Her *jihād* is not necessarily an outward one, yet it is the foundation for active *jihād*. Imam 'Alī said, "The first kind of *jihād* that will overpower you is the *jihād* of your hands, then of your tongues, then of your hearts. He whose heart neither knows right conduct nor disapproves of indecency has a heart that has been turned upside down".[103] While *jihād* with words or actions may be deemed either inevitable or contingent, *jihād* with the heart is indispensable, and without it the human becomes misshapen.[104] The latter kind is perhaps the easiest among the three, but it is also the most basic kind of *jihād* and the prerequisite for the other two.

Moses' bride

During Moses' adult life circumstances led him to kill an Egyptian. He received news that people were planning for retaliation, so he fled to Madyan, "And when he came to the waters of Madyan he found a company of the people there drawing water, and he found, apart from them, two women holding back their flocks. He said, 'What is your business?' They said, 'We do not draw water until the shepherds drive off; and our father is passing old'" [28: 23]. Moses watered their flocks for them, and then left them to sit in the shade where he addressed God saying, "O my Lord, surely I have need of whatever good Thou shalt have sent down upon me" [28: 24]. Then, one of the two women came to him "walking bashfully" inviting him to her father who wished to reward him for his help [28: 25]. Moses told his story to the old man, who assured him that he is now safe from the oppressors. One of the women then asked her father to hire him, "surely the best man thou canst hire is the one strong and trusty" [28: 26]. The old man then expressed his wish to marry Moses to one of his two daughters, on the condition that he would hire himself to the old man for eight or ten years, an offer which Moses accepted [28: 27–8].

Even though women's work has not traditionally been an issue, some modern Muslim literature has seen in this story proof that women's work outside the house is acceptable only when unavoidable and as long as it does not involve association with men.[105] Traditions from Ḥuwayzī's exegesis do not explain that story thus, rather, they mention that the women were lean, and that the job Moses did for them required the equivalent of ten men.[106] Another tradition explains the woman's words describing Moses as "the strong and trusty", that she saw his strength in the job he performed, and his trustworthiness because while she was leading him to her father, he preferred to walk in front of her rather than behind her so as not to see her figure.[107] In fact, Moses seems to have considered their situation of not watering their flock to be odd, which is why he asked them what the problem was, the expression he used, "*mā khaṭbukumā*", denotes surprise because of a grave situation.[108] These explanations might shed light on why the women told Moses that their father was an old man. It is not necessarily to justify their working outside the home, but could be understood that they were explaining why a physically demanding job was being done by themselves. Ṭabāṭabā'ī combines the classical point of view with the modern one when he says that the women were waiting aside, partly because of modesty, and partly because the people oppressed them by not considering giving them space.[109]

Of course, the element of modesty is clearly present in the story when the Qur'an describes the woman's bashful walk (*tamshī 'ala-stiḥyā'in*), and the tradition above points out Moses' modest gaze. The theme of segregation between the sexes and women's proper workplace is a later interpretation because it is not discussed either in the early and classical exegeses or in the traditions.

The element of attraction the woman felt towards Moses, and perhaps he to her, exists, albeit subtly, in the text. Her words asking her father to hire Moses, and describing him as strong and trustworthy, were immediately followed by her father expressing his wish to marry Moses to one of his daughters, as if her father realised what she had hinted at.[110] This has not gone unnoticed and traditions confirm that the woman he married was the one who asked her father to hire him.[111] This woman, therefore, gives an example of someone who can be honest in their attraction to a member of the opposite sex, but with modesty.

Notice that as soon as Moses expressed to God his need for any good that he might send down for him, the woman came to him and invited him to her father, who eventually gave him a job and a wife.

In *Sūrat Ṭā Hā*, the Qur'an narrates how God spoke to Moses and informed him of his mission. Moses then asked that his brother Aaron be made his minister, so that he may share the task and help Moses be strong. God granted Moses his request and reminded him of other favours he had conferred upon him, when he inspired his mother to cast him in the river, when their enemy picked him up and he was endowed with love, when his sister traced him and brought him back to their mother so that she does not grieve, when he killed a man and God saved him from distress and made it a severe test for the prophet, and finally when he tarried among the people of Madyan until a time [20: 37–40]. Thus, God told him, "I produced you for myself" [20: 41]. Notice that four out of the five people who worked God's plan which was a favour upon Moses were these four women who have just been discussed (and the fifth was the man who warned him of the Egyptians' plan to retaliate [28: 20]). These verses mention Moses' mother's inspiration to cast him in the river, and his sister tracing and returning him. The love that he was endued with is a reference to Āsiyā who loved him and convinced Pharaoh to adopt him.[112] As for his years in Madyan, it has been shown that this was organised for him primarily through his bride.

God sent these women to Moses to help in his making. When Moses' prophethood began, he was reminded of those favours. The women's relevance, however, particularly his mother and Āsiyā, is not limited to their contribution to Moses. His mother received an inspiration or sign, and even though this is not divine revelation, it nonetheless signals a spiritual experience. Her spiritual state may be confirmed in the expression that her heart became empty, which has been understood to be empty of fear and grief, a psychological state that exists among the *awliyā'* and the people of paradise. Āsiyā also is not confined to the Moses story. Although she is only explicitly mentioned in one verse, she is made an example to the believers, because she prayed to be delivered from Pharaoh's work and to be placed close to God. This experience of Āsiyā hints not only at a religious struggle, but also contains a political element considering that her fight was, in her words, against Pharaoh and the evildoers.

The Queen of Sheba

In *Sūrat al-Naml* the Qur'an briefly narrates the encounter between King Solomon and the Queen of Sheba, whom traditions name Bilqīs. This encounter culminated in the queen's conversion to monotheism, the religion of Solomon. The queen's conversion, the most important event in the story, describes a gradual change in the queen's heart. The throne that is mentioned repeatedly in the story is controversial, due to its political symbolism. However, the throne may also have religious meanings which would make it the central element in the story. Being a powerful female sovereign remembered favourably in the Qur'an, Bilqīs' mind, including her political tactics, will be examined.

Her conversion

Solomon's hoopoe once came back to him with news of the kingdom of Sheba: "I have come from Sheba to thee with a sure tiding. I found a woman ruling over them, and she has been given of everything, and she possesses a mighty throne" [27: 23]. She and her people, however, prostrated to the sun instead of God, and Satan had made their works alluring to them [27: 24]. Solomon sent the hoopoe to them with a letter, which the queen described to her people as a "generous/noble letter" [27: 28–9]. She then proceeded to explain that it was from Solomon and it reads, "In the Name of God, the Merciful, the Compassionate. Rise not up against me, but come to me in surrender/as Muslims (*muslimīn*)" [27: 30–1]. The queen sought the advice of the eminent ones and added, "I am not used to decide an affair until you bear me witness" [27: 32]. They assured her that they are lords of might and great prowess, and added, "The affair rests with thee; so consider what thou wilt command" [27: 33]. She said, "Kings, when they enter a city, disorder it and make the honourable ones of its inhabitants abased. Even so they too will do" [27: 34]. She then decided to send them presents and wait for the response [27: 35]. Solomon refused the gifts and rebuked her messengers, saying, "What, would you succour me with wealth, and what God gave me is better than what He has given you? Nay, it is you who exult in your gift" [27: 36]. He told the queen's messenger to return, and threatened, "we shall assuredly come against them with hosts they have not power to resist, and we shall expel them from there with shame, and they will be abased" [27: 37]. However, Solomon somehow knew that the queen will decide to go to him, and asked for her throne to be brought to him before she arrives in submission/as a Muslim [27: 38]. He brought her throne to himself within a glance,[113] and ordered his people to disguise her throne, to see whether she will be guided or not [27: 41]. When asked, "Is thy throne like this?" the queen answered, "(It is) as though it were the very one" [27: 42]. The verse continues, "And we were given the knowledge before this, and we were in surrender/Muslims" [27: 42]. Finally, when asked to enter the pavilion she deemed it a pool and bared her legs, but Solomon informed her that it was smooth glass. At that point, the queen turned to God saying, "My Lord, indeed I have wronged myself, and I surrender with Solomon to God, the Lord of all Being" [27: 44]. This is where her story ends.

It has been proposed that the queen's conversion in the Qur'anic narrative is too sudden, and questioned whether an architectural oddity is a good reason for a great queen to bend to the will of a foreign ruler.[114] In answer to this it has been proposed that the conversion did not happen in a moment but that it was a culmination of a process of change in the queen's heart.[115] This issue is important here as part of the examination of the *jihād al-nafs* theme and the evaluation of this queen's heart and mind.

Upon receiving Solomon's letter, the queen described it as noble, generous (*kitābun karīm*), and then continued, as though to justify her judgement regarding its nobility, adding that it was from Solomon, and that it opened with the name of the merciful God.[116] She decided to send presents which were her test to Solomon, but he refused her luxurious gifts which showed her that he was not a mere worldly king.[117] She went to visit him and was faced with the test of the throne. While Solomon was arranging to disguise her throne, he described that test as a "guidance" (*nanẓur atahtadī am takūnu min al-ladhīna lā yahtadūn*), which signifies the importance that Solomon attached to this test.[118] The queen gave a non-definitive answer as to whether that was her throne, which exegetes interpret as a sign of her intelligence.[119] The verse then continues, "And we were given the knowledge before this (*min qablihā*), and we were in surrender/Muslims" [27: 42]. Some have attributed this last statement to Solomon, but such a reading has been considered weak.[120] If Solomon were the speaker then he would have been saying that he was given knowledge before her, that is the queen, and that he had been a Muslim. Whereas, if the queen were the speaker, the statement then shows the queen's admission that she had been given the knowledge, of Solomon's power, before this sign (*āya*), and we have surrendered to Solomon, although not yet to God.[121] Indeed, if the statement were Solomon's then it would be redundant because Solomon was a prophet and was already showing her the signs, so he need not have said that he had been given knowledge and is a Muslim. The very next verse explains, "but that she served, apart from God, barred her, for she was of a people of unbelievers" [27: 43]. This suggests that, while she had inwardly acknowledged the supremacy of Solomon, the pressure of her people's idolatrous tradition kept her from actually converting.[122] Upon witnessing the sign of the glass floor, she immediately turned to God confessing having wronged herself and modelled her faith on that of Solomon's, when she said that she submit along with Solomon, to the Lord of all worlds.[123] By acknowledging that God is the Lord of all worlds, she confirmed that she worships nothing else with him.[124]

According to the Qur'an, the disbelievers' hindrance from following the path of the prophets is always the pressure, or the excuse, of following the existing culture as it had been inherited from the fathers [2: 170, 5: 104, 10: 78, 21: 53, 26: 74, and 31: 21]. The Queen of Sheba also experienced that hindrance but soon overcame it.

There is something to be said concerning the nature of the signs that were given to Bilqīs, starting with the bird delivering a letter, passing through the throne which had arrived to Solomon's palace before her, and ending with the "architectural oddity" of the glass floor she presumed to be water. The Qur'an elsewhere tells that Solomon had prayed, "My Lord, forgive me, and give me a kingdom (*mulk*) such as may not befall anyone after me" [38: 35]. The verses continue to describe how the wind and the devils were subservient to his command, and that Solomon has a place near God [38: 36–40]. A tradition from the seventh Imam al-Kāẓim explains these verses, saying that, thus the people in his time and after him realised that his reign/estate/authority (*mulk*) is unlike that of other sovereigns, whether they had been chosen by the people or ruled by tyranny and oppression.[125] This indicates that one of Solomon's ways of proving his prophethood to people was through his exquisite *mulk*. A tradition from Imam al-Ṣādiq tells that a prophet always speaks to people in the language that could convince them. That is why, for example, Moses brought magic, and Muhammad brought a literary masterpiece.[126] Their people thought that they have excelled in the respective field, until the prophet excelled over them, as a sign of his prophethood. Now, the Qur'an tells that Bilqīs had been given of everything. Ṭūsī understands the phrase "*'ūtiyat min kulli shay'in*" to exaggerate the fact that she had been given much worldly things and a vast kingdom.[127] Ṭabāṭabā'ī adds that she possessed all the components of a great kingdom, including her personal attributes of firmness, resolution and sway, in addition to a vast kingdom and treasures, a strong army, and an obedient people.[128] In spite of all that she had however, Solomon demonstrated his sway over elements in nature, and treasures that were beyond her grasp. Perhaps this is how the queen was able to associate with those signs and comprehend them as convincing proofs.

The intersection of the theme of worldly power and abundance with the theme of religion and spirituality add an extra dimension to the story, as will be seen in the sign of the throne.

The Throne

The symbol of the throne is poignant due to its carrying within it both political and religious meanings.

One feminist author, Fatima Mernissi, saw that the throne and its transfer from the female to the male is the clear message of the story.[129]

It has been observed above that Solomon acted in his capacities, as both prophet and king. His letter inviting the queen and her people not to be haughty with him and to go to him in submission (*muslimīn*) carries in it religious as well as political meanings.[130] However, Solomon's threatening letter was sent after the hoopoe gave news of the kingdom that prostrates to the sun rather than God, and made a short speech about the oddity of people not prostrating to God. As it was pointed out above, at the sign of the disguised throne, the queen submitted to Solomon's authority, but not yet to the Creator. Nevertheless, Solomon continued to show the queen the signs until she converted. This interpretation leads to the understanding that had he desired political dominion only, he could have stopped at the sign of the throne. Therefore, according to one point of view, "the Muslim prophet wishes to subdue her for one reason and one reason alone: she is an unbeliever".[131] Her submission to his worldly rule was not enough, she had to submit to his God, otherwise the tale would not have been believable to Muslims.[132]

When the queen accepted the new faith, her final, crucial statement was not a submission to Solomon; rather it was a submission to God, with (*ma'*) Solomon, thus putting herself shoulder to shoulder with the king.

The Qur'an and traditions do not speak of what happened next. Therefore it is difficult to speculate further on the problem of whether the transfer of the throne necessarily indicates his taking over her kingdom. It is as one medieval person put it, "the last I have heard of her (Bilqīs) is that she said, 'I surrender with Solomon to God, the Lord of all Being'".[133] Drawing on Islamic history, however, it would seem that since Solomon was a prophet whom the queen accepted, that he would have had the ultimate authority even if she continued to rule her nation.[134]

Even so, the question remains whether the transfer of the throne from the female to the male really is "the clear message of the story". This claim is difficult to justify, since the Qur'an does not raise any issue regarding the queen's femaleness throughout. The sole incident when this is mentioned is at the very beginning when the hoopoe tells Solomon, "I found a woman ruling over them". This statement seems to be free from any value judgement, even though it might contain a hint of surprise. It is the hoopoe's following statement on the faith of her nation that has a moral judgement. Throughout the rest of the story the issue of the queen's gender is never raised. Rather, Solomon was inviting Bilqīs to see his power, and the truth of his faith.

The transfer of the throne, as the throne itself, may have meanings beyond politics and gender. When Solomon saw the queen's throne brought in front of him in the twinkling of an eye, he thanked his Lord in what has been described as "a rather puzzling statement":[135] "This is of my Lord's bounty that He may try me (*li yabluwanī*), whether I am thankful or ungrateful. Whosoever gives thanks gives thanks only for his own soul's good, and whosoever is ungrateful – my Lord is surely All-sufficient, All-generous" [27: 40]. This statement, through the transfer of the throne, brings about in the middle of the story's events, the moral that power and possessions are a test for gratitude.

The Qur'an repeatedly teaches that money is a severe trial [8: 28, 64: 15], and that the wealth and power human beings have over each other are most often an affliction (*balā'*) [6: 165]. Moreover, whenever a prophet spoke, the affluent elite (*mutrafūn*) were always the ones to hinder and fight him [34: 34, 43: 23].[136] Solomon had been given much, and here it is shown that even though he was a prophet, he continued to consider everything God gave him a trial. In his statement, Solomon contrasts gratitude (*shukr*) with ingratitude (*kufr*), also the term for disbelief. This theme again has to do with the nature of Solomon's signs to Bilqīs, and Solomon's statement perhaps sheds light on the trial that Bilqīs herself was about to experience.

The divine throne is an oft repeated Qur'anic term. After the hoopoe mentions that the Queen of Sheba has a mighty throne (*wa lahā 'arshun 'aẓīm*) [27: 23], the verses continue, "God: there is no god but He, the Lord of the Mighty Throne (*rabbu-l-'arsh al-'aẓīm*)" [27: 26]. There is a parallel there,[137] which perhaps gives a comparison/contrast between her worldly throne and the divine throne. The religious test of gratitude may be further developed into a spiritual meaning when the queen's throne is set against the theme of God's tremendous throne.

Another element in the story that combines the divine throne and political threat is the *basmala* in the beginning of Solomon's letter, which invoked the name of God with the typically Islamic formula "*bism-i-llāh al-raḥmān al-raḥīm*". It is reported that the Prophet said that the opening of the Qur'an (*fātiḥa*) is "the noblest of the treasures of the Throne", and that it was an honour given to Muhammad alone among the prophets, with the exception of Solomon who was given a part of it, namely, the *basmala* that Bilqīs received from him.[138] Thus, another relationship is established between the throne and the exchange between Solomon and Bilqīs. It could be that bringing this tradition here is reading too much into the text, however the tradition sheds light on what is already within the Qur'anic text, that Solomon gave Bilqīs the *basmala*. It may therefore be argued that the prophet wanted political dominion as symbolised by her throne indeed, but he wished to give in return what was, in his view at least, a nobler and more enduring piece of the divine throne.

Her politics

Some modern authors suggested that the story of Bilqīs is a story of a woman who has a weakness that is usually praised in women,[139] and that she was submissive in politics until her throne was stolen from her.[140] This reading may be valid from the strictly political point of view, but not from the religious one.

The Qur'an describes in some detail how Bilqīs dealt with the political problem. Upon receiving the threatening letter, the queen recognised its noble character. She sought consultation with the notable persons among her people, and informed them that she would not make a decision without their presence. They assured her that they were strong militarily and otherwise, and then confirmed that the matter was for her to decide. She sought wise counsel, and as her chiefs said, it was her final word that mattered. Indeed, even though she listened to them, she decided on a path that was different from what they were disposed towards. She made an interesting statement, "Kings, when they enter a city, disorder it and make the honourable ones of its inhabitants abased. Even so they too will do". Her next step was to send gifts to Solomon. Most exegetes understand this move as a ploy to know more about Solomon. They say that she decided that if he accepted the gifts, it would mean that he was a mere worldly king, and therefore he would not be able to vanquish her people.[141] Therefore, she was not in favour of war, but did not rule out the possibility; rather she decided to take the course of war only if necessary.[142] Solomon's ridicule to her messenger of their contentment with their gifts, and his statement that he, Solomon, had been given better than what they had been given, plainly revealed to her what she wanted to know. She wished to know her enemy, and the gifts did indeed serve their purpose. This would mean that after Solomon returned the gifts and she consequently went to visit him, it was not only in submission to a more powerful king, but in awe of an unusual king who had a balanced view of the relationship between this world and the next.[143]

The queen's statement on the nature of war is set against her chiefs' assurances of their military might. This demonstrates that her aversion to war was not out of fear, but out of disdain for war in general. She said that soldiers always behave in the same manner, destroying towns and degrading people. In fact, Bilqīs' view on war is repeated twice more in the story. First, Bilqīs' words are confirmed by Solomon himself who said as the messenger was leaving with the gifts, "we shall assuredly come against them with hosts they have not power to resist, and we shall expel them from there with shame, and they will be abased". The second statement was made by the ant after which this chapter was named. This occurred in a valley where Solomon's soldiers were passing and one of the ants there screamed, "Ants, enter your dwelling-places, lest Solomon and his hosts crush you, being unaware" [27: 18]. At that point, Solomon smiled with amusement at her speech, thanked God for the blessings he bestowed on him and his parents, and prayed that he would do good and pleasing work [27: 19].[144] This incident occurs right before the hoopoe episode. These three statements paint a violent picture of kings and soldiers, and affirm that war by its very nature always incurs destruction and humiliation.[145]

Finally, a comparison between Bilqīs and other sovereigns mentioned in the Qur'an would help put her experience into perspective. The Qur'an narrates the debate between Abraham and the ruling king, and a point was reached when the king could not find any more replies to Abraham's propositions, "Then the unbeliever was confounded/astonished. God guides not the people of the evildoers" [2: 258]. The king saw a moment of truth, but unlike this queen, his experience was not fruitful because he was a wrongdoer. Another example is Pharaoh, to whom Moses and Aaron were sent. Pharaoh, the Qur'an says, was an oppressor who corrupted his people instead of guiding them [7: 123, 20: 79], he was arrogant in front of God's signs [23: 25–7], and he plainly declared that he was the god [26: 29]. Pharaoh according to the Qur'an did not have a happy ending either worldly or other-worldly. Perhaps the only king remembered favourably was the one who freed Joseph from prison and made him governor, although nothing is told of that king in terms of a spiritual journey or acceptance of Joseph's faith.

The Queen of Sheba may therefore be the antithesis of Pharaoh and the king who argued with Abraham, in the sense that she was in their position, but she made the opposite choice. If the inner consistency of the Qur'an were to be considered, it cannot be said that Bilqīs is portrayed as a vanquished leader, but a victorious soul.

The queen attempted to understand her enemy. This may be seen as political tact, but this also led her to see that his authority was higher than hers. The story of her gradual conversion shows that the queen had inner dilemmas. Political consciousness and pride might have been one of them at the start, when she acknowledged the generosity and nobleness of Solomon's letter but refused to yield, and discussed the choice of war. She decided to send him presents to test him and found that he was an unusual king. Then, it was Solomon's turn to test her with the throne, which Solomon considered a test of guidance. At that point, the queen accepted Solomon's authority as a matter of fact. Her pride was not a hindrance to conversion, but her idolatrous heritage was. Upon the final test, she proclaimed that she had wronged herself and that she submits to God.

Throughout the story there is tension between her heart and her head. That is not to say that she did not reveal qualities of intelligence, but quite the opposite. Her intelligence seems to be exemplary from the religious point of view, precisely because it was neither vain nor stubborn, but led to submission to God. If understanding and softness are feminine qualities, these seem to be favoured in this case.

Mary

The bulk of the story of Mary is told in two passages in the Qur'an. Her consecration and birth, election and purification in her early life, and then the annunciation of the conception in *Sūrat Āl-'Imrān* [3: 33–7, 42–8], and the story of her pregnancy and delivery of Jesus in the chapter named after her, *Sūrat Maryam* [19: 16–29]. Some of the major themes in Mary's story are the Qur'anic statement upon her birth that "the male is not as the female", her election and purification by God, the nature of the provisions that she was given since early childhood, and the annunciation and delivery of Jesus. Finally, the limited debate on whether she was a prophet will be briefly presented, and followed by a wider discussion on her representation in the Qur'an.

"The male is not as the female"

In *Sūrat Āl-'Imrān*, the passage concerning Mary's family, the house of 'Imrān, starts, "God chose Adam and Noah and the House of Abraham and the House of 'Imrān above all beings, the seed of one another; God hears and knows" [3: 33–4]. The passage then continues to narrate the story when the wife of 'Imrān, Mary's mother, while pregnant pledged to consecrate what is in her womb for God's service at the temple, "And when she gave birth to her she said, 'Lord, I have given birth to her, a female'-And God knew very well what she had given birth to; the male is not as the female-[146] 'And I have named her Mary, and commend her to Thee with her seed, to protect them from the accursed Satan'" [3: 36].

Most exegetes understood the phrase "the male is not as the female" to be the utterance of Mary's mother. Some claim, based on inauthentic traditions, that the male is not like the female because the latter menstruates, and therefore cannot be consecrated to the temple, for she would have to leave the temple during those days,[147] or that the female is better at service, and therefore she is more adequate to serve the people in the temple.[148] Others interpret the difference between the sexes, based on an authentic tradition, that the female cannot be God's messenger.[149] These traditions seem to find that the Qur'anic statement prefers the male, with the exception of the interpretation that women are better fit for service.

Ṭabāṭabā'ī, however, is clear that in terms of language, the structure of the statement "the male is not as the female (*wa laysa-dh-dhakaru ka-l-unthā*)" expresses preference to the latter, which is the female. He further explains that Mary's mother, based on the custom of consecrating only the males to the temple, expressed regret when she delivered a female child for not being able to fulfil her pledge, "Lord, I have given birth to her, a female". Ṭabāṭabā'ī confirms that the statement "And God knew very well what she had given birth to; the male is not as the female" is all God's speech intercepting that of Mary's mother. Otherwise, due to the regret Mary's mother felt, she ought to have said "the female is not as the male", preferring the male. He adds that God's first statement confirms that he already knew that it was a female, and that he wished to fulfil the mother's wishes of consecrating the child in the best way possible. For if the mother knew God's reason for making what was in her womb a female, she would not have expressed regret. He continues that this female child was to fulfil her role better than a male child would have done, and ultimately it is this female that would bring Jesus into the world. Ṭabāṭabā'ī reprimands earlier exegetes for considering the statement to belong to Mary's mother, and their pretension that it expresses preference to the male.[150]

The passage continues to describe the election and purification of Mary. After the two intercepting statements, the mother gives her newborn daughter the name Mary and the passage continues, "Her Lord received the child with gracious favour, and by His goodness she grew up comely" [3: 37]. The story then shifts to Mary's conversation with her guardian Zechariah, and his subsequent supplication for a child of his own. Then it shifts back to Mary, "And when the angels said, 'Mary, God has chosen thee (*iṣṭafāki*), and purified thee (*wa ṭahharaki*); He has chosen thee above all women (*thumma-ṣṭafāki 'alā nisā' al-'ālamīn*)'" [3: 42]. Ṭabāṭabā'ī finds that God's reception of her with gracious favour and her growing up comely in [3: 37] correspond respectively to his choosing her and purifying her in [3: 42]. These, he adds, are the answers to her mother's prayers, whereas the second election in [3: 42] is in reference to her delivery of Jesus, and to her being with him a sign to the worlds. To Ṭabāṭabā'ī, the second election above the women of the worlds is a confirmation of the previous statement, "the male is not as the female".[151]

Ṭabāṭabā'ī's interpretation thus connects the preference for the female to Mary's miraculous conception. This is an interesting connection, although not entirely clear. That is because the Qur'an generalises the preference to the female sex (*al-untha*), but Mary's election for the miraculous conception is unique to her.

There is a tradition from Imam al-Ṣādiq, not in reference to Mary but in his answer to a man who expressed grief over his wife giving birth to a girl. The Imam explained to him a particular reference in the Qur'anic story of the journey that Moses took with al-Khiḍr, when among the three things that al-Khiḍr did but Moses misunderstood was the killing of a boy who seemed innocent. Part of the Qur'anic defence of al-Khiḍr's actions was that the boy was an infidel and cruel to his good parents, and God wished to replace him for their sake, with one better in purity and nearer to mercy [18: 80–1]. In this authentic tradition, the Imam explained that God replaced the boy with a girl who gave birth to seventy prophets.[152] The Imam's answer is in the context of changing the man's opinion concerning his sorrow at the birth of a female. He argued giving the example of an infidel and cruel boy, as opposed to a pure and merciful girl who gave birth to prophets.

To pursue the claims of Ṭabāṭabā'ī, the common denominator between the female sex in general and Mary's particular conception is perhaps the ability to conceive and deliver great human beings. One may conclude from this, in conjunction with the tradition above, that part of the preference of the female over the male as it is expressed in the Qur'an, is in her potential for delivering prophets.

Her rizq

> Her Lord received the child with gracious favour, and by His goodness she grew up comely, Zechariah taking charge of her. Whenever Zechariah went in to her in the Sanctuary, he found her provisioned. "Mary", he

> said, "how comes this to thee?" "From God", she said. Truly God provisions whomsoever He will without reckoning. At that, Zachariah prayed to his Lord saying, "Lord, give me of Thy goodness a goodly offspring".
>
> [3: 37–8]

The key word here is provision/bounty (*rizq*). It is a reference to what is for the human being to benefit from, without anyone being able to withhold it.[153] In Arabic as in the Qur'an, *rizq* may be restricted to food [2: 233], or generalised to include many services and kindnesses including knowledge and prophethood [11: 88].[154] Kāshānī speculates that it is possible that what is meant here is spiritual food in the form of esoteric knowledge and wisdom.[155] The nature of her provision is not clearly defined, but it seems to be implied that it was something unusual.[156]

The statement "Truly God provisions whomsoever He will without reckoning" is either a continuation of Mary's speech or a narration of God's words.[157] It was the miracles granted to Mary that provoked Zechariah to pray for a son.[158]

Most exegetes narrate weak traditions which identify Mary's provision as summer fruits in the winter time and winter fruits in the summer time, and they add that that is what inspired Zechariah to pray for a child out of the usual time, meaning in his old age.[159] Ṭabāṭabā'ī's point of view, however, is that it was what Zechariah saw of Mary's sincere worship and her honour in the eyes of her Lord, that provoked him to ask for a good progeny. He finds that *rizq* as related to fruit has no proof in the text, but relates Mary's *rizq* with her dignity, which the sequence of verses prior to this passage actually refers to.[160] Ṭūsī narrates several opinions of his day, among them that this was a foundation for the prophethood of Jesus.[161]

Annunciation and parturition

In *Sūrat Āl-'Imrān* is a brief recounting of the event when the angels gave Mary the good tidings of the birth of her son, and Mary's subsequent surprise at the miracle [3: 45–7]. However, in *Sūrat Maryam* is a more detailed description of the events of the conception and parturition.

> And mention in the Book Mary when she withdrew from her people to an eastern place, and she took a veil apart from them; then We sent unto her Our Spirit that presented himself to her a man without fault. She said, "I take refuge in the All-Merciful from thee if thou fearest God!" … He said, "I am but a messenger come from thy Lord, to give thee a boy most pure." She said, "How shall I have a son whom no mortal has touched, neither have I been unchaste?" He said, "Even so thy Lord has said: 'Easy is that for me; and that We may appoint him a sign unto humans and a mercy from Us; it is a thing decreed'". So she conceived

> him, and withdrew with him to a distant place. And the birth pangs surprised her by the trunk of the palm-tree. She said, "Would I had died ere this, and become a thing forgotten!" But the one that was below her called to her, "Nay, do not sorrow; see, thy Lord has set below thee a rivulet. Shake also to thee the palm-trunk, and there shall come tumbling upon thee dates fresh and ripe. Eat therefore, and drink, and be comforted; and if thou shouldst see any mortal, say, 'I have vowed to the All-merciful a fast, and today I will not speak to any human'".
>
> [19: 16–26]

Exegetes generally agree that the Spirit in this passage is a reference to Gabriel, who appeared to her as a fully formed man.[162] She was at first wary of him and pleaded for his piety, until he revealed his identity and his message to her from her Lord.[163] Mary expressed surprise to have become pregnant when no man had touched her, and Gabriel implied that he did not know the workings of this miracle either, but confirmed that God had said that this is easy for him, that the child will be made a sign and a mercy, and that it is decreed.[164] Mary conceived and withdrew to a distant place.[165] The pangs of birth led her to the palm tree, perhaps to hold on to it.[166] She wished she had died before this and been utterly forgotten. This to most exegetes is in reference to the "scandal" of her pregnancy, and the fear of people's talk.[167] At this sentiment, or after giving birth, "the one below her" who is sometimes identified as Gabriel, but most often as Jesus, drew her attention to a little stream of water that was made to flow beneath her and invited her to shake the branch of the palm tree towards herself in order to receive some fruit.[168] It has also been suggested that the dry branch producing fruit upon her touch is one of Mary's miracles.[169] As she carried her newborn back into her town, the people reproached Mary, expressing their surprise at the strange thing she had done,[170] and reminded her of her noble ancestry and good parents [19: 27–8].[171] As instructed, Mary maintained her fast of silence and pointed at the newborn who spoke miraculously [19: 29–33].

Many interpretations of Mary's experience have been interpreted by Sufis in highly spiritual terms. Mary's withdrawal to an eastern place (*makānan sharqiyyā*), according to most exegetes, simply means that she withdrew from people and her family towards an eastern corner for religious purposes, and that the veil (*ḥijāb*) in the verse emphasises her detachment and aloneness.[172] The term *intabadhat* does not only mean seclusion, but it implies throwing away something of little or no value.[173] Sufis, however, interpret the eastern place as the source of divine lights.[174]

The choice of Mary in the miracle/scandal "clearly involve(s) the relation of gender to social authority in religious imagination".[175] The image of an innocent girl standing accused for reasons which might seem self-evident to her accusers, surely stirs up much feeling and emotion on both sides. The people's rejection of Mary and her "illegitimate" son "become emblematic of resistance to the prophet's emergence".[176]

Another issue is Mary's wish to have died before this. This is quite a curious statement which is normally explained as her reaction to the "scandal". Indeed, a tradition, although weak, explains that this was her reaction to the so-called scandal and her knowledge that none of her folk was knowledgeable enough to diagnose her innocence.[177] However, another tradition, also unauthenticated, from Imam al-Ṣādiq explains that she wished to have died before she saw her heart attached to something other than God.[178]

Perhaps the element of physical pain added to Mary's wish. The pain of parturition is clear when the pangs drove her to the palm tree. Moreover, several traditions explain that the Qur'anic scene teaches post-natal women that the dates of the palm tree are healing for them.[179] In one tradition, a man comes to Imam al-Bāqir telling him that his wife is dying from the pain of labour, the Imam instructed the man to read this passage on Mary's labour [19: 23–5], in conjunction with another Qur'anic passage [16: 78] and pray for a safe delivery.[180] There is, therefore, other than the universal spirituality, something in the description of Mary's experience that is uniquely feminine and relevant for women.

The overlap between the spiritual and feminine elements of Mary's experience will be further discussed in the meaning of her prophethood.

Her prophethood

The debate surrounding the prophethood of Mary could be open-ended. That is partly because the distinguishing traits of prophets and messengers are not identified clearly in the Qur'an and traditions.

The different categories of messenger, prophet, and *muḥaddath* will be discussed here with emphasis on Mary's place among them. Moreover, it will be suggested that Mary's representation in the Qur'an indicates an elevated status and places her among the prophets.

*Messengers, prophets, and "*muḥaddathūn*"*

The debate on the prophethood of Mary is not a modern one. Several traditional scholars, but especially Mālikīs, were convinced of Mary's prophethood.[181] The major discussion on this took place in Andalusia, where, however, the debate on the prophethood of women was closely connected to the debate on the miracles of the saints.[182]

The view that Mary was not a prophet because prophethood is exclusively the domain of men remains the dominant view of Muslims. The proofs that are normally given for this are some Qur'anic verses that say to the prophet Muhammad "We sent not (*mā arsalnā*) forth any before thee, but men (*illā rijālan*) We revealed to" [12: 109, 16: 43, 21: 7]. Ibn Ḥazm (d.456/1064), however, a pioneer among the dissenting voices that confirmed Mary's prophethood,[183] argued that that the above verse is in reference to messengers, which is separate from the argument on women as prophets.[184] Ṭabāṭabā'ī acknowledges that a strict reading of the word *rijāl*, which necessarily excludes women and children from prophethood, would be problematic. He says that while being "sent" has been utilised in the Qur'an in reference to both prophets and messengers [22: 52], the examples of John [19: 12] and Jesus [19: 30], who were both children when they were prophets, ascertain that the aim of the word *rijāl* in this context is to stress the humanity of prophets, as opposed to their being supernatural creatures. He finds his opinion confirmed in the context of those verses, especially [21: 7–8].[185] Ṭabāṭabā'ī, as we shall see, does not extend this argument to potentially include women among the prophets.

Prophet is more general than messenger, and the difference between them is that the latter is sent with a particular message, to complete a mission, and consequently has to function as a just judge among the people, either to preserve and bestow favour upon his nation or to destroy it [10: 47].[186]

It is important to further clarify the differences between the three categories, messenger, prophet, and "the one spoken to" (*muḥaddath*). There are many traditions on this categorisation, and with some variations, they generally agree that the messenger is the one who sees Gabriel and speaks to him, the prophet is the one who sees the inspiration/revelation in a dream or a vision, and the *muḥaddath* hears the angels when they speak but does not see them. Being a prophet and a messenger could coexist in one person. According to one tradition the prophet Muhammad was a prophet in his early life, and after Gabriel visited him he became a messenger.[187]

Ṭabāṭabā'ī, however, interprets the traditions concerning the *muḥaddath* hearing but not seeing the angel, in the sense that he does not need to see the angel even though he may. As proof he cites the examples of Sarah and Mary who saw the angels as they spoke to them [11: 71, 19: 17]. He expands on this saying that the *muḥaddath* does not see the reality and essence of the angel even though he might see the form, or possibly that the *muḥaddath* does not see the angel in the sense of not receiving legal revelations from the angel.[188] It is interesting that Ṭabāṭabā'ī's argument is derived from the examples of the two women Sarah and Mary, based on the assumption that they could not have been prophets or messengers. The next chapter will also show Fāṭima as a *muḥaddatha*.

What is problematic however is that Mary was visited by the archangel himself, she saw his form and was informed of his identity and there is no dispute over interpreting this among exegetes. She was also given news of a burden that she had to carry for the sake of God. Therefore, considering Mary as only a *muḥaddatha* might be inconsistent with the traditions. On the other hand, excluding women, including Mary, from the potentially vulnerable and violent mission of the messenger might be seen to be in line with Islamic reasoning that military *jihād* is a burden not incumbent upon women.

Mary's representation in the Qur'an

Mary's election and purification, discussed above, is often taken as proof of her *'iṣma* (impeccability/sinlessness).[189] While this does not necessarily imply prophetic status, exegetes do speak of Mary as one of the *awliyā'*.[190] Interestingly, one tradition describes her first election as an election to be of the progeny of prophets (*dhurriyyat al-anbiyā'*).[191]

Consider the verses, "God chose (*iṣṭafā*) Adam and Noah and the House of Abraham and the House of 'Imrān above all beings, the seed (*dhurriyyatan*) of one another; God hears, and knows" [3: 33–4]. In addition to this instance where families are mentioned, being elected/purified (*iṣṭifā'*) occurs in reference to Abraham in [2: 130], to Mary in [3: 42], and to Moses in [7: 144]. One of the names of the prophet Muhammad is also *al-Muṣṭafa*.

Ṭūsī considers the election/purification in [3: 33] to refer to three possibilities, that God elected/purified their religion, or that he elected them to be prophets, or that he elected them in preference over others.[192] Moreover, their being of one another here is seen either as a reference to them being an assembly around the truth, or as the term *dhurriyya* specifies, a progeny in the genealogical sense.[193]

Ṭabāṭabā'ī observes that the family of Abraham here must be confined to a small group, for all the Israeli prophets and the Arabian prophet were from his offspring. That would have included the family of 'Imrān by implication, but being mentioned in a separate category, shows that the family of Abraham intended here is a smaller group of people.[194] He adds that the verse that follows, "When the wife of 'Imrān said, 'Lord, I have vowed to Thee, in dedication (*muḥarrarā*), what is within my womb'" [3: 34] is an explanation of the election of the house of 'Imrān.[195] Thus, the election of *Āl 'Imrān* is explained through the story of 'Imrān's wife and unborn daughter, and later their son Jesus. 'Imrān himself is never independently discussed in the Qur'an or in the traditions. This gives the impression that the reference to his *ahl al-bayt* is made in order to include the remaining people within his family that are mentioned in the *sūra*, first among them Mary's mother and her child.[196]

That the mention of the household of a prophet (*ahl al-bayt*) may include particular women of that house is seen on other occasions. Among the family of Abraham, the angels address Sarah personally, "The mercy of God and His blessings be upon you, O people of the House (*ahl al-bayt*)" [11: 73]. Therefore, Sarah was included in the expression *ahl al-bayt*, also employed above as *Āl Ibrāhīm*. Another occasion is the inclusion of Fāṭima among *Āl Muḥammad* [33: 33] (to be discussed in the next chapter).

It has been observed by several authors that the Qur'an mentions Mary among the prophets in *Sūrat Maryam* and in *Sūrat al-Anbiyā'*.[197] It may be added that she is mentioned in a style that shows continuity in naming prophets. *Sūrat Maryam* names a list of prophets and concludes the list by explicitly stating that these were prophets:

> The mention of thy Lord's mercy unto His servant Zechariah ... [19: 1], and mention in the Book Mary ... [19: 16], and mention in the Book Abraham ... [19: 41], and mention in the Book Moses ... [19: 51], and mention in the Book Ishmael ... [19: 53], and mention in the Book

> Idrīs … [19: 56].[198] These are they whom God has blessed among the Prophets of the seed of Adam, and of those We bore with Noah, and of the seed of Abraham and Israel, and of those We guided and chose [19: 58].

Exegetes generally agree that the latter verse says that the people mentioned are some of the prophets, for not all have not been mentioned, and that these prophets are divided here into four categories as described in the verse.[199]

In *Sūrat al-Anbiyā'* a long list of prophets is mentioned along with some of their exalted traits and experiences:

> and We delivered him (Abraham), and Lot, unto the land that We had blessed for all beings. And We gave him Isaac and Jacob … And Lot – to him We gave judgment and knowledge … And Noah – when he called before, and We answered him, and delivered him and his people from the great distress … And David and Solomon – We bore witness to their judgment; and We made Solomon to understand it, and unto each gave We judgment and knowledge. And with David We subjected the mountains to give glory … And We taught him the fashioning of garments for you, to fortify you against your violence … And to Solomon the wind, strongly blowing, that ran at his command unto the land that We had blessed … And Job – when he called unto his Lord … So We answered him, and removed the affliction … And Ishmael, Idrīs, Dhu-l-Kifl – each was of the patient … And Dhu-l-Nūn – when he went forth enraged and thought that We would have no power over him; then he called out in the darkness, "There is no god but Thou. Glory be to Thee! I have done evil" … And Zachariah … So We answered him, and bestowed on him John, and We set his wife right for him; truly they vied with one another, hastening to good works, and called upon Us out of yearning and awe; and they were humble to Us. And she who guarded her chastity, so We breathed into her of Our spirit and appointed her and her son to be a sign unto all beings. "Surely this community of yours is one community, and I am your Lord; so serve Me".
>
> [21: 71–92]

Mary is again mentioned among the prophets in her own right, and then Jesus was bestowed, and both of them are a sign for humanity.[200]

Ṭabāṭabā'ī points out that even though Mary and Jesus are considered one sign, Mary is older in this partnership. However he continues that she is honoured to be mentioned among the prophets even though she is not one of them.[201] Hamza Yusuf, the contemporary American teacher of traditional Islam, observes that in a great number of Qur'anic verses Jesus is referred to as the son of Mary, but never Mary as the mother of Jesus (*Umm 'Īsa*). This to him shows that it is part of the honour of Jesus to be the son of Mary.[202] In fact, out of thirty times Jesus is mentioned in the Qur'an, twenty-three times his name is accompanied by "son of Mary". In the brief account of the annunciation the angels say, "Mary, God gives thee good tidings of a Word from Him whose name is Messiah, Jesus, son of Mary" [3: 45], making "son of Mary" a part of his proper name. Mary is described as Jesus' mother three times in the Qur'an, but only after he is called her son, such as in the expression "and We made Mary's son, and his mother (*ibna Maryama wa ummahu*), to be a sign" [23: 50 and 5: 17, 75], thereby always giving preference to her name.

A study has shown that the Arabic words and sounds of the Qur'anic passages that describe the conception of Jesus are almost identical to the text of *Sūrat al-Qadr* (which speaks of the blessed night, awaited every year in the month of Ramadan, when the Qur'an descended on the heart of Muhammad):[203]

> The implicit metaphor in the Sura of Destiny [*sic*] is night, personified as a woman, conceiving the prophetic message through the Spirit. This conception by the night of destiny is almost identical, in the language used to depict it, to the conception by Maryam of Jesus through the Spirit.[204]

Mary's motherhood in this sense is not seen as strictly biological but as a spiritual experience of awaiting and receiving the descent of Spirit, and being impregnated with the prophetic message. This reading might help explain why Mary's (spiritual) motherhood experience is listed among the prophets' experiences, and why this very peculiar convergence between motherhood and spirituality is made an example for all believers in [66: 11–12], "God has struck a similitude for the believers ... And Mary, 'Imrān's daughter, who guarded her chastity, so We breathed into her of Our Spirit, and she confirmed the Words of her Lord and His Books, and became one of the obedient".

The meaning of her prophethood

Jesus is identified in the Qur'an thus, "The Messiah, Jesus son of Mary, was only the Messenger of God, and His Word (*wa kalimatuhu*) that He committed to Mary, and a Spirit from Him" [4: 171]. In modern discourse, an analogy has been repeatedly drawn between the Qur'an as the word of God, and Jesus as the word of God. Moreover, a comparison has been made between Mary and the prophet Muhammad who were both visited by the Spirit which is said to be Gabriel,[205] and both were thus agents of their Lord through the conception of Jesus and the reception of the Qur'an respectively.[206] This likening of Mary to Muhammad and Jesus to the Qur'an necessarily invites a look into the Qur'anic understanding of Jesus as God's word because it would be directly related to the nature and meaning of Mary's prophethood, if she were a prophet.

Furthermore, the conception of Jesus and his own role have been linked, "the spirit-as-support-for Jesus passages (2: 87, 2: 253, 5: 110) and the

Jesus-as-spirit passage (4: 171) echo, in sound quality and vocabulary, the Qur'anic account of the conception of Jesus".[207] Therefore, while Jesus as "word" and "spirit" communicate very different meanings in Christianity than they do in Islam, they are relevant to the Qur'anic discourse nevertheless.

Most exegetes consider the description of Jesus as "word" to be a reference to the word "Be (*kun*)", which is God's command with which he created Jesus without a father [3: 47].[208] Ṭabāṭabā'ī considers this to be from the ambiguous verses (*mutashābihāt*).[209] He inclines to the explanation of the "word" being "Be", because he considers everything to be the word of God because everything exists as a result of his command.[210] Indeed, the Qur'an affirms in another context that God's words are endless [18: 109].

However, in reference to the Qur'anic verse in which Jesus addressed Jewish rabbis and scholars of the scripture, "Be you masters (*rabbāniyyīn*) in that you know the Book, and in that you study" [3: 79], Ṭabāṭabā'ī explains that Jesus is the "word" because he clarified for the scholars what they had missed from their scripture.[211] Here, Jesus as word is related to his capacity to interpret scripture.

In exegesis, the "*rabbānī*" is someone who is a lord in that he manages people's affairs and/or someone wise and pious. The main meanings of the admonishment to be *rabbāniyyīn*, is to be people who deserve this title by learning the real divine scripture, teaching it to others, and behaving in accordance with it.[212] To Kāshānī, "*rabbānī*" is the perfect human being in terms of knowledge and action.[213]

It has been proposed by a contemporary Sufi sheikh that the Messiah was "the existential reality of lawfulness, in its organic sense", and that he was not recognised by the Jews because they had turned what was meant to be a scientific law about man "into a legalistic structure exterior to and imposed on man".[214] This portrays Jesus not only as a primary interpreter of scripture, but also Jesus as a living scripture.

Thus, Jesus' emphasis that people should be *rabbāniyyīn* seems to be a reflection of his own experience that scripture should be lived, and that it was not sent merely to be studied and taught.

In that sense, the functions of Mary as mother and as prophet may take an additional meaning to reception of and impregnation by Spirit; it is the prophet's job, as is the mother's, generally speaking, to raise human beings and help them grow. Jesus' teaching on the place of the human being in relation to scripture, that making people *rabbāniyyīn* is the goal of scripture, stresses the importance of Mary's religious contribution as a mother.

The idea of being as scripture also resounds in the Shī'ī view of the Imam as the "Speaking Qur'an",[215] and in this sense Mary as mother of Jesus and Fāṭima as mother of the Imams will have particular affinities.

This also brings to mind Rūḥullāh Khumaynī's statement which makes women partners to the Qur'an, "The noble Qur'an raises the human being, and the woman also raises the human being. Women's job is to raise the human being".[216]

The question of Mary's prophethood leaves one with more questions than answers. It has been argued that since all prophets were men, that men have a monopoly over the connection with the divine.[217] However, some cases beg the question whether Mary's prophethood or lack of it increases or diminishes her essential value, because those titles sometimes seem to have more to do with worldly mission than spiritual status.[218] Moreover, if Mary is deemed a prophet, does this break the monopoly of men or is it a case of an exception that proves the rule? The overlap between her role as mother and as prophet seems to imply that she manifests her exceptional state through her femininity, and therefore, that these two categories are not mutually exclusive but may be corresponding. Mary's example has been further seen to "profoundly redraw(s) the general image of the Qur'anic prophet along gynocentric lines".[219]

Mary was consecrated to the temple before her birth. God's choice to make her a female reveals in retrospect that she was destined for her role. The divine proclamation at her birth that "the male is not as the female" has been linked in the exegesis to her election above the women of all worlds. It was also read here in light of an authentic tradition to refer more generally to the females' capacity to deliver prophets. Mary's second election over the women of the worlds was actualised when she conceived and then went to a distant place to give birth to her son, in a scene that combined spiritual hints with images of a woman in pain, namely, the bitterness of a social scandal and the physical anguish of labour. It has been argued that Mary could have been a prophet not only because she saw and spoke to the archangel Gabriel who delivered to her a divine message, but also because she was listed among the prophets in the Qur'an. Even though Mary did not bring a scripture as such, she bore a perfected being who was himself a living scripture. In this sense, likening Mary's conception of Jesus to Muhammad's conception of the Qur'an is plausible as a similar, and no inferior, contribution, with Mary's legacy being distinctly feminine.

The wives of the prophet Muhammad and other Muslim women

Unlike the stories of the past prophets, when the Qur'an speaks of the wives of the prophet Muhammad and other Muslim women, it evokes incidents which occurred during the time of Islamic revelation. As such, it will be shown that the historical context becomes a part of the Qur'anic context. The wives of the Prophet are spoken to directly, reminded of the difficulty of their position and the sacrifices it entails, and told that they will not be judged by the same standards as other women. The seclusion of the Prophet's wives has sometimes been understood as a model worthy of emulation by other women; however, the Qur'an portrays Muslim women around Muhammad as present, both in their moral and political allegiance to the Prophet, as well as in their engagement with the process of revelation.

Mothers of the believers

Sūrat al-Taḥrīm was mentioned above as the context of the verses on the two women who are made examples for the disbelievers and the two who are examples for the believers. The Qur'anic chapter begins, however, by discussing a problem the Prophet had with two of his wives, asking him why he bans himself from what God has made lawful for him, seeking the pleasure of his wives, and continues that Muslims may absolve this kind of oaths [66: 1–2].[220] Then the story is told that the Prophet had confided something to one of his wives, but she then went and told her co-wife of it, and the Prophet knew about that [66: 3]. The Qur'an then admonishes the two wives who aided each other against their husband to repent because they have cause to do so (*in tatūbā ila-llāhi fa-qad ṣaghat qulūbukumā*), and reminds that if they persist in plotting against the Prophet, then Gabriel, the good believers, and the angels will be his protectors [66: 4]. The wives are then warned that it may happen that if the Prophet divorces them, God will substitute for him better wives, faithful and pious, previously married and virgins [66: 5]. The Qur'an does not clarify the specifics, and even with the given historical contexts some issues remain blurred.[221] There are different stories about the details surrounding the occasion of revelation, but what is widely agreed upon is that it was a matter of jealousy that caused the co-wives, 'Ā'isha and Ḥafṣa, to devise some plot so that the Prophet withdraws from one or more of his other wives, in most versions this was about Māriya.[222] The women were not ordered to repent as such, but were given the choice of either repentance or the futile alternative of aiding one another against one who is supported by the angels and the righteous believers, followed by the expectation that they may be substituted by better women.[223] The reference to the potential marriage to virgins is seen to be directed at 'Ā'isha who was the only maiden the Prophet had married, and something she was proud of.[224] While jealousy between the wives of Abraham was only mentioned in the *ḥadīth*, here, the Qur'an shows that at least some of the Prophet's wives felt jealous and took action against their husband and co-wives.[225]

The main passage on the Prophet's wives occurs in *Sūrat al-Aḥzāb*. It begins by asking the Prophet to tell his wives, "If you desire the present life and its adornment, come now, I will make you provision, and set you free with kindliness. But if you desire God and His Messenger and the Last Abode, surely God has prepared for those amongst you such as do good a mighty wage" [33: 28–9]. Commentators usually agree that the occasion of revelation was some or all the wives' demands for an increased allowance,[226] and some add that there were also issues of jealousy and that this is the incident when the Prophet reportedly withdrew from all his wives for a lunar month, and then returned to them with this ultimatum.[227] The options that were given to the wives were either to be provisioned for and let go without dispute or enmity, or to stay with the Prophet and not have desire for the material world, but for the one to come.[228] God was therefore informing these women that they were in a difficult situation because of their esteem and honour.[229] It is due to their being examples, that the following verses warn and promise the wives double the punishments and double the rewards of other people:

> Wives of the Prophet, whosoever among you commits a flagrant indecency, for her the chastisement shall be doubled; that is easy for God. But whosoever of you is obedient to God and His Messenger, and does righteousness, We shall pay her her wage twice over; We have prepared for her a generous provision.
>
> [33: 30–1][230]

These promises are for their afterlife and the generous provision is paradise.[231] However, when the wives at that point reportedly each chose the Prophet, they were given the honorific title "*Ummahāt al-Mu'minīn* (Mothers of the Believers) [33: 6]" in recompense.[232] Therefore, it is not marriage to the Prophet itself that gives them honour, but the Qur'an couples this with their actions, as elsewhere in the Qur'an when judgement is always connected to actions, which is why the following verse again mentions their high status, and connects it directly to their piety, "Wives of the Prophet, you are not as other women if you are god-fearing" [33: 32].[233] If they choose to remain married to the Prophet but do not behave accordingly, then they would have lost both this world and the next, and would have gone even further away from God with evil results.[234] It has been observed that after having addressed the Prophet (*yā ayyuha-n-nabiyyu qul li-azwājika*) in [33: 28–9], God redirected his speech and addressed the women personally (*yā nisā' al-nabiyyi*) in [33: 30–5] in order to warrant their responsibilities.[235] The Qur'an then continues to define the behaviour that is proper to them:

> be not abject in your speech, so that he in whose heart is sickness may be lustful; but speak honourable words. Remain in your houses; and display not your finery, as did the pagans of old. And perform the prayer, and pay the alms, and obey God and His Messenger. (People of the House, God only desires to put away from you abomination and to cleanse you.)[236] And remember that which is recited in your houses of the signs of God and the Wisdom; God is All-subtle, All-aware.
>
> [33: 32–4]

While these stipulations are generally applicable to all women and to all Muslims, the verses here emphasise that since the Prophet's wives are not like others, they ought to exaggerate in abiding by these guidelines, and be more careful than other women.[237]

The theme of protecting the Prophet's wives from potentially harmful men continues within the context of teaching Muslims to be respectful when they visit the Prophet in his home, and this has been revealed on the night of his marriage ceremony to Zaynab bint Jaḥsh,[238] when some people stayed lingering about,[239] "And when you ask his wives for any object, ask them from behind a curtain; that is cleaner for your hearts and theirs. It is not for you to hurt God's Messenger, neither to marry his wives after him, ever; surely that would be, in God's sight, a monstrous thing" [33: 53]. It is reported that some people in Medina were saying that when the Prophet dies, they would marry this or that of his wives, which is why the *ḥijāb* was revealed, thereby restricting further the wives' movements, with the repeated warning that no one is allowed to marry any one of the Prophet's wives after he passes away.[240]

The affair of the lie (*'ifk*) [24: 11] is another example where hypocrites attempted to cause considerable harm to the Prophet and the Muslim community, by falsely accusing one of his wives of indecent behaviour.[241] Indeed, there are ample such examples where the Prophet and other Muslims in general were being harmed by the hypocrites of Medina through harming their women; subsequently modest dress (*jilbāb* and *khimār*) was incurred on Muslim women and seclusion (*ḥijāb*) on the Prophet's wives [33: 53–62].

The Prophet's marriage to Zaynab and the subsequent descent of the *ḥijāb* has been used by many as the gender-defining event in Islam, and as a reference to the Prophet's views on women and sexuality.[242] While the Muslim tradition itself plays a part in advocating such stereotypes, upon reading the Qur'an it may be seen that these two instances are highly contextual.[243]

The Prophet, who is normally considered a perfect example, is not necessarily a legal example in matters of marital relations, considering the freedoms as well as constraints that are unique to him [30: 50–2].[244] His wives are also exceptional women in at least three ways. First, they are "mothers of the believers" even though no other woman is any man's mother except the one she actually gives birth to [58: 2]. Second, they carry double the punishments and rewards of the rest of Muslims. Third, they are the only women addressed in the Qur'an with the second person (*mukhāṭab*) rather than the third person (*ghā'ib*). This in itself may point to the androcentricity of the Qur'an as text,[245] but it also signifies that these are really "not as other women". This however does not mean that these verses are of no relevance at all outside that particular historical context.

Barabara Stowasser's extensive study of the Prophet's wives in the Qur'an concludes that:

> The Prophet's polygamous household here becomes a prime example of Qur'anic reasoning in favor of righteous institutions over individual aspirations. At the same time … the Qur'anic legislation also signifies aspects of the principle of ethical individualism in its linkage between individual select status and individual virtue, clearly expressed in the "verse of choice". [33: 28–9][246]

What strengthens this analysis is the tradition that when a man told the fourth Imam Zayn al-'Ābidīn that "you *ahl al-bayt* are always forgiven", the

Imam felt troubled with the connotations of that statement and explained that, if anything, *ahl al-bayt* have the status of the Prophet's wives in that they would incur double the punishments and rewards.[247]

Bay'at al-Nisā'

Sūrat al-Mumtaḥana, where the text of the women's *bay'a* (pledge of allegiance) occurs, has three main themes. These are, severing relationships with the pagans in Mecca [60: 1–9 and 13], legal stipulations where severing ties involves spouses [60: 10–11], and finally the pledge of allegiance that the newcomers to Medina must give the Prophet [60: 12], after their faith had been examined [60: 10].[248] The text of the pledge reads thus:

> O Prophet, when believing women come to thee, swearing fealty to thee upon the terms that they will not associate with God anything, and will not steal, neither commit adultery, nor slay their children, nor bring a calumny they forge between their hands and their feet, nor disobey thee in aught honourable, ask God's forgiveness for them; God is All-forgiving, All-compassionate.
>
> [60: 12]

Exegetes explain these terms much more narrowly than the text appears to be. The prohibition of stealing they take to mean stealing from their husband's house primarily. Slaying the children they identify as either infanticide or abortion. The forged calumny between their hands and legs is described as ascribing illegitimate children to their husbands. They do not however explain how ascribing an illegitimate child to their husband is related to women's hands, but Ṭabaṭabā'ī elaborates that when a woman gives birth, the child falls between her legs and into her hands. Obeying the Prophet in what is good they understand to be a prohibition of mourning and lamenting the dead in the pre-Islamic manners of women striking their face, tearing their clothes, and dishevelling their hair.[249]

Obeying the Prophet in what is good does not seem to have a clear interpretation, because one presumes that everything the Prophet orders is good. The semantic meaning of *bi-l-ma'rūf* which may be translated as something recognised, beneficent, or reputable, is taken to mean something that the intellect recognises as good, which in any case applies to all that the Prophet orders.[250] Ṭabāṭabā'ī finds that the *sunna* of the Prophet, rather than God's commands as such, is what is meant as something recognisable to Muslims.[251]

It has been correctly pointed out, however, that the text of the *bay'a* actually enshrines the condition of membership in the *umma* (Islamic community/nation), "in terms of sins/crimes foresworn that are applicable to all believers regardless of gender: polytheism, theft, fornication, infanticide, slander, and disobedience to the Prophet".[252] In fact, according to the early historian Ibn Isḥāq, men initially pledged their allegiance to the Prophet, in the first 'Aqaba meeting, in the exact wording of the women's fealty, until war became a part of men's duties.[253] Furthermore, there were a few women who reportedly gave the men's pledge when they went to war with the Prophet.[254] The exegetes discussed above, however, collectively fail to mention that the text of *bay'at al-nisā'* (women's fealty) was given by men as well, or at least to mention that there is an early and reliable report to that effect.[255] This seems to help them redefine its terms in very gender-specific language, which is unlike the gender-neutral text itself.[256]

al-Mujādila

It is reported that a woman named Khawla bint Khuwaylid came to the Prophet complaining of her husband. She explained that after having disseminated her belly for him, and helped him in the affairs of his world and hereafter, he said the words of *ẓihār* to her; a pre-Islamic practice whereby the man declared that his wife is as his mother to him, thereby dismissing her sexually without actually letting her go by way of divorce. After much debate with the Prophet, he informed her that he cannot issue a ruling without God guiding him to it, so she directed her complaint towards God.[257] Later, revelation decided, "God has heard the words of her that disputes with thee concerning her husband, and makes complaint unto God. God hears the two of you conversing together; surely God is All-hearing, All-seeing" [58: 1]. The very beginning of the verse *qad sami'a-llāh* indicates that prayers have been answered and relief arrived.[258] The revelation continues to prohibit the practice [58: 2].[259]

This is not the only incident by which revelation descended in answer to a question, whether from a man or woman. However, the acknowledgment of this particular women's pain in the Qur'an is indeed noteworthy. There is a sense of intimacy when God reassures that he had been listening to her whole argument, as well as to her complaint to him. This, however, opens the question for contemporary women, whether God is still listening, and how to debate with revelation today? Khawla's *jadal*, her "manoeuvring left and right in debate",[260] has been described as a "critique of male religio-legal rulings".[261] There is indeed a sense to that in this verse, especially in what may be a universally deep pain for women, to feel used and discarded after beauty and strength had perished. Yet, there is also in this story a proposition that God indeed responds to one who puts questions forth skilfully.

Unlike most of the personalities in the Qur'an, the Prophet's wives seem subservient to their husband's command, and perhaps some of their individuality is lost because of the political situation in Medina, where the women were included in the cold war that the hypocrites waged on the Prophet. As a group, the Prophet's wives may be seen to carry the theme of *jihād al-nafs* in so far as a prominent position in society requires a more stringent struggle to set an example, and that when one is in an eminent position or a leadership role, individual sacrifices be made for the sake of the collective good. The women's *bay'a* in the Qur'an shows women as citizens in the *umma*, and since this was revealed after the verses on the seclusion of the Prophet's wives and the modesty of Muslim women, it "acknowledged for the Muslim woman her legal competence to participate in the public act of pledging her moral and political allegiance and stipulated women's admission to citizenship in the *umma* on conditions exclusive of clothing restrictions".[262] The *mujādila* model similarly shows women's participation in the debate with revelation, and it is hopeful that these may be skilful in their arguments, and that they might win over the men in their rights. Away from the more abstract themes in the stories of the previous personalities, the models of the Muslim women around the prophet Muhammad, as an institution or group (irrespective of the debate on polygamy), as citizens, and as conversers with revelation, are relevant models today in as far as living in the world is concerned.

The women of paradise (*al-Ḥūr al-'Īn*)

The hereafter and its women in the Qur'an may be considered as an altogether separate category which does not belong to the earth, and does not fit into human experience as we know it. For example, heavenly fruit resembles earthly fruit but tastes different [2: 25], the milk there does not change taste [47: 15], and the wine does not cause intoxication [37: 47, 52: 23].

Paradise is often depicted as a place of soberness and joy. There is no idle, sinful, or lying talk there [56: 25, 78: 35, 88: 11], there is no fear or sorrow [7: 49, 10: 62, 43: 68]. The people of paradise are brought nearer to God [56: 11], and the two will take mutual pleasure in each other [5: 119, 9: 100, 58: 22, 98: 8]. There is also a degree of sensuality in paradise, with gardens and rivers, meat and fruit for food, silk and jewellery for clothing, and many beautiful maidens. It has been observed, however, that pleasure there is produced without an earthly counterpart, for there is no excretion or pregnancy in paradise.[263] There is an unusual combination of the utterly spiritual with the utterly sensual. Perhaps that is why some have observed that the Qur'an refers to its own depiction of paradise as a "*mathal*" [13: 35, 47: 15]. This has been translated as parable, similitude, or likeness.[264] Ṭabāṭabā'ī understands the term *mathal* as description, but adds that perhaps *mathal* here may be understood in what he calls its known meaning. In which case, referring to those descriptions as *mathal* would be saying that paradise is higher and nobler than to be described and limited by words, but that these illustrations function as metaphors to bring paradise closer to the minds.[265]

There is in the Qur'an an emphasis on pairing the men and women of paradise. For example, in paradise the believers will have "spouses purified (*azwājun muṭahharatun*)" [2: 25, 3: 15, 4: 57]. There are also other references to this pairing, "when the souls shall be coupled (*wa idha-l-nufūsu zuwwijat*)" [81: 7].[266] In these cases the grammar is gender-neutral and it seems therefore to apply to both men and women. However, the majority of verses that speak of marriage in paradise refer to the maidens that are reserved for believing men, known as *al-ḥūr al-ʿīn*, or simply as *ḥūr*.[267]

The *ḥūr* (singular, *ḥawrāʾ*), a perfect beauty according to the Arabs, is a woman whose iris and pupil are very black, against a very white background in the eye. Moreover, a woman is not *ḥawrāʾ* unless she has very white skin.[268] *Al-ʿīn* (singular, *ʿaynāʾ*) is a reference to black and very wide eyes.[269]

Some of the Qur'anic verses that describe the *ḥūr* of paradise are, "houris, cloistered in cool pavilions ... untouched before them by any man or jinn" [55: 72–4], "and wide-eyed houris as the likeness of hidden pearls ... Perfectly We formed them, perfect, and We made them spotless virgins, chastely amorous (*ʿurban atrāban*), like of age for the Companions of the Right" [56: 22–3, 35–8]. The *ḥūr* also have "and with them wide-eyed maidens restraining their glances as if they were hidden eggs" [37: 48–9], and again "and with them maidens restraining their glances" [38: 53], and finally they are "maidens with swelling breasts (*kawāʿiba atrābā*), like of age" [78: 33].

Among these descriptions are also the "maidens good and comely (*khayrātun ḥisān*)" [55: 70]. According to authentic traditions, these, unlike the *ḥūr*, are actually the believing women of this world who go to heaven, and they are more beautiful than the *ḥūr*.[270]

In Qummī's early exegesis, the "maidens restraining their glances (*qāṣirātu-t-ṭarfi*)" has been consistently understood to mean that the maidens, due to their brightness, cause the men that look at them to restrain their glances.[271] This, however, is not what later exegetes say, for they understand these verses to mean that the maidens do not look at any man other than their husbands.[272] Their being cloistered in the pavilions (*maqsūrātun fi-l-khiyām*) seems to give precedence to the latter meaning.

The entire depiction of those maidens, with the exception of [55: 70] which is supposed to be about believing women not the *ḥūr*, focuses on two aspects. First, there is focus on their physical beauty by describing them as *ḥūr ʿīn* and emphasising their eternal youth by describing their swelling breasts (*kawāʿib*).[273] Second, there is focus on their extreme modesty through the repeated reminder of their modest gaze, being secluded in pavilions, and guarded as pearls and ostrich eggs.[274]

It has been argued that the Qur'anic depiction of paradise is subjective to the Arab view of comfort.[275] On the other hand, it has been suggested that the sensuous picture of heaven need not be understood from a historico-critical perspective but as an appreciation of fundamental human nature as the monotheistic tradition perceives it.[276] One study of various descriptions of paradise among ancient cultures suggests that since most ancient cultures have portrayed a similar vision of paradise, then that place must exist as such.[277] Regardless of the validity of this conclusion, the study is a case in point. It succeeds in showing great similarities in peoples' depictions of paradise, but it neglects certain elements that are culturally specific. One such example describes that in the Japanese paradise robes are hung on their sacred *sakaki* tree.[278]

In any case, the Qur'anic emphasis that in paradise, people will get whatever they wish for [16: 31, 25: 16, 39: 34, 42: 22, 50: 35, 36: 57] hints at the subjectivity of paradise.

Al-Ḥūr al-ʿīn may be seen to portray a femininity that is utterly submissive. Women in paradise are how men want them to be, very beautiful and completely secluded as a sign of their devotion to their husbands. Alternatively, at least according to Qummī, the *ḥūr* possess the power of mysteriousness and allure. So while they may be waiting for men and created to be devoted to them, they can still attract men and hold them in some form of subjection.

Traditions tell that the *khayrātun ḥisān*, who are this world's believing women, are more beautiful than the *ḥūr*. It could be argued, then, that the emphasis on youthfulness and beauty is appealing to women themselves, and that would certainly be a valid point. Considering what has been mentioned above regarding the subjectivity of paradise, and the possibility of its description being a metaphor, the *ḥūr* may be regarded as a male fantasy. However, the real issue at stake will be noted in the final chapter, where much of the *ḥadīth* literature and subsequently Islamic law projects this personality onto the women of this world, not in the emphasis on physical appearance, but in regard to extreme seclusion and submission to the husband.

Summary and conclusions

In the end, it might be useful to compare and contrast all these personalities with one another, then final and more general conclusions will be made.

First, the mothers of several prophets are portrayed as participants in God's plans, and indeed were the hands through which God worked to prepare their sons for their missions. This is particularly true of Hagar, the mother of Moses, and Mary. One may argue that there is a strong matriarchal element in their stories, where Hagar survived alone in the desert, brought water and even a ritual, Moses' mother was responsible for receiving and acting on her inspiration and thus changed Moses' life, and Mary was complete without a man. Moreover, the fathers of Moses and Mary are conspicuously absent from their accounts.

Second, Mary has been seen as impeccable and among the *awliyā'*, perhaps even a prophet. The mother of Moses has been described similarly to the *awliyā'* as well. The stories of these two women particularly have been told in connection to their motherly bodies, through the emphasis on Moses' mother breastfeeding and Mary's delivery. It may be that these feminine experiences which are normally seen by men as merely biological functions are elevated in people's eyes when they are told thus.

Third, in the story of Mary the statement that "the male is not as the female" is the only explicit statement that differentiates between the two sexes. It has been argued that the preference here is for the female and that the preference may be due to the female's capacity to conceive and deliver prophets. This has been linked to Mary's legacy and the feminine portrayal of spirituality in the Qur'an.

Fourth, Sarah and Mary both saw the angels and conversed with them and both have been included in the term *ahl al-bayt* of Abraham and of 'Imrān.

Fifth, the personalities of the women of the *qaṣaṣ* are so varied that it is near impossible to speak of a certain personality of woman that is being portrayed. The daughters of Lot were offered in marriage by their father to the Sodomites, presumably without their consultation, whereas one of the two sisters of Madyan herself hinted to her father about a marriage proposition. Zulaykha's pursuit of Joseph is condemned whereas the pursuit of Moses' bride is acceptable. Zulaykha and Bilqīs are similar in that they are perhaps the only characters not related to a prophet by blood or marriage, yet they each gave two very different stories. Zulaykha opposed the will of a prophet, while Bilqīs allied herself with him. Where Zulaykha showed the drunkenness of emotion, Bilqīs showed intelligence at its best, that is when it leads to faith. Bilqīs may be compared to Āsiyā the wife of Pharaoh. Neither cared for the palaces or thrones of this world, but hoped to be near to God, although Bilqīs did not suffer a husband's tyranny.

Sixth, most of the female personalities of the *qaṣaṣ* tell stories of the spiritual *jihād* or *jihād al-nafs*. The wives of Noah and Lot were betrayers and spiritually dead, therefore they were doomed. Zulaykha was an example of the lower appetitive soul, but one that was eventually able to judge her actions and therefore progress. The mother of Moses reveals deep trust in God's inspiration and promise, even though she needed divine support to strengthen her heart at the most difficult time. Bilqīs tells a story of the inner mental struggle, between inherited cultural ideas and novel ones which are true to the heart. Mary is a character who did not show much signs of struggle, rather the emphasis was on her submission to God's will and the fruits that she reaped as a result. The wives of the Prophet Muhammad were given a choice between leaving the Prophet's household or struggling in the soul's *jihād*. Being in a position of responsibility as role models for their community, and given the honorific title "mothers of the believers" entailed double the rewards and punishments. The stories of Hagar and Āsiyā, however, next to their spiritual *jihād* tell a story of a more active *jihād*. Due to her activeness and earthly pursuit Hagar was miraculously given water that appeared in a barren valley. The wife of Pharaoh underwent a spiritual *jihād* when she had faith in the message of Moses, but that was coupled with a basic form of political *jihād* whereby she refused, with her heart and words, the false claims and tyrannical actions of her husband. Even though these characters are women and some aspects of their stories have much to do with their being women, such as being mothers or men's consorts, they do transcend their sex and they speak of the human *nafs* and its varied aspirations.

Seventh, while the personalities of the *qaṣaṣ* were not subject to but often rebellious against male authority, the wives of the Prophet after the warnings, and the *ḥūr* of paradise do portray the image of women dedicated to their husbands, and the theme of women's seclusion as part of that devotion occurs both times. Both these examples however are portrayed as exceptions rather than the rule for normal women.

Eighth, the *ḥūr* of paradise differ much from the women of the *qaṣaṣ*. The maidens of the hereafter are beautiful and do not say or do anything that reveals a personality behind the beauty, with the exception of their modesty of course. The women of the *qaṣaṣ* have interesting personalities; whether pious or impious they are strong and dynamic, and significantly, often act independently of men.

The group of verses from *Sūrat al-Taḥrīm* [66: 10–12] best summarise this chapter. These verses pick certain female personalities from the *qaṣaṣ* and present them as examples to believing men and women, whereby the wives of Noah and Lot are examples for the disbelievers, and the wife of Pharaoh and Mary are examples for the believers.

Two important observations about these verses are particularly striking. First, the example of women is given in all cases. Second, there is a balance in that there are two examples for the disbelievers and the same number for the believers. Perhaps, this group of verses speaks of women's humanity. This is done by portraying women as examples for all human beings, disbelievers and believers. The exclusive use of female characters here is remarkable. Moreover, by giving the same number of women in each category, a profound statement about women's common humanity is implied. Women are neither idealised nor vilified. They are not put on a pedestal nor are they debased. These two are in fact the sides of the same coin, because when women are put on a pedestal, any error on the part of a woman would make her fall very low in people's eyes. Also, because of the same number of female examples on both sides, it can hardly be argued, as the *ḥadīth* consistently does, that women may be put into a general category that lacks faith and is destined for either heaven or hell.

The two examples for the believers are Āsiyā and Mary. The first portrays a spiritual *jihād* followed by a political one, and the second portrays the epitome of spirituality which yields its fruits through perfect motherhood and the birth of children who are true interpreters of scripture.

The next chapter will move to the female personalities in the *sunna* of the prophet Muhammad, and particularly the three main women of *ahl al-bayt* because through these women, some of the major findings in this chapter may be affirmed. The theme of the striving of the human *nafs* will continue. The idea of motherhood as a spiritual experience that makes impeccable children will be confirmed in the personality of Fāṭima. The political *jihād* as performed by Āsiyā will become fully developed by the women of *ahl al-bayt*.

Notes

1 Lawson, B.T. (1993) "Akhbari Shi'i approaches to tafsir". In Hawting, G. and Shareef, A.-K.A. (eds) *Approaches to the Qur'an*. London: Routledge, p. 184.
2 Pauliny, J. (1998) "Some remarks on the *qisas al-anbiya'* works in Arabic literature". In Rippin, A. (ed.) *The Qur'an: formative interpretation*. Aldershot: Ashgate Variorum, pp. 321–3.

3 Pauliny (1998, p. 326).
4 Ahmad, A. (2010) *Qur'anic concepts of human psyche* [online]. Available from: www.biblioislam.net/en/ELibrary/FullText.aspx?tblid=3&id=44 [Accessed 18.07.2011].
5 Sands, K.Z. (2006) *Sufi commentaries on the Qur'an in classical Islam*. Oxon: Routledge, p. 100.
6 al-Kulaynī, Muḥammad Ibn Ya'qūb (1388h) *al-Kāfī*. 3rd edn. 8 volumes. Tehran: Dār al-Kutub al-Islāmiyya, vol. 5, p. 12.
7 For example: Wadud-Muhsin, A. (1994) *Qur'an and woman*. Kuala Lumpur: Penerbit Fajar Bakti, p. 32.
8 al-Khaṭīb, 'Abd al-Karīm (1964) *al-Qaṣaṣ al-Qur'ānī fī manṭūqihī wa mafhūmihī*. Cairo: Maṭba'at al-Sunna al-Muḥammadiyya, p. 118.
9 Abdel Haleem, M. (1999) *Understanding the Qur'an: themes and style*. London: Tauris, p. 132.
10 Stowasser, B. (1994) *Women in the Qur'an, traditions, and interpretation*. New York: Oxford University Press, p. 39.
11 al-Ṭūsī, Muḥammad Ibn Ḥasan (1409h) *al-Tibyān fī tafsīr al-Qur'ān*. 10 volumes. Qum: Maktab al-I'lām al-Islāmī, vol. 10, pp. 52–3. al-Ṭabrisī, al-Faḍl Ibn al-Ḥasan (1415h) *Majma' al-Bayān*. 10 volumes. Beirut: Mu'assasat al-A'lamī, vol. 10, p. 64.
12 Ṭūsī (1409h, vol. 10, p. 53).
13 al-Ṭabāṭabā'ī, Muaḥmmad Ḥusayn (1402h) *al-Mizān fī tafsīr al-Qur'ān*. 20 volumes. Qum: Mu'assasat al-Nashr al-Islāmī, vol. 19, pp. 342–3.
14 al-Iṣfahānī, al-Rāghib, al-Ḥusayn Ibn Mufaḍḍal (1404h) *al-Mufradāt fī gharīb al-Qur'ān*. Tehran: Daftar Nashr al-Kitāb, p. 163.
15 al-Fayrūz Ābādī, Muḥammad Ibn Ya'qūb (n.d.) *al-Qāmūs al-muḥīṭ*. 4 volumes. Cairo: Muḥammad 'Abd al-Ḥamīd, vol. 4, p. 220.
16 Ibn Manẓūr, Muḥammad Ibn Mukarram (1405h) *Lisān al-'Arab*. 15 volumes. Qum: Nashr Adab al-Ḥawza, vol. 13, p. 144.
17 Also note that the status of vicegerency is referred to in the Qur'an as "the Trust" [33: 72], and therefore, perhaps there is a hint at the women betraying "the Trust", although their betrayal of their husbands the prophets is the more explicit indication here.
18 Stowasser (1994, p. 41) quotes Ibn Kathīr and al-Kisā'ī.
19 Ṭabāṭabā'ī (1402h, vol. 10, pp. 235–6).
20 Ṭūsī (1409h, vol. 10, p. 52). Ṭabrisī (1415h, vol. 10, p. 64).
21 al-'Ayyāshī, Muḥammad Ibn Mas'ūd (n.d.) *Tafsīr al-Qur'ān*. 2 volumes. Tehran: al-Maktaba al-'Ilmiyya al-Islāmiyya, vol. 2, p. 151.
22 Ṭabrisī (1415h, vol. 5, p. 285; and vol. 10, p. 64).
23 The objection however is not only feminist based but an Islamic one against believing men and especially women being offered in marriage to disbelievers. It might be, however, that Lot knew already the Sodomites would not accept because they were not interested in women, but made the offer anyway for some reason such as to save face in front of his guests, or to give proof to the Sodomites that they acted out of greed not out of need, which is why he described them as "*musrifūn*".
24 Ṭabāṭabā'ī (1402h, vol. 19, p. 343).
25 Faḍlallāh, Muḥammad Ḥusayn (1998) *Dunyā al-mar'a*. Beirut: Dār al-Malāk, p. 270.
26 Kulaynī (1388h, vol. 8, p. 370).
27 Kulaynī (1388h, vol. 8, pp. 372–3).
28 al-Ṭabarī, Muḥammad Ibn Jarīr (1879) *Tarīkh al-'umam wa al-mulūk*. 8 volumes. Beirut: Mu'assasat al-A'lamī, vol. 1, pp. 189–90.
29 Kulaynī (1388h, vol. 4, pp. 203–4), and al-Qummī, 'Alī Ibn Ibrāhīm (1404h) *Tafsīr al-Qur'ān*. 3rd edn. 2 volumes. Qum: Mu'assasat Dār al-Kitāb, vol. 1, pp. 351–2.
30 Ṭūsī (1409h, vol. 6, p. 29). Ṭabāṭabā'ī (1402h, vol. 10, p. 323).
31 Ibn Manẓūr (1405h, vol. 10, pp. 459–60).

32 Ṭabāṭabā'ī (1402h, vol. 10, p. 323).
33 Ṭabāṭabā'ī (1402h, vol. 10, p. 323).
34 Iṣfahānī (1404h, p. 292), where he describes *ḍaḥik* not as laughter but an expression that reveals the two front teeth, more like a smile then, which would make it plausible in this context.
35 Stowasser (1994, p. 46) quoting Ibn Kathīr.
36 The idea that Sarah's reactions stress the inconceivability of the event has been noted by: Reynolds, G.S. (2007) "The Qur'anic Sarah as prototype of Mary". In Thomas, D.R. (ed.) *The Bible in Arab Christianity*. Leiden: Brill, p. 196.
37 Kulaynī (1388h, vol. 6, pp. 35–6).
38 Ibn Manẓūr (1405h, vol. 14, p. 286).
39 Stowasser (1994, p. 44).
40 Kulaynī (1388h, vol. 4, pp. 201–5).
41 Kulaynī (1388h, vol. 4, p. 202).
42 Ibn Manẓūr (1405h, vol. 14, p. 385).
43 al-Māzandarānī, Muḥammad Ṣāliḥ (2000) *Sharḥ uṣūl al-kāfī*. 12 volumes. Beirut: Dār Iḥyā' al-Turāth al-'Arabī, vol. 5, p. 50.
44 Kulaynī (1388h, vol. 4, p. 434).
45 Abdel Haleem (1999, pp. 33, 38–9).
46 Kulaynī (1388h, vol. 4, pp. 430–1), etc.
47 Abugideiri, H. (2001) "Hagar: a historical model for 'gender jihad'". In Haddad, Y.Y. and Esposito, J.L. (eds) *Daughters of Abraham: feminist thought in Judaism, Christianity, and Islam*. Gainesville: University Press of Florida, p. 83.
48 Najmabadi, A. (1998) "Feminism in an Islamic republic: years of hardship, years of growth". In Haddad, Y.Y. and Esposito, J.L. (eds) *Islam, gender, and social change*. New York: Oxford University Press, p. 62.
49 Abugideiri (2001, pp. 83–4).
50 The theme of sacred space is strong in the story of Abraham, Hagar, and Ishmael. The two hilltops where Hagar walked have been shown to be a sacred space referred to in the Qur'an as "*al-Sa'y*" in Calder, N. (1986) "The sa'y and the jabīn: some notes on Qur'an 37: 102–3". *Journal of Semitic Studies*, 31: 17–26. Hagar is also buried in *Ḥijr Ismā'īl*, a semi-circular wall at the north-western side of the Ka'ba, where Ishmael placed the first stones there in order to disallow stepping on her grave, and the space is a burial site for many prophets (Kulaynī, 1388h, vol. 4, p. 210).
51 al-Nīsabūrī, al-Wāḥidī, 'Alī Ibn Aḥmad (1388h) *Asbāb nuzūl al-āyāt*. Cairo: Mu'assasat al-Ḥalabi & Co, p. 182, says that the Arabs demanded to hear stories (presumably for entertainment), so the Qur'an decided to give them "*aḥsan al-qaṣaṣ*".
52 Merguerian, G.K. and Najmabadi, A. (1997) "Zulaykha and Yusuf: whose 'best story'?" *International Journal of Middle East Studies*, 29 (4): 485–508.
53 Keeler, A. (2006) *Sufi hermeneutics: the Qur'an commentary of Rashid al-Din Maybudi*. Oxford: Oxford University Press in association with the Institute of Isma'ili Studies, p. 285.
54 It is Ṭabāṭabā'ī who maintains that Joseph's fidelity towards what he calls "*rabbī*" is meant towards God not the governor, because according to his reasoning, the whole tale shows that Joseph would have no "lord" besides God.
55 Stowasser (1994, p. 55) quoting Sayyid Qutb.
56 Johns, A.J. (1981) "Joseph in the Qur'an: dramatic dialogue, human emotion and prophetic wisdom". *Islamic Quarterly*, 7: 37.
57 Other ironic aspects of the brothers' guile have been noted in: Johns (1981, p. 35).
58 Also pointed out in: Johns (1981, p. 35).
59 Ṭūsī (1409h, vol. 6, pp. 123, 127).
60 Ṭabāṭabā'ī (1402h, vol. 11, p. 143).
61 Merguerian and Najmabadi (1997, pp. 485–508).

62 Ṭabāṭabā'ī (1402h, vol. 11, pp. 144–5).
63 Merguerian and Najmabadi (1997, pp. 485–508).
64 Merguerian and Najmabadi (1997, pp. 485–508).
65 Najmabadi, A. (1999) "Reading and enjoying 'wiles of women' stories as a feminist". *Iranian Studies*, 32 (2): 203–22.
66 Kulaynī (1388h, vol. 5, p. 516, and vol. 6, p. 49).
67 Some of this tension is also expressed in the diverse depictions of Zulaykha, sometimes as an image of love as in Persian poetry, and other times as a *fitna* as in the legalistic tradition (Stowasser, 1994, pp. 55–6).
68 Keeler (2006, p. 282).
69 Ṭabāṭabā'ī (1402h, vol. 11, p. 240).
70 Ibn Manẓūr (1405h, vol. 9, p. 179). Imam al-Ṣādiq has been quoted in this context as saying, "*Shaghaf* is like a cloud; it obscures the lover's heart from contemplating other than Him and from preoccupation with other than him" (Keeler, 2006, p. 290).
71 Ṭabāṭabā'ī (1402h, vol. 11, pp. 122–5).
72 Keeler (2006, pp. 289–92).
73 Keeler (2006, p. 300).
74 Ṭabāṭabā'ī (1402h, vol. 11, p. 246). He adds that this is not in defiance to the Islamic command that people prostrate to none other than God, because Joseph here was a sign (*āya*), just like Adam was to the angels and the Ka'ba is to Muslims. Prostration before the sign does not imply worshipping it, and worship remains for God (Ṭabāṭabā'ī, 1402h, vol. 11, p. 247).
75 Ṭabāṭabā'ī (1402h, vol. 11, p. 119).
76 Qummī (1404h, vol. 1, p.346).
77 Ṭabrisī (1415h, vol. 5, pp. 414–15). al-Kāshānī, Muḥsin Fayḍ (1416h) *al-Ṣāfī fī tafsīr kalam Allāh al-wāfī*. 2nd edn. 5 volumes. Tehran: Maktabat al-Ṣadr, vol. 3, p. 26.
78 Ṭūsī (1409h, vol. 6, pp. 154–6).
79 Ṭabāṭabā'ī (1402h, vol. 11, pp. 199–200).
80 Ṭabāṭabā'ī (1402h, vol. 11, p. 194).
81 Qummī (1404h, vol. 1, p. 344).
82 Ṭabāṭabā'ī (1402h, vol. 11, pp. 169–70).
83 Perhaps in refrence to 'Ayyāshī (n.d., vol. 2, pp. 173–4) among other exegetes.
84 Ṭabāṭabā'ī (1402h, vol. 11, p. 133).
85 Al-Ḥuwayzī, 'Abd 'Alī Ibn Jumu'a al-'Arūsī (1412h) *Nūr al-thaqalayn*. 4th edn. 5 volumes. Qum: Mu'assasat Ismā ilyān, vol. 2, p. 419.
86 Ṭabāṭabā'ī (1402h, vol. 11, pp. 129–30).
87 Ṭabāṭabā'ī (1402h, vol. 11, p. 153).
88 Ḥuwayzī (1412h, vol. 2, p. 421).
89 Ḥuwayzī (1412h, vol. 2, p. 421).
90 Ṭabāṭabā'ī (1402h, vol. 11, pp. 204–5).
91 Refer to: Stowasser (1994, p. 77).
92 Iṣfahānī (1404h, p. 515).
93 Fayrūz Ābādī (n.d., vol. 4, p. 399).
94 Ṭabrisī (1415h, vol. 7, p. 418). Ṭūsī (1409h, vol. 8, pp. 132–3).
95 Ṭabāṭabā'ī (1402h, vol. 16, pp. 12–13).
96 Lane, E.W. (n.d.) *Arabic-English lexicon* [online]. Available from: www. studyquran.co.uk/PRLonline.htm: *w-l-y*.
97 Ṭabāṭabā'ī (1402h, vol. 16, p. 13).
98 Al-'Āmilī, Muḥammad Ibn al-Ḥasan al-Ḥurr (1414h) *Wasā'il al-Shī'a*. 30 volumes. Qum: Mu'assasat Ahl al-Bayt.
99 Ṭūsī (1409h, vol. 10, p. 54).
100 Ṭabāṭabā'ī (1402h, vol. 19, p. 344).

101 Ṭabāṭabā'ī (1402h, vol. 19, p. 344).
102 Khaṭīb (1964, p. 106).
103 al-Raḍī, al-Sharīf, Muḥammad Ibn al-Ḥusayn (n.d.c) *Nahj al-balāgha*. 4 volumes. Beirut: Dār al-Ma'rifa, vol. 4, p. 90.
104 Ibn Abi al-Ḥadīd (n.d., vol. 19, p. 312).
105 Stowasser (1994, p. 61).
106 Ḥuwayzī (1412h, vol. 4, pp. 121–2).
107 Ḥuwayzī (1412h, vol. 4, p. 123).
108 Ṭabrisī (1415h, vol. 7, p. 426).
109 Ṭabāṭabā'ī (1402h, vol. 16, p. 25).
110 Khaṭīb (1964, pp. 108–10), also claims that strength and trustworthiness are two qualities women admire most in men, and further clarifies the father's reasoning in doing justice towards both daughters.
111 Ḥuwayzī (1412h, vol. 4, p. 125).
112 Ḥuwayzī (1412h, vol. 3, p. 379). Ṭabāṭabā'ī (1402h, vol. 16, p. 11).
113 There is a debate on who brought the throne from Sheba to Solomon, but this is not relevant here.
114 Lassner, J. (1993) *Demonizing the Queen of Sheba: boundaries of gender and culture in postbiblical Judaism and medieval Islam*. Chicago: The University of Chicago Press, p. 43.
115 Mir, M. (2007) "The queen of Sheba's conversion in Q. 27:44: a problem examined". *Journal of Qur'anic Studies*, 9 (2): 43–56.
116 Ṭabāṭabā'ī (1402h, vol. 15, pp. 358–9).
117 Mir (2007, p. 49).
118 Mir (2007, p. 46).
119 Ṭabrisī (1415h, vol. 7, p. 387). Ṭabāṭabā'ī (1402h, vol. 15, p. 365).
120 Ṭabāṭabā'ī, Muḥammad Ḥusayn (1402h) *al-Mīzān fī tafsīr al-Qur'ān*. 20 volumes. Qum: Mu'assasat al-Nashr al-Islami.
121 Ṭabāṭabā'ī (1402h, vol. 15, pp. 366–7).
122 Mir (2007, p. 45), based on Iṣlāḥī's exegesis.
123 Mir (2007, p. 50).
124 Ṭabāṭabā'ī (1402h, vol. 15, p. 367).
125 Al-Ṣadūq, Muḥammad Ibn 'Alī Ibn Bābawayh (1379h) *Ma'ānī al-akhbār*. Qum: Intisharat Islami.
126 Kulaynī (1388h, vol. 1, pp. 24–5). Jesus is said to have brought medical miracles which people needed (rather than excelled in), and the tradition continues that in the Imams' time, intellect/reason (*'aql*) is the way to prove the existence of God.
127 Ṭūsī (1409h, vol. 8, pp. 88–9).
128 Ṭabāṭabā'ī (1402h, vol. 15, p. 355). Although, one wonders why being given of everything has to be understood in the narrow meaning of everything pertaining to her role as queen. Normally, being given of everything would include a wide variety of things such as health, good manners, intelligence, beauty, etc. al-Qummī, 'Alī Ibn Ibrāhīm (1404h) *Tafsīr al-Qur'ān*. 3rd edn. 2 volumes. Qum: Mu'assasat Dār al-Kitāb, vol. 1, p. 7, explains that he understands this general statement to be specific because she had not been given many things including the remembrance of God, and a beard.
129 Mernissi (1993, p. 142).
130 Ṭūsī (1409h, vol. 8, p. 88).
131 Lassner (1993, p. 41).
132 Lassner (1993, p. 93).
133 Ṭabrisī (1415h, vol. 7, p. 388).
134 Although, attempting to apply Islamic law to that ancient event may not necessarily give certain answers because prophets had some variations in the laws that they brought, and therefore Islamic law need not be considered applicable to

Solomon's experience. On another note, in *Sūrat Saba'*, verse [34: 14] describes Solomon's death, and the following verses [34: 15–16] describe the state of Sheba, whereby its inhabitants were given "a fair land and a forgiving Lord", but they did not show gratitude so they were punished through the flooding of their dam, and subsequently their land produced bitter fruit. These verses have not normally been seen to be connected, and it may well be that [34: 14] marks the end of one passage, and [34: 15] the beginning of another. However, considering the Qur'anic link between Solomon and Sheba, is it possible that these verses imply that its people reverted after his death? If so, does this establish that he indeed ruled Sheba directly or indirectly?

135 Lassner (1993, p. 38).

136 On this subject, refer to: Mūsa, Faraḥ (1997) *al-Anbiyā' wa al-mutrafūn fi al-Qur'ān*. Beirut: Dār al-Hādī.

137 Ṭabāṭabā'ī (1402h, vol. 15, p. 357).

138 al-Ṣadūq, Muḥammad Ibn 'Alī Ibn Bābawayh (1404hb) *'Uyūn akhbār al-Riḍā*. 2 volumes. Beirut: Mu'assasat al-A'lamī li al-Matbū'āt, vol. 2, p. 270. al-'Āmilī, al-Ḥurr, Muḥammad Ibn al-Ḥasan (1414h) *Wasā'il al-Shī'a*. 30 volumes. Qum: Mu'assasat Ahl al-Bayt, vol. 6, p. 233.

139 Khalafallāh, Muḥammad Aḥmad (1999) *al-Fann al-qasasī fi al-Qur'ān al-karīm*. 4th edn. Beirut: Sīna li al-Nashr, p. 308.

140 Mernissi, F. (1993) *The forgotten queens of Islam*. Cambridge: Polity Press, p. 142.

141 Qummī (1404h, vol. 2, p. 128). Ṭūsī (1409h, vol. 8, pp. 93–4). Ṭabrisī (1415h, vol. 7, p. 380).

142 Ṭabāṭabā'ī (1402h, vol. 15, p. 360).

143 Mir (2007, p. 49).

144 It is worth pointing out that Ṭabāṭabā'ī (1402h, vol. 15, pp. 353–4) infers from Solomon's mention of both his parents here, that his mother was from the people of the straight path whom God bestowed "*ni'am*", and therefore she belongs to one of four categories of righteous people listed in [4: 69], namely, prophets, saints, martyrs, and the righteous.

145 This is in reference to the nature of war, while acknowledging that there is under Islamic law the distinction between legal and illegal war. The point here is that even though some wars might be legal and necessary, this does not make war in itself a beautiful experience.

146 Brackets exist in Arberry's original.

147 'Ayyāshī (n.d., vol. 1, p. 170). Ṭūsī (1409h, vol. 2, p. 444). Ḥuwayzī (1412h, vol. 1, p. 332).

148 'Ayyashī (n.d., vol. 1, p. 170). Ḥuwayzī (1412h, vol. 1, p. 332).

149 Ṣadūq (1404h, vol. 1, p. 101). Ḥuwayzī (n.d., vol. 1, p. 334), based on Kulaynī (1388h, vol. 1, p. 535). Ṭabāṭabā'ī (1402h, vol. 3, pp. 183–4) insists, however, that this does not conform to Arabic grammar because it presumes the preference to be to the former.

150 Ṭabāṭabā'ī (1402h, vol. 3, pp. 170–2).

151 Ṭabāṭabā'ī (1402h, vol. 3, pp. 165, 174).

152 Kulaynī (1388h, vol. 6, pp. 6–7.)

153 Ṭūsī (1409h, vol. 2, p. 447).

154 Ṭabāṭabā'ī (1402h, vol. 3, pp. 137–8).

155 Sands (2006, p. 102), quoting Kāshānī's *Ta'wilāt*.

156 Ṭabāṭabā'ī (1402h, vol. 3, p. 174).

157 Ṭūsī (1409h, vol. 2, p. 448).

158 Ṭūsī (1409h, vol. 2, p. 448).

159 Qummī (1404h, vol. 1, p. 101). Ṭūsī (1409h, vol. 2, pp. 448–9). Ḥuwayzī (1412h, vol. 1, p. 332, and vol. 3, p. 323).

160 Ṭabāṭabā'ī (1402h, vol. 14, pp. 10–15).

161 Ṭūsī (1409h, vol. 2, p. 447).
162 Qummī (1404h, vol. 2, p. 49). Ṭūsī (1409h, vol. 7, p. 114).
163 Ṭūsī (1409h, vol. 7, p. 114). Ṭabāṭabā'ī (1402h, vol. 14, p. 41).
164 Qummī (1404h, vol. 2, p. 49).
165 Ṭūsī (1409h, vol. 7, p. 116).
166 Ṭabrisī (1415h, vol. 6, p. 417).
167 Qummī (1404h, vol. 2, p. 49). Ṭūsī (1409h, vol. 7, pp. 119–20).
168 Ṭūsī (1409h, vol. 7, p. 117). Ṭabrisī (1415h, vol. 6, pp. 417–18).
169 Ṭūsī (1409h, vol. 7, p. 119). Ṭabrisī (1415h, vol. 6, p. 418).
170 Ṭūsī (1409h, vol. 7, p. 122). Although "*fariyya*" could also mean a lie, in this context they prefer the meaning of strange due to what the people have known of her family and her seclusion and prayer (Ṭabāṭabā'ī, 1402h, vol. 14, p. 44).
171 There is some debate as to why the people called her "sister of Aaron", but that is not relevant here.
172 Ṭūsī (1409h, vol. 7, p. 114). Ṭabrisī (1415h, vol. 6, p. 410).
173 Ṭūsī (1409h, vol. 7, p. 114). Ṭabāṭabā'ī (1402h, vol. 14, p. 34).
174 Sands (2006, p. 107).
175 Lybarger, L.D. (2000) "Gender and prophetic authority in the Qur'anic story of Maryam: a literary approach". *The Journal of Religion*, 80 (2): 258.
176 Lybarger (2000, p. 248).
177 Ḥuwayzī (1412h, vol. 3, p. 330).
178 Sands (2006, p. 105), quoting *Le Tafsir Mystique*.
179 Ḥuwayzī (1412h, vol. 3, pp. 330–1).
180 Ḥuwayzī (1412h, vol. 3, pp. 329–30).
181 Yusuf-Hanson, H. (n.d.) *Men and women in Islam* [online audio]. Available from: www.youtube.com/watch?v=BhEirLTl8ig [Accessed 20.02.2014].
182 Fierro, M. (2002) "Women as prophets in Islam". In Marin, M. and Deguilhem, R. (eds) *Writing the feminine: women in Arab sources*. New York: I.B. Tauris, pp. 183–94.
183 Haddad, Y.Y. and Smith, J.I. (1989) "The Virgin Mary in Islamic tradition and commentary". *The Muslim World*, 79 (3–4): 178.
184 Schleifer, A. (1998) *Mary, the blessed virgin of Islam*. Louisville: Islamic Texts Society, pp. 82–3, quoting *Kitāb al-Fiṣal* of Ibn Ḥazm.
185 Ṭabāṭabā'ī (1402h, vol. 12, pp. 256–7), also (vol. 1, p. 85) for more on this notion. In (vol. 11, p. 278), he excludes women from prophethood because "men were closer to knowledge than the women who are veiled traditionally (*dhawāt al-khidr*)".
186 Ṭabāṭabā'ī (1402h, vol. 3, p. 198).
187 Kulaynī (1388h, vol. 1, pp. 176–7).
188 Ṭabāṭabā'ī (1402h, vol. 3, pp. 221–2). It is important to mention here that when Lot's wife and his people saw his guests who were in reality angels, and when the Prophet's companions saw Gabriel in the famous *Ḥadīth Jibrā'īl* tradition, they were not aware of the identity of the angels until after the event, and thus they are not related to the *muḥaddath* category.
189 Ṭabāṭabā'ī (1402h, vol. 3, p. 188).
190 Ṭūsī (1409h, vol. 2, p. 457), particularly due to her miracles.
191 Ṭūsī (1409h, vol. 2, p. 456). Ṭabāṭabā'ī (1402h, vol. 3, p. 214).
192 Ṭūsī (1409h, vol. 2, p. 440).
193 Ṭūsī (1409h, vol. 2, p. 441).
194 Ṭabāṭabā'ī (1402h, vol. 3, pp. 165–6).
195 Ṭabāṭabā'ī (1402h, vol. 3, p. 188).
196 If Zechariah's wife was Mary's sister as some traditions and exegeses point out (Qummī, 1404h, vol. 2, p. 48. Ḥuwayzī, 1412h, vol. 3, p. 323.), then she, being another daughter of 'Imrān, and her son John the Baptist might be included here too (although according to Ṭabrisī, she was her maternal aunt, 1415h, vol. 6, p. 410).

197 Schleifer (1998, p. 94).
198 Note that the Qur'an in this verse [19: 56] describes Idrīs as "*ṣiddīqan nabiyyā*", that is, a man of truth and a prophet. Therefore, the Qur'anic description of Mary as *ṣiddīqa* (honest, truthful) in [5: 75] need not limit her to the category of the *ṣiddīqīn* and it does not necessarily exclude her from the category of the prophets or *nabiyyīn*, as regards the Qur'anic verse [4: 69].
199 Ṭūsī (1409h, vol. 7, pp. 135–6). Ṭabāṭabā'ī (1402h, vol. 14, p. 75).
200 For an interesting and innovative analysis of this verse in reference to its sounds and their relation to spirit, gender, and prophethood, refer to: Sells, M. (1999) *Approaching the Qur'an: the early revelations.* 2nd edn. Oregon: White Cloud Press, pp. 203–9.
201 Ṭabāṭabā'ī (1402h, vol. 14, p. 317).
202 Yusuf-Hanson (n.d.).
203 Ṭabāṭabā'ī (1402h, vol. 20, pp. 330–3).
204 Sells (1999, pp. 208–9).
205 Exegetes normally concede that the Spirit is Gabriel, however there are some authentic traditions that identify the Spirit as an entity that is different from the angels (Kulaynī, 1388h, vol. 1, pp. 274, 386).
206 Robinson, N. (2001) "Jesus and Mary in the Qur'an: some neglected affinities". In Rippin, A. (ed.) *The Qur'an: style and contents.* Aldershot: Ashgate.
207 Sells (1999, p. 203).
208 Ṭabrisī (1415h, vol. 3, p. 347).
209 Ṭabāṭabā'ī (1402h, vol. 3, p. 37).
210 Ṭabāṭabā'ī (1402h, vol. 3, pp. 193–4).
211 Ṭabāṭabā'ī (1402h, vol. 3, p. 277).
212 Ṭūsī (1409h, vol. 2, pp. 511–12). Ṭabrisī (1415h, vol. 2, pp. 331–2).
213 Kāshānī (1416h, vol. 1, p. 350).
214 Sufi, A. (2002) *The way of Muhammad.* London: Madinah Press, p. 81.
215 Ayoub, M.M. (1988) "The speaking Qur'an and the silent Qur'an: a study of the principles and development of Imami Shi'i tafsir". In Rippin, A. (ed.) *Approaches to the history of the interpretation of the Qur'an.* Oxford: Clarendon Press.
216 al-Khumaynī, Rūḥullāh (n.d.) *Makānat al-mar'a fī fikr al-Imām al-Khumaynī.* Damascus: Iranian Embassy, p. 78.
217 Fierro (2002, p. 183), where she has a quote analysing men's monopoly on the connection with the divine, and a subsequent hierarchy of authority.
218 For example while al-Khiḍr is described in the Qur'an merely as one of God's servants unto whom mercy and knowledge were given [18: 65], and while some traditions identify him as a prophet, his encounter with Moses, a messenger, strangely but clearly reveals that al-Khiḍr had more esoteric knowledge than Moses [18: 78]. For further analysis of this, refer to: Keeler (2006, p. 265). Another example would be the comparison between King Solomon and Imam 'Alī in some exegeses, refer to: Ṭabāṭabā'ī (1402h, vol. 11, p. 388, and vol. 15, pp. 362–71).
219 Lybarger (2000, p. 269).
220 In which case, one would have to pay a *kaffāra* (Ṭūsī, 1409h, vol. 10, p. 46).
221 Ṭabāṭabā'ī (1402h, vol. 19, pp. 329–30, and p. 338) where he observes that the stories do not clarify "he made known part of it, and turned aside from part" [66: 3].
222 Qummī (1404h, vol. 2, pp. 375–6). Ṭūsī (1409h, vol. 10, pp. 44–7). Ṭabrisī (1415h, vol. 10, pp. 55–6). Ḥuwayzī (1412h, vol. 5, pp. 367–71). Ṭabāṭabā'ī (1402h, vol. 19, pp. 337–40). Also in the Sunni tradition: Stowasser (1994, p. 80).
223 Ṭabāṭabā'ī (1402h, vol. 19, pp. 332–3).
224 Qummī (1404h, vol. 2, p. 377).
225 Bint al-Shāṭi' reports much of the jealousies and plotting that took place among his wives, and she contends that the Prophet's wives were divided into two groups

('Abd al-Raḥmān, 'A'isha (1967) *Nisā' al-nabī*, Beirut: Dār al-Kitāb al-'Arabī, pp. 84–100); that the wives were of two groups is attributed to al-Ṭabarī's "*al-Ṣimt al-Thamīn*" in her footnote on p. 99.

226 Qummī (1404h, vol. 2, pp. 192–3). Ṭūsī (1409h, vol. 8, p. 334). Ṭabāṭabā'ī (1402h, vol. 16, p. 305, and 314–16).

227 Ṭabrisī (1415h, vol. 8, p. 151). Ḥuwayzī (1412h, vol. 4, p. 264).

228 Ṭabrisī (1415h, vol. 8. p. 152). Ṭabāṭabā'ī (1402h, vol. 16, p. 306).

229 Ṭabāṭabā'ī (1402h, vol. 16, p. 305).

230 Ṭūsī (1409h, vol. 8, pp. 334–5, and 337). Ṭabāṭabā'ī (1402h, vol. 16, p. 305).

231 Qummī (1404h, vol. 2, p. 193). Ṭūsī (1409h, vol. 8, p. 338). Ṭabāṭabā'ī (1402h, vol. 16, p. 308).

232 Ṭūsī (1409h, vol. 8, p. 334).

233 Ṭabāṭabā'ī (1402h, vol. 16, p. 306). Ḥuwayzī (1412h, vol. 4, p. 238, and vol. 5, p. 372).

234 Ṭabāṭabā'ī (1402h, vol. 16, pp. 307–8).

235 Ṭabāṭabā'ī (1402h, vol. 16, pp. 307–8), where he also notes that the punishments are spoken in the passive form to denote farness (*yuḍā'af laha-l-'adhābu ḍi'fayni*), and the rewards in the active to denote closeness (*nu'tihā ajrahā marratayni*).

236 The parentheses here are not in Arberry's but are added to avoid confusion, because it will be soon explained that this phrase, to all Shī'ī exegetes and some Sunni ones, is not a part of God's speech to the wives. Ibn Sa'd, Muḥammad (n.d.) *al-Ṭabaqāt al-kubrā*. 8 volumes. Beirut: Dār Ṣāder, vol. 8, p. 199, finds that this verse is part of God's address to the Prophet's wives. Muslim, Ibn al-Ḥajjaj (n.d.) *al-Ṣaḥīḥ*. 8 volumes. Beirut: Dār al-Fikr, vol. 7, p. 123, reports that the term *ahl al-bayt* does not include the Prophet's wives but those members of his family who are not allowed to accept alms after him. al-Ḥākim, al-Nīsabūrī, Muḥammad Ibn 'Abdallāh (1406h) *al-Mustadrak 'ala al-Ṣaḥīḥayn*. 4 volumes. Beirut: Dār al Ma'rifa, vol. 2, p. 416, and vol. 3, pp. 147, 158 and Ibn Ḥanbal, Aḥmad (n.d.) *Musnad*. 6 volumes. Beirut: Dār Ṣāder (vol. 1, p. 331, vol. 3, pp. 259, and 285, vol. 4, p. 107, vol. 6, p. 292) and others find that the term *ahl al-bayt* in the *sunna* is a reference to the members of the house of Fāṭima. Shī'ī scholars are all of the latter view: Qummī (1404h, vol. 2, pp. 193–4). Ṭūsī (1409h, vol. 8, pp. 339–41). Ṭabrisī (1415h, vol. 8, pp. 156–7). Ṭabāṭabā'ī (1402h, vol. 16, pp. 309–12). In addition to the context of the verse as it is described in traditions – which is about "the five people of the cloak" from the Prophet's family – scholars note that the whole passage addressing the Prophet's wives is in the grammatically feminine plural form, whereas this verse is in the masculine plural. Therefore, there is a discontinuation, and this verse is not part of God's speech to the wives. Moreover, this verse has been understood as proof of the impeccability of *ahl al-bayt*, and will be discussed in the section on Fāṭima.

237 Ṭabāṭabā'ī (1402h, vol. 16, p. 308).

238 Qur'anic verses [33: 36–40] deal with the issue of Zaynab's marriage. Zaynab, the Prophet's cousin, was twice the means for the divine command issuing some change in the community's cultural perceptions. In the first arrangement of her marriage to the Prophet's adopted son Zayd, the desired change was reportedly that people should be humble and intermarry with others from lower social strata. In the second marriage to the Prophet himself, that adopted sons are not real sons. She is portrayed to have been audibly unhappy upon and during her first marriage, but very pleased with the second. If the proud and beautiful Zaynab was after prestige, she did in the end get the most prestigious marriage she could wish for, and indeed the second might have not been possible without the first. A legitimate question for the tradition would be why only the modern exegetes and authors were dismissive of the story regarding the Prophet's uncontrollable physical attraction to Zaynab, which allegedly led to her divorce from her husband and subsequent marriage to the Prophet himself (even though

she was his first cousin whom he must have interacted with during his life even before Islam). Is it because the earlier exegetes were less sceptical of traditions in general and the alleged incident describing his attraction to her in particular, even though they maintained that there was a divine command for the Prophet's marriage to her? Is it that the modern authors, aware of orientalists' galling depictions of the prophet of Islam as a sensual man, more observing of the incompatibility of that report with the Prophet's excellent character? Is it that modern men/exegetes' views on sex differ from those of their medieval counterparts, and do they therefore project different expectations on to the Prophet's behaviour? In any case, the Prophet's marriage to Zaynab is probably less problematic today than it was to the pagan Arabs because after Islam, adopted sons are not seen as real blood sons whatsoever. However, it is some of the Prophet's other conjugations, such as those within the institution of concubinage, which were not controversial in his day and therefore did not warrant any explanation in the Qur'an, that are seen as problematic today. On this latter point, refer to the discussion in reference to the relevance of the Prophet's example in: Ali, K. (2006) *Sexual ethics and Islam: feminist reflections on Qur'an, hadith, and jurisprudence.* Oxford: Oneworld, p. 137.

239 Qummī (1404h, vol. 2, p. 195). Ṭabāṭabā'ī (1402h, vol. 16, p. 343).

240 Qummī (1404h, vol. 2, p. 195). Ṭūsī (1409h, vol. 8, pp. 357–8). Ṭabrisī (1415h, vol. 8, pp. 173–7). Ḥuwayzī (1412h, vol. 5, p. 298). Ṭabāṭabā'ī (1402h, vol. 16, p. 337).

241 The traditions explain that it was in reference to the gossip about one of the Prophet's wives, either 'Ā'isha or Māriya, who had arrived to the site of her caravan late only to find that her people had gone, so that a young man accompanied her back to her folk. Some accused her of indecent behaviour, but the verse came to her rescue and further set stipulations on people who accuse decent women unjustly, that the punishments should be carried on the accusers and that their words not be trusted after that, unless they repent [24: 4–5]. That some people created this fuss to hurt the Prophet and the believers more generally is implied in verse [24: 11] which says that those who spread the slander are a "gang among you (*'iṣbatun minkum*)". Despite Sunni opinion that this incident was about 'Ā'isha, several Shī'ī scholars like Qummī maintain it was Māriya. This is not to say – as some have wrongly understood – that 'Ā'isha remains accused, rather, that 'Ā'isha was not suspect in the first place (Qummī, 1404h, vol. 2, p. 99), (Ṭabāṭabā'ī, 1402h, vol. 15, p. 89), etc.

242 Varisco, D.M. (2005) *Islam obscured: the rhetoric of anthropological representation.* New York: Palgrave Macmillan, p. 84, and ch. 3 more generally.

243 I am referring to a textual context that is discernible in these particular verses of the Qur'an. This is not the same as Fatima Mernissi's central argument on the relationship between the politics of Muhammad's Medina, and subsequent verses and traditions on women, where she speaks of two opposing forces in the Prophet's city of Medina, at the time of the fifth year after *hijra* (Mernissi, F. (1991) *The veil and the male elite: a feminist interpretation of women's rights in Islam.* Reading, MA: Addison-Wesley. Translated by M.J. Lakeland, ch. 7 and 8). Mernissi departs from other modernists in her treatment of the Qur'anic verses as being tied up to the historical events surrounding them; thus the *asbāb al-nuzūl*, "occasions of revelation" tacitly become "occasions for revelation". Stowasser (1994, pp. 133–4). For a critique of Mernissi's method, including inconsistencies in her use of primary sources, refer to: Scott, R.M. (2009) "A contextual approach to women's rights in the Qur'an: readings of 4:34". *The Muslim World,* 99: 68–9.

244 For a legal debate on this, refer to: Ali (2003).

245 Kecia Ali rightly contends that the Qur'an is androcentric though not misogynist (2006, p. 132).

246 Stowasser (1994, pp. 102–3).
247 Ṭabrisī (1415h, vol. 8, p. 153).
248 Stowasser, B. (2009) "The women's bay'a in Qur'an and sira". *The Muslim World*, 99 (1): 90. It must be added, though, that this short Qur'anic chapter is about women emigrants to Medina but not the men, because after the Treaty of Ḥudaybiyya, the Prophet had a mutual agreement with the pagan Arabs not to accept newcomer convert men and that they in turn would not take in people from Medina either. The Prophet did not promise the same about women however: Ṭabāṭabā'ī (1402h, vol. 19, p. 240). When women arrived in Medina, their faith was to be examined by swearing that they have come to Medina for nothing other than love of God and his Prophet, their dowers were to be returned to their husbands so that they would be divorced from them, and the women were expected to take the pledge of allegiance to the Prophet: Qummī (1404h, vol. 2, pp. 362–3). Ṭūsī (1409h, vol. 9, pp. 583–7). Ṭabāṭabā'ī (1402h, vol. 19, pp. 239–41).
249 Qummī (1404h, vol. 2, p. 364). Ṭūsī (1409h, vol. 9, p. 588). Ṭabrisī (1415h, vol. 9, p. 456). Ṭabāṭabā'ī (1402h, vol. 19, p. 242). They also elaborate on women's *bay'a* in terms of segregation, such as the stories on the Prophet refusing to shake hands with women. Also refer to: Stowasser (2009, pp. 92–3).
250 Ṭūsī (1409h, vol. 9, p. 588). Ṭabrisī (1415h, vol. 9, p. 456).
251 Ṭabāṭabā'ī (1402h, vol. 19, p. 242).
252 Stowasser (2009, pp. 90–1).
253 Ibn Hishām, 'Abd al-Malik (1383h) *Sīrat al-Nabī*. 4 volumes. Cairo: Maktabat Muḥammad 'Alī Ṣabīḥ, vol. 2, pp. 294–5. Moreover, the men's fealty before war was "in the terminology of the historians ... called *Bay'atun Nisa*'" (Subhani, J. (1984) *The message*. Tehran: Be'that Foundation, p. 299).
254 Stowasser (2009, p. 91).
255 Ṭūsī (1409h, vol. 9, p. 587) completely neglects the event of men giving the women's *bay'a* when he explains that women gave *bay'a* even though they do not fight, in order to secure their good behaviour towards themselves and their husbands.
256 Stowasser (2009, pp. 91–2 and 94–5).
257 Qummī (1404h, vol. 2, pp. 353–4). Ḥuwayzī (1412h, vol. 5, pp. 254–5).
258 Ṭabāṭabā'ī (1402h, vol. 19, p. 178).
259 Qummī (1404h, vol. 2, p. 354). Ḥuwayzī (1412h, vol. 5, p. 255).
260 Kahf, M. (2000) "Braiding the stories: women's eloquence in the early Islamic era". In Webb, G. (ed.) *Windows of faith: Muslim scholar-activist in North America*. New York: Syracuse University Press, p. 157. *Jadal* means "to braid" and "to compete in dispute and compare evidence": Ṭabrisī (1415h, vol. 3, p. 183). Lane, E.W. (n.d.: *j-d-l*).
261 Kahf (2000, p. 159).
262 Stowasser, B. (1996) "Women and citizenship in the Qur'an". In Sonbol, A. (ed.) *Women, the family, and divorce laws in Islamic history*. New York: Syracuse University Press, p. 32.
263 Bouhdiba, A. (1998) *Sexuality in Islam*. London: Saqi Books, p. 84.
264 Abdel Haleem (1999, p. 106).
265 Ṭabāṭabā'ī (1402h, vol. 18, p. 232). It is worthy to mention here that on another note, Imam 'Alī had explained that the ordeals of this world give an illustration of the ordeals of the world to come, and the pleasures of this world create eagerness for the pleasures to come (al-Raḍī, n.d.c, vol. 4, p. 31).
266 Refer to: Qummī (1404h, vol. 2, p. 407).
267 Robinson, N. (1996) *Discovering the Qur'an: a contemporary approach to a veiled text*. London: SCM Press, pp. 68, 88, 95, etc., has a valuable though inconclusive argument on how the chronology of the Qur'anic verses might affect the progressive description of the women of paradise from sexualised to "purified".
268 Ibn Manẓūr (1405h, vol. 4, p. 219).

269 Ibn Manẓūr (1405h, vol. 13, p. 302).
270 Kulaynī (1388h, vol. 8, p. 156). Ṣadūq (1404h*a*, vol. 3, p. 469).
271 Qummī (1404h, vol. 2, p. 346), where he also understands "*maqṣūrāt*" in a similar vein. Ḥuwayzī (1412h, vol. 5, p. 198).
272 Ṭūsī (1409h, vol. 9, p. 481, 485). Ḥuwayzī (1412h, vol. 5, p. 198).
273 Ṭūsī (1409h, vol. 9, p. 482) reports that their comparison to pearls and coral gems emphasises their whiteness.
274 Perhaps the comparison to pearls and eggs refer to both whiteness of skin and seclusion, and perhaps these two ideas are related anyway, since rich secluded women who do not work do not see the sun much and therefore are not tanned.
275 Wadud (1994).
276 Rippin (1996, p. 134).
277 Surty, M.I.H. (1986) "Reflections on the Qur'anic concept of paradise". *The Islamic Quarterly*, 30: 179–88.
278 Surty (1986, p. 180).

3 Female personalities in the *sunna*

Introduction

In Arabic, *sunna* is a line of conduct, or mode of life, and as a verb it means to establish the law, or follow a path.[1] In Islam, and probably during the Prophet's lifetime, the term was applied to his activities and rulings, although after his death, the term came to be applied to the standards set by others.[2] The Qur'an itself does not mention the *sunna* of Muhammad as such, but it does advise that the example of the Prophet is a good example (*uswatun ḥasana*) [33: 21].[3]

Another important reason for studying the *sunna* of the Prophet is that it is the context of the Qur'an: "If one approaches the Qur'an without any preconceptions based on subsequent tradition, one discovers that it contains very few clues to help to determine the provenance of the revelations with any accuracy."[4] References in the Qur'an to people or events in the Prophet's life are often vague and very difficult to comprehend without some knowledge of his biography (*sīra*) and the time and space he lived in, "Indeed, it would be fair to say that a 'passage' of the Qur'an was a 'passage' in the incidence of inspiration. To that extent *wahy* and *Sirah*, what came *into* speech and *on* to the page came with a psychic awareness without which it could have had neither setting nor relevance".[5]

There are difficulties in determining the authenticity of events in the Prophet's biography,[6] but the problems there are similar to those of history writing in general, such as the nature and availability of the earliest sources, as well as the various agendas of the compilers and historians.[7] The earliest sources are generally seen as more authentic than the later ones.[8] Drawing on those earliest sources might therefore be the only option if one were to fill in the sketch (between the Qur'an and provenance of the revelations) and sharpen its focus.[9]

The problem of historical authenticity is more severe regarding female personalities, as history often saw women and their activities to be on the periphery of events, and therefore not worthy of documenting.[10] In any case, historical authenticity is not the direct concern of this chapter. Rather, it is the portrayal of certain female personalities of the *sunna* in the major sources of the Shī'ī Muslim tradition.

Here, female personalities of the *sunna* are primarily not all the women who were around the Prophet; rather those who are themselves authorities and carriers of his *sunna*.

Therefore, the three most prominent women of *ahl al-bayt*, Khadīja, Fāṭima, and Zaynab, those who have come to be seen as the major female contributors to the very making of Shīʿī Muslim identity, will be discussed here. Unlike the previous chapter which discusses female personalities who were directly mentioned in the Qur'an, references in the Qur'an to female personalities of Muhammad's *sunna* are obscure and need to be supported by exegeses and traditions. Moreover, some of the women discussed here are among the Prophet's descendants and therefore their roles were played after the Qur'anic revelations. For these reasons, some of the main sources of this chapter will be the exegeses and the earlier books of traditions. While history is not in itself the concern here, some historical sources are needed to set the framework of the discussion, particularly because political *jihād* is one of the major legacies of these women. The major historical sources of the Muslim tradition, those which have come to be seen as reliable by Muslims in general, will be referred to. *Asbāb al-nuzūl* are not necessary here as an independent genre because they occur in exegesis and they originate in the *sīra*.[11]

In the previous chapter, female personalities of the Qur'an were discussed. It was shown that some personalities were negative examples and others were positive role-models. Women in the stories of the prophets were portrayed as being at different stages of *jihād al-nafs*. Other than the more general themes of *jihād al-nafs*, the examples of Mary and Āsiyā stood out. It was argued that Mary's perfect motherhood is understood in a spiritual sense, whereby a holy mother becomes a receptive vessel and brings a holy child. Āsiyā's *jihād* was shown to have extended into a religio-political one through her defiant words to Pharaoh. In this chapter, *jihād al-nafs* is a more inconspicuous theme, perhaps due to the nature of the sources examined here. While the Qur'an as divine speech would be able to narrate the internal struggles of the heart, traditions and history books are not in a position to do that. However, the idea of a religio-political *jihād* will be expanded here. The three prominent women of *ahl al-bayt* will be shown to be examples for diverse aspects of *jihād*. Other than *jihād al-nafs*, Khadīja's *jihād* is mainly financial. Fāṭima's *jihād* is primarily in worship and gaining knowledge, and then political and oratorical. Zaynab's *jihād* is political, oratorical, and activist. One might argue that the outer *jihād* performed by the women of *ahl al-bayt* in the most troubling times is necessarily an indication of an already accomplished *jihād al-nafs*.

The technical use of the term "*Ahl al-Bayt*" as we shall see includes five people, namely the prophet Muhammad, his daughter Fāṭima, his cousin and son-in-law ʿAlī Ibn Abī Ṭālib, and their male children, Ḥasan and Ḥusayn. Therefore, Fāṭima is the only female among *ahl al-bayt* in the strict sense of the five impeccable individuals of the Prophet's family. More broadly, however, the term may include other members such as the sisters and daughters of the Imams. This chapter is on three generations of women, the impeccable Fāṭima, her mother Khadīja, and her daughter Zaynab.

Khadīja *al-Kubrā*

Khadīja is included here among the women of *ahl al-bayt* even though she overlaps with the category of the wives of the Prophet, because of her circumstances and different status, to the Shī'a at least, from the rest of the Prophet's wives. She was the Prophet's only wife throughout their life together in Mecca,[12] and therefore she is not directly included in the Qur'anic verses which address the multiple wives the Prophet lived with in Medina. Moreover, she is the mother of Fāṭima and the grandmother of the Imams, and suffice to say that Khadīja is often included in the supplications, taught by the Imams themselves, which send peace and blessings towards the members of *ahl al-bayt*.[13]

Traditions credit Khadīja with two main contributions; her reassurance for her husband the Prophet upon receiving his first revelation, and her financial assistance in teaching and spreading his monotheistic message.

Khadīja bint Khuwaylid, according to the dominant story, was a successful businesswoman widowed twice and already a mother to two or three children,[14] when she employed Muhammad, who was perhaps fifteen years her senior, then offered to marry him.[15] This woman is portrayed as unbound by conventions, such as when she offered to pay her own dowry due to the Prophet's poverty, a move which caused controversy among the elders of Mecca.[16]

When the first revelation came to him, the Prophet is said to have returned to Khadīja trembling, asking her to cover him. He was worried he might have become a jinn-inspired poet, or a man possessed.[17] Khadīja reportedly was supportive with a crucial *ḥadīth* reminding Muhammad of his excellent qualities, saying, "Nay by God, God will never disgrace you; you do good unto the kindred, bear the burden of the infirm, bestow alms on the poor, entertain the guest, and you help in cases of recurring obligations".[18] This tradition implies that Khadīja believed in a God that was good and just, thus her reassurance to her husband, that since you are good to people, God will be good to you.[19] Muslim tradition also adds that she then went to her uncle Waraqa Ibn Nawfal, a Christian scholar, and confided in him, but Waraqa assured the couple that this was the very angel that had spoke to the prophet Moses before.[20]

Thus Khadīja became the first person to accept Islam,[21] followed by 'Alī Ibn Abī Ṭālib, the Prophet's cousin who was in his care and a member of his household.[22] The sources describe how early on, these three, namely the Prophet, Khadīja, and 'Alī, were the first to perform the Muslim style prayers in the vicinity of the Ka'ba while it was as yet an unusual form of worship to the Arabs.[23]

Khadīja was with the Prophet and Muslims when they starved in the desert as a result of the boycott imposed by the Prophet's tribe of *Quraysh*, on all his clan of *Banū Hāshim* and the Muslims.[24] Soon after the annulment of the ban, Khadīja died, and was followed by Abū Ṭālib who had been the Prophet's uncle and protector.[25] Her status as not only a wife and supporter but protector is revealed in an authentic tradition which confirms that the Prophet felt insecure in Mecca without her.[26]

Khadīja is renowned for spending her wealth in the cause of Islam. One Qur'anic verse addresses the Prophet, "Did he (God) not find you destitute and enrich you?" [93: 8] is widely interpreted as a reference to Khadīja's money which she put in the service of the Prophet of Islam.[27] Moreover, it is reported that the Prophet declared, "No money has been more useful to me than that of Khadīja".[28] The Qur'an very often encourages financial *jihād* as a necessary and intrinsic aspect of *jihād*, "Such believers as sit at home – unless they have an injury – are not the equals of those who struggle in the path of God with their possessions and their selves. God has preferred in rank those who struggle with their possessions and their selves over the ones who sit at home" [4: 95].[29]

Perhaps the main aspect of traditions featuring Khadīja's piety, portray the presence of Gabriel in her house, in addition to promising her paradise.[30] For example, it is narrated that while in her home, Gabriel asked the Prophet to send to Khadīja his regards/peace, to which Khadīja replied, "Verily, God is peace, from him is peace and to him is peace, and upon Gabriel may there be peace".[31] A widely reported tradition mentions that she is among four women who are "the most excellent women of paradise"; these are Khadīja, Fāṭima, Mary, and Āsiyā,[32] thereby crucially putting Khadīja and her daughter Fāṭima next to the two examples for the believers in the Qur'an.

Khadīja is therefore credited with two favours to the Prophet. The first one is her positive reassurance to him regarding his sanity when he was in self-doubt. She is portrayed as the voice of calm and reason during his emotional distress. The second one is her financial *jihād*.

Khadīja is an interesting example because she is a woman of both the so-called *Jāhiliyya* period as well as Islam. She is seen by later Muslims themselves as a financially independent woman, and along with Abū Ṭālib, as the Prophet's protector in Mecca, so much so that her death was a major instigator for Muslim emigration to Medina. Especially significant for women today, is that she is the example of financial independence being a necessary step towards forcing social and even religious change.

Fāṭima *al-Zahrā'*

Fāṭima is a member of *ahl al-bayt* and considered by the Shī'a to be one of the "Fourteen Impeccables",[33] which include the prophet Muhammad, his daughter Fāṭima, and the twelve Imams beginning with her husband 'Alī, their children Ḥasan and Ḥusayn, followed by the nine descendants of the latter. Not much is known about her by way of biography, but this is compensated for in the compilations of *ḥadīth*, and she is considered a role-model for Muslim women.[34] A mystical doctrine has developed around Fāṭima, particularly in Ismāʿīlī and later Imāmī texts.[35] This section is based on the earlier and more authoritative sources.

Among ahl al-bayt

Fāṭima assembles the elect family of the Prophet. She is often seen among *ahl al-bayt* as a group, and is not necessarily singled out, although what is said about the group certainly is meant to apply to her individually as well. However, it does not seem that Shīʿī piety has seen her simply as a daughter, wife, and mother; even though this indeed is an important aspect of her persona. Looking at the verses and traditions on *ahl al-bayt*, and what is said of their piety, knowledge, generosity, and authority, one finds that Fāṭima's motherhood is, more often than not, depicted as the origin of all those qualities in her sons the Imams.

In the Qur'an

The Qur'anic reference to *al-Kawthar* [108: 1] is interpreted as a reference to Fāṭima: "Surely We have given thee abundance (*al-kawthar*); so pray unto thy Lord and sacrifice. Surely he that hates thee, he is the one cut off/without posterity (*al-abtar*)" [108: 1–3]. In language, *al-kawthar* is a derivative of the word "many" and means "much goodness", and in religion it is a river in paradise.[36] Some exegetes add to both those meanings an inference regarding the purified descendants of the Prophet through his daughter Fāṭima.[37] This revelation was an answer to the people who tried to slander the Prophet because he had no sons, and without this interpretation, the final verse, that his insulter is the one without posterity, would be meaningless.[38] Fāṭima's children were the only surviving descendants of the Prophet, but since her children were not yet born at the time of this revelation, *al-Kawthar* is understood as a reference to Fāṭima herself, and the children she would bear in the future.[39]

Other verses are on *ahl al-bayt* as a collective, four of these clarify the status of *ahl al-bayt* in Shīʿī circles.

First is the "verse of purification", "People of the House (*ahl al-bayt*), God only desires to put away from you abomination and to cleanse you with a thorough cleansing/purification" [33: 33]. A tradition from the Prophet's wife Umm Salama explains that the Prophet had called on Fāṭima, ʿAlī, Ḥasan, and Ḥusayn to sit with him under his cloak, and he prayed for their purification.[40] Therefore, the verse is understood as proof that these five individuals are immune from sin.[41]

Second is the "verse of the challenge/earnest supplication followed by imprecation (*al-mubāhala*)":

> And whoso disputes with thee concerning him (Jesus), after the knowledge that has come to thee, say: "Come now, let us call our sons and your sons, our women and your women, our selves and your selves, then let us humbly pray and so lay God's curse upon the ones who lie".
>
> [3: 61]

The occasion of revelation is that a Christian delegation debated with the Prophet about Islam and the nature of Jesus, as the passage preceding this verse indicates. Then, when the conversation reached a deadlock, this verse was revealed and the Prophet proposed the challenge. Muslim traditions record that the Prophet took with him to the challenge 'Alī, Fāṭima, Ḥasan, and Ḥusayn,[42] and Shī'ī scholars view this incident as highly significant.

Ṭabāṭabā'ī notes that the two statements about the knowledge that has come to the Prophet, and the invitation to the challenge are linked grammatically with the letter *f* (*fa qul*), which makes the challenge a branch or a result of that knowledge. He adds that the prayer to invoke the curse of God upon the liars infers that the people present at both sides are all participants in certain claims, because lying does not occur except in someone who has a claim. To him, this makes *ahl al-bayt* present at the challenge, partners with the Prophet in his claims and calling.[43] He did not bring members of his community even though they were believers, because faith alone has no stakes in such a challenge that involves a curse and punishment.[44] As far as Fāṭima is concerned, this is very important because it situates her as a partner in her father's calling and at the forefront of his mission.

Third is the "verse of the relatives", "Say: 'I do not ask of you a wage for this, except love for the kinsfolk" [42: 23]. In traditions and Shī'ī exegeses, this is love for the Prophet's kindred, particularly *ahl al-bayt* and the Imams.[45] They find that specifying love for the Prophet's kin as a fee means that it is a part of accepting the message.[46] Moreover, this fee of love for *ahl al-bayt* is understood as a means to explain to people that they ought to refer to them in all matters of religious knowledge, if they wish to be on the path towards God.[47] A religious and philosophical argument on the relationship between love and authority has been made elsewhere.[48]

Fourth is an interesting passage which describes the heavenly rewards of the righteous, that these are those who fulfil their vows, fear the day of judgement, and give food in spite of their love for it, to the needy, the orphan, and the captive [76: 5–10]. It is narrated, with slight variation, that the occasion of revelation of this was when 'Ālī and Fāṭima had vowed to fast three days due to their sons' illness. Each day consecutively, a needy person, an orphan, and a captive appeared at their door and the family gave their bread away despite their hunger for it.[49] The Qur'anic passage continues to describe the heavenly rewards for these righteous people [76: 11–22]. This particular passage does not mention *al-Ḥūr al-'Īn* even though it describes luxurious rewards, and even though the *ḥūr* are normally among the frequently described rewards of paradise, which has been interpreted as a token of respect for Fāṭima who is intended in this passage.[50]

In the sunna

Biographical information about Fāṭima is alarmingly lacking in the *sīra* literature; and yet she occupies a fairly dominant space in the earliest compilations of *ḥadīth* within both the Sunni and Shī'ī traditions.[51] Some biographical information would describe her feeding the poor,[52] nursing her father, and cleaning her husband's swords after battle,[53] as well as paying regular visits to the grave of her martyred great-uncle Ḥamza.[54]

In the *ḥadīth*, which is the main concern here, Fāṭima's life takes on another dimension; sometimes she is venerated, and other times, the seemingly mundane events of her life are regarded as sacrosanct.

The event of her marriage to 'Alī, traditions say, had come from above when the angel informed the Prophet to "marry the light to the light".[55] Another report from the Prophet praises Fāṭima in particular when he says that, had God not created 'Alī for Fāṭima, she would have never found her match.[56] Several traditions describe the couple's cooperation in the housework,[57] as well as resolving their differences.[58] 'Alī did not marry another woman in Fāṭima's lifetime.[59]

Traditions speak of the material poverty this exemplary couple lived in.[60] One pictures Fāṭima after her marriage, crying to her father because of her scant dowry, but the Prophet comforts her that she married the best of men and that God had given her the *khums* (a tax that is due to the Prophet and *ahl al-bayt* [8: 41]).[61] One moral of this story is stated within the *ḥadīth* compilation it is listed in, that Muslim women ought not to demand expensive dowries. When she went to her father to complain about her heavy work, asking for a maid to help her, he instructed her a set of words of praise which are now named after her, "the Praise of *al-Zahrā'* (*Tasbīḥ al-Zahrā'*)".[62] Perhaps the moral in this is that this kind of prayer is the best servant a person could have.

Later *ḥadīth* compilations especially, emphasise Fāṭima's generosity and alms giving. These serve various purposes, such as to show her contentment with the little that she had, or to teach the moral that alms return to the person who gives them, or to show that *ahl al-bayt* are required to be servants and live as the poorest in their community.[63] In one tradition, the Prophet was disquieted by seeing Fāṭima wearing a gold necklace, he asked her not to give people an opportunity to say that the daughter of Muḥammad wears the clothes of oppressors, so Fāṭima bought a slave with that necklace and freed him.[64]

Perhaps the most important feature of *ahl al-bayt* is the depiction that they were taught privately by the Prophet, all aspects of the Qur'an and its meanings. There is a long tradition from 'Alī, in which he explains how the Prophet would privately teach him the Qur'an, its esoteric interpretation, and all the various aspects of it. He adds that these sittings would happen mostly in his own house, in which case neither Fāṭima nor any one of their children were asked to leave. That is contrary to when anyone other than *ahl al-bayt* was present.[65]

There are a few traditions which describe Fāṭima's appreciation and recording of knowledge. In one report, a man came to her asking her to teach him something, she asked her maid for the writing piece, when she couldn't find it, she said, "Get it, it is for me equal to Ḥasan and Ḥusayn. This is the inheritance of the messenger of God".[66] She equated the knowledge she inherited from her father, with her own children. This narration also suggests that Fāṭima used to be visited by people and answer their religious queries.[67]

The famous and mysterious book of Fāṭima (*Muṣḥaf Fāṭima*) is said to be a book three times the size of the Qur'an. Traditions report that when the Prophet died, the angels used to speak to Fāṭima to comfort her, tell her of her father's station, and the future of her descendants. She told this to ʿAlī, and complained about not being able to memorise all that she was told by the angel, so he suggested that she tell him what she hears and that he would record it. One tradition explains that there is no information on the legal and the prohibited in the book but revelations concerning future events. Another tradition explains that in this book is not another Qur'an – as some accusations against the Shīʿa suggest – but it contains what makes the people refer to the Imams for knowledge, while the Imams refer to no one. Another report says that in the book is Fāṭima's will.[68] In an authentic tradition that is in line with the view of Fāṭima as the source of the Imams' knowledge, the eighth Imam al-Riḍā explains that the rightful Imam is the one who is in possession of *Muṣḥaf Fāṭima*.[69]

Muḥammad Ḥusayn Faḍlallāh (d.1431/2010),[70] a controversial yet prominent Lebanese religious teacher and author, considers Fāṭima as "the first author in Islam", in reference to *Muṣḥaf Fāṭima*,[71] even though Fāṭima's authorship of the book named after her is not claimed in the authentic traditions.[72] Yet, she is portrayed as a devoted student and a woman keen to record the knowledge that had reached her, for the sake of future generations.

While the above traditions and several others indicate that Fāṭima and *ahl al-bayt* were advised to study and act righteously in order to actually gain their status,[73] their capacity to excel over others was determined before their birth. In some traditions, it is the transmission of light from the Prophet to his heirs which is the most important element in their heirdom (*waṣiyya*).[74] These narrate that before the creation of the world, God made a luminous ray spring forth from his own divine light, and from that ray he made a second one. The first ray is that of Muhammad and prophethood, and is the domain of exoteric knowledge; the second ray is that of ʿAlī and the *imāma* or *wilāya* (guardianship) and is the domain of the esoteric.[75] Of course, the Prophet also has the esoteric knowledge and is therefore also a *walī*, but he reserves teaching this to the Imams. On the other hand, the Imam is never considered a prophet.[76] Fāṭima's light is placed at the junction of the two lights of prophethood and *imāma*. She is therefore known as the "Confluence of the Two Lights (*Majmaʿ al-Nūrayn*)".[77]

In an authentic tradition, however, Fāṭima herself is the origin of the light of the Imams, and this is traced back to the Qur'an. Imam al-Ṣādiq was asked about the Qur'anic "verse of light" [24: 35]:

> Concerning God's word, may He be exalted, "God is the light of the heavens and of the earth. His light may be likened to a lamp-niche," Abū 'Abd Allāh (the sixth Imam), peace be upon him, said the following: Fāṭima, peace be upon her, "Within her is a lamp." Ḥasan is "the lamp within a glass." Ḥusayn is "the glass, like unto a glittering star." Fāṭima is a "glittering star" among the women of the people of the lower world, a star that "is enkindled from a blessed tree." Abraham, upon him be peace, is "an olive tree, neither of the east nor of the west," neither Jewish nor Christian. "Its oil gives light almost of itself": Knowledge virtually bursts forth by means of it. "Even if untouched by fire. Light upon light": that is, one Imam after another proceeds therefrom.[78] Here, the lamp-niche is interpreted as Fāṭima, in a womb-metaphor which describes her as the birthplace and the very source of light of the Imams.[79]

This image of Fāṭima is reminiscent of her as *al-Kawthar*; in both cases she is the origin of the elevated status of the Imams, and she is either water or light, originating from heaven.

While she shares the knowledge and impeccability of the Imams, the men of *ahl al-bayt* normally take precedence as religious teachers of the wider community. Fāṭima serves a different role; her motherhood of the Imams becomes celebrated in itself.

It has been shown that much of what is said of Fāṭima in the Qur'an and authentic *ḥadīth* compilations is associated with the larger group of *ahl al-bayt*. In all the verses, except for *al-Kawthar*, Fāṭima is one of five. Fāṭima is also the only female among the fourteen impeccable persons. Even her daughters from 'Alī are not technically part of *ahl al-bayt*, and therefore not considered impeccable. In that way she may be seen in a traditional role as daughter, wife, and mother of impeccable men. Perhaps, it is this very role that requires her impeccability, that is, to ascertain the greatness of her children the Imams, their continuity from the Prophet, and their distinction from other men.

Another way to view her position among them is that she is central, as one author noted that "without her, they would not be brought together nor would their number be complete".[80] This point of view may gain credence in light of the Imams' traditions which sometimes do put Fāṭima at the centre, by offering prayers and peace "upon Fāṭima and her father, her husband and her sons (*Fāṭima wa abīha wa ba'lihā wa banīhā*)".[81] Other times, the phrase "*wa-s-sirri-l-mustawda'i fīhā*" (and the secret deposited within her) is added.[82]

Fāṭima's relationship with the Imams is reciprocal. She may be seen as designated impeccable due to them, but they also gain their authority from her. In early Islamic history, after the death of the Prophet, many attempted revolts against the state were made in the name of the Prophet's family.[83] Traditions, however, came to define the rightful Imams as "sons of Fāṭima",[84] not sons of 'Alī because he had descendants through other women after her. As mentioned above, another one of the defining traits of the Imams which narrows down the list of contenders even further, is that the rightful Imam possesses *Muṣḥaf Fāṭima*. Therefore, Fāṭima as in *al-Kawthar* and the authentic tradition explaining the verse of light [24: 35] above, is the origin of the light and knowledge of the Imams.

Similarly, while her description as "Confluence of the Two Lights" is ambiguous considering that she is in effect neither a prophet nor an Imam, without her the two would not have been brought together in the sense that there would have been no adequate heirs of the Prophet's esoteric knowledge. Similar to the case of Mary, Shī'ī religious texts seem to infer that while impeccable men function as prophets and Imams, impeccable women contribute by bearing impeccable children. Both women, however, purified themselves and became heirs of divine knowledge in their own right before they could bear their children. This latter point cannot be overemphasised. Therefore it may be concluded that the impeccable female differs from the impeccable male, not in essence, but in the manner that their status is manifested.

It has been suggested that a part of Fāṭima's revolutionary role was in her being a daughter rather than a son, to carry the Prophet's message and his line of successors, but this point has been received with some sarcasm.[85] While it is clear that glorifying biological functions and destiny is far from being unique or revolutionary, the proposition ought not to be dismissed entirely. Certainly, the Arabs understood that biologically children are attributed to their mothers as well as fathers, but they gave all moral weight and legal rights to the father's line, and so they did not consider a man's grandsons through his daughters to be real sons.[86] That is why until the late Umayyad period the Imams were explaining that they are sons of the Prophet, even though through his daughter.[87] The Prophet set this example of honouring lineage through women not only for his daughter, but for his own ancestry as well. It is reported that he used to say, "I am the son of *al-'Awātik*, I am the son of *al-Fawāṭim*", in reference and courtesy to several of his female ancestors who were named 'Ātika and Fāṭima.[88]

Her names and traits

There is an array of names given to Fāṭima in the traditions, usually nine but the number grows in variant texts.[89] However, few of her names as well as nicknames are especially particular to her, and carry within them concepts that identify Fāṭima most distinctly. Two of those relate her to the Prophet, and four mark her as the best of women and reveal some similarities she shares with Mary.

Fāṭima is the *biḍ'a*; because the Prophet reportedly said of his daughter, "Fāṭima is a part and parcel of me (*biḍ'atun minnī*), whoever angers her has angered me",[90] and in another version that God gets angry for her anger, and is pleased when she is pleased.[91] Being a part of the Prophet is understood to mean more than a physical biological part of him, but an organic connection with the Prophet.[92] The reference given her anger and her satisfaction indicates that Fāṭima's emotions are given credence, because when Fāṭima gets angry it is for the sake of God and religion.[93] This is quite a unique turn because while women's emotions may normally be subject to ridicule and even contempt, Fāṭima's emotions are cause for reverence, considering what they may be telling of God's own feelings.

The idea that Fāṭima's anger causes divine anger sets Fāṭima as a criterion by way of whom actions may be judged. This statement will prove crucial for the Shī'a who define themselves in relation to Fāṭima's satisfaction in this world, by being on her side in her religio-political stance, and in the hereafter by hoping for her intercession (*shafāʿa*).

She is also known as her father's mother (*umm abīhā*),[94] although not much else is known about that name.[95]

One of the earliest and most widely circulated of Fāṭima's names is the title said to be given to her by the Prophet, "doyenne of the women of the worlds (*Sayyidat Nisā' al-ʿĀlamīn*)", and her husband 'Alī is portrayed to have taken pride in it.[96] However, there are some variants of this title. Some other authentic traditions refer to her as the "doyenne of the women of Paradise",[97] and in other reports, more common among Muslims in general, she is the "doyenne of the women of the *umma*".[98] Some traditions report that the Prophet said that Fāṭima is the doyenne of women, with the exception of Mary.[99] These variations point out to the tension between the claim that Fāṭima is the doyenne of all women and the Qur'anic description of Mary as having been elected over all women [3: 42]. In Ṭabāṭabā'ī's interpretation of the verse, he explains that confining Mary's excellence to the women of her world and age is not compatible with the generality expressed in the verse.[100] On the other hand, Ṭūsī mentions an opinion that the election of Mary over all women is only in reference to the miraculous birth of her son.[101]

The most commonly used name for Fatima is *al-Zahrā'*, which means "the radiant". Traditions explain that she was named *al-Zahrā'* because God created her from the light of his grandness (as he created the Prophet and Imams), and another tradition explains that when she prayed, her light shone to the people of heaven like the light of the planets shines to the people of the earth.[102]

Another one of her names is *al-Batūl*. *Al-Batūl*, in language, is originally a description of a palm branch that is disconnected from its mother and does not need it.[103] In its religious meaning, it is to be disconnected from the world and loyal to God, as for example in the Qur'an [73: 8].[104] The woman *batūl* is one who is detached from men and has no desire for them, or is a virgin and does not marry.[105] Thus, according to the lexicon, Mary was called *Batūl* in the Islamic tradition because she was a virgin and had no desire to marry, and Fāṭima was called *Batūl* because she departed from the women of her time and her nation in that she exceeded them in favour, religious path, and lineage.[106]

In Shī'ī *ḥadīth*, however, *al-Batūl* takes an unusual meaning, which is to be cut off from menstruation. One authentic tradition says that God instructed the Prophet to name his daughter Fāṭima (literally "the woman who weans") because "God had weaned her on knowledge, and off menstruation (*innī faṭamtuki bi-l-'ilm wa faṭamtuki 'an al-ṭamath*)".[107] However, in what may seem as a contradiction, a tradition that discusses legal tenets pertaining to menstruants indicates that this is what the Prophet instructed Fāṭima and what Fāṭima taught Muslim women, and in another version that he instructed this to Fāṭima and his wives.[108] The editor's footnote explains that this is not a reference to Fāṭima *al-Zahrā'*, but another woman named Fāṭima who happens to be mentioned often in legal books due to her long menstrual periods. However, the manner in which Fāṭima is mentioned here, as the one who taught the rest of the Muslim women, or as one who received the Prophet's instructions along with his wives, gives the impression that this was the Prophet's daughter and that he gave these kinds of instructions only to the female members of his household due to the intimacy of the matter, expecting them in turn to teach it to other women.

The fact that the term *batūl* has several meanings is evident in a tradition which narrates that a woman came to the Prophet and told him that she is a *mutabattila*. He asked her "what does *tabattul* mean for you?" She answered that she does not marry, so the Prophet inquired about the reason, and she answered that she seeks God's favours. The Prophet responded saying that if there were any favour in that, Fāṭima would have done it before her for no one exceeds Fāṭima in grace.[109]

Another name seems to combine the themes of light, as in *al-Zahra'*, and that of virginity or physical purity, as in *al-Batūl*, and that is her designation as *ḥawrā' insiyya* (the human *ḥawrā'*, female angel).[110] Shī'ī scholars maintain a supernatural conception of Fāṭima, which followed the Prophet eating from the fruit of heaven, hence, the prophetic statement elaborates, "Fāṭima is *ḥawrā' insiyya*, so any time I miss the smell of Paradise I smell my daughter Fāṭima".[111]

It has been argued that having impeccable women, like Mary and Fāṭima, is an indication to women that they, like men, may reach the highest levels of exaltedness.[112] However, this argument is not without its shortcomings, because both women are portrayed as distinguished from other women, at the basic biological level.

There is a competitive edge regarding the two women in the Islamic texts.[113] This is clear in the contradictory traditions over who "the doyenne of all women" really is, and who is only "the doyenne of the women of her age". This is also evident in the other name the two women share, *al-Batūl*, even though it seems to mean a different thing for each. Fāṭima as *Batūl* predominantly refers to her lacking menstruation. If this uncommon meaning of *Batūl* were an honour bestowed on Fāṭima, as a physical purity coupled with her spiritual purity, then such an understanding would be demeaning to the female body.

One viewpoint reasons that if those traditions were true, they might be referring to a case of amenorrhoea not honour.[114] This has been criticised and is almost considered a dissident opinion.[115]

To give these traditions on Fāṭima the benefit of the doubt, one may propose that they be seen as part of a wider circle of traditions about the physical purity of the Prophet and Imams. This proposition about the Prophet exists in Sunni Islam which reports him saying that he was honoured by being born circumcised so that nobody saw his pudendum.[116] This tendency extends to the Imams in Shī'ī Islam where an authentic tradition claims that the Imams are born with their umbilical cord cut (*masrūr*) and already circumcised (*makhtūn*).[117] Following the prophetic tradition, the contention here appears to be that nobody, or perhaps more correctly, no stranger such as a midwife, needed to look at their private parts.

In any case, understanding the traditions on Fāṭima's physical purity in this context is limiting because it simplifies a complex problem. Being born circumcised cannot be equated with lacking menses for two reasons. First, is the issue of ritual purity (*ṭahāra*). There is the widely circulated understanding of Fāṭima's lack of menses, being a corollary of the Qur'anic verse "They will question thee concerning the monthly course. Say: It is hurt (*adha*); so go apart from women during the monthly course, and do not approach them till they are clean" [2: 222].[118] This verse describes menstrual blood as a pollutant, but in a specific context of sexual intercourse.[119] In this sense, a more suitable male parallel would not be circumcision, but seminal fluid, which is described in the Qur'an as "mean water (*mā'in mahīn*)" [32: 8, 77: 20].[120] Yet, it had never been proposed that the impeccable male lacks seminal fluid, probably because this would be insulting to the virility of men.

The second issue with menses, and why it cannot be equated with circumcision, is the tradition on Fāṭima's name referenced above which declares that she is Fāṭima because she was "weaned on knowledge and off menstruation". This implies that knowledge and a body that menstruates cannot coexist. Moreover, a very similar attitude has been discussed in a tradition on Eve, where she was not taught by God the names of all things as Adam was, but was given partial knowledge by her husband as a dowry. Therefore there seems to be a pattern in the traditions of disassociating the female body from knowledge. Therefore, the Imam being born circumcised and Fāṭima's lack of menses are not analogous to one another.

One theory in the anthropology of menstruation is particularly insightful in Fāṭima's case:

> On the one hand a society may have a consciously developed *ideology* of male superiority but, on the other, it may also permit women access to at least some kinds of power, thereby in a sense undermining its own ideology of male dominance. The common fact of menstruation among all women challenges the social order of a male-dominated society and defines and bounds a female subgroup within the society, thereby creating a new separate and dangerous order. Here is a social situation, then, that contains a powerful contradiction, and … it is in such societies that strong concept [*sic*] of menstrual pollution will arise, signalling the contradiction.[121]

In the present context, it is the contradiction between men's monopoly over the positions of prophethood and *imāma*, and the inclusion of Fāṭima among the impeccable persons of *ahl al-bayt*, that demands an explanation. By portraying her as different from other women at the basic physiological level, the impeccable Fāṭima is excluded from the female group and the structure is maintained.

In later Shīʿī texts, Fāṭima as *Batūl* comes to mean "virgin", even though this clearly cannot be taken at face value, since she was married and had children. That is why Christopher Clohessy proposes a sort of "esoteric virginity".[122] Interestingly, he adds:

> In this, Fatima is in fact closer to some of the pagan goddesses than she is to Mary in Catholic dogma. As numerous authors point out, in the case of such goddesses, "virgin" and "chastity" (not in the sense of the virtue, but in the sense of not indulging in any sexual activity) [brackets in original] were not necessarily synonymous. Venus, Ishtar, Astarte and Anat, all love-goddesses of the Near East and of classical mythology, were all called "virgin", and yet none of them practiced sexual chastity, but took many lovers. In the case of Artemis, Hippolyte and Athene Parthenos, their virginity was not for any reason of morality or in favor of the virtue of purity: they remained virgins, rejecting male advances because they were paramount, autonomous and alone … But Fatima is different, even from these pagan goddesses, for she was married to one husband, and in that sense had no freedom of choice.[123]

In fact Fāṭima *al-Batūl* represents the "golden mean". Her pleasure is in a committed relationship with a man who is her match. She remains unblemished despite knowing her husband, and her innocence is perpetual. This is not pessimistic of sexual relationships, quite the opposite; it reconciles sexual intimacy with chastity, while denigrating lust as a state of mind.

Mary and Fāṭima are two impeccable women who gave birth to impeccable men. One author gives further insight on the similarities between the two women:

> As the female was increasingly identified as the core of the family unit, she also emerged as a politically galvanizing symbol for the group she represented. With the establishment of a matriarchal figure at its center, what might otherwise be just another political faction was transformed into a spiritual family – the social group that creates the deepest affective bond among its members.[124]

This statement was not made about the historical Mary or Fāṭima but of their portrayal in their respective traditions. It has been shown that the majority of Sunni sources do accept Fāṭima as the doyenne of women.[125] Shīʿī identity in particular is very much dependent on Fāṭima. This is evident not only through the link she forms between Muhammad and the Shīʿī Imams, but also very significantly through the public political role she played towards the end of her life and in the manner of her death.

When the authentic tradition (that will be discussed below) suggests that the first Shīʿa are those who attended Fāṭima's burial, it is highlighting Fāṭima's defiance as it is expressed in her secret burial, along with the idea that these persons were allowed to attend her burial and therefore are not included in Fāṭima's anger, which begets God's anger. This tradition in particular moves out of the politics of succession into the feminine/spiritual domain of *ahl al-bayt*. The event of the burial binds the Shīʿa in a feeling of sorrow coupled with self-assurance that they were there to honour the last of the Prophet's offspring. In later Shīʿī sources, the image of Fāṭima also functions as the emotional glue of the community when she is portrayed as a weeping mother mourning the sufferings of her children the Imams, even while she dwells in paradise, and the one who will offer intercession on judgement day to protect her Shīʿa from hellfire.[126] The intercession (*shafāʿa*) of Fāṭima is for those who share her grief and cry for Imam Ḥusayn especially.[127]

Moreover, despite differences between Mary and Fāṭima's sons, Jesus and Ḥusayn, they too have striking affinities in their respective traditions, and that is why it has been proposed that "what most deeply binds Mary and Fatima together is the joint image of mistress of sorrows".[128] This sorrow that brings Fāṭima's Shīʿa closer to her is the subject of the following section on her *jihād*.

Fāṭima's impeccability is manifested through her motherhood to the Imams, not only physically but also morally. This, and her religio-political stance at the event of her father's passing, both play a major role in defining Shīʿī identity.

Her jihād

There are no reports on Fāṭima's involvement in politics except after her father's death. The scale of her contribution is relative; it mostly revolves around one major speech directed at the new caliph, and some talks to the people and women of Medina, in addition to her will regarding her burial arrangements. To understand the reasons for her fierce political stance and the relevance of her contribution, some background is needed. In the final analysis, there will be a discussion of her religious and political legacies, as they have been described by her modern hagiographers, or even ignored, to suit their particular aims.

Background: Ghadīr Khum, Saqīfa, *and* Fadak

There are a number of verses and traditions which the Shīʿa understand to be on the heirdom and guardianship of ʿAlī after the Prophet.[129] Perhaps the most important among them is the Prophet's declaration at Ghadīr Khum.

After his last pilgrimage, on the way back to Medina, the Prophet and Muslims stopped at Ghadīr Khum, where they all prayed, "and then he took 'Alī by the hand and said to the people: 'Do you not acknowledge that I have a greater claim on each of the believers than they have on themselves?' And they replied: 'Yes!' And he took 'Alī's hand and said: 'Of whomsoever I am lord, then 'Alī is also his lord (*man kuntu mawlāhu fa 'Aliyun mawlāh*). O God! Be thou the supporter of whoever supports 'Alī and the enemy of whoever opposes him'".[130] While the Shī'a understand the word *mawla* as master and patron, others understand it as a friend, nearest kin, and confidant.[131]

The main disagreement among Muslims upon their Prophet's death was a disagreement on the issue of succession. This, to the Shī'a at least, was not merely a political disagreement but essentially a religious one as well.

According to the early biography of Ibn Isḥāq, upon the Prophet's death, the *anṣār* ("helpers", people of Medina who welcomed and supported the Prophet and Islam) gathered in the hall (*saqīfa*) of Banū Sā'ida inclining towards the leadership of a man from them. A few companions had withdrawn with Banū Hāshim (the Prophet's immediate clan) into the house of Fāṭima, while the rest of the *muhājirūn* ("emigrants", converts to Islam who migrated with the Prophet from Mecca to Medina) gathered around Abū Bakr. At that point the Prophet's body was still in his house, the burial arrangements not yet completed, and his family had closed the door of the house.[132] The Prophet's companions 'Umar and Abū Bakr went to the *anṣār* at their meeting place, and after a lot of clamour, and tribal feuds had been rekindled,[133] it was decided that there must be one leader to the unified community and that he ought to be from Quraysh.[134] Finally, Abū Bakr exacted homage for himself,[135] but the popular and official pledge of allegiance, however, occurred the next day at the mosque.[136]

According to accounts, *ahl al-bayt* were meanwhile taking care of the Prophet's body. When later they were summoned to the mosque for the formal pledge of allegiance to consolidate Abū Bakr's caliphate, they refused to go and gathered with Banū Hāshim and some other companions in Fāṭima's house.[137] 'Alī was opposed to the procedure and decision of the *saqīfa* gathering. He expressed to the group that came to his house to exact homage, that this office belongs to *ahl al-bayt*, as long as they have among them the one who is truly knowledgeable.[138] In another version, Fāṭima reproached the band for deciding among themselves without consulting or respecting the rights of *ahl al-bayt*.[139] In some accounts, it was when the tension almost erupted into violence that Fāṭima came out of her house reproaching the people and threatening to dishevel her hair and cry out to God if they did not leave immediately.[140] This apparently stopped the problem for a while, and 'Alī with all Banū Hāshim as well as some of his friends withheld their pledge of allegiance until after the death of Fāṭima, which was around six months after the death of the Prophet and the events at the *saqīfa*.[141]

The problems between the new caliph and Banū Hāshim did not end there. Abū Bakr dispossessed Fāṭima of her estate of Fadak, instead he claimed that he had heard the Prophet say that "we, the company of prophets do not give an inheritance, whatever we leave is alms (*ṣadaqa*)".[142] He explained that he would follow the example of the Prophet in that the Prophet's family may live from the estate, but he added that they shall not own it.[143] The Prophet's wife Umm Salama found it difficult to believe that the Prophet would have made that statement without informing the people it concerns about it.[144] The Shī'a also maintain that Fadak had already been given by the Prophet to Fāṭima, and that it was in her possession when the Prophet died.[145] Therefore, Fāṭima took the case to the caliph with two witnesses, but 'Alī's word was refused because he is her husband, and the word of Umm Ayman alone was not considered. 'Alī then debated with Abū Bakr, defending Fāṭima's witness as well as her rights. Sending Fāṭima's agent away from Fadak, 'Alī found illegal because it is the person who is reclaiming the estate that needs proof, not the one who is already managing it. He further defended Fāṭima's word as she is described as impeccable in the Qur'an.[146]

The issue remained the subject of much debate, and indeed the estate was repeatedly given to Fāṭima's heirs by some caliphs and then withdrawn from them by others.[147] In the interpretation of verse [8: 41], the Imam explains that land taken without a fight, referred to as *anfāl*, totally belongs to the Prophet and the Imam after him, to do with as he sees fit, and Fadak was from the *anfāl*.[148] Therefore, the attitude of *ahl al-bayt* in confirming their rights to Fadak, even though they considered themselves above material desire, is that they saw this inheritance from the Prophet as a token of their authority status, and that is why it is viewed as an extension of the problem of succession.[149]

Her speech

While historians generally remark that after being denied Fadak Fāṭima never spoke to Abū Bakr again until her death,[150] Shī'ī authentic sources narrate a speech she gave, presumably at the mosque in Medina, in which she spoke about religion, succession to the Prophet, and Fadak. In the authenticated books it is reported on the authority of her daughter Zaynab bint 'Alī,[151] and the Shī'a insist that the elders of the house of Abū Ṭālib transmitted this speech from their parents and taught it to their children.[152]

Upon hearing the news regarding Fadak, Fāṭima put on her head-scarf and went to Abū Bakr, accompanied by her daughters, helpers, and a group of women. She hung her robe, sat down and sighed, then spoke.[153]

She began by offering her gratitude to God, briefly spoke about *tawḥīd*, prophethood, the pre-Islamic era, and the accomplishments of Muhammad. She reminded Muslims of their place, "You are God's worshippers … trustees towards yourselves, and his messengers to the nations. The Prophet enjoined you to do what is right, and gave you a covenant, a remnant to succeed him, the speaking book of God, and the truthful Qur'an".[154] Reference to the "speaking book of God" as separate from the Qur'an is understood to mean the right interpreter of it from *ahl al-bayt*, as the variations of this statement indicate, which again points out to the relation between prophet/Imam and scripture. She continued to speak about the Qur'an and explain the reasoning behind several of the *sharī'a*'s main tenets, among these "obedience to us the order of the nation, and our leadership a security from separation", where she included herself in the leadership (*imāmatanā*), although the technical use of the term is usually the domain of the designated men of *ahl al-bayt*. She then reminded the people of her own status, saying, "Know that I am Fāṭima, and my father is Muhammad … I do not say what I say wrongfully, and I do not do what I do unjustly". Therefore, she spoke both on her own authority and excellence, as well as that derived from her father. This also seems reminiscent of Fāṭima as the *biḍ'a*, a part of the Prophet, and the woman whose anger invokes God's anger. She spoke of the difficulties the Prophet faced during his mission, how he educated and purified his people with religion, and united a humiliated warring Arabia, primarily through the services of 'Alī. She explained that upon his death, discord among Muslims became apparent even while the Prophet's body had not been buried, adding, "and now you claim that we have no inheritance, 'is it the judgement of pagandom then that they are seeking?' [5: 50]". She incorporated this Qur'anic verse here, in reference to the pre-Islamic custom of not giving women an inheritance.[155] Therefore, she referred to the inheritance of *ahl al-bayt* in the plural, and then to her own material inheritance which she was denied as a woman. She then reproached the new caliph saying, "O son of Abī Qaḥāfa! Is it in the book of God that you inherit from your father and I do not inherit from mine? … Have you (plural) purposefully left the book of God and threw it behind your backs, whence it says, 'And Solomon was David's heir' [27: 16]". She continued to recite a number of Qur'anic verses which speak about prophets leaving an inheritance to their children [19: 6], about inheritance in general [8: 75, 2: 180], and women's inheritance in particular [4: 11].[156] Therefore, this was her attempt to combat the reported tradition from the Prophet that he left no inheritance, by use of Qur'anic verses and interpretation, thereby providing evidence for her claims in Fadak. She challenged whether they know the generals and particulars of the Qur'an better than her father and her husband. Here, despite her own arguments, she is portrayed to have referred the people to the knowledge of her father and husband, and it is not clear whether she considered the Imam's knowledge fuller than hers even though she is his partner in *ahl al-bayt*, or whether referral to male authority was to persuade the people. She ended her address to Abū Bakr telling him to take Fadak and with a last piece of advice warning that the estate will meet him again during his judgement. It is as though she were aware that change was not going to happen, but felt the need to make a statement anyway. She then moved to the *anṣār*,[157] reminded them of their stature and services to Islam, wondered at their heedlessness regarding her rights and reminded them of the Prophet's saying "a man is preserved through his children". She expressed deep disappointment that inviolability was lost after his death, blamed their changed position towards *ahl al-bayt* on their fear and the weakness of their souls, and rhetorically asked as the Qur'an does, whether after the Prophet's death they would return to their old state [3: 144]. Here, Fāṭima diagnosed the first split in the community as an essentially spiritual weakness of souls, thereby linking the religious and political aspects of *jihād* together. Indeed, this is also how her speech began, whence she reminded Muslims of the depth of their religious principles and its laws, and reminded them of their position as trustees over themselves and as the Prophet's messengers to the nations. Her words bring to mind the theme of vicegerency, with the extra obligation incurred on Muslims because of the last message having been sent to them. In that sense, her speech may be characterised as holistic, because the talk about succession and her inheritance was not merely political and legal, but was put into a larger framework of theology and history. Even though her words sound more disappointed than optimistic, they nonetheless serve as a summary, after her father's death, of the meaning of Islam, the sacrifices people had made for the sake of emerging out of the *jāhliyya*, and crucially at that critical moment, it is a reminder of the idea that the *jihād* is not finished, and that as individuals and as a group the struggle continues for the souls and for proper guardianship of the community in order to continue walking in the Prophet's footsteps.

Abū Bakr insisted that he had heard the Prophet say the *ḥadīth* that prophets' inheritance becomes alms after their death.[158]

There are a few points to highlight in Fāṭima's speech. First, her talk about *tawḥīd*, prophecy and the reasons for the various *sharī'a* articles are considered gems of theological, religious, and literary value independent of the politics of her speech.[159] In fact, her words are quoted in Shī'ī sources most often as religious teachings rather than as a political stance, although the latter surely has been a major instigator of Shī'ī sentiments. This shows that she is studied by Shī'ī scholars as an authoritative teacher despite being a woman. In other words, her status as they understood it in the Qur'an and traditions to be a possessor of divine knowledge and an impeccable woman, was indeed taken seriously, even though unfortunately, not very much else besides this speech has been reported from her.[160] Second, she talked about the *imāma* of *ahl al-bayt* and the obedience that is due to them, herself among them, as well as her disappointment at the events that transpired concerning their inviolability after the Prophet's death. Therefore after delving at length into the religious dimension, she moved into the religio-political issue of the heirdom of prophethood. While the issue of her inheritance is reported as the direct occasion for her talk, the speech itself only mentioned Fadak briefly, but she fit it into a larger religious and political framework. This is evident in the way her discussion progressed from religion to guardianship to her own estate, and finally back to religio-political awareness in her address to the *anṣār*. Third, her mention of her own genealogy and character traits portrays a great deal of self-confidence, even while she was going against the caliph and the majority of Muslims. If one considers the Prophet's reported statement on his daughter as a part of himself (*biḍʻa*) and then his linking that to the idea that her anger and satisfaction are the ultimate criteria, then her mention of her genealogy and the truthfulness of her words and actions might be taken to indicate Fāṭima's understanding of the responsibility the Prophet had placed on her shoulders as a part of him and as a guide to her community, interestingly enough, through the expression of her feelings. This understanding would explain her fierceness here and her insistence on talking, despite the apparent embitterment, because of a sense of duty. Fourth, she argued strongly for her right to her inheritance, using Qur'anic verses to prove her claims to it, but also pointing out that denying a woman her inheritance is a remnant of the pre-Islamic customs. Her insistence on arguing even for a material inheritance is normally commended as a legitimate claim and an example for people not to give up on their rights in general.[161] This legacy of an oppressed person who, nonetheless, assertively stands up for their rights will continue with her daughter Zaynab in the next section and with later Imams. More than this, however, Fāṭima is in this speech, conscious of being denied her rights *as a woman*. This insistence on even the material rights from someone who is normally depicted as completely detached from the material, as well as her awareness of the role of gender in oppressive tactics, both might be seen as useful models for modern Muslim women.

It was not a solitary sermon that Fāṭima contributed, but she was reportedly active in attempting to procure her and her family's rights. One account describes ʻAlī and Fāṭima visiting people in their homes in Medina encouraging them to rise, but to no avail.[162] During her final illness preceding her death, Fāṭima was reportedly visited by a group of women, and she again explained to them why she had become withdrawn from them. She expressed odiousness to their men, who were persecuting her husband saying:

> And what do they hate about Abu al-Ḥasan (Imam ʻAlī)? By God, they hate the pungency of his sword, his carelessness about his own death, the firmness of his tread and his punishments which give severe warnings (to others than those being punished), and his tiger-like anger in matters of God. By God, had they desisted from (holding) the bridle the Prophet left behind, he (ʻAlī) would have led them through a pleasant journey, without injury to the mount or annoyance to the rider, to a place of rest where water overflows, and they would have advanced with fulfilment … "And which is worthier to be followed – he who guides to the truth, or he who guides not unless he is guided?" [10: 35].[163]

After lamenting the loss of the opportunity to chose the right successor, she warned them of the results of their choices, continuing with the analogy of the camel as the nation (*umma*), saying:

> I swear, it has conceived, but wait until it produces, then draw from it barrels of fluid blood, and a bitter and fatal poison. It is then that the

> men of falsehood will lose, and the latter generation will know the effects of what the former had founded. Then, enjoy yourselves, be content with the affliction composedly, and rejoice in the tidings of a stern sword, total injury, and the oppression of tyrants who will reckon your monetary rights of little value, and will slay your community. Woe to you, what will be done to you! And it is obscure from you; do we make it (this understanding or the *wilāya* of *ahl al-bayt*) incumbent upon you while you are averted from it?![164]

These revelations of Fāṭima concerning the future of the nation have not been considered a case of knowledge of the unseen, but foresight based on an understanding of causal relations.[165]

Muḥammad Bāqir al-Ṣadr (d.1400/1980), the Iraqi religious authority, activist and weighty philosopher,[166] observes that the Qur'an presents history as a science in that it functions according to laws, and these laws pertain to people's adherence to divine guidance.[167] When people abandon their revealed laws, they become annihilated, for there is a definite relationship between the injustice of the elite and the ensuing destruction of the nation.[168] Societies, as do individuals, have an appointed time, but unlike individual judgement, when social death happens, it is both the culprit and the innocent that suffer the results because the rulers' acts are performed at least with the tacit consent of the community.[169] With this in mind, it becomes easy to contend that Fāṭima in this case diagnosed the situation based on a clear understanding of history as it is taught in the Qur'an. If there are recognisable laws, then they can be manipulated,[170] thus she significantly pointed out to the women who came to her, that it is the actions of the early Muslims which will shape their future.

Fāṭima's ideas are also politically significant; whether they played a defining role or not, they do reflect Twelver Shīʿī political theory which "adopted an attitude towards the administration of divine authority that ruled out any compromise leading to the identification of actual power with divine authority".[171]

According to authentic traditions, Fāṭima asked to be buried secretly as she did not wish for the caliph and the larger community to attend her funeral.[172] Following her will, Imam ʿAlī performed the burial rituals but kept the location of her grave secret.[173] Crucially, traditions describe the first "*Shīʿa*" (other than the Prophet's family) as the three, or seven, people who prayed over Fāṭima.[174]

The clandestine burial of the Prophet's daughter at night, in order to avoid the attendance of the caliph, would have been a clear message that she died in a state of resentment.[175] Therefore, Fāṭima continued to express her indignation even beyond her last breath. It is not entirely clear why ʿAlī paid homage to Abū Bakr only after Fāṭima's death. One modern historian attributes two factors to this, the first being the demoralising factor of Fāṭima's death, and the other possibly being the eruption of apostasy and rebellion among the Arab tribes after the Prophet's death, which would have compelled ʿAlī to reconcile with the existing order so that Islam stays unified in those troubling times.[176]

Even though Fāṭima's everyday life is not normally taken much notice of, with attention given to her spiritual status, she is portrayed in the sources as having stepped up to action when the situation demanded it, and indeed is shown to have been very fierce at that. First, she forceably calmed the situation at her house when it was threatened, then she took the case of her inheritance to court followed up by a fiery speech to Muslims, and finally she used her own death as an occasion to express her disapproval of the events that culminated after the Prophet's passing away. The contents of her speech and then her talk to the women reveal a well versed woman, knowledgeable in religion, and with an understanding of history and politics. Her mannerism, train of thoughts, and clear expression do not seem to indicate petty emotion. She is depicted as confident in the righteousness of her cause and in her person. When she used her own death as a protest, she was well aware of her position in the community. Her speech and her burial became landmarks in defining the earliest Shīʿa and their stance.

It is quite curious that she is seen, in the reports on those events, as far more vocal than her husband in their objection to the manner in which the succession was carried out. Perhaps her intervention and reproach would have been more palatable to the Muslims, considering that she is their Prophet's daughter. Also, perhaps since Fadak was her own affair, she was the one to defend it, and there was no need to call ʿAlī for her plight. In any case, she is often commended for realising her responsibility to act for what she believed was the common good, and for not remaining silent about anything concerning her personal rights.

Therefore, this chapter of her life is incompatible with the often propagated image of a domesticated and segregated Fāṭima. Later traditions, particularly, tend to put Fāṭima's "ontological value before her sociological value".[177] The prevailing image of her as a victim is strange when compared to the politically active Fāṭima who could easily inspire others to similar action.[178] The question as to why Fāṭima is not present at the centre of events, except in the time of crisis, is open. In any case, Fāṭima's actions indicate an awareness of responsibility to action. In other words, her previous inaction was not necessarily a passivity, but simply that there was no situation that demanded her interference.

To push the argument further in evaluating Fāṭima's politics, the critical question of *bayʿat al-nisāʾ* must be brought to the picture. While the Prophet's homage was paid by men and women of the community, his successors only received the allegiance of men. This was of course damaging to women's standing in the community.[179] One might argue that the troubling times following his death did not allow the Prophet's ideal model to be practised; however, in modern times also, women's rights and say are very often pushed to the back. The underlying perception seems to be that women's opinion and participation in social and political affairs is a bonus, not a necessary requirement for sound decision-making. Fāṭima cannot be blamed for not standing up for the women's vote, because such a critique would be highly anachronistic. She did however express her consciousness that she was being wronged as a woman, that is that women may be doubly subject to oppression, because they are women, and in this is a useful model.

A recent study has shown that religious Shīʿī women today do find a political role for themselves, but place it within a framework of their motherhood towards society. While this "culture of motherhood" has certainly allowed political participation, the tension between this idea of motherhood and the powerlessness of women in society may be seen to have restricted women who remain "kept outside the main circles of power and decision making".[180] Here, it would be useful to note that despite what has been said on Fāṭima's prominence as mother, it was shown that the authoritative religious texts emphasise this strictly in the religious dimension of her relationship to the Imams. As a political role-model, Fāṭima provides an example of not only political participation, but leadership exhibited with confidence and courage, despite swimming against the current. She made it a point to speak from a position of authority, both as daughter of the Prophet, and as her own self whose moral character she considered to be well-known to the people.

Being *Sayyidat al-Nisāʾ*, the representation of the life of Fāṭima necessarily overlaps with her hagiographer's views on how a Muslim woman should live. Modern conservative hagiographies of Fāṭima consider her the perfect example for Muslim women, because she fulfilled her maternal duties, upheld her religion, and guarded her chastity.[181] To Khumaynī, Fāṭima is an example for women to give up western clothes in favour of a more modest traditional dress, but he ignores the more public aspects of her life.[182] Another modern hagiographer, before discussing the contents of her speech, mentions that she entered the mosque and sat "in the place made for her behind a curtain", although he does not reference this piece of information which does not exist anywhere else.[183] Conservative hagiographies and popular culture also tend to portray her as a woman weeping incessantly on earth and in heaven, in order to emphasise the suffering of *ahl al-bayt* after the Prophet, and of her progeny after her.[184]

Contrary to these, however, ʿAlī Sharīʿatī, the intellectual of pre-revolutionary Iran, drew an image of Fāṭima that seems closer to his socialist and revolutionary ideas.[185] He objected such portrayals of Fāṭima among the traditionalists, but also the hollow "westernised" woman of his day whose model he considered without endurance. He finds that the former does not adequately educate his people but tries to turn back time, and the latter who uncritically borrows only what is superficial in the west, a useless observer.[186] Therefore, he contrasted the hard-working Fāṭima with the trivial existence of the consumer woman.[187] In his opinion, Fāṭima is "an ideal woman whom no one has yet become", because no one has yet come to know.[188]

Similarly, Muḥammad Ḥusayn Faḍlallāh criticises the emphasis in legendary compilations of traditions on the metaphysical stories of Fāṭima's creation of celestial light and her marriage ceremony to ʿAlī in heaven, and explains that the transmitters ought to have emphasised her religious, social, and political activities. To him, Fāṭima could become a model for modern Muslim women to participate in the social and cultural life, while preserving their morality, and who may even attain the highest level of religious authority as *mujtahida* and *marja' taqlīd.*[189]

To conclude, the various aspects of Fāṭima as impeccable mother of the Imams have been discussed. It was argued that she may be seen in the traditional role of daughter, wife, and mother, and that she may also be seen as the centre that brings *ahl al-bayt* together. While she is described as the source of the Imams' light and knowledge, it is also said that her name denotes that she was weaned on knowledge and off menstruation. If this tradition were to be accepted, it would be problematic because it promotes an image of Fāṭima being impeccable because she is exceptionally outside of womanhood, which in turn, maintains men's monopoly over spirituality and divine knowledge. It was also shown that her motherhood symbolically extends beyond the Imams to cover her adherents, making her a spiritual mother that binds the group into a family. Fāṭima's political role, however, was one she did not play as a mother. She sought to get some authority by linking herself to the Prophet; however she stressed her own personal character as her authority. As a warning, she expressed her view of history as a constant movement in which individuals in a society collectively reap what they sow. She was vocal about her rights as a woman, and possibly defining later Shī'ī political theory, she considered the *imāma* of *ahl al-bayt* as the only divine authority. Her very politics were framed in terms of theology, law, vicegerency, guardianship, history, and the soul's struggle for the sake of individual and common good.

Zaynab *al-'Aqīla*[190]

The importance of Zaynab in the Shī'i tradition is primarily due to her role in the aftermath of the battle of Karbalā'. Hers is neither the traditional female role of nursing, nor the combat which is reserved for men. Like her mother, her contribution is oratorical. Moreover, Zaynab's particular situation made her oratorical role necessarily coupled with religious preaching and political activism. Being Ḥusayn's partner in his mission, an understanding of Zaynab is necessarily preceded by a brief understanding of Ḥusayn. Then, her role after the battle of Karbalā' will be examined. Finally, her *jihād* will be discussed within the context of women's *jihād* in Islam, and it will be evaluated as a possible model for today's women.

Historical background

Following the rule of the "four rightly guided caliphs", Mu'āwiya Ibn Abī Sufyān took charge. Muslim historians normally viewed Mu'āwiya unfavourably.[191] The character of his son Yazīd, whom he tried to secure homage to, is portrayed as having been highly offensive to pious Muslims.[192] Thus, Mu'āwiya was cautioned by his advisors to mend his son's ways.[193]

Traditional Muslim historians record that the Kufans soon started writing to Ḥusayn who was in Mecca, complaining of Yazīd's oppression, and pressing him to come to them.[194] At the same time, Ḥusayn's envoys to Kūfa were being killed, and he understood that it was either allegiance to Yazīd or death.[195] 'Abd Allāh Ibn Ja'far Ibn Abī Ṭālib, Zaynab's husband, wrote to Ḥusayn inviting him to come to a friend's house in Ṭā'if for security, Ḥusayn thanked him but preferred to stay on his path.[196] This is possibly the only record of the role of Zaynab's husband in Ḥusayn's movement, and it will be a matter of controversy for modern interpreters wishing to excuse Zaynab's movement independently of her husband. An army was sent to Karbalā', where Ḥusayn had settled with his family and friends, and the Umayyad army blocked their access to the Euphrates so that they suffered terribly from thirst.[197] On the fateful day, the tenth day of the month of Muḥarram (*'Āshūrā'*), all the men were killed.[198] According to Ṭabarī, Ḥusayn was slain, decapitated, and his was the "first head (in Islamic history to be) hung on a spear".[199] The wailing women, with the young Imam 'Alī Zayn al-'Ābidīn who did not fight due to his illness,[200] were taken as prisoners to Ibn Ziyād the governor of Kūfa, and then to Yazīd in Damascus.

In a letter to Yazīd, the Prophet's companion Ibn 'Abbās considered that even worse than the slaughter of Ḥusayn and his family, was the captivation and parading of the women and girls of Banū 'Abd al-Muṭṭalib from Kūfa to Damascus, for the sake of showing victory and power.[201] Zaynab, Ḥusayn's sister, was twice the defender of the family. When Ibn Ziyād ordered the only surviving son, 'Alī, to be killed, and again in Yazīd's court when a man asked the caliph to grant him one of Ḥusayn's daughters.[202] These events will be discussed more thoroughly in Zaynab's role. However, to better understand the values she defended, it is important to take a closer look at the objectives of Ḥusayn's mission.

It has been shown that Ḥusayn did not heed any advice about the lack of support he would find in Kūfa because he felt committed to his word, and that he doesn't seem to have tried to mobilise an army for his cause even when he met empathetic people along the way,[203] therefore, Shī'ī historians contend that Ḥusayn's movement was not merely a political one but that "from the very beginning Ḥusayn was planning for a complete revolution in the religious consciousness of the Muslims", because in any case a political victory would have been temporal, but a victory made through sacrifice would leave a permanent imprint on the consciousness.[204] It is in this two-fold mission of the battle itself and the battle for its aftermath that Zaynab becomes, in the Shī'ī tradition, truly Ḥusayn's partner in his calling.

Zaynab*: the aftermath of* Karbalā'

The first lamentation rites took place in Karbalā' itself, over the dead bodies, then in the palace in Damascus, and finally in Medina upon the women's return. There are also reports on spontaneous rites that took place in Kūfa and Medina when news was dispatched.[205] Lamentation poetry attributed to the women captives addressing the people of Kūfa abound.[206] For the sake of limiting the discussion, only the major stances and speeches of Zaynab will be discussed here.

Before entering Ibn Ziyād's court Zaynab tried to disguise herself, but he asked about her, and while she did not answer him others did. He told her, "Gratitude to God who exposed your vices, killed you, and disclaimed your innovation". She said, "Gratitude to God who honoured us with Muhammad prayers and peace be upon him, and purified us a thorough purification, not as you say, but it is the wicked who is exposed and the deviate who lies". Note the reference to the "verse of purification" discussed with regard to Fāṭima, and here repeated by Zaynab. He said, "Then how do you perceive what God has done to your household?" She said, "Murder was ordained for them, so they went forth towards their resting place, and God will assemble you with them so that you dispute with him and altercate in front of him". Ibn Ziyād got angry and one of his men advised him that she is a woman and therefore cannot be blamed for what she says. The former persisted, "God has cured my soul from your tyrants and the disobedient rebels of your household". Zaynab wept, then said, "I swear you have killed my middle age, stabbed my family members, severed my branch, and pulled out my roots, if this is your cure then you have been cured". Ibn Ziyād said, "She is a rhymist! I swear, your father was a rhymist and poet!" She answered, "What does this woman have to do with rhyme? I am diverted into my affairs, and only blurting out what I say".[207]

When Ibn Ziyād ordered 'Alī the young son of Ḥusayn to be killed, Zaynab objected, "Ibn Ziyād, enough of our blood!", then enfolded her nephew and asked to be killed before him.[208] This move spared the young Imam, and with it the line of Imams was protected. It was also common practice after Karbalā' for the Shī'a to use Zaynab's name instead of her nephew's, 'Alī Zayn al-'Ābidīn, in the transmission of knowledge and the narration of traditions for the sake of protecting the Imam's identity.[209] Therefore, at the time of his youth and vulnerability, Zaynab stepped in and the Shī'a would continue to use her name in lieu of the Imam's.

When brought to Yazīd, Zaynab again had to protect her niece Fāṭima bint al-Ḥusayn with the power of her words, when a man in Yazīd's court wanted to take her. Zaynab forbid it, Yazīd answered that he can do whatever he wishes, but Zaynab concluded that if he does it then he will have officially renounced the religion and departed from the practices of their community. Yazīd said, "You come to me with these words! Indeed it is your father and brother who extricated themselves from the religion". She answered, "It is through the religion of God, the religion of my father, brother, and grandfather that you, your father and grandfather are guided". He said, "You lie you enemy of God". She said, "You are an autocratic commander, you curse wrongfully, and oppress with your dominion". After these words were exchanged, the man in his court repeated his wish to be granted the young Fāṭima but Yazīd angrily wished that God grant the man death.[210]

On this incident and others like it, Shī'ī interpretations find that Yazīd may indeed have harmed the women if he so wished, but Zaynab's words seem to have swayed some of the people in his court and especially his women, so that he felt the need to eventually disassociate himself from the event of Karbalā' and later blame it on Ibn Ziyād, the governor of Kūfa.[211]

When Ḥusayn's head was brought to Yazīd, he struck its still mouth and allegedly said some poetry, gloating that he has avenged his family members killed in the battle of Badr (the first battle in which Muslims fought the pagan Arabs). It is at this point that Zaynab stood up and spoke.[212] She expressed gratitude to God, and then rhetorically asked Yazīd whether he believed that his power and captivation of her family was due to God's contempt towards them, and beneficence and honour for him. She described him as having raised his nose in pride, and shown amazement and jubilation when he saw that the world is driven by his command, then she added, "This is God's saying, 'And let not the unbelievers suppose that the indulgence We grant them is better for them; We grant them indulgence only that they may increase in sin; and there awaits them a humbling chastisement' [3: 178]". She addressed him as "the son of *al-ṭulaqā'* ('freedmen', those who were pardoned by the Prophet upon his victorious return to Mecca)" and asked whether it were just that he keeps his women guarded, while the daughters of the Prophet are paraded in the streets for all sorts of men to stare at. She continued:

> I swear, you have scraped the wound and rooted calamity, by shedding the blood of the Prophet's progeny … you will arrive at God's presence soon where they have arrived, then you will wish you had been made blind and mute and that you had not said (the poetry of vengeance for Badr).

She ironically told them to carry on their rejoicing and jubilation, and then turned to God asking him to avenge her family and their rights. She then warned Yazīd, "You only cut your own flesh, and your opulence is only skin-deep". She explained that her speech is not out of any delusion that words might benefit him, "but because the eyes are tearful and the chests vehement; Ḥusayn is killed and the party of Satan is giving us to the party of the foolish, giving them God's money to violate his prohibitions … so if you take us as booty, you will also take perdition". She closed her speech with the vital words:

> I swear, I have not feared except God, and my complaints are for none other than him. Then devise your schemes, seek what you will, and exert your efforts, for by God who honoured us with revelation and the book, and prophethood and purification, you will not overtake our time, you will not reach our destination, you will not erase our memory, and the shame of it (Karbalā') will not be washed off you. Is your opinion but

> falsehood, your days but numbered, and your gathering but dispersed when the caller summons God to curse the wrongful transgressor? Gratitude is for God who decreed happiness to his friends, and impressed martyrdom upon his elect.[213]

Muḥammad Jawād Mughniyya (d.1400/1979) – one of the most prominent Lebanese jurisprudents of the past century, whose concerns included modernising *ijtihād* (the analytical process of deriving laws from scripture), reforming Islamic seminaries, and bringing Islamic sects closer together – comments on Zaynab's words, when she was sarcastically asked how she viewed what God had done to her family, and replied "I have not seen anything except that it was beautiful (*mā ra'aytu illā jamīlā*)"; he writes, "that spirit which addressed Yazīd in that atmosphere does not in any way resemble our spirits, the people of the earth".[214] Therefore, the strength of her vision and political stance is understood to have necessarily derived from a calibre of spirit which is not found except in *ahl al-bayt*, as Mughniyya contends.

It is reported that the first commemoration of Ḥusayn was held by Zaynab in her captivity in Yazīd's very palace, when for three days the women of Mu'āwiya's house joined the captives in mourning.[215] Commemorating the journey of Ḥusayn, its religious and political motives as well as the massacre itself was Zaynab's preoccupation for the remainder of her life.[216] It is normally accepted among the Shī'a that Ḥusayn took the women on his journey, in order to fulfil that particular role.[217] However, Zaynab's role in the aftermath is not recorded in detail. Scholars normally maintain that upon her return to Medina, she focused her solemn commemoration gatherings on lamenting Ḥusayn and discussing the religio-political situation of the day and the reasons for Ḥusayn's movement and martyrdom.[218] To some, this served Ḥusayn's purpose of causing a stir that would eventually destroy the Umayyad government.[219] There is agreement that the "propaganda" role she played was eventually the reason she was forced into exile from Medina.[220] Despite the significance of this task, the sources unfortunately do not elaborate much on it. This role, however, is always implied particularly because it is presumed to be essential for the completion of the story of Karbalā'. Ḥusayn had taken the women and children with him because he knew that this would publicise his message, and make him a lasting reminder for Muslims to distinguish between Islamic norms and the character of rulers.[221]

Zaynab is fully recognised by the Shī'ī tradition as Ḥusayn's partner in his *jihād*. She is seen to have defended Islam and the *sharī'a* of her grandfather the Prophet. She is described as eloquent, steadfast, not submissive to tyrants, fearless except of God, speaks the truth sincerely, not moved by storms nor removed by tempests, and truly the sister of Ḥusayn and his partner in his ideology and *jihād*.[222]

Zaynab's stance in the face of Yazīd, informing him of the victory of her family and his impending doom, completely turned the understanding of the results of the battle of Karbalā' upside down. Her commemoration gatherings revived Ḥusayn's memory, and she told the story from the point of view of those who had perished. Her work was so important that it became institutionalised and carried on after her by the Imams themselves. In fact, it seems that both the structure of these first rites, as well as the style of the lamentation poetry, has been preserved by the Imams, who also urged weeping on this occasion.[223] Therefore, a replication of the women's experience and Zaynab's reaction to the event, more particularly, has become a very popular devotional rite.

Zaynab's legacies

It has been shown in various Karbalā' narratives that women were present in the events leading up to the battle, helping Ḥusayn's envoys and encouraging their husbands and children to join Ḥusayn.[224] They are also portrayed as brave and steadfast women, so that their own fate after the battle had to be overcome for the sake of preserving Ḥusayn's cause and attaining moral victory. It has also been shown that Zaynab's precedent in commemorating *'Āshūrā'* has been carried on by the Imams and their Shī'a until today. Such commemoration rituals occur during the first days of the month of Muḥarram, and they typically include religio-political sermons, followed by narrations of the stories of Karbalā', and conclude on the tenth day of *'Āshūrā'* with a procession on the streets of major Shī'ī towns. It is in these rituals that tension around the portrayal of Karbalā's women, Zaynab in particular, become apparent.

One contemporary author has outlined the main themes of the Karbalā' narratives and divided them into two categories, one is gender-neutral and the other gendered. Gender-neutral themes include loyalty to Ḥusayn, courage, self-sacrifice for Islam, and general moral conduct.[225] Leadership, fighting, and martyrdom are specifically male activities, for men are associated with martyrdom and women with mourning.[226] Gendered themes pertaining to women are women as victims of humiliation through captivity, women as mourners of the dead, women as the conscience of the community – evident in Kūfan women mourning after the battle as well as the women of Mu'āwiya's house – and finally, women as spokespersons, preservers, and transmitters of Ḥusayn's message.[227] This latter theme is significant because it assures women, particularly Zaynab, centrality to the story.[228] Men and women, however, are encouraged to take on the gender-neutral traits from models of the opposite sex. Moreover, Ḥusyan, and sometimes Zaynab, are role-models for both.[229] Therefore, these are "not rigidly exclusive categories but tendencies within a fluid dynamic of interpretation".[230]

Another author commenting on Zaynab's prominence and her protection of the young 'Alī Zayn al-'Ābidīn, finds that "Male helplessness among the survivors of Karbala led to role reversals and unexpected inversions of traditional gender-linked behaviour".[231] He attributes the tension surrounding the figure of Zaynab in devotional and political writings to this role reversal.[232]

A further problem with Zaynab's experience seems to be her husband's absence from her mission. He did not accompany her to Karbalā' even though he was sympathetic to Ḥusayn.[233] This issue has been most problematic for Zaynab's hagiographers who do not seem to agree about where to place her husband within the events of her life.[234] They normally find that her husband was loyal to the Imams, and even though he did not accompany Ḥusayn, he did send his children to battle with him.[235] However, they also feel the need to explain that Zaynab herself would not have acted so publicly were it not for a sacred duty that needed to be done.[236] Therefore, despite her success in playing a central role, her example is contained by continuous mention of Ḥusayn's *need* for these women.

To conservative clerics, Zaynab's forceful emergence into the public domain constitutes a problem. In Iran before the revolution, the Shah was likened to Yazīd, and women were encouraged to emulate Zaynab. After the revolution succeeded and things were put in the "right order", they found Zaynab's model no longer useful and propagated a return to the more "peaceful" model of Fāṭima.[237] This break between the two women might have existed only in some clerics' minds; for some others outside revolutionary Iran, Zaynab's strength could only have been possible as a result of the seeds her mother Fāṭima had planted in her, and they find even the manner of Zaynab's speaking to be reminiscent of Fāṭima's.[238] In the Lebanese context, a shift occurred in the last three decades from what has been termed a "traditional" understanding of *'Āshūrā'* to an "authenticated" one.[239] With it, the image of Zaynab has shifted from a mourner to a revolutionary role-model, and the commemorations are no longer merely lamentation gatherings but an education about the meanings of the tragedy.[240] Here, Zaynab teaches women to stand strong in the face of oppression. Whether due to political contexts or to women's increasing awareness, or both, there seems to be a need in modern times to associate with Zaynab her more active public role than her more passive lamenting one.

On the domain of Karbalā's women's *jihād*, it has been suggested that even though (the female role of) crying for Ḥusayn has always been considered worthy of merit, it is not the same as that (male role) of martyrdom.[241] This point of view, however, supposes that the only real sacrifice occurs in combat; therefore it devalues the sufferings of those who actually survive the atrocities, especially mothers who have to outlive their children. If Islam did not force military *jihād* on women, it follows that women do not miss a reward by not fighting.[242] What the retellings of the event of Karbalā' have always maintained, is that the sacrifices and sufferings of women are genuine contributions which are worthy of merit. This traditional viewpoint seems to honour women's part in war for itself, instead of forcing men's experience on them as more admirable, the way that some modern interpretations do.

The major element in Zaynab's *jihād* is not nursing and perhaps not even lamenting, but it is her activist role in the aftermath of the battle. Imam 'Alī had said, "The finest *jihād* is a word of justice said to a ruling tyrant".[243] Imam al-Ṣādiq further explained that this is so, provided one follows those words with action.[244] Zaynab's model is of a woman who spoke sharply and fearlessly of the truth as she saw it, and she did so in the courts of the rulers. Then, she followed this by continuous commemorations of Karbalā', with what that entails regarding teaching Ḥusayn's message, and being subject to danger from the authorities. Perhaps the most important legacy of Zaynab is that the literary recounting of the Shī'a's pivotal event survived through her, and has acquired further religious significance by being "regarded as an act of covenant renewal between the Holy Family and their followers".[245] In this regard, Zaynab's role seems very similar to Fāṭima's religio-political task culminating in her burial, which came to define Shī'ī identity.

Two notions in the model of Karbalā's women must be examined critically. First, the idea that women play a central role during times of "male helplessness" might be exploited negatively in a way that keeps women behind the scenes at all other times. Here, the example of Fāṭima who played her role while 'Alī was alive may be useful to remember along with Zaynab's. Indeed, Mughniyya has argued that Fāṭima was the first to speak, and actually spoke for 'Alī, when she set the standard of defending the rights of *ahl al-bayt*, making the case for their supreme status and demanding the people's allegiance, and he finds that this model was followed by none other than Zaynab.[246] In this sense, Zaynab seen as an extension of Fāṭima is important for a better understanding of their joint example of women's *jihād*. Zaynab's task may have been more public and activist, but Fāṭima's role was not due to male absence. The second notion in the narratives on Karbalā's women that needs to be examined critically is self-sacrifice, which has often (and perhaps worldwide) been an ideal that is promoted to the detriment of women. This perceived virtue is required of women mostly in respect to the men of the family/society. In Islamic Iran, while men were expected to modernise economically, socially, and politically, the image of Karbalā's women was utilised as "a preservationist model of womanhood, according to which the women of the nation are to preserve and pass on the 'true' nature of the Iranian nation".[247] Thus, Karbalā' symbolism was used to promote women as a symbol of resistance to foreign moral corruption.[248] The idea that women in particular are expected to uphold traditional values in the face of westernisation is a discourse that has also been used outside Iran and therefore points towards a pattern.[249] However, why is this role restricted to women, and what does it have to do with Zaynab?

In the twentieth century, many Muslim women were disillusioned by being permitted and even encouraged to be politically active, but then as soon as the war of independence was won or the revolution succeeded, the new order forced women to go back to their domestic place.[250] This seems to be a trend. Thus, a major concern for Muslim women today is not mere political participation, but the need to advocate a programme that guarantees their inclusion in decision-making and execution.

There might be a need to be wary for what cause women sacrifice themselves, and which understanding of Zaynab they accept. Self-sacrifice merely for the sake of other members of the family or the preservation of traditional patriarchal values might prove destructive to women, whereas self-sacrifice for an understanding of Ḥusayn's vision as one of freedom from tyranny and oppression might prove constructive. For example, one may chose to emphasise Ḥusayn's words on those ultimate human values, such as when he spoke in Karbalā', in universal terms where he told some Umayyad soldiers, "if you have no religion and do not fear judgement day, then be free persons of esteem, in the affairs of your world".[251]

In conclusion, Zaynab's main role as Ḥusayn's partner was to transform through her *jihād* the battle of Karbalā' from a tragedy into a victory. Her activism was at once religious and political, and it has been argued that women's *jihād*, whether it is through losing loved ones and remaining steadfast, or through their struggles with their words and actions to change the status quo, both are seen from the tradition's point of view, as a parallel to actual military combat. Zaynab's strong image in the aftermath of Karbalā' even makes the men around her fade into the background. She offers an innovative kind of *jihād* which does not fit into the traditional female role, although it is not military either. This activism of Zaynab in public affairs, albeit without taking on typically male activities, makes her a perplexing image. There is a gender role-reversal in Karbalā' narratives regarding women's strength and their taking charge, but this has been accompanied by a focus on Ḥusayn's need for these women, as though to justify their very public roles. The women's loss of their men in the battle and their own captivity and suffering has come to promote women's self-sacrifice for the sake of tradition and nation. However, one may also argue that, quite the opposite of this, Zaynab is not portrayed to have sacrificed a grain of her beliefs. In fact, she refused to keep quiet even in front of Yazīd. It is through her faith and commitment to her cause, in addition to her unceasing defiance and activism, that Zaynab becomes a valuable role-model for women today.

Summary and conclusions

In this chapter, the three most prominent women of *ahl al-bayt* have been studied as women whose life constitutes an extension of the Prophet's *sunna*. The main theme in all three experiences is their *jihād*, and it has been shown that even though *jihād al-nafs* is not the major theme here as it was in the Qur'anic personalities; the political struggles of the women of *ahl al-bayt* are often portrayed in the literature as subsidiary to their religious achievements. Furthermore, the female personalities of the *sunna* exemplify three types of religio-political *jihād*, financial, pedagogical oratory, and activist. Khadīja believed in monotheism and the prophethood of her husband, therefore she spent her wealth in that cause. Fāṭima's stance against the new caliph and community was explained to the people through a skilled religious argument. In the end, she utilised her body as the final statement of resistance, and her burial an event to distinguish her Shīʿa. Zaynab similarly used her literary talents in order to reap the victory of Karbalāʾ. Zaynab lived in different circumstances, however, and she is said to have committed her life to activism, the product of which was a rite that is still held every year as the Shīʿa's allegiance to *ahl al-bayt*. Furthermore, just as it was pointed out in Khadīja's case, that the Qur'an consistently couples financial *jihād* with the *jihād* with one's self, traditions also maintain that even though excessive weeping for the dead is normally considered reprehensible, grieving and weeping for the tragedy of Karbalāʾ are religious activities which bring reward. All three women were in the similar position of being anti-establishment, and none of them conceded or compromised their vision until their death. Their ability to withstand such pressures hints at an inner strength that is drawn from faith.

While both Khadīja and Fāṭima are placed next to Āsiyā and Mary as the best of women, Fāṭima is more distinguished in her spiritual rank. While all of them are highly revered in the Shīʿī tradition, Fāṭima is considered impeccable. It has been argued that her exceptional status might mean that her impeccability is not entirely liberating for women. However, in view of Khadīja and Zaynab, it must also be considered that it is liberating to have revered females who are not technically considered sinless.[252] While all male role models are impeccable (Prophet and Imams), having highly revered non-impeccable women makes their example more feasible to accomplish by ordinary women. In any case, Fāṭima, similar to Mary, through her uniqueness serves to stress the value of the feminine in religion. Like Mary, she is an impeccable mother that bore impeccable children. Her very emotions, normally despised in women, are seen to be foretelling of God's feelings. Being the only woman among *ahl al-bayt* serves as glue in linking the holy family together, as well as joining their Shīʿa at a deeper emotional level. Her power as mother and possessor of *shafāʿa* makes her akin to a matriarch for her devotees. In the next chapter, female personality in the *ḥadīth* literature will be set against the female personalities of the Qur'an and *sunna* studied thus far.

Notes

1 Lane, E.W. (n.d.) *Arabic-English lexicon* [online]. Available from: www.studyquran.co.uk/PRLonline.htm: *s-n-n*.
2 Juynboll, G.H.A. (1987) "Some new ideas on the development of sunna as a technical term in early Islam". *Jerusalem Studies in Arabic and Islam*, 10: 98–101.
3 Juynboll (1987, p. 101). Refer to the Qur'an, verses [17: 77, 33: 38, 62, 40: 85, 43: 62, and 48: 23] for the "*sunna* of God". *Sunna* is also used in a negative sense in reference to previous peoples [8: 38, 15: 13, 17: 77, and 18: 55]. Both *sunna* and *uswa ḥasana* are used in reference to previous prophets and their community of believers [17: 77, 60: 4, 6].
4 Robinson, N. (1996) *Discovering the Qur'an: a contemporary approach to a veiled text*. London: SCM Press, p. 30.
5 Cragg, K. (2001) *Muhammad in the Qur'an: the task and the text*. London: Melisende, p. 22.

6 There is an interesting but inconclusive debate on whether *sīra* writing preceded exegesis or followed it, with the ensuing contention that if *sīra* accounts are exegetical, then they are not historical. In: Rippin, A. (1997) "Book review: eye of the beholder: the life of Muhammad as viewed by the early Muslims. A textual analysis". *Journal of the American Oriental Society*, 117 (4): 768–70. Also refer to: Guillaume, A. (1954) "The biography of the Prophet in recent research". *Islamic Quarterly*, I: 5–11. Motzki, H. (2000) "The biography of Muhammad: the issue of the sources". *Journal of Law and Religion*, 15 (1/2): 627–32.

7 Refer to: Donner, F.M. (1998) *Narratives of Islamic origins: the beginnings of Islamic historical writing*. Princeton: The Darwin Press, pp. 280–3.

8 Donner (1998, pp. 282–90).

9 Robinson (1996, pp. 44–5).

10 Refer to: Fiorenza, E.S. (1990) *Bread not stone: the challenge of feminist Biblical interpretation*. Edinburgh: T& t Clark, p. 109.

11 Rubin, U. (1995) *The eye of the beholder: the life of Muhammad as viewed by the early Muslims: a textual analysis*. Princeton: Darwin Press, p. 227. For a further discussion of Asbāb al-Nuzūl, refer to: Rippin, A. (1988) "The function of 'Asbāb al-Nuzūl' in Qur'anic exegesis". *Bulletin of the School of Oriental and African Studies*, 51 (1): 1–20.

12 al-Kulaynī, Muḥammad Ibn Yaʿqūb (1388h) *al-Kāfī*. 3rd edn. 8 volumes. Tehran: Dār al-Kutub al-Islāmiyya, vol. 5, p. 391. Ibn Hishām, 'Abd al-Malik (1383h) *Sī rat al-Nabī*. 4 volumes. Cairo: Maktabat Muḥammad 'Alī Ṣabīḥ, vol. 1, p. 122. Also, Khadīja is the only woman who bore children to the Prophet, with the exception of Māriya the Copt, who bore him Ibrahīm who died as an infant. Khadīja bore him before the onset of his prophetic career, al-Qāsim, Ruqayya, Zaynab, and Umm Kulthūm, and after the revelations al-Ṭāhir, al-Ṭayyib, and Fāṭima, and some said that only Fāṭima was born after the revelations began (Kulaynī, 1388h, vol. 1, p. 439; Ibn Hishām, 1383h, vol. 1, pp. 122–3). All his male children died in infancy, and all his female children died in adulthood before their father. Only Fāṭima survived for a short time after the death of the Prophet. Fāṭima's children are also the only descendants of the Prophet to survive past him and into adulthood.

13 Kulaynī (1388h, vol. 4, p. 577). al-Ṣadūq, Muḥammad Ibn 'Alī Ibn Bābawayh (1404ha) *Man lā yaḥḍuruhu al-fuqīh*. 2nd edn. 4 volumes. Qum: Jāmi'at al-Mudarrisīn, vol. 2, p. 596. al-Ṭūsī, Muḥammad Ibn Ḥasan (1390hb) *Tahdhīb al-aḥkām*. 10 volumes. Tehran: Dār al-Kutub al-Islāmiyya, vol. 6, p. 118.

14 Kister, M.J. (1997) *Concepts and ideas at the dawn of Islam*. Aldershot: Ashgate, pp. 123–5. Ṣubḥānī, J. (1984) *The message*. Tehran: Be'that Foundation, p. 156.

15 Ibn Hishām (1383h, vol. 1, p. 121). al-Ṭabarī, Muḥammad Ibn Jarīr (1879) *Tarīkh al-'umam wa al-mulūk*. 8 volumes. Beirut: Mu'assasat al-A'lamī (1879, vol. 2, pp. 34–5). Ṣubḥānī (1984, pp. 147–56).

16 Kulaynī (1388h, vol. 5, pp. 374–5).

17 Lings, M. (1994) *Muhammad: his life based on the earliest sources*. 5th edn. Lahore: Suhail Academy, p. 44.

18 Ḥadīth translation from: Kister, M.J. (1965) "God will never disgrace thee: the interpretation of an early hadith". *Journal of the Royal Asiatic Society of Great Britain and Ireland*, pp. 27–32. Other traditions additionally narrate that Khadīja recognised that Gabriel was an angel not a demon when he was sitting in her house, and then the Prophet informed her that Gabriel left when she and her husband started getting intimate. Refer to: Ibn Hishām (1383h, vol. 1, p. 157).

19 For various interpretations regarding her crucial statement, refer to: Kister (1965), and Dutton, Y. (n.d.) *Ibn Warraq's "Origins of the Koran": a critical analysis* [online]. Available from: www.bismikaallahuma.org/archives/2005/ibn-warraqs-origins-of-the-koran-a-critical-analysis [Accessed 20.02.2014].

20 Ibn Hishām (1383h, vol. 1, pp. 123 and 156). al-Nīsābūrī, 'Alī Ibn Aḥmad al-Wāḥidī (1388h) *Asbāb nuzūl al-ayāt*. Cairo: Mu'assasat al-Ḥalabī & Co, vol. 3, p. 184.

21 Ibn Hishām (1383h, vol. 1, pp. 158–9).

22 Ibn Hishām (1383h, vol. 1, p. 162). al-Ḥākim, Muḥammad Ibn 'Abdallāh al-Nī sabūrī (1406h) *al-Mustadrak 'ala al-Ṣaḥīḥayn*. 4 volumes. Beirut: Dār al Ma'rifa, vol. 3, p. 133.

23 Kulaynī (1388h, vol. 1, p. 250). Ṭabarī (1879, vol. 2, p. 56). Ibn Sa'd, Muḥammad (n.d.) *al-Ṭabaqāt al-kubrā*. 8 volumes. Beirut: Dār Ṣāder (n.d., vol. 8, p. 18). Ḥākim (1406h, vol. 3, p. 183).

24 Ibn Hishām (1383h, vol. 1, pp. 234 and 251–4). Ṣubḥānī (1984, pp. 260–4).

25 Ibn Hishām (1383h, vol. 2, p. 282). This came to be known as "the year of sadness". In: Lings (1994, p. 96).

26 Kulaynī (1388h, vol. 8, p. 340).

27 al-Kūfī, Furāt (1410h) *Tafsīr al-Qur'ān*. Tehran: al-Tābi'a li-Wizārat al-Thaqāfa wa al-Irshād, p. 569. al-Ṭabāṭabā'ī, Muḥammad Ḥusayn (1402h) *al-Mizān fī tafsīr al-Qur'ān*. 20 volumes. Qum: Mu'assasat al-Nashr al-Islāmī, vol. 20, p. 311.

28 al-Ṭūsī, Muḥammad Ibn Ḥasan (1414h) *al-Amālī*. Qum: Dar al-Thaqāfa, p. 468. Several other traditions exist around the value of Khadīja's money to the Prophet and to Islam, but these have not been authenticated.

29 Other verses that mention financial *jihād* are: [8: 72], [9: 20, 44, 81, and 88], and [49: 51].

30 On the promise of paradise, refer to: Kulaynī (1388h, vol. 3, pp. 218, 219), and Ḥākim (1406h, vol. 3, p. 185).

31 Al-'Ayyāshī, Muḥammad Ibn Mas'ūd (n.d.) *Tafsīr al-Qur'ān*. 2 volumes. Tehran: al-Maktaba al-'Ilmiyya al-Islāmiyya (n.d., vol. 2, p. 279). Ibn Hishām (1383h, vol. 1, pp. 158–9).

32 al-Ḥuwayzī, 'Abd 'Alī Ibn Jumu'a al-'Arūsī (1412h) *Nūr al-thaqalayn*. 4th edn. 5 volumes. Qum: Mu'assasat Ismā'ilyān, vol. 5, p. 377. Ḥākim (1406h, vol. 2, p. 497, and vol. 3, pp. 185–6). There is a variation, perhaps even a crude corruption, of this tradition in: Ṣadūq (1404ha, vol. 1, p. 139). I say it is a corruption, not least because of the expression it uses for co-wives, the pre-Islamic "*ḍarā'ir*" which was not used in Islam because it comes from the word *ḍarar* or harm, signifying that polygamy is harmful to the wives (Ibn Manẓūr, 1405h, vol. 4, pp. 486–7). It is crude because the "four best women" are made his wives in the afterlife, but of course the fourth is not his daughter Fāṭima but is replaced by Kulthūm, Moses' sister.

33 Amir-Moezzi, M.A. (1994) *The divine guide in early Shi'ism*. New York: State University of New York Press, p. 22.

34 Christopher Paul Clohessy addresses the issue of the sources aptly and thoroughly. Clohessy, C. (2009) *Fatima, daughter of Muhammad*. Series: Gorgias dissertations in Arabic and Islamic Studies, 40. Piscataway: Gorgias Press, pp. 1–67 and 225–37.

35 Amir-Moezzi (1994, p. 159, footnote no. 152). For a thorough discussion of later Imami texts, and their comparison with Sunnī sources, refer to: Clohessy (2009). Also refer to: Lawson, T. (2007) "The authority of the feminine and Fatima's place in an early work by the bab". *Online Journal of Baha'i Studies*, 1: 137–70, pp. 149–50, where the author briefly discusses the differing views of each of Lammens and Massignon on Fāṭima.

36 al-Ṭabrisī, Faḍl Ibn Ḥasan (1415h) *Majma' al-Bayān*. 10 volumes. Beirut: Mu'assasat al-A'lamī, vol. 10, pp. 458–60. Ṭūsī (1409h, vol. 10, pp. 417–18).

37 Kāshanī (1416h, vol. 5, p. 382). Ṭabāṭabā'ī (1402h, vol. 20, pp. 370–1).

38 Ṭabāṭabā'ī (1402h, vol. 20, p. 370). For the occasion of revelation, refer to: Nīsābūrī (1388h, pp. 306–7).

39 Refer to: Faḍlallāh, M.H. (2002) *The infallible Fatimah: a role model for men and women.* Beirut: Dār al-Malāk, pp. 13–14.

40 According to traditions, the Prophet brought himself and those four individuals together under his cloak and spoke to God saying these are my family and my elite (in another version, my weight) so purify them a thorough purification. Umm Salama, the Prophet's wife whose house they were in, wished to come under the cloak with them and asked the Prophet, "Am I not of your family?" He did not allow her to join them but answered, "You are on the right path". Nī sābūrī (1388h, p. 239). Kulaynī (1388h, vol. 1, p. 287). Muslim, Ibn al-Ḥajjāj (n.d.) *al-Ṣaḥīḥ*. 8 volumes. Beirut: Dār al-Fikr, vol. 7, p. 130. Although this verse occurs in the passage addressing the Prophet's wives, as was pointed out in the previous chapter, neither the occasion of revelation nor the grammatically masculine tone of the verse points to the Prophet's wives, but that it was revealed for the five members of *ahl al-bayt*.

41 Ṭūsī (1409h, vol. 8, pp. 339–41). Moreover, in the traditions, the Prophet is said to have advised his community that the Qur'an and *ahl al-bayt* are "the two weighty matters (*al-thaqalayn*)" which he is leaving behind, and that these two will not separate until they meet him in the pool of *al-kawthar* in Paradise, in: Kulaynī (1388h, vol. 1, p. 294). Muslim (n.d., vol. 7, p. 123).

42 Nīsābūrī (1388h, pp. 67–8). Muslim (n.d., vol. 7, pp. 120–1).

43 Ṭabāṭabā'ī (1402h, vol. 3, pp. 222–7). He further explains that extending the invitation to women and children aims that each side shows conviction in its claims, by putting those they love most in potential danger, which is why the verse starts with the children first, the most beloved, then the women, and finally the adult males.

44 Ṭabāṭabā'ī (1402h, vol. 3, p. 226), where he adds that the Prophet did not merely bring with him a sample of his community, because the verse commands that he bring with him children, women, and men, all in the plural form (neither singular nor the Arabic grammatical dual). Yet the Prophet brought two men, two children, and one woman, which is taken to mean that he found none other than these individuals to supplicate with.

45 Kulaynī (1388h, vol. 1, p. 413, vol. 8, p. 93). al-Qummī, 'Alī Ibn Ibrāhīm (1404h) *Tafsīr al-Qur'ān*. 3rd edn. 2 volumes. Qum: Mu'assasat Dār al-Kitāb, vol. 2, pp. 275–6. One tradition elaborates with the observation that other prophets, particularly Noah and Hūd, say in the Qur'an that they ask for no fee and that God will give them their due fee, whereas Muhammad asked for love for his kindred because, the tradition contends, God knew that they would always be on the path of truth (Ḥuwayzī, 1412h, vol. 2, pp. 349 and 372).

46 Ṭabāṭabā'ī (1402h, vol. 18, pp. 42–3). Moreover, Ṭabāṭabā'ī goes through the various other interpretations of *al-qurbā*. He says that the idea that the verse asks Quraysh to love him for his kinship if not for his prophecy is wrong because Quraysh did not accept Islam so they could not be asked for a fee. Moreover, if they did accept it then accepting Muhammad as Prophet would have erased hatred from their hearts and no such love for kin would have been asked. Asking for a fee assumes their genuine faith and gratitude for what he brought. The second opinion that this could be addressed to the *anṣār* since they are related to the Prophet from his mother's side is also untenable because they are the people who welcomed him and the emigrants of Mecca with him. Third, as for the fee being a love for kindred in general, Ṭabāṭabā'ī explains that even though love for kindred is highly recommended in Islam, it is in the sense of maintaining good relations with them and supporting them financially, but Islam is not concerned about love for family members as such, because religion is only concerned about love for God and equates nothing with it. In this respect, Ṭabāṭabā'ī refers his readers to the Qur'anic verse [58: 22]. Moreover, Ṭabāṭabā'ī reminds us that

pagans also love their kin, therefore that may hardly be considered a fee for the Prophet's message (Ṭabāṭabā'ī, 1402h, vol. 18, pp. 43–6).

47 Ṭabāṭabā'ī (1402h, vol. 18, p. 46). He adds that this does not negate the other verses whereby the Prophet, as the ones before him, asks for no fee [12: 104] because this is a reminder for human kind, and [25: 57] where he further explains that he asks for no fee, except that whomsoever wills may take a way unto his Lord. However, since God has prescribed love for all believers, the Prophet would consider love for his kin, who are among the believers, to be his fee.

48 Lawson (2007, pp. 167–70).

49 Nīsābūrī (1388h, p. 296). Qummī (1404h, vol. 2, p. 398).

50 Ṭabāṭabā'ī (1402h, vol. 20, p. 131).

51 Clohessy (2009, pp. 226–9 and 235–6).

52 Lings (1994, p. 168), claims that before her marriage she was the hostess as it were, of the "people of the bench" or *ahl al-ṣaffa*, who were the poorest of Medina.

53 Ibn Hishām (1383h, vol. 3, p. 614).

54 Ibn Sa'd (n.d., vol. 3, p. 19). Ṣadūq (1404ha, vol. 1, p. 180).

55 Kulaynī (1388h, vol. 1, pp. 460–1), and upon the Prophet's further enquiry the angel explained that he meant Fāṭima to 'Alī. It is reported that Fāṭima had several suitors but the Prophet always refused them politely saying that he was awaiting God's command regarding Fāṭima. 'Alī was advised by some men to propose, but he was hesitant either because he felt shy or because of his extreme poverty. Possibly, upon the Prophet's hint he felt encouraged and proposed (Lings, 1994, p. 163). The Prophet asked his daughter's permission and she accepted; when the Prophet mentioned 'Alī to her, Fāṭima kept silent and the Prophet did not see any hostility in her face, therefore he found that she is shy and that her silence is her acceptance (al-'Āmilī, al-Ḥurr, Muḥammad Ibn al-Ḥasan (1414h) *Wasā'il al-Shī'a*. 30 volumes. Qum: Mu'assasat Ahl al-Bayt, vol. 20, p. 275). Fāṭima's dowry was 'Alī's armour (Kulaynī, 1388h, vol. 5, pp. 377–8).

56 Kulaynī (1388h, vol. 1, p. 461). Ṣadūq (1404ha, vol. 3, p. 393).

57 One tradition states that "The Prince/Commander of the Faithful ('Alī) would chop the wood, irrigate, and sweep the floor, while Fāṭima would grind, knead, and bake" (Kulaynī, 1388h, vol. 5, p. 86, pp. 377–8 and 528–9).

58 It is reported that when they had a disagreement, 'Alī would not argue with her but put dust on his head – possibly to calm himself, which is why the Prophet nicknamed him *Abū Turāb* (Ibn Hishām, 1383h, vol. 2, p. 434).

59 Ṭabarī (1879, vol. 4, p. 118). Some have claimed that Imam 'Alī wished to marry another woman while married to Fāṭima, and that the Prophet forbade it for the sake of his daughter's feelings. The Shī'a refuse this story categorically, not only because of the conspicuous choice of bride which is alleged to be the daughter of Abū Jahl, an arch enemy of Islam and the Prophet, but more importantly because they consider it a hypocrisy not characteristic of the Prophet, that he would allow polygamy based on the Qur'an, and practise it himself, yet make an exception for his daughter's feelings (al-Qazwīnī, Muḥammad Kāẓim (1991) *Fāṭima al-Zahrā': min al-mahd ila al-laḥd*. Beirut: Mu'assasat al-Nūr 1991, pp. 143–7). One of the things mentioned in her will is her wish that her husband marry her niece Umāma after her so that she may take care of her children, which he did (Kulaynī, 1388h, vol. 5, p. 555).

60 Kulaynī (1388h, vol. 5, pp. 377–8). Clohessy finds that the reason for discrepancies in the *ḥadīth* between some which describe her as very poor, and those which describe her as reasonably well off, is because of some wealth she acquired after the siege of Khaybar (Clohessy, 2009, p. 36).

61 Kulaynī (1388h, vol. 5, p. 378).

62 Ṣadūq (1404ha, vol. 1, pp. 320–2). There are several other forms of worship that are attributed to Fāṭima, for example, the particular set of prayers named after her, *Ṣalāt Fāṭima* (Kulaynī, 1388h, vol. 3, pp. 368–9).
63 al-Majlisī, Muḥammad Bāqir (1403h) *Biḥār al-anwār*. Beirut: Mu'assasat al-Wafā', vol. 43, pp. 81–9.
64 al-Ṣadūq, Muḥammad Ibn 'Alī Ibn Bābawayh (1404hb) *'Uyūn akhbār al-Riḍā*. 2 volumes. Beirut: Mu'assasat al-A'lamī li al-Maṭbu'āt, vol. 1, p. 49.
65 Kulaynī (1388h, vol. 1, pp. 63–4). Here 'Alī describes the differences among the companions in their capacities for knowledge. He adds that he used to regularly sit and learn from the Prophet twice a day, once during the day and another at night. The only companion allowed was Salmān the Persian, who as traditions report, was considered among *ahl al-bayt*.
66 Kulaynī (1388h, vol. 1, p. 6).
67 Faḍlallāh (2002, p. 47).
68 Kulaynī (1388h, vol. 1, pp. 238–41). Another tradition explains that the Imam does not know the hidden (*ghayb*) except if he asks to know (Kulaynī, 1388h, vol. 1, p. 257). There is also another narration about a tablet presented to her by the Prophet upon the birth of *al-Ḥasan* with the names of the twelve Imams written in it. A man had seen her carrying it and enquired about, so she gave it to him to read it. The same man years later found it with the Imam (Kulaynī, 1388h, vol. 1, p. 8).
69 Ṣadūq (1404ha, vol. 4, pp. 418–19).
70 Refer to: Sankari, J. (2005) *Fadlallah: the making of a radical Shi'ite leader*. London: Saqi.
71 Faḍlallāh (2002, p. 49).
72 Modarressi, H. (2003) *Tradition and survival: a bibliographical survey of early Shi'ite literature – Volume 1*. Oxford: Oneworld, pp. 17–20, where the author puts forward all the possibilities concerning the authorship of *Muṣḥaf Fāṭima*, and especially pp. 17–18 which shows that most reports suggest, as this chapter had done above based on *al-Kāfī*, that the angels talked to Fāṭima, and 'Alī recorded what was said. The suggestion that the book was God's word to Fāṭima, dictated by the Prophet to 'Alī, is actually an attempt to compromise two reports, the one which says it was given by Gabriel to Fāṭima and recorded by 'Alī, and another which says it was revealed by God, and dictated by the Prophet to 'Alī. Majlisī, however, finds the expression that it was dictated by "the messenger of God" as a probable reference to Gabriel.
73 Such as what he reportedly told his daughter, "Fāṭima be active (do good deeds), for I have no power to support you against God". (Majlisī, 1403h, vol. 22, p. 465). That is what Sharī'atī means when he says that "Fāṭima must become Fāṭima herself", Bakhtiar, L. (1996) *Shariati on Shariati and the Muslim woman*. Chicago: ABC International Group, p. 183.
74 Amir-Moezzi (1994, p. 42).
75 Amir-Moezzi (1994, pp. 29–30).
76 Amir-Moezzi (1994, pp. 29–30). Other traditions relate how the primordial light that was derived from divine light belongs to *ahl al-bayt* altogether; the five "people of the cloak", or to the "Fourteen Impeccables", Muhammad, Fāṭima, and the twelve Imams, quoting Ibn Babūye among others.
77 Amir-Moezzi (1994, pp. 29–30). Sometimes, however, Fāṭima and her light are passed over in silence in favour of the light of the Prophet and Imams.
78 Kulaynī (1388h, vol. 1, p. 195). This translation is borrowed from Pinault, D. (1998) "Zaynab bint 'Ali and the place of the women of the households of the first imams in Shi'ite devotional literature". In Hambly, G.R.G. (ed.) *Women in the medieval Islamic world: power, patronage, and piety*. Basingstoke: Macmillan, p. 74, although Pinault understands Abū 'Abd Allāh as Imam Ḥusayn.

79 Pinault (1998, pp. 74–5).
80 al-Mārandī, Abū al-Ḥasan (1328h) *Majma' al-nūrayn*. Qum: Mu'assasat Taḥqīqāt wa Nashr Ma'ārif Ahl al-Bayt, p. 10.
81 Kulaynī (1388h, vol. 8, p. 165).
82 al-Qayyūmī, Jawād (1373h) *Ṣaḥīfat al-Zahrā'*. Qum: Daftar Intishārat Islamī, p. 304.
83 Momen, M. (1985) *An introduction to Shi'i Islam*. New Haven: Yale University Press, pp. 61–84, such as the Abbasids from the Prophet's uncle al-'Abbās, and Muḥammad Ibn al-Ḥanafiyya, Imam 'Alī's son from another woman.
84 Kulaynī (1388h, vol. 1, p. 215).
85 Kashani-Sabet, F. (2005) "Who is Fatima? Gender, culture, and representation in Islam". *Journal of Middle East Women's Studies*, 1 (2): 16, where the author explains Dr 'Alī Sharī'atī's point with the remark, "Fāṭima's unique position, then, as the surviving heir of the prophet is revolutionary in and of itself".
86 Ṭabāṭabā'ī (1402h, vol. 7, pp. 261–4), where he includes two verses from Arabic poetry, one to the effect that real sons are the sons of our sons, and the sons of our daughters belong to distant men, and the other considers mothers as mere reservoirs and that genealogy belongs to men.
87 Kulaynī (1388h, vol. 8, pp. 317–18).
88 Al-Ya'qūbī, Aḥmad Ibn Isḥāq (n.d.) *Tārīkh*. 2 volumes. Beirut: Dār Ṣāder, vol. 2, pp. 120–2, identifies twelve *'Awātik* and four *Fawāṭim*. Ibn Sa'd (n.d., vol. 1, pp. 61–6) identifies thirteen *'Awātik* and ten *Fawāṭim*. Kulaynī also, but separately mentions *al-Fawāṭim* (1388h, vol. 1, p. 303), and *al-'Awātik* (1388h, vol. 5, p. 51).
89 Enumerated and translated in: Clohessy (2009, pp. 86–90).
90 Ṣadūq (1404ha, vol. 4, p. 125). al-Bukhārī, Muḥammad Ibn Ismā'īl (1401h) *al-Ṣaḥīḥ*. 8 volumes. Beirut: Dār al-Fikr, vol. 4, pp. 210, 219.
91 Ṣadūq (1404hb, vol. 1, p. 51). Ḥākim (1406h, vol. 3, p. 154).
92 Faḍlallāh, Muḥammad Ḥusayn (1421h) *al-Zahrā' al-qudwa*. Also available from: http://arabic. bayynat.org.lb/books/alzahraa_index.htm.
93 Faḍlallāh (1421h). The seriousness of this statement causes Faḍlallāh to stress that, being God's messenger, the Prophet does not speak out of his personal inclinations [53: 3], particularly when he makes statements with such far-reaching consequences as Fāṭima's anger being an extension of God's anger, or that she is the doyenne of women.
94 Murtaḍā, Ja'far (1995) *al-Ṣaḥīḥ min Sīrat al-Nabī al-A'ẓam*. 4th edn. 11 volumes. Beirut: Dār al-Hādi, vol. 6, p. 229.
95 According to Faḍlallāh, history, as it would, did not record the details of the special relationship between Fāṭima and her father; however this description as *ummu abīhā* summarises the attentive care Fāṭima showed her father, her feeling of responsibility towards his well-being, and the important emotional support she provided for the Prophet during his lifetime (Faḍlallāh, 1421h). In the days of persecution in Mecca, the young daughter of Muhammad would clean her father and weep when filthy things were thrown at him (Lings, 1994, p. 98). In Medina, Fāṭima would be the last person the Prophet saw before he travelled, and upon his return he would pray in the mosque and then visit Fāṭima first. It is also reported that when she would enter his house he would stand up for her, kiss her hand, and make her sit in his place, and that she used to do the same for him (Qazwīnī, 1991, pp. 185–8). According to 'Alī Sharī'atī, this humility of the Prophet towards his youngest daughter "taught man to come down from his Pharaoh-like throne … it taught women … to put aside old feelings of inferiority and baseness" (Bakhtiar, 1996, p. 161).
96 Kulaynī (1388h, vol. 1, p. 459). al-Ṭūsī, Muḥammad Ibn Ḥasan (1390hb) *Tahdhīb al-aḥkām*. 10 volumes. Tehran: Dār al-Kutub al-Islāmiyya, vol. 6, p. 118. Ḥuwayzī (1412h, vol. 1, p. 336 and vol. 5, p. 599).

97 Ṣadūq (1404ha, vol. 2, p. 603). She is referred to as such in the possibly earliest available Shī'ī text, *Kitāb Sulaym bin Qays*, circa 80/662 (Clohessy, 2009, p. 3, fn. 4). Ḥākim (1406h, vol. 3, p. 151). Al-Ṣadūq, Muḥammad Ibn 'Alī Ibn Bābawayh (1386h) *'Ilal al-sharāi'*. 2 volumes. Najaf: al-Maktaba al-Ḥaydariyya, reports a tradition which claims that the angels used to speak to Fāṭima and tell her that she has been elected, purified, and elected over the women of all worlds, in exactly the same words with which the Qur'an narrates Mary's episode. So Fāṭima enquires whether this is not the place of Mary, to which the angels answer that Mary was the doyenne of women of her age, while you Fāṭima are the doyenne of women of her age and your age, and the doyenne of the first and the last women (Ṣadūq, 1386h, p. 182). But Ṣadūq himself did not include the latter in his authentic compilation (1404ha).

98 Ṣadūq (1404ha, vol. 2, p. 420). Bukhārī (1401h, vol. 4, pp. 183, 209, 219, and vol. 7, p. 142). Muslim (n.d., vol. 7, pp. 143–4). Ibn Sa'd (n.d., vol. 2, p. 248).

99 Ḥākim (1406h, vol. 3, p. 154, vol. 4, p. 44).

100 Ṭabāṭabā'ī (1402h, vol. 3, p. 189).

101 Ṭūsī (1409h, vol. 2, p. 456).

102 Ṣadūq (1386h, vol. 1, pp. 179–81).

103 Ibn Manẓūr (1405h, vol. 11, pp. 42–3).

104 Ibn Manẓūr (1405h, vol. 11 pp. 42–3).

105 Ibn Manẓūr (1405h, vol. 11, pp. 42–3).

106 Ibn Manẓūr (1405h, vol. 11, pp. 42–3), who adds that Fāṭima was disconnected from the material world, and the same statement exists in the editor's footnote in: Kulaynī (1388h, vol. 5, p. 509).

107 Kulaynī (1388h, vol. 1, p. 460). Another tradition in *al-Kāfī* claims that all daughters of prophets do not menstruate (Kulaynī, 1388h, vol. 1, p. 458), although this has not been traced in Fāṭima's sisters for instance. Clohessy reports a number of traditions which indicate that the root of her name (f-ṭ-m) refers to her separating her adherents (*shī'a*) from hellfire (Clohessy, 2009, pp. 81–91).

108 Kulaynī (1388h, vol. 3, pp. 104–5, and vol. 4, p. 136).

109 (Kulaynī, 1388h, vol. 5, p. 509).

110 It is Clohessy who notes those two aspects of this name (Clohessy, 2009, pp. 115–16).

111 One story is that the Prophet was instructed to withdraw from Khadīja for forty days and forty nights and spend them fasting and praying. On the final night he was told to conjugate with Khadīja, with the promise that a pure offspring will be conceived. Other traditions report that the Prophet had said that during his ascension to heaven Gabriel offered him a date fruit from Paradise. He ate the fruit and it became the fluid in his loins. When he returned to earth, he conjugated with Khadīja, and Fāṭima was conceived. Ṣadūq (1404hb, vol. 2, p. 107). Ṣadūq (1417h, p. 546). Qazwīnī (1991, pp. 31–9).

112 Faḍlallāh (2002, p. 65).

113 The similarities have been restricted here to those discernible in the authentic sources. However, if one were to consult later traditions, one finds that the similarities and competition grow into an extreme. There are for example the narrations that 'Alī would find food brought to Fāṭima miraculously, and the Prophet would then explain to 'Alī that his is similar to the case of Zechariah when he would see Mary provisioned, sometimes the traditions add that the Prophet expressed gratitude to God for letting him live to see of his daughter what Zechariah saw of Mary (Ṭūsī, 1414h, pp. 615–17; Majlisī, 1403h, vol. 14, pp. 197–200, vol. 21, p. 20, vol. 37, pp. 104–6, vol. 41, p. 30, vol. 43, pp. 29, 31, 50, etc.). Even more than that, in *Biḥār al-Anwār*, Fāṭima is sometimes referred to as "The Grander Mary (*Maryam al-Kubrā*)" (Majlisī, 1403h, vol. 22, p. 484, vol. 43, p. 16, vol. 88, p. 376, vol. 89, p. 113, vol. 99, p. 201, with the exception of vol. 30, p. 81 where Fāṭima is *Sayyidat al-Nisā'* after *Maryam al-Kubrā*). These traditions serve the opposite purpose of what they set out to do. They try to stress Fāṭima's

exalted position by forcing upon her a competition with Mary. To my mind, Fāṭima needs to be appreciated on her own terms.

114 Rosiny, S. (2001) "The tragedy of Fatima al-Zahra': in the debate of two Shiite theologians in Lebanon". In Brunner, R. and Ende, W. (eds) *The Twelver Shi'a in modern times: religious culture & political culture*. Leiden: Brill, p. 214, fn. 19, which quotes a book (Nūr al-Dīn's *Ma'sāt Kitāb al-Ma'sāt*) that defends this point of view of Faḍlallāh.

115 al-ʿĀmilī, Jaʿfar Murtaḍā (1997) *Ma'sāt al-Zahrā'*. Beirut: Dār al-Sīrah. Also available at: www.shiaweb.org/books/maasat_alzahraa_1/ and www.shiaweb.org/books/maasat_alzahraa_2 [Accessed 18.07.2011].

116 For example, refer to: Kister (1997, p. 12).

117 Kulaynī (1388h, vol. 1, pp. 384–9).

118 For example, refer to: 'Āmilī (1997, p. 93).

119 For an enlightening discussion of this verse, refer to: Naguib, S. (2010) "Horizons and limitations of Muslim feminist hermeneutics: reflections on the menstruation verse". In Anderson, P.S. (ed.) *New topics in feminist philosophy of religion, Feminist Philosophy Collection*. Dordrecht: Springer Press, pp. 33–49.

120 In exegeses, this despised fluid is "*al-nuṭfa al-manī*", a reference to the male *nuṭfa* rather than the female *nuṭfa* (Qummī, 1404h, vol. 2, p. 168; Kāshanī, 1416h, vol. 4, p. 154; Ḥuwayzī, 1412h, vol. 4, p. 222).

121 Buckley, T. and Gottlieb, A. (eds) (1988) *Blood magic: the anthropology of menstruation*. California: University of California Press, pp. 28–9. The lengthy Introduction where this quote is located convincingly argues that this particular theory has been beneficial but also limiting. While accepting its limitations in some cases, it seems to be beneficial and very relevant here.

122 Clohessy (2009, pp. 108 and 229–31).

123 Clohessy (2009, p. 232).

124 Thurlkill, M.F. (2007) *Chosen among women: Mary and Fatima in medieval Christianity and Shi'ite Islam*. Indiana: University of Notre Dame Press, p. 68.

125 McAuliffe, J.D. (1981) "Chosen of all women: Mary and Fatima in Qur'anic exegesis." *Islamic Quarterly*, 7, pp. 19–28. Also refer to Spellberg's thorough investigation of this position of Fāṭima versus 'Ā'isha, in relation to the variant traditions on the four most excellent women (Spellberg, D.A. (1994) *Politics, gender, and the Islamic past: the legacy of 'A'isha bint Abi Bakr*. New York: Columbia University Press, pp. 156–78).

126 Ayoub, M.M. (1978) *Redemptive suffering in Islam: a study of the devotional aspects of 'Ashura' in Twelver Shi'ism*. The Hague: Mouton, pp. 48, 212–16, etc.

127 Ayoub (1978, pp. 142–5).

128 Stowasser (1994, p. 80).

129 For a concise list of such traditions and their various Sunnī and Shī'ī sources, refer to: Momen (1985, pp. 12–17). Also refer to [5: 55] and its "occasion of revelation" as the proclamation of the *wilāya* of 'Alī.

130 Kulaynī (1388h, vol. 1, pp. 287, 294–6, vol. 4, p. 566, vol. 8, p. 27). Translation from: Momen (1985, p. 15), who quotes Ibn Ḥanbal's version, although for some odd reason the author writes lord with a capital "L". The context of this tradition is sometimes told that some people had complained about 'Alī upon their return with him from a campaign to Yemen. His army wished to wear some of their acquired linen clothing to meet the Prophet in pilgrimage, but 'Alī ordered them that the booty must be handed to the Prophet untouched. When the Prophet heard of their resentment towards 'Alī, he told the people not to blame 'Alī for being too scrupulous in his path towards God, and then made the famous declaration, in: Lings (1994, p. 335), and Ṣubḥānī (1984, pp. 743–4).

131 Jafri (1979, p. 21). Also refer to Ibn Saʿd (n.d., vol. 5, p. 320), who shows that while the tradition is widely accepted, its meaning is subject to disagreement.

132 It seems that the reason the Prophet's family closed the door is that there was a row around the Prophet. While he was on his deathbed (Ṭabarī, 1879, vol. 2, p. 436, and 439), and the incident was hinted at by Ibn Hishām (1383h, vol. 4, pp. 302–3).
133 Ayoub, M.M. (2003) *The crisis of Muslim history: religion and politics in early Islam*. Oxford: Oneworld, p. 12, where he suggests that Abū Bakr played a role in this.
134 Ibn Hishām (1383h, vol. 4, pp. 306–8).
135 Ibn Hishām (1383h, vol. 4, p. 309).
136 Ibn Hishām (1383h, vol. 4, pp. 309–10).
137 Jafri, S.H.M. (1979) *Origins and early development of Shi'a Islam*. London: Longman, p. 50, with an analysis of the different timing in the various sources.
138 Ayoub (2003, pp. 17–18 and 49), based on Ibn Qutayba. Imam 'Alī expressed in poetry his surprise and disagreement with the actions and arguments at the *saqī fa*; that if homage to Abū Bakr was decided through consultation, then how is it that the weighty men to be consulted were absent, and if homage was exacted on the basis of proximity to the Prophet, then others are closer heirs to the Prophet and nearer to him (Raḍī, n.d.*c*, vol. 4, pp. 43–4).
139 Jafri (1979, p. 51), quoting Baladhūrī.
140 Kulaynī (1388h, vol. 8, p. 238). Ya'qūbī (n.d., vol. 2, p. 126), and in Ṭabarī (1879, vol. 2, p. 443), the incident is mentioned without Fāṭima.
141 Ṭabarī (1879, vol. 2, p. 448).
142 Ṭabarī (1879, vol. 2, p. 448).
143 Ṭabarī (1879, vol. 2, p. 448).
144 Qazwīnī (1991, pp. 348–9).
145 When the verse [17: 26] was revealed: Kulaynī (1388h, vol. 1, p. 543), and ('Ayyāshī, n.d., vol. 2, p. 287).
146 Qummī (1404h, vol. 2, pp. 155–9), where Abū Bakr insisted that he has the words of Aws Ibn al-Ḥadthān, 'Ā'isha his daughter, and Ḥafṣa 'Umar's daughter, therefore, a man and two women, concerning the *ḥadīth* that prophets do not leave an inheritance.
147 For example, the Umayyad calīph 'Umar Ibn 'Abd al-'Azīz returned it to Imam 'Alī Ibn al-Ḥusayn, then it was taken back from them, then the 'Abbasid calīph al-Ma'mūn returned it to the heirs of Fāṭima, and so on (Ibn Abi al-Ḥadīd, al-Mu'tazilī, 'Izz al-Dīn Ibn Hibatallāh (n.d.) *Sharḥ nahj al-balāghah*. 20 volumes. Cairo: Dar Iḥyā' al-Kutub al-'Arabiyya, vol. 16, pp. 216–17).
148 Kulaynī (1388h, vol. 1, pp. 538–9).
149 Jafri (1979, p. 63). In other words, that it were a *fay'* that belongs to all Muslims as Abū Bakr and 'Umar contended, then having been under Fāṭima's management also proves her authority over Muslims.
150 For example: Ṭabarī (1879, vol. 2, p. 448).
151 Ṣadūq (1404ha, vol. 3, pp. 567–8). Ṭūsī (1390hb, vol. 10, p. 27), refers to a book which interprets the *khuṭba*.
152 Ibn Abī al-Ḥadīd (n.d., vol. 16, pp. 252–3).
153 Ibn Ṭayfūr, Ibn Abū Ṭāher (n.d.) *Balāghāt al-nisā'*. Qum: Basirati (n.d., pp. 12–19), where two versions, with slight variations between them are given.
154 Notably, in Ibn Ṭayfūr's other version, she continues, "and us (*ahl al-bayt*) a remnant to succeed him, and with us the book of God". The two versions might well carry the same meaning since "the speaking book" is normally understood as a reference to the Imam. Her contention here is clearly a reminder of "*ḥadīth al-thaqalayn*".
155 Qazwīnī (1991, pp. 300–1).
156 For the exegeses of these two verses, and the debates surrounding them, that prophets' inheritance in the Qur'an refers to material inheritance, refer to: Ṭabāṭabā'ī (1402h, vol. 15, p. 349, and vol. 14, pp. 22–4).

157 This is the second version of her speech, reported by Zaynab in: Ibn Ṭayfūr (n.d., pp. 14–18).
158 Ibn Ṭayfūr (n.d., pp. 18–19).
159 Ṣadūq (1404ha, vol. 3, pp. 567–8).
160 There are several supplications (*du'ā*) attributed to Fāṭima, as well as some *ḥadīths*. These are compiled in Qazwīnī's second edition: al-Qazwīnī, Muḥammad Kāẓim (1414h, 2nd edn) *Fāṭima al-Zahrā': min al-mahd ila al-laḥd*. Qum: Basirati, pp. 220–5 and 233–40.
161 Qazwīnī (1991, pp. 232–3), among others.
162 Faḍlallāh (2002, p. 55). Qazwīnī (1991, p. 441), based on Ibn Abi-l-Ḥadīd.
163 Ibn Ṭayfūr (n.d., p. 19).
164 Ibn Ṭayfūr (n.d., p. 20).
165 Qazwīnī (1991, p. 392).
166 His book on Islamic economics has been rendered into English as: al-Sadr, Muhammad Baqir (2010) *The Islamic economic doctrine: a comparative study*. 2nd edn. MECI Ltd. Edited and translated by Shubber, K.J. His book on Islamic philosophy: al-Sadr, Muhammad Baqir (1989) *Our philosophy*. 2nd edn. Iran: Ansariyan Publications. Edited and translated by Inati, Sh.C. For his political activism, refer to: Al-Rikabi, J. (2012) "Baqir al-Sadr and the Islamic state: a theory for Islamic democracy". *Journal of Shi'a Islamic Studies*, 5 (3): 249–75. Bernhardt, F. (2011) "The legitimacy of party politics and the authority of the 'ulama' in Iraq's Shi'a Islamist movement: the example of the Islamic Da'wah Party (1957–88)". *Journal of Shi'a Islamic Studies*, 4 (2): 163–82.
167 al-Ṣadr, Muḥammad Bāqir (1991) *Trends of history in the Qur'an*. London: al-Khoei Foundation, pp. 78–83.
168 Ṣadr (1991, pp. 91–2).
169 Ṣadr (1991, pp. 85–90, 107–8, and 86–90 especially deal with the difficult notion of an all-encompassing punishment).
170 Ṣadr (1991, p. 94).
171 Eliash, J. (1969) "The Ithna 'ashari-Shi'i juristic theory of political and legal authority". *Studia Islamica*, 29: 28. This, however, was written before the Islamic revolution in Iran, where arguably political power and divine authority are presented as one.
172 Ṭabarī (1879, vol. 2, p. 448).
173 Kulaynī (1388h, vol. 1, pp. 458–9). al-Raḍī, al-Sharīf, Muḥammad Ibn al-Ḥusayn (n.d.c) *Nahj al-balāgha*. 4 volumes. Beirut: Dār al-Ma'rifa, vol. 2, pp. 182–3.
174 Kulaynī (1388h, vol. 2, p. 244 with footnote).
175 Madelung, W. (1998) *The succession to Muhammad*. Cambridge: Cambridge University Press, p. 52.
176 Jafri (1979, p. 59).
177 Lawson (2007, p. 163).
178 Lawson (2007, p. 152).
179 Ziyādā, Asmā' Aḥmad Muḥammad (2001) *Dawr al-mar'a al-siyāsī fī 'ahd al-nabī wa al-khulafā' al-rāshidīn: wa bihā taḥqīq tārīkhī wa fiqhī wa tashrī'ī li fahm dawr al-sayyidah 'Ā'isha fī aḥdāth al-fitna*. Cairo: Dār al-Salām, pp. 210–13.
180 Zaatari, Z. (2006) "The culture of motherhood: an avenue for women's civil participation in south Lebanon". *Journal of Middle East Women's Studies*, 2 (1): 35–6 and 41.
181 Kashani-Sabet (2005, pp. 1–3).
182 Afshar, H. (1982) "Khomeini's teachings and their implications for women". *Feminist Review*, 12: 63.
183 Qazwīnī (1991, p. 235).
184 For example, refer to: Pelly, L. (1879) *The miracle play of Hasan and Husain*. London: W.H. Allen. Although, it has to be mentioned that authentic traditions

confirm that Fāṭima did not smile after her father's death (Kulaynī, 1388h, vol. 4, p. 561). There is also an incident when she asked Bilāl, who had decided not to do the *adhān* to anyone after the Prophet, to do it once more for her sake, but then upon hearing his voice and remembering the days of her father she fainted and Bilāl stopped (Ṣadūq, 1404ha, vol. 1, pp. 297–8).

185 Kashani-Sabet (2005, pp. 9–10, 14).

186 Bakhtiar (1996, pp. 117–18), he actually names female pioneers in the west and argues that Muslims have not emulated those progressive models, but the fashion models and beauty queens.

187 Kashani-Sabet (2005, p. 18).

188 Bakhtiar (1996, pp. 93–9).

189 Rosiny (2001, p. 210).

190 The Shī'a know her as *al-'aqīla* (Abū Mikhnaf, Lūṭ Ibn Yaḥyā (1398h) *Maqtal al-Ḥusayn*. Qum: al-Maktaba al-'ilmiyya, p. 165), and (Iṣfahānī, Abū al-Faraj (1385h) *Maqātil al-Ṭalibiyyīn*. Qum: Dār al-Kitāb, p. 60), meaning the honourable and precious lady (Ibn Manẓūr, Muḥammad Ibn Mukarram (1405h) *Lisān al-'Arab*. 15 volumes. Qum: Nashr Adab al-Ḥawza, vol. 11, p. 463).

191 Hitti, P.K. (1970) *History of the Arabs*. 10th edn. London: Macmillan, p. 197, because he was the first king (*malik*), an idea abhorrent to the Arabs, in addition to his secularising Islam and changing the theocratic caliphate into a temporal sovereignty.

192 Jafri (1979, pp. 167–8 and 174). He needed in particular the allegiance of five prominent individuals, including Imam Ḥusayn, and he went to Medina to try to secure their allegiance, but it is not clear what happened there, and they might have escaped to Mecca at night. In other versions he kept a will for his son to seek the allegiance of these individuals, or to have them killed, but to deal respectfully with Ḥusayn who is loved and revered in the community (Ya'qūbī, n.d., vol. 2, p. 240).

193 Ṭabarī (1879, vol. 4, pp. 224–6). Jafri (1979, pp. 180–1).

194 Ṭabarī (1879, vol. 4, pp. 261–2).

195 Ṭabarī (1879, vol. 4, pp. 299–300), and adds that Ḥusayn considered there is no good living after those good men had been killed. Jafri (1979, p. 185) adds that Ḥusayn at that point gave his companions the option to leave him.

196 Ṭabarī (1879, vol. 4, pp. 291–2).

197 Ya'qūbī (n.d., vol. 2, p. 243). Ṭabarī (1879, vol. 4, pp. 308–12) so he sent his half brother 'Abbas b. 'Alī with others to fetch water but they were unsuccessful.

198 Ya'qūbī (n.d., vol. 2, p. 245).

199 Ṭabarī (1879, vol. 4, p. 297). For a discussion of the political significance of the move, refer to: Shams al-Dīn, Muḥammad Mahdī (1981) *Anṣār al-Ḥusayn*. 2nd edn. al-Dār al-Islāmiyya, pp. 225–33.

200 Ya'qūbī (n.d., vol. 2, p. 244).

201 Ya'qūbī (n.d., vol. 2, pp. 248–50).

202 Ṭabarī (1879, vol. 4, p. 293).

203 Jafri (1979, p. 200). Ḥusayn reportedly got a timely offer of refuge in unreachable mountains by his travel guide who proposed to mobilise his own tribe and strike the Umayyads in due time with an army of 20,000 men. He simply refused and answered that he is committed to his word, and will go to Kūfa no matter what happens (Ṭabarī, 1879, vol. 4, pp. 306–7; Jafri, 1979, p. 201).

204 Jafri (1979, pp. 201–2).

205 Shams al-Dīn, M.M. (n.d.) *The revolution of Imam al-Husayn: its impact on the consciousness of Muslim society*. [online]. Available from: www.al-islam.org/revolution-imam-al-husayn-shaykh-muhammad-mahdi-shams-ad-din-al-amili; Rites of remembrance for al-Ḥusayn: Part I, section 2 [Accessed 20.02.2014]. (Ṭabarī, 1879, vol. 4, p. 348).

206 Ibn Ṭayfūr (n.d., p. 23). al-Ṭabrisī, Faḍl Ibn Ḥasan (1386h) *al-Iḥtijāj*. 2 volumes. Najaf: Dār al-Nu'mān, vol. 2, p. 29. al-Ṭūsī, Muḥammad Ibn Ḥasan (1414h) *al-Amālī*. Qum: Dār al-Thaqafa, p. 92. al-Mufīd, Muḥammad Ibn al-Nu'mān (1403h) *al-Amālī*. Qum: Jami'at al-Mudarrisīn fi al-Ḥawza, pp. 321–2. For a far more comprehensive reference of the women's words, refer to: al-Shirāzī, Ḥasan (2000) *Kalimat al-Sayyida Zaynab wa rubaybāt al-risāla*. Beirut: Dār al-Qāri'. Commemoration rituals are dominated by poetry attributed to various women of Ḥusayn's family: Ayoub (1978, pp. 129–32, 173–6).

207 Ṭabarī (1879, vol. 4, p. 350). Abū Mikhnaf (1398h, p. 205), al-Mufīd, Muḥammad Ibn al-Nu'mān (1413h) *al-Irshād*. 2 volumes. Beirut: Dār al-Mufīd, vol. 2, pp. 115–16. Ṣadūq (1417h, pp. 229–30).

208 Ibn Sa'd (n.d., vol. 5, p. 212). Ṭabarī (1879, vol. 4, p. 350). Abū Mikhnaf (1398h, p. 206).

209 Ṭūsī (1411h, p. 230).

210 Ṭabarī (1879, vol. 4, p. 353). Abū Mikhnaf (1398h, p. 214). al-Ṣadūq, Muḥammad Ibn 'Alī Ibn Bābawayh (1417h) *al-Amālī*. Qum: Mu'assasat al-Ba'tha, p. 231.

211 Mughniyya, Muḥammad Jawād (1992) *Ma' baṭalat Karbalā': Zaynab bint Amīr al-Mu'minīn*. 5th edn. Beirut: Dār al-Ṭalī'a and Dār al-Jawād, p. 66.

212 Ṭabrisī (1386h, vol. 2, p. 34). Ibn Ṭayfūr (n.d., pp. 20–1). Abū Mikhnaf (1398h, p. 225 footnote). At that, one of the Prophet's companions present in the court objected that he had seen the Prophet kissing that mouth (Ya'qūbī, n.d., vol. 2, p. 245). He then went out and cried some words reminiscent of Fāṭima's warnings, "O Arabs, slaves you have become from this day; you killed the son of Fāṭima, and gave the son of Marjāna (Ibn Ziyād) your command, he is killing the good ones among you and enslaving the evil, you have accepted humiliation" (Ṭabarī, 1879, vol. 4, p. 349), where the narrator adds that had Ibn Ziyād heard him he would have killed him. The incident of striking the mouth is sometimes attributed to Yazīd, and sometimes to Ibn Ziyād.

213 Ṭabrisī (1386h, vol. 2, pp. 35–7). Ibn Ṭayfūr (n.d., pp. 22–3). Abū Mikhnaf (1398h, pp. 226–7 footnote).

214 Mughniyya (1992, pp. 61 and 65).

215 Ṭabarī (1879, vol. 4, pp. 353, 355). Abū Mikhnaf (1398h, p. 215). Shams al-Dīn (n.d., Rites of Remembrance: Part I, section 2b). Also noted in: Pinault (1998, p. 71) and Hamdar, A. (2009) "Jihad of words: gender and contemporary Karbala narratives". In Tate, A. (ed.) *Yearbook of English Studies*, 39 (1–2): 84–100. Special Issue on Literature and Religion, p. 86.

216 Jawād, Ibrāhīm Muḥammad (2005) *al-Sayyida Zaynab: thawra lā tahda' wa dam'a lā tarqa'*. Beirut: Dār al-Maḥajja al-Bayḍā', pp. 275–8.

217 Mughniyya (1992, pp. 52–4).

218 Jawād (2005, p. 279). Shams al-Dīn (n.d., Rites of Remembrance: Part I, section 2c).

219 Mughniyya (1992, pp. 54–5).

220 Jawād (2005, pp. 279–80). Shams al-Dīn (n.d., Rites of Remembrance: Part I, section 2c).

221 Jafri (1979, p. 204). A similar idea is expressed in: Pinault (1998, p. 72).

222 al-Khū'ī, Abu al-Qāsim Ibn 'Alī Akbar (1413h) *Mu'jam rijāl al-ḥadīth*. 5th edn. 24 volumes. Qum: Lajnat Taḥqīq Turāth al-Shaykh al-A'ẓam, vol. 24, p. 219.

223 Ayoub (1978, pp. 148–53), on the early stages of *ta'ziya* rituals including the Imams' impetus. Shams al-Dīn (n.d., The Ziyāra, Rites of Remembrance: Part I, section 2c, and Weeping).

224 Several women are remembered as champions in Karbalā', among them are some who pushed their husbands to go to Ḥusayn and fight on his side, and Ibn Sa'd's wife who held a sword and proceeded towards Ḥusayn 's tents to protect the daughters of the Prophet (Ayati, 1991, pp. 146–9). About the hostess of Muslim Ibn 'Aqīl, and the wife of Zuhayr Ibn al-Qayn, refer to: Ṭabarī (1879, vol. 4, pp. 263

and 299, respectively). An observation has been made that Ḥusayn personally asked the women who were on the site of the battle to withdraw to the tents and work on nursing the injured. Two examples have been given, one is of a woman called Umm Wahab who progressed to protect her husband, and the other was Zaynab (Aghaie, K.S. (2004) *Martyrs of Karbala: Shi'i symbols and rituals in modern Iran*. Seattle: University of Washington Press, pp. 119–20). In the case of Umm Wahab, it is reported that when she saw her husband in danger, she took up a pole and went to him encouraging him to fight for the good people. Her husband then tried to push her back towards the women, but she kept holding his garment and said, "I will not let go until I die with you". It is then that Ḥusayn interfered thanking her for her good will towards his family and asking her to join the ranks of women because women are not required to fight. From this account, it seems as though Umm Wahab was not behaving in a confident manner regarding her fighting skills, but she was throwing herself into death for the sake of honouring *ahl al-bayt* and dying with her husband. In Zaynab's case, it is reported that upon the death of one of Ḥusayn's children, 'Alī al-Akbar, she threw herself on him crying. Ḥusayn took her hand and accompanied her back to the tent. Again, Zaynab was lamenting rather than fighting, and Ḥusayn took a protective measure walking her away from the scene (Ṭabarī, 1879, vol. 4, p. 341). Abū Mikhnaf (1398h, p. 164). Furthermore, it has been pointed out that women's participation on the battlefield as nurses, in addition to providing water and food, is a *sunna* and must be considered a necessary and vital contribution in battle (Ziyāda, 2001, pp. 220–78).

225 Aghaie (2004, p. 118).
226 Aghaie (2004, pp. 118–19).
227 Aghaie (2004, pp. 121–2).
228 Aghaie (2004, p. 122).
229 Aghaie (2004, p. 123).
230 Aghaie (2004, p. 123).
231 Pinault (1998, p. 83).
232 Pinault (1998, p. 83).
233 As in Ṭabarī's account described above.
234 Aghaie (2004, pp. 127–8). Some said he was too old, others suggested she was divorced, but others (not mentioned in Aghaie) claimed that she had stipulated in her marriage contract the condition that she would be allowed to accompany her brother to Karbalā', the assumption being that *ahl al-bayt* foresaw the future.
235 Mughniyya (1992, pp. 35–8).
236 For example: Mughniyya (1992, p. 54).
237 Pinault (1998, pp. 94–5).
238 Mughniyya (1992, pp. 60–6). Husseini, R. (2008) "Women, work, and political participation in Lebanese Shi'a contemporary thought: the writings of Ayatollahs Fadlallah and Shams al-din". *Comparative Studies of South Asia, Africa and the Middle East*, 28 (2): 273–82.
239 Deeb, L.Z. (2005) "From mourning to activism: Sayyedeh Zaynab, Lebanese Shi'i women, and the transformation of Ashura". In Aghaie, K.S. (ed.) *The women of Karbala: ritual performance and symbolic discourse in modern Shi'i Islam*. Austin: University of Texas Press, p. 244.
240 Deeb (2005, pp. 253–8).
241 Aghaie (2004, p. 121).
242 al-Ṭūsī, Muḥammad Ibn Ḥasan (1409h) *al-Tibyān fī tafsīr al-Qur'ān*. 10 volumes. Qum: Maktab al-I'lām al-Islāmī, vol. 3, pp. 184–5.
243 Raḍī (n.d.c, vol. 4, p. 90). The observation of this *ḥadīth* regarding Zaynab has also been made in: Hamdar (2009, p. 90).
244 Kulaynī (1388h, vol. 5, p. 60).

245 Ayoub (1978, p. 184), where the author makes his remark in reference to *ziyāra*, an act of physical or literal visitation of the shrine of Ḥusayn in Karbalā'.
246 Mughniyya (1992, pp. 58–61).
247 Aghaie (2004, p. 115).
248 Aghaie (2004, p. 116).
249 Zaatari (2006, pp. 43–4).
250 For the Algerian example, refer to: Helie-Lucas, M.-A. (1990) "Women, nationalism and religion in the Algerian liberation struggle". In Badran, M. and Cooke, M. (eds) *Opening the gates: a century of Arab feminist writing*. Bloomington: Indiana University Press, pp. 106–12. For the Iranian example, refer to: Afshar, H. (1998) *Islam and feminisms: an Iranian case-study*. Basingstoke: Macmillan, pp. 43–5.
251 Ṭabarī (1879, vol. 4, p. 344). Another statement from Ḥusayn again explains his point of view, "The adopted, son of the adopted (reference to Ibn Ziyād's unknown grandfather) has given us two choices, war or humiliation. Humiliation is far from us! God refuses this for us, as do his messenger, and the believers, and (people with) pleasant bosoms/hearts, purified barriers/genitals, vehement noses/ pride, and souls noncompliant, to prefer obedience to the depraved over the deaths of the honourable!" (al-Ḥusaynī, Ibn Tāwūs, 'Alī Ibn Mūsa (1417h) *al-Luhūf fī qatla al-ṭufūf*. Tehran: Mehr, p. 59). (Ṭabrisī, 1386h, pp. 24–5).
252 For a brief account of the life of Imam Riḍā's sister who popularly came to be known and called the "impeccable (maʿṣūma)", though not technically so from the theological point of view, refer to: Waddy (1980, pp. 49–55).

4 Female personality in the *ḥadīth*

Introduction

Ḥadīth in Arabic may mean something new or recent, something which came into existence, or the relation of discourse.[1] In Islam, the term was applied to the human record of the Prophet's words and deeds, and came to mean a "tradition".[2] It is therefore considered the second source of Islamic knowledge after the Qur'an. However, the two are not of equal value, but differ in "their provenance and roles, as well as their form and style".[3]

The subject of *ḥadīth* has been one of much controversy since the beginning of the twentieth century, when voices that rejected the authority or authenticity of the *ḥadīth* were heard throughout the Islamic world.[4] In fact, the history of *ḥadīth* from its outset was one of continuous scrutiny to find the best ways to determine whether traditions were authentic or not. That gave rise to different grades marking the degree of authenticity of individual traditions, in addition to different collections of *ḥadīth* varying in esteem. In traditional Islam, emphasis is placed on the *ḥadīth* as complementary to the Qur'an, because it helps explain it. There are several Qur'anic verses that ask Muslims to obey God and the Prophet, to follow the Prophet's example, and indeed to take everything the Prophet had given them and to refrain from everything that he had forbidden.[5] This shows that the *ḥadīth* is authoritative by virtue of the Qur'anic command itself. It is also known that the family and companions of the Prophet were recording his traditions during his lifetime.[6] For these reasons, the argument of those who wish to neglect the *ḥadīth* and focus solely on the Qur'an in the name of scripturalism, that is, a return to the pure Islam,[7] is unfounded.

It is important, however, to question the lack of distinction between *ḥadīth* and *sunna*. This is apparent in western as well as modern Muslim scholarship, which actually reflects "the post-Shāfiʿī, 'classical', view that, although the two terms are not the same, the *ḥadīth* is nevertheless the total record of the *sunna* and thus the *sunna* can be reconstituted from *ḥadīth*".[8] However, for the more ancient schools the two terms were always distinct, moreover, "the rejection of certain *ḥadīths* was in no way considered a rejection of the *sunna* of the Prophet: on the contrary, it was considered a clarification of it".[9] In fact, it is acknowledged by the Muslim tradition itself, which created a science out of the authentication process,[10] that "the Hadith as vehicle of the prophetic *sunnah* is mutable and historically contingent".[11]

While the *ḥadīth* in Sunni Islam consists mainly of traditions from the Prophet, in Shī'ī Islam, *ḥadīth* expands to include traditions from all the impeccable/sinless persons (*ma'ṣūmīn*).[12] The Imam himself is an authority in transmission and need not find a chain of narrators leading back to the Prophet. Imam al-Ṣadiq explains this when he says that the *ḥadīth* of every Imam is the same as the *ḥadīth* of the Imam before him, in a chain that goes back to the first Imam 'Alī, the Prophet, and ultimately to God.[13] One implication of this is the doctrine of the "unity" of the teachings of the Imams, which therefore need to be understood in an integral manner.[14] This is why all traditions, no matter from which impeccable person, will be considered together as co-texts when relevant.

In the Shī'ī tradition, besides the authentication process of the chain of transmitters leading to the Imam, the meaning of the content of a tradition is a main criterion for determining its authenticity.[15] One authentic tradition explains, "Everything should be in accordance with the Qur'an and *sunna*, and every *ḥadīth* that contradicts the Qur'an is an embellishment".[16]

However, discovering the meaning of the Qur'an is not a simple task, and as it will be seen in the variety of interpretations of even a single verse, the Qur'an itself allows for multiple meanings. As Imam 'Alī said, "Do not altercate with them using the Qur'an, because it carries many angles so that you will say (something) and they will say (something else), rather dispute with them using the *sunna*, because it is clear and they cannot run from it".[17] The mention of *sunna* instead of *ḥadīth* here is duly noted.

Therefore, in dealing with the meanings of traditions and their authenticity, a balance needs to be found among the interpretation of the Qur'an, the normative established *sunna* of the Prophet, and other traditions as representative of the unity of the teachings of the *ma'ṣūmīn*.

Four books came to be known as the most authoritative Shī'ī *ḥadīth* collections,[18] and their authenticity has been examined.[19] Not among those is the monumental work entitled *Nahj al-Balāgha*, meaning "the path of eloquence".[20] This was collected by al-Sharīf al-Raḍī (d.406/1015) and is attributed to Imam 'Alī (d.40/661). The book comprises sermons, letters, and sayings attributed to 'Alī. Part of the book's charm is perhaps that it combines the language and imagery of ancient Bedouin Arabia, with Islamic teachings and wisdom.[21] The issue of this book's sources has been subject to some speculation, but it has recently been shown that large portions of it may indeed be attributed to 'Alī.[22] Yet, when Henri Corbin enquired about the sources of this book, Ṭabāṭabā'ī simply answered, "For us, whoever wrote *Nahj al-Balāgha* is 'Alī, even if he lived a century ago".[23] In line with this sentiment, and Shī'ī attitudes towards *ḥadīth* in general, the discussion here will focus on the content of the traditions, not their chain of transmission (although their grade will be noted in the footnotes).

The *ḥadīth* literature is especially controversial for the study of the status of women in Islam considering its often misogynist attitudes. Perhaps this is why it has been neglected by most feminist and feminist-informed Muslim scholars and is normally addressed in broad terms. For example, Riffat Hassan criticised the high reverence that Muslims and their jurisprudence give the authentic *ḥadīth* collections,[24] while Amina Wadud advised that women's reinterpretation of scripture extend to the traditions.[25] However, women's studies on *ḥadīth* are scarce, and Islamic feminism seems to have a tendency towards "Qur'an-only" hermeneutics. This attitude risks abandoning a necessary agent in explaining even the basic precepts of Islamic thought and practice. Moreover, some traditions are actually beneficial to women in the way they interpret the Qur'an or even affect the issuing of certain laws.[26] It will be seen in what follows that the single most problematic verse for women in the Qur'an [4: 34] is made much milder by use of the *ḥadīth*.[27]

In this chapter, traditions from *Nahj al-Balāgha* will be the main focus of discussion due to the high popularity of the book and its general acceptance among Arabs and Muslims as an unimpeachable authority, and because it is perceived by Shī'ī scholars and laypeople as unsurpassed except by the Qur'an, thereby making its sayings most relevant for Shī'ī thought on women. Out of eleven statements on woman/women in *Nahj al-Balāgha*, four will be taken as samples here. These four are singled out mainly because they reflect the major themes on women in the *ḥadīth* literature more generally, but also because they correspond to the areas that have been discussed in the previous chapters. The other seven traditions on women in *Nahj al-Balāgha* are unique in their content compared to the wider traditions on women, so even though they would make for a necessary and interesting discussion of Imam 'Alī's views on gender, they will be left for another occasion. The four traditions that will be discussed here seem to describe woman as evil, women as deficient in faith and intellect, women's seclusion, and woman's *jihād* as towards her husband. Therefore, they elaborate on the themes discussed in the previous chapters, such as the full personhood of women and their potential vicegerency, particularly in reference to their faith and intellect, women's greater and lesser *jihād*, and their private and public roles. Finally, a brief analysis of the few traditions with positive tones towards women in the "four books" will be included, and compared to the prevailing views on women in the *ḥadīth*. That is in order to get a better picture of what the *ḥadīth* literature amounts to. In the conclusion, it will be proposed that these apparently misogynist traditions seem to depart from descriptions of Imam 'Alī's extremely tolerant, even sympathetic, attitude towards women. This again is a useful reminder that the *sunna* as practice and *ḥadīth* as written record ought to be considered together before any conclusions are reached.

The method of analysis will be textual and comparative. One traditional method of authentication by applying each tradition to the Qur'an and *sunna* will be used, making use of the preceding chapters on the female personalities there. Further, comparisons with co-texts, that is, variations of the same tradition, or even traditions discussing a similar issue will be made. The aim of this chapter is to attempt to switch the reading of *ḥadīth* from a body of literature that informs Islamic law, into one that is subject to the Islamic tradition's broader views on womanhood, in light of the conclusions already made on the female personalities. This chapter will therefore deconstruct these four sample traditions and show how, unlike the colourful and varied female personalities of the Qur'an and *sunna*, woman here is repeatedly presented as a monolithic personality, which is usually lesser than man, particularly in relation to her husband.

It has to be noted between parentheses, that not everything written in every tradition is considered an article of the law; rather, deriving laws from the *ḥadīth* is a complicated process that attempts to make use of the totality of texts and contexts available, in addition to analytical reasoning. Therefore, when reading the *ḥadīth* here, we are looking into what "image" of women it portrays. Even if it speaks in legal terms, every individual tradition is not necessarily in itself a binding law for Muslims. This will become apparent within the analysis.

Woman as evil and necessary

Consider the tradition, "Woman is wholly evil (*al-mar'a sharrun kulluhā*), and the worst of her evil is that she must needs be (*wa sharru mā fīhā annahu lā budda minhā*)".[28]

The first part of this tradition seemingly proclaims womankind as evil. The generalisation that this is about womankind stems from the use of the word "*al-mar'a*", meaning woman in the singular, which in turn implies a generalisation based on sort. The second part of this tradition, however, complicates the meaning by linking the evilness of woman with the necessity of her existence. It is not saying that woman is a "necessary evil", but that she is wholly evil because she is absolutely necessary.

In another tradition, Imam 'Alī describes three qualities that are favourable in women but not so in men,[29] and it has been suggested that this shows that the Imam does not regard woman as totally evil but that both women and men have positive and negative traits.[30]

It was argued in the chapter on Eve that woman was created a full person, and that the human being and the human soul are described in the Qur'an in general terms, irrespective of sex, as containing the good and the evil within them, "We indeed created the human being in the fairest stature, then We restored him the lowest of the low – save those who believe, and do righteous deeds" [95: 4–6]. Faḍlallāh finds that this tradition's apparent meaning is irreconcilable with the foundations of Islam, unless another meaning is intended.[31] If the first part of this tradition cannot mean what it appears to mean, perhaps the second part explains it.

A few Qur'anic verses may be taken to express a similar sentiment of wariness from women, "O believers, among your spouses and children there is an enemy to you; so beware of them … Your wealth and your children are only a trial; and with God is a mighty wage" [64: 14–15]. In exegesis, this has been taken to refer to some, not all, spouses and children, who try to pull people away from religion. These are a trial because they cause distress to the soul which is forbidding itself from following desire.[32] In another verse, wealth and sons are described as adornments of this world, and the good deeds which endure are described as better in the sight of God and better in expectation [18: 46]. Wealth and sons are not a problem in themselves and are indeed necessary tools for a good life in human society.[33] However, the problem is in the hearts which cling to these things expecting ultimate benefit and endurance from them.[34]

In this context, where something is condemned which is not necessarily wicked in itself, an incident comes to mind, when a man cursed the illusory ephemeral world (*dunyā*) in front of Imam 'Alī. Now, 'Alī himself had often condemned this world for its changeability, its danger, and its misleading hopes, and declared that he had "divorced" it irrevocably.[35] However, when this man cursed the world in front of him, 'Alī criticised him and asked rhetorically whether the man should be accusing the world or whether it is the world that ought to be accusing him. He continued to describe the man's situation reproachfully, saying to him that it was he who was seduced by this world and then he accuses it, even though the world is actually clear about its ephemeral nature, and is not deceptive. Then he went on to describe all the hints and the possibilities for growth that the world offers.[36] Therefore, even when the Imam condemned this world, his condemnation was mistakenly understood to mean that the problem originates in the ephemeral world itself. Perhaps this example might also be taken as a warning against misunderstanding his condemnation of woman in a similar manner.

Another tradition from Imam 'Alī might help understand his literary style, he says, "To God be attributed the good that has proceeded from envy; how just it is! It originates with its possessor and then it struggles with/kills him".[37] Here, he begins by praising envy and therefore immediately captures the listener's attention with the unlikely declaration. Then he continues to explain that envy is just, because it punishes the person who produces it. This tradition might help understand the link between the first part of the tradition on woman as evil, and its second explanatory part on the peak of her evil being her indispensability, because there is a paradoxical meaning between woman's evilness and the necessity of her existence.

The context of this aphoristic tradition has not been narrated with it, and one wonders how much the context would have defined the meaning of these words.[38] It is especially true of a literary text that:

> It is necessary to take the viewpoint of the hearer or the reader and to treat the novelty of the emergent meaning as the counterpart, on the author's side, of a construction on the side of the reader. Thus the process of explanation is the only access to the process of creation … In the

> asymmetrical relation between the text and the reader, one of the partners speaks for both. Bringing a text to language is always something other than hearing someone and listening to his speech.[39]

It has been argued that this extremist language leaving no space for goodness in woman is inconsistent with the Qur'an, and even with Imam 'Alī's own views on favourable traits in men and women. His statement might however be in line with the Qur'anic warning from spouses, children, and wealth that are a trial for the clinging hearts. Moreover, one can understand from the incident with the man condemning the world, that even though 'Alī appears to have done so himself, such condemnation coming from that man was considered a lack of understanding and was corrected by the Imam. The literary style of shocking the listener with an unusual declaration and then turning the meaning around had been used by 'Alī on at least one other occasion. The unavailable context leaves the meaning of this tradition open for interpretation. However, the Qur'anic context and the co-texts of Imam 'Alī's more general outlook and style, may inform the understanding that the tradition does not simply say that woman is evil, but points at woman's necessity and, possibly, her place in the hearts of men. It cannot be a sentiment against the full personhood of woman and her potential for vicegerency.

Women as deficient in faith, fortune, and intellect

With this *ḥadīth*, interestingly, the context is recorded as "after the War of the Camel". Imam 'Alī said:

> O multitude of people, indeed women are deficient in faith (*nawāqis al-ī mān*), deficient in fortune (*nawāqis al-ḥuẓūẓ*), and deficient in intellect (*nawāqis al-'uqūl*). As for their deficiency in faith, it is in their refraining from prayer and fasting during their menstruation, as for their deficiency in fortune, it is in their share of inheritance being half the men's share, and as for their deficiency in intellect, it is in the statement of two women witnesses being equivalent to the statement of one man. Therefore, guard yourselves from evil women and be cautious of the good ones among them. Do not obey them in good deeds so that they do not get greedy for your obedience in bad deeds.[40]

To begin with, the recorded occasion of this tradition is after the War of the Camel. This was named so in reference to 'Ā'isha's camel which was the rallying point for the soldiers rebelling against 'Alī's caliphate and it was the first civil war among Muslims.[41] The occasion is interesting because that time seems to have had strong anti-women sentiments. For example, in Sunni authentic *ḥadīth* literature a tradition occurred around that time, which condemns women's political leadership.[42] The opinion of the esteemed religious scholar, Muḥammad Mahdī Shams al-Dīn (1422 h/2001 A.D.), is that Imam

'Alī wanted to warn people from following 'Ā'isha in a manner that did not offend her personally, so he resorted to describing some of the particulars of Islamic law regarding women, as his way of showing that despite 'Ā'isha's position as the Prophet's wife, she is still a woman like all women and Muslims have no obligation to follow her, particularly because she did not listen to admonishments nor feared sedition, and she did not abide by the Qur'anic command for the wives of the Prophet to stay in their homes.[43] This brings Shams al-Dīn to the second part of the tradition which recommends being wary of women and not obeying them in any matter. He explains the admonishment to be wary of good women as only pertaining to situations when such women do not abide by the practice of consultation and the law.[44] The aim, Shams al-Dīn says, was to protect the public from following 'Ā'isha who is in the view of the majority Muslims a good woman.[45] The question remains, if he did not wish to discredit her personally, why would he allow himself to discredit all women on her part? It may be correctly argued that intending the individual by referring to the general is a well-known rhetorical device (known in Arabic as *iṭlāq al-kull 'ala-l-ba'ḍ*). This may have been so in its given context; however since this statement has too often been used as a confirmation of women's inferior capabilities, it needs to be deconstructed, particularly because of the grave theological and legal consequences of its inner reasoning.

To claim that women are deficient in faith is perhaps the most dangerous, from a religious point of view. The Qur'an repeatedly and clearly puts men and women on an equal footing in matters of faith:

> Men and women who have surrendered, believing men and believing women, obedient men and obedient women, truthful men and truthful women, enduring men and enduring women, humble men and humble women, men and women who give in charity, men who fast and women who fast, men and women who guard their private parts, men and women who remember God oft – for them God has prepared forgiveness and a mighty wage.
>
> [33: 35][46]

It has been argued in the previous chapters that women are represented in the Qur'an as being on various levels of the *jihād al-nafs*, with some of them, like the mother of Moses, Āsiyā, and Mary reaching exalted levels, and others like Bilqīs overcoming their conditioning and accepting the new message of the prophets. Moreover, Khadīja is portrayed as the first person to accept Islam and support the prophecy of Muhammad. There were also many women who left their families and everything they had in Mecca and migrated to Medina to proclaim their faith, as is evident in the occasion of revelation of verse [60: 10].[47] To accept the claim that women are deficient in faith, not only goes against the Qur'an, but also betrays those pioneers.

The legal aspects mentioned here, that women's deficient faith is in their abstention from fasts and prayers during menstruation, is peculiar. Faḍlallāh argues that by refraining from prayer and fasts during menstruation, women are actually obeying God's legal commands. Moreover, he poses the question whether people's faith becomes reduced during travel, because according to Islamic law prayers should be shortened and fasts broken during travel.[48]

While the Qur'an accords spiritual equality between men and women, the *ḥadīth* is far from this because it often warns them of their situation in the hereafter. For example, in one tradition the Prophet urged a group of women to give alms as much as possible because most of them are the firewood of hell, the women objected reminding him of the good natured ones among them, this made the Prophet tender so he explained that were it not for the harm they cause their husbands, no prayerful woman would enter hell.[49] The position towards women shifted from being the firewood of hell to the assertion that no prayerful woman would enter hell, based solely on the women's attitude towards their husbands. On the other hand, the Prophet allegedly told women not to lengthen their prayers in order to hold back their husbands from their sexual rights, for such women are cursed by the angels.[50] When the traditions are brought together, it will be observed that their inner reasoning is not clear. If a woman lacks in faith and is doomed, it would be sensible to encourage her to increase her worship, particularly her prayer. However, the advice that these traditions give is that she does not cause harm to her husband and that she allows him sexual access. It is not specified here what kind of harm is supposed, nor is the character of each husband taken into consideration. What redeems women in any case, is their relationship with their husbands, not with other people or with God.

Therefore, while the Qur'an does not support the claim of women's deficient faith, and while the legal reasoning provided here is inconsistent, traditions tend to carry this point of view and break from the Qur'an when they put service to the husband before service to God.[51]

The claim about women's lack of fortune is not found in any of the other variations of this tradition. The lack in fortune is portrayed as a lack in oneself. This is very different from the Qur'anic point of view:

> So he went forth unto his people in his adornment. Those who desired the present life said, "Would that we possessed the like of that Korah has been given! Surely he is a man of mighty fortune (*ḥaẓẓin 'aẓīm*)". But those to whom knowledge had been given said, "Woe upon you! The reward of God is better for him who believes, and works righteousness; and none shall receive it except the steadfast".
>
> [28: 79–80]

As far as the legal aspect of this statement is concerned, a quick reading of the Qur'anic passage on inheritance would readily show that women's share being half of men's is only one possible situation within the very complicated inheritance laws. The proportion of two-to-one is the general rule, but not applicable in every situation [4: 11–12].[52] In addition to that, a tradition from

Imam al-Ṣādiq explains that women generally have a lesser share in inheritance because men have the extra responsibilities of financial support (*nafaqa*), *jihād*, and the payment of blood money (*diyya*).[53] According to this point of view, the men's larger share in inheritance is due to their larger spending responsibilities as well as their military *jihād*.[54] Therefore, it cannot be said that women are lacking in fortune because the lesser share in inheritance functions as part of a system that sees itself to be distributing the wealth and the responsibilities fairly. Moreover, wealth and fortune cannot be measured by inheritance alone. Khadīja was far wealthier than her husband, and Mary surprised Zechariah with the *rizq* that descended upon her as a young girl.

With the claim of men's greater intellectual capacity, the issue becomes more complicated because this idea has weight among many religious scholars (*'ulamā'*). In the previous chapters, it was shown that women in the Qur'an and *sunna* are often presented as intelligent. This is particularly the case with Bilqīs who is portrayed as having correctly calculated every step she took, political and religious, as well as Āsiyā who had a much better understanding of the message of the prophets than did her husband. Fāṭima is represented in the sources as having the mental capacity to grasp esoteric religious knowledge, which was not the case with men outside of *ahl al-bayt*, and she is portrayed to have possessed a profound understanding of politics and history, which enabled her to foresee the destiny of her nation.

One verse in the Qur'an may be seen to contend females' incapacity to engage in debate. The verse reads, "What, one who is reared amid ornaments and, in dispute cannot make himself plain?" [43: 18].[55] This verse is located within a passage that reproaches the pagan Arabs for claiming that the angels are females and that they are God's daughters instead of God's creatures and servants [43: 15–16, and 19]. The passage criticises the discrepancy between allocating female daughters to God, but when an Arab man is given tidings of what he had attributed to God, that is the birth of a daughter, his face darkens with suppressed sorrow and rage [43: 17]. The passage criticises their whole system of thought, especially that the angels are not material to be identified by either sex,[56] and that they look down on daughters but attribute them to God.[57] In this context of looking down on the female, the verse [43: 18] is located and the exegetes do understand it to be about women in general.[58] To them, woman is naturally more passionate and more compassionate, as she is less intellectual compared to man, and one sign of her powerful emotion is her love for ornaments and adornments, while she is weak in her intellect and therefore cannot provide effectual arguments.[59] Interestingly, an early tradition, even though not authenticated, does portray the verse as being applicable to men, when it is narrated in reference to Moses.[60] Indeed, despite the fact that the context of this verse is about females, its grammar is masculine which implies that it is not exclusive to females (*awa-man yunashsha'u fi-l-ḥilyati wa huwa fi-l-khiṣāmi ghayru mubī nin*). Most importantly, unlike the exegetes' understanding that this is woman's nature, the verse itself expresses nurture when it says that one, male or female, who is bred in ornaments cannot make himself clear in dispute.[61]

Imam 'Alī said, "Every container becomes narrow when it is filled, except for the container of knowledge, it becomes wider", in reference to the intellect (*'aql*).[62] Imam al-Ṣādiq, when asked whether a woman may perform the pilgrimage rites on behalf of a man he answered, "a woman may be more knowledgeable (*afqah*) than a man".[63]

These traditions assert that the intellect may grow when the mind is fed with knowledge, and when that happens, a woman may excel over a man. This is different from the contention of the main tradition being discussed here, which portrays a deterministic sense of women's inferior intellectual capacities, by utilising a tenet of Islamic law to draw conclusions about women's nature.

This brings the discussion to the legal aspect on women's intellect which is the Qur'anic verse on witnessing, where two female witnesses are required for every male, "that if one of the two women errs the other will remind her" [2: 282]. This verse, however, begins by advising believers to record their debt contracts.

Every other instance in which the Qur'an prescribes witnesses, it mentions the number of witnesses needed and their piety, but not their gender.[64] A tradition from Imam al-Ṣādiq narrates that 'Alī himself allowed the witnessing of two women alone in some cases, and when asked about the verse on two female witnesses as equal to one man, Imam al-Ṣādiq answered that this is in reference to the recording of debts.[65]

In modern times, it has again been argued that the verse in question "is the product of a specific context in which women were under-educated and did not normally engage in business. Consequently, if we no longer believe that a woman, or all women, will 'forget', there is no justification for the two women for one man rule, in debts or otherwise".[66]

The early and medieval Muslim scholars did not necessarily relate the witnessing verse with women's mental capacities. The testimony of women had been accepted by all Muslims in the narration of *ḥadīth*, which involves the very making of Islamic scripture.[67] Shams al-Dīn argues that there is absolutely no proof for women's incapacity to occupy the position of an Islamic judge for example, which is a bigger responsibility than witnessing. In fact, there is no consensus on the issue because there is no text or *sunna* regarding it. Any talk about manhood being a prerequisite in a judge, is based on the personal opinions of jurists, not on any solid grounds.[68]

If the verse on female witnesses is understood by traditions to be only in the recording of debts, and today it is being argued further that this given context is not necessarily applicable anymore, then what remains of the Imam's contention that women lack in intellect because their word in court counts for half a man's? Indeed, "The cultural evaluation of a woman was transmitted in some of the *ḥadīth* reports that were used to overcome the conditional denotation of the Qur'anic law of evidence".[69] Rather than allowing the law to make use of the Qur'anic contextualisation, this tradition uses the verse to make generalisations about women, at once fixing Islamic law and fixing "women's nature" into a comprehensive system, which then becomes very difficult to mend. This is a very important point that will be revisited below.

The tradition ends with the admonishment to be guarded from evil women and to be cautious of the good ones, and not to obey them in any thing they might demand.[70] Some have claimed that there is nothing wrong with this conclusion. They explain that it is only saying that people should be careful in their relationships, and that it is a valid advice to tell men not to grant women too much lest they get spoiled and start manipulating men's feelings and desires for their own personal advantage.[71] Shams al-Dīn finds that to ask men to disobey women's demands even when the demands are good is not reasonable and needs further interpretation. He suggests that the meaning is that goodness must be done regardless who demands it, whether it is a woman or a man, because these are not the source of *sharīʿa*. He adds that women must not be obeyed when they become autocratic in their opinions and powers, and this applies to men as well.[72] This opinion attempts to make sense of the tradition, but seems apologetic. It is a clear expression here that women in particular, not men, must not be obeyed in any matter, even the good. Faḍlallāh repeats that this is a sensible precaution so that women do not use all their powers over men, but adds that the Imam in another occasion warned one of fully trusting his brother for similar reasons to what Shams al-Dīn describes.[73] What would inhibit this otherwise helpful understanding is not just the context of the phrase within this tradition, but also a co-text where another tradition, perhaps realising the tension between such admonishments and the reports that the Prophet sometimes consulted his wives,[74] explains that he consulted them and then did the opposite of what they said.[75]

Some thoughts on the issue of intellect versus emotion

Conservative clerics tend to generalise that woman's emotional nature interferes in her affairs to the detriment of her intellect, and that is why she is incapable of anything more than child-rearing and household duties.[76] Shams al-Dīn argues differently. He says that experience has shown that women are not lesser than men in their intellectual capabilities. Therefore, he suggests that what is meant here is the role emotions play on most women in some situations, in addition to their occupation with household duties in most cases. He adds that if a woman has knowledge and experience then this does not affect her.[77]

The contemporary Persian mystically inclined scholar, Javādī Āmulī, provides several examples that indicate that the Qur'an and *ḥadīth* present the heart as more favourable than the intellect in matters of faith.[78] For example, he explains that the prophets in the Qur'anic narrative seem to have convinced their people of their message as far as the intellect was concerned, but the disbelievers were unable to allow their hearts to follow what they acknowledged in their heads, therefore their knowledge remained devoid of resolve.[79] Āmulī continues that according to the Qur'an, faith is precisely in the unity between the head and the heart.[80] He adds that discussions ought not to be about the size of the brain of each sex, because if a woman cries faster than a man, it is a signal that her heart is alive.[81]

One contemporary feminist discussing Western philosophy, which has systematically condemned the way of the heart and raised the way of the intellect that it attributed to the male, as the ultimate human achievement, says:

> even if the contention that women are emotional or more susceptible to compassion than men are is actually true, it does not prove that they do not reason but live on an animal-like level of subjective intuitions. And the corollary to this is that the desire to make loving kindness a cardinal virtue of morality ... does not mean that one is asking for a return to savagery. What it does mean is that the rationalist attempt to construe morality as a peculiarly masculine achievement, as one that depends on the subject-object dyad and on the suppression of feelings, is tantamount to the assertion that what we normally call goodness is something of which men must logically be incapable ... At any rate, to think that feelings are important and have their place only in human life is not to commit oneself to a denial of objectivity and the possibility of knowledge because, as we saw above (in the author's analysis of the compassionate behaviour of some female characters to be not out of selfish egoism but of moral wisdom), the notion of objectivity need not be restricted to those activities which are independent of feelings and emotions.[82]

One may elaborate on this that in *Ḥadīth Junūd al-'Aql*, compassion is recommended and contrasted with anger, as knowledge is contrasted with ignorance.[83] This poses the difficult and very pertinent question as to why "women's compassion" is considered an emotion in the first place, and why emotions such as anger, which, according to traditions, prevail in many men and divert away from reason and destroy faith,[84] are not included in discussions on women's emotions versus men's intellect.

"Women's deficiency" and Islamic law

The tradition discussed above claims that women are deficient in intellect and in faith, which are arguably two characteristics which define a human being and would make him or her a potential vicegerent of God on earth. It portrays women as naturally inferior and wretched creatures at every level of their being. Therefore, the woman here is presented as less than a full person. Some have passed by this narration very lightly. They would explain it away, saying for instance that it is only explaining legal issues, and that it is not really condemning women because it is saying that God has made them this way and therefore all these problems are beyond women's control.[85] According to that rationalisation, God has created women deficient and given them roles to fit their deficiency, so this seems reasonable and merciful. However, if other aspects of Islamic law were considered, it will be found that it does not treat women as inferiors as far as religious duties and the penal code are concerned. Particularly with regard to accountability for one's actions, the law has consideration for the circumstances of each individual who trespasses the limits, for example a married adulterer would get a bigger punishment than the non-married one, and an insane person is excused.[86] Following this precision in judgement, if women lack in faith and intellect, then it should follow that women should receive lesser punishments for the same crimes committed by men. This, however, is not the case.

One of the main problems with this tradition is that it uses some tenets of the law to draw conclusions about women, disregarding the historic and Qur'anic contexts of those tenets. Women are seen as lacking in faith, despite evidence to the contrary, based solely on the fact that they do not perform their religious rituals during menstruation. Herein lays the conundrum of setting nature against scripture. Women's deficiency in faith is explained at the biological level so that it is seen as predetermined, and the *sharī'a* is equally portrayed as immutable, so that women remain in this situation where their nature and scripture cause a constant strain. Women's lesser share in inheritance is explained as a lesser fortune, disregarding the situations when women get an equal share in inheritance, and more importantly, disregarding the economic system for which these shares were set, especially men's greater financial responsibilities towards women. Finally, women's lesser weight in testifying does not take into account the contextualisation of this verse and the example of Imam 'Alī himself, who took women's word in evidence. Therefore, rather than viewing legal tenets as depending on situational contexts and aiming at a just society for all its members, this tradition interprets them as pertaining to women's inherent deficiency. What might have been a situational law becomes a law that understates women's existence. This gives a pessimistic view of womanhood, and an equally pessimistic view of Islamic law:

> It should be noted that what might be called the "facts" of women's oppression – etc. – may be assimilated within a number of competing explanatory frameworks. The meaning adduced from such facts will differ depending upon the logic of explanation within which the facts are lodged. Facts are given meaning through their absorption into a conceptual framework.[87]

When the law is explained not as a result of a social system or a larger system of justice, but as a result of women's inherent deficiency, the meaning of these legal "facts" becomes oppressive to women. Faḍlallāh, who does try to explain the tradition, finds that if it had stopped at describing women as deficient in faith and intellect, one may have left it open for interpretation, however, the justifications of these premises are strange and refutable.[88]

Women as flowers to be secluded

Towards the end of his will to his son, Imam ʿAlī allegedly wrote a few lines about women:

> Do not consult women because their view is deficient and their determination feeble. Hold back their sight by keeping them behind the veil because strictness of veiling preserves them. Their going out is not more intense than your allowing an unreliable man to visit them. If you can manage that they not know anyone (meaning any strange man) other than yourself, do so. Do not give woman control over her affairs beyond those pertaining to her self, because woman is a fragrant flower not a subduer. Do not show excessive honour that would stretch beyond herself, and do not encourage her to intercede for others. Do not show jealousy out of place, for this invites the healthy woman to illness and the innocent woman to suspicion.[89]

It has been suggested that this being a will to his son, possibly also an Imam,[90] ʿAlī was giving advice not to common Muslims but for the leader not to put the affairs of the state under women's command.[91] The widespread interpretation for this, as it was also mentioned above with regard to not consulting women, is more generally understood in the sense of not allowing relatives to make use of a man's prominent position for personal gains. This however does not explain the rest of the tradition describing women's opinion and determination as feeble, which is similar to their weaker intellects described in the tradition above, and again widely understood to be contingent on women's level of education, particularly in the time this text was produced or uttered. For example, Shams al-Dīn observes that in another version of this tradition, the advice against consulting women is followed with the statement, "except for the one whose fullness of intellect has been tested."[92] To him, this particularisation of consulting only the capable women is more appropriate than claiming that they are all weak in intellect, which is not realistic.[93] Then, there is the issue of advising women's extreme seclusion, and disallowing them control over their own affairs, except what pertains directly to their person. If this tradition is to be understood as particularly the will of one Imam to another, it contradicts the example set by the women of *ahl al-bayt*, as described in the previous chapter. Fāṭima and Zaynab were shown to be, as far as Shīʿī sources are concerned, among the makers of Shīʿī identity and the preservers of the Prophet and Imams' religio-political legacies. Keeping women away from the Imams' political affairs is the direct opposite of what the renowned speeches of Fāṭima and Zaynab stand for, this is besides Khadīja's funding of the Prophet's early movement.

Shams al-Dīn considers the strict veiling of women prescribed here problematic, because juridical texts have proven that women's veiling is restricted to their modest dress, and that the decent mixing between men and women is allowed.[94] Moreover, he rejects the claim that a woman should not manage her own personal affairs, partly because this statement from *Nahj al-Balāgha* is not found in other variations of the tradition,[95] and partly because juridical texts prove that a mature woman is fully responsible for herself, and that she shares this responsibility with others in only two particular situations.[96]

While there is an agreement that women's seclusion is not an absolute requirement, some consider it a question of morality. Morteza Muṭahharī (d.1399/1979) the Iranian revolution ideologue,[97] understands this tradition to advise the total seclusion of women, but he adds that jurists do not find this obligatory for lack of evidence and indeed for the existence of evidence otherwise. Still, he insists that this tradition be accepted as a moral requirement even if it is not legal.[98] This, however, is a question of moral relativism. The "moral" seclusion of women is questionable from a religious point of view. As far as the Qur'an is concerned, keeping women inside their homes is a punishment for indecent action [4: 15].[99] Muṭahharī also understands the implications of this verse to be against the seclusion of women, but he tries to find middle ground when he adds that Islam allows neither the imprisonment of women nor their total interaction with men.[100] There is an inconsistency, however, between the Qur'an considering women's imprisonment as a punishment for indecent action, and the tradition's admonishment for the total seclusion of women as a moral procedure. What this reveals is an underlying mentality that women are guilty until proven innocent, because the act of punishment is advised for all women as a precautionary measure.

Another religious problem with this is best portrayed in another tradition, when Imam al-Ṣādiq said concerning a man who, despite the admonishment to study religion, preferred to stay in his house and did not meet his brethren, "How does this man understand his religion?!"[101] This implies that the seclusion of any person will be a hindrance from acquiring first-hand knowledge. From a feminist point of view this is equally problematic; "human beings need to live with and among others in relations of concrete particularity, in space, extending over and through time. If we are deprived of such relations we are damaged and distorted in body and spirit".[102]

Finally, the statements on seclusion to the extent that this tradition goes, that is to advise the man that, if possible, his women shall not know any man other than himself, is soon followed by the advice not to show jealousy out of place because this corrupts the good woman and makes the innocent one become doubtful. This is an inner contradiction within the text; if not allowing a woman to know any man is not jealousy out of place, then what is?

Some attention needs to be given to the comparison of "woman" to a fragrant flower (*al-mar'a rayḥāna wa laysat bi-qahrumāna*). Another version of this tradition says, "If you can manage that she does not control affairs beyond those pertaining to herself then do it, for this prolongs her beauty and affords her well-being … indeed woman is a flower, not a subduer/warden".[103] This has been understood to be referring to the wife in particular because women in general may be employed, but one's wife must not be made for service.[104] Of course, this is only helpful when women have the options available to them. Khadīja easily sets an example of both a career and family woman. However, this ḥadīth is pre-industrial, and even though it is not clear whether it is the outcome of a rural or urban setting, one cannot be certain that the delineation of an economy centred outside the home in jobs and professions is what is meant here.[105] This is doubtful to my mind, and it seems that the Imam may be referring to something else. After all, the statement declares that its concern here is women's well-being. Perhaps Imam 'Alī makes a significant point that excusing women from performing particular roles in the world has retained women's internal and external beauty. Still, not giving women any responsibility and limiting their experiences, also inhibits their maturity and growth. In the previous chapters, it was seen that women often took control of difficult situations, and then grew stronger with them. For example, Hagar was left alone in the desert to fend for herself and her child. Her very *sa'y*, however, was the reason that the water of Zamzam was sent to her. The mother of Moses had to decide for herself what to do with her child in the face of Pharaoh's oppression, and her acting upon the sign she received not only saved her son who was a messenger to the world, but it also strengthened her heart and her submission to God. Zaynab had to witness the massacre of her family, and then she was given the banner of *ahl al-bayt*, so to speak, in order to preserve their message. Without the suffering and the responsibility, it is doubtful that she would have been pictured as an altogether different calibre of spirit, the way she has been throughout the ages. The danger with this rhetoric and this genre of traditions more broadly, is that the women of this world become like *al-Ḥūr al-'Īn*, the women of the hereafter who are confined to their pavilions. These women belong to the realm of paradise, which is in every way different from the earthly realm. In view of the extreme seclusion that is advised, it seems to be the case that this dreamlike world, which is the promised reward for believing men in the hereafter, is being presently demanded of the women of this world.

Woman's *jihād* towards her husband

"Prayer is the *qurbān* (offering/means of access to God) of the pious, pilgrimage is the *jihād* (striving) of the feeble, and for everything there is a *zakāt* (levy); the *zakāt* of the body is fasting, and the *jihād* of woman is *ḥusn al-taba''ul*."[106]

The meaning of *ḥusn* ranges between seeming good, beautiful, comely, pleasing, conferring benefit upon someone, and acting graciously towards them. According to one lexicon, when *taba''ul* is said concerning a woman, its meanings include, taking a husband, being obedient to her husband, as well as adorning herself for him.[107] There are various sound traditions which indeed describe the good wife as one with physical and moral beauty, in addition to her obedience to her husband.[108] The meaning of taking a husband, however, is never emphasised.

The recommended personality of the wife is interpreted differently, often depending on the interpreter's understanding of the Qur'anic verse [4: 34]:

> Men are the managers of the affairs of women (*qawwāmūn 'ala al-nisā'*) for that God has preferred in bounty one of them over another (*bimā faḍḍala allāhu ba'ḍahum 'alā ba'ḍ*), and for that they have expended of their property (*wa bimā anfaqū min amwālihim*). Righteous women are therefore obedient (*qānitāt*), guarding the secret for God's guarding. And those you fear may be rebellious (*nushūzahunna*) admonish; banish them to their beds apart,[109] and beat them (*wa-ḍribūhunna*). If they then obey you (*fa-in aṭa'nakum*), look not for any way against them; God is All-high, All-great.

This verse is normally regarded as the most problematic for women, and its interpretation is not final.[110] While the patriarchal meaning of the verse remains near impossible to challenge, there are legitimate questions whether the *qiwāma* of men is applicable when the two conditions of *faḍl* and *nafaqa* cease to exist or are reversed, and whether the *nushūz* of wives means disobedience, and whether it is disobedience towards the husband or towards God. Azizah al-Hibri has pointed out the nuance in the verse that the *faḍl* is given to some men over some women and is therefore not for all men over all women as traditional exegesis maintained.[111] One difficulty with taking this argument further is that *faḍl* has not yet been clearly defined. Others have noticed that if the man does not support his family financially (*nafaqa*) which is a condition of his *qiwāma*, then he loses his status. Faḍlallāh, however, contends that even though the man may lose one aspect of his *qiwāma* if he is not the financial sustainer of his wife and family, the verse still accords him the degree of *faḍl* and therefore the *qiwāma* of men cannot be fully annulled nor reversed.[112] Moreover, while traditional exegesis usually understood women's *nushūz* as disobedience to the husband,[113] modern interpretations have observed that another verse which mentions the husband's *nushūz* is not taken to mean disobedience to his wife [4: 128].[114] Furthermore, if leaving the marital bed is what constitutes women's *nushūz*, as it is surprisingly vastly held,[115] then it would seem illogical that the retribution for this would be the man leaving his wife's bed. Some classical, but especially modern interpretations, tend to utilise the Prophetic statements on *nushūz* and *ḍarb* to make the verse less severe by pointing out the Prophet's identification of *nushūz* as a prohibited act or indecent behaviour (*fāḥisha mubīna*),[116] in addition to his extreme repugnance towards wife beating.[117] Ṭabāṭabā'ī, for example, lists the Prophetic traditions on honouring the wife and refusing her beating, and then without explicitly giving his opinion regarding the apparent contradiction between the Qur'anic verse and the Prophet's sentiments and example, he advises the reader to meditate on the traditions in order to understand Islam's position on the matter.[118] Classical exegetes based on the *sunna* context of the verse and its sequential retribution of the wife, understood it to be restricting male violence.[119]

It has been correctly pointed out that even though the verse shows a hierarchy between men and women, which may not be removed without doing violence to the text itself, it is also the case that the verse must not be read in isolation of scriptural and social contexts.[120] There are discrepancies for example between the *faḍl* men have over women in this verse [4: 34], and the mutual friendship/guardianship (*wilāya*) of men and women over each other in [9: 71].[121]

It may be pointed out that *ṭā'a* in Arabic does not only mean obedience, but also to consent, to act with effort, to act voluntarily, or to be capable of something.[122] The notion of total obedience to the husband does not take into consideration larger Shī'ī theology and *fiqh* which prohibit obedience to anyone other than an impeccable person.[123] In fact, those who restrict her obedience consider the Qur'anic description of the marital relationship as good (*ma'rūf*) [2: 228, and 4: 19] and tranquil (*sakan*) [7: 189, and 30: 21], to be incompatible with the notion of obedience.[124] This particular tradition on the woman's *jihād* as *ḥusn al-taba''ul*, is in this case understood as a recommendation for the wife to show her husband kindness, not because of a right that is due but out of graciousness.[125] In fact, an authentic variation of this tradition describes that the women's *jihād* which parallels the military one incumbent on the man, is for her to be patient with her husband's hurt and jealousy.[126] Put differently, the tradition points out to the wife that the marriage relationship is a struggle (*jihād*) to overcome petty issues, and service out of love even if it were not out of duty, in order to ensure closeness to God by providing a good family environment, just as one would perform optional prayers and serve other people not out of obligation but in seeking nearness to God.[127]

In an effort to understand "*jihād al-mar'a ḥusn al-taba''ul*" further, in the context of the *ḥadīth* literature, attention must be drawn to the two available "pools of meaning" in traditions about the marital relationship. The first category includes traditions which describe the wife as in complete servitude towards her husband. The second category includes traditions which speak of the man and woman's efforts towards creating a peaceful and prosperous home environment.

In the first group, the woman is portrayed as submissive and that the husband's needed approval (*riḍā*) is a result of her obedience.[128] Other weaker traditions claim that a woman serving water to her husband qualifies her entry to paradise, and is better for her in the afterlife than prayers and fasts.[129] While these are considered weak, they are sometimes taken to represent that it is recommended for the wife to serve her husband. Shams al-Dīn, however, felt that they might have been forged traditions and was very wary of their message.[130] Such traditions reduce the woman's capacities and role in life to the menial service of the husband. Her relationship with God becomes indirect and mediated by her husband, thereby reducing her to a sub-human level.

It is perhaps in this context that one can understand the following authenticated tradition. When a woman came to the Prophet and asked about the wife's marital obligations, he repeated what has been discussed above, such as her obedience, allowing her husband sexual access even if she were on the back of a camel, that she does not leave the house without his permission, and so on. So the woman asked, "Do I not have the same rights over him as he does over me?", the Prophet answered, "No, and not even in a proportion of one to a hundred", so the woman answered, "I swear by the One who sent you as a Prophet of Truth, no man shall ever own me (*lā yamliku raqbatī rajulun abadan*)".[131] The tradition ends here. Irrespective of the legal issues on marital duties it raises, it seems abrupt. If the Prophet sang the praises of marriage and recommended it as his *sunna* as other traditions report,[132] one wonders why he did not in this instance try to persuade this woman of the benefits of marriage after he had dissuaded her from it. According to Khaled Abou El Fadl, who finds that the *ḥadīth* literature poses the intriguing problem of "multiple authorship":

> These traditions and their counter-traditions are indicative of the vibrant negotiative process that took place in early Islam – a process that most certainly included the re-definition of gender relations ... The responses of the women who refuse the institution of marriage altogether can be read as a protest against the patriarchal religious dogma that places women in a submissive and degrading position. The symbolism of these reports conveys a compelling message: if need be, women will just have to do without men.[133]

The second available pool of meaning regarding marital relationships is mutual kindness, rather than unilateral obedience, within the home environment. One tradition confirms that "The one (masculine) who toils for the sake of his family/household, is the same as the one who fights the *jihād* in the path of God".[134] In other authentic traditions, the care for daughters in particular brings rewards and paradise closer.[135] Such traditions show that a man's care for his family is also akin to fighting the *jihād*. Wadud's reading of woman's place in the Qur'an understands that, "The family acts as the initial arena of practice. Surely, as the Prophet says, 'The best of you is he who is best to his family'".[136]

It may be argued that the traditions are not entirely reciprocal, because the man's *jihād* is towards his dependents in general, whereas the woman's *jihād* is specifically towards her husband. However, it is also the case that men's family responsibilities are legally prescribed duties, and the husbands' duty of kindness (*iḥsān*) towards their wives is already stipulated in the Qur'an [2: 228].[137] On the other hand, women's domestic roles are not required by law, perhaps this is because Islam wants women's particular role to be performed out of a spirit of giving, not under obligation.[138] According to this point of view, the tradition discusses the marital relationship because it is here that there might be trouble and where the woman might not wish to be kind.

The first group of traditions then understands obedience as absolute, and reflects on [4: 34] thus. The second group of traditions procures a family environment of servitude among its members. This understands the wife's obedience being towards God primarily, and to her husband in so far as God's law gives the husband certain rights, as it gives the wife certain rights as well. This tradition on woman's *jihād* seems less harsh than [4: 34] in that it asks of the woman *ḥusn* rather than *ṭā'a*, and in that it describes this not as an obligation, but a beautiful struggle. This tradition is not incompatible with the Qur'an and might shed new light on the interpretation of verse [4: 34].

More importantly for the purpose of this study, it has been argued in the previous chapters that the Qur'an and *sunna* portray female personalities as primarily concerned with spiritual *jihad* as well as political *jihād*. This tradition about woman's *jihād* as *ḥusn al-taba''ul* might lead some to believe that this is her only *jihād*.[139] This however would be incompatible with the detailed depiction of the *jihād* of virtually every female personality of the Qur'an and *sunna* that has been discussed throughout this book. Yet, this tradition need not be seen as incompatible with those examples; rather it is referring in particular to the physical exertion aspect of military *jihād*, in its variants, and when it affirms that pilgrimage is the *jihād* of the feeble. Therefore, the tradition does not mean that women ought not to perform the *jihād* in its social and cultural aspects, but it aims at elevating women's domestic role by making its reward equivalent to that of men's *jihād*.[140] The spiritual and earthly *jihād* of the female personalities offer women indisputable models of actualising women's potential outside the domain of the family.

Women-friendly traditions in the "Four Books"

There are a few authentic traditions which exalt women and which might seem to oppose the general tone of the *ḥadīth*. For example, one authentic tradition states, "Among the morals/disposition of prophets, is the love for women",[141] and another one similarly finds that love for women increases when faith increases.[142] In other traditions the Prophet says, "I love nothing of your world, except women and perfume",[143] or, "(God) made the relief of my eyes in prayer, and my pleasure in women".[144]

One problem with this trend is the explicit contradiction it poses to other more numerous traditions on women's inferiority. For example, while many traditions speak of the rarity of the good believing women, that most of them are doomed to hell, and that women and anger are the army of Satan,[145] one authentic tradition claims that, "Most goodness is in women".[146] The fact that this tradition stands alone in view of the more pessimistic ones, makes it difficult to take it at face value.

For argument's sake, if their inferior mind is not necessarily incompatible with the prophets' love for women, let's say due to their heart. The incompatibility between traditions that warn of women's inferior faith, and then a few others elevating women to the extent that love for them becomes a measure of a man's faith, is difficult to fathom.

There is every possibility that a meaning which is not made clear may be retrieved from those traditions, but if one were to accept what was proposed above, on the *ḥadīth* literature being a space where negotiations on gender were being made, the question becomes whether these positive-toned traditions are a part of that negotiation process? Moreover, if these positive traditions are not genuine, then are they consolatory?

What is a commonly problematic feature of all traditions, negative and positive, is that they constantly group women together, as though assuming that women have no individuality. It has been shown in the verses [66: 10–12] that the Qur'an offers two women as negative examples and two as positive role-models for all people. It was argued that this group of verses portrays women as human without showing any tendency to abase them or elevate them as a group, but presents individual female personalities as negative and positive models for men and women together. The *ḥadīth* literature, on the other hand, often speaks of woman in the singular or generalises about women in the plural, in a manner which it does not do with men as a gender. Where the Qur'an assumes women's common humanity and therefore their separate individualities, the *ḥadīth* literature seems to assume that women are a category that is separate from men, even in basic matters which the Qur'an teaches are universally human issues pertaining to the human *nafs*.

Conclusions

It has been explained in the introduction to this chapter that any authentication process of the *ḥadīth* must apply each tradition to the Qur'an and *sunna*. This has been done here in a limited capacity and in direct relation to the Qur'anic verses and *sunna* traditions which have already been analysed in the previous chapters. It would require another study to compare and contrast Imam 'Alī's particularly harsh statements on woman/women in *Nahj al-Balāgha*, with his renowned leniency towards women in his jurisprudence and daily life. Several authors have pointed out details of his compassionate attitude towards women:[147]

> Stories of 'Ali's sympathy for female victims of unfortunate circumstances or malicious oppression indicates another thread running throughout the Shi'ite perspective on women – namely, an intrinsic sympathy for, and even identification with, the oppressed and helpless members of society.[148]

Therefore, a comparison of the Imam's reported words and his reported actions is necessary before reaching any conclusions about his views on women.

In any case, these traditions were picked as representatives of the *ḥadīth* literature at large, in its perception and portrayal of women. Not all traditions can or need be dismissed due to the complicated issues of context and varying texts. Most of these traditions are descriptive of women, and prescriptive of men's attitude towards them, but for this reason they may be seen as self-fulfilling prophecies. The examples of female personalities in the Qur'an and *sunna* counter these deterministic prophecies and offer one way out of the loop.

Notes

1 Lane, E.W. (n.d.) *Arabic-English lexicon* [online]. Available from: www.studyquran.co.uk/PRLonline.htm: *ḥ-d-th*.
2 Denny, F.M. (1993) "Islam: Qur'an and hadith". In Denny, F.M. and Taylor, R.L. (eds) *The Holy Book in comparative perspective*. Columbia: University of South Carolina Pres, p. 99.
3 Denny (1993, p. 104).
4 About the twentieth century debate around *ḥadīth*, refer to: Brown, D.W. (1996) *Rethinking tradition in modern Islamic thought*. Cambridge: Cambridge University Press.
5 Refer to the Qur'anic verses [8:20], [3:21], and [59:7].
6 Azami, M.M. (1992) *Studies in early hadith literature*. Indianapolis: American Trust Publications, pp. 18–60. Also, Azami (1992, pp. 8–15) on some orientalist misconceptions of this literature.
7 Brown (1996, p. 40).
8 Dutton, Y. (1999) *The origins of Islamic law: the Qur'an, the muwatta' and madinan 'amal*. Richmond: Curzon, pp. 168–9).
9 Dutton (1999, p. 173).
10 Such as *'ilm al-rijāl*, or knowledge of the men and women transmitters of *ḥadīth*, particularly their piety, the times they lived in, and whether it is likely that they met the persons preceding and following them in the "chain of transmitters".
11 Graham, W.A. (1977) *Divine word and prophetic word in early Islam*. The Hague: Mouton Publishers, p. 14.
12 Shī'ī *ḥadīth* and therefore also its apostolic age stretch over a period of two centuries. The sayings of the Imams are not only a continuation of the Prophet's, but also a kind of commentary and elucidation of prophetic traditions, "often with the aim of bringing out the esoteric teachings of Islam" (Ṭabāṭabā'ī, M.H. (1980) *A Shi'ite anthology*. London: Muhammadi Trust of Great Britain & Northern Ireland, pp. 6–7).
13 al-Kulaynī, Muḥammad Ibn Ya'qūb (1388h) *al-Kāfī*. 3rd edn. 8 volumes. Tehran: Dār al-Kutub al-Islāmiyya, vol. 1, p. 53.
14 Amir-Moezzi, M.A. (1994) *The divine guide in early Shi'ism*. New York: State University of New York Press, p. 24.
15 Amir-Moezzi (1994, pp. 25–6).
16 Kulaynī (1388h, vol. 1, p. 69).
17 al-Raḍī, al-Sharīf; Muḥammad Ibn al-Ḥusayn (n.d.c) *Nahj al-balāgha*. 4 volumes. Beirut: Dār al-Ma'rifa, vol. 3, p. 136, in his instruction to Ibn al-'Abbās' altercation with the *Khawārij*.

18 Amir-Moezzi (1994, pp. 27–8). The four books are: al-Kulaynī, Muḥammad Ibn Ya'qūb (1388h) *al-Kāfī*. 3rd edn. 8 volumes. Tehran: Dār al-Kutub al-Islāmiyya. al-Ṣadūq, Muḥammad Ibn 'Alī Ibn Bbāawayh (1404ha) *Man la yaḥḍuruhū al-faqī h*. 2nd edn. 4 volumes. Qum: Jāmi'at al-Mudarrisīn. al-Ṭūsī, Muḥammad Ibn Ḥasan (1390hb) *Tahdhīb al-aḥkām*. 10 volumes. Tehran: Dār al-Kutub al-Islāmiyya, and al-Ṭūsī, Muḥammad Ibn Ḥasan (1390ha) *al-Istibṣār*. 4th edn. 4 volumes. Tehran: Dār al-Kutub al-Islāmiyya. On the "four books", also refer to: Newman, A.J. (2000) *The formative period of Twelver Shi'ism: hadith as discourse between Qum and Baghdad*. London: Routledge. Newman, A.J. (2013) *Twelver Shi'ism: unity and diversity in the life of Islam, 632 to 1722*. Edinburgh: Edinburgh University Press.

19 Refer to Kohlberg, E. (1987) "al-Uṣūl al-arba'umi'a". *Jerusalem Studies in Arabic and Islam*, 10: 128–66.

20 It has been translated as "The Peak of Eloquence" in the book's translation edited by Yasin T. al-Jiboury (al-Raḍī, Sh. (1996) *Peak of eloquence*. 7th edn. New York: Tahrike Tarsile Qur'an. Translated by Y.T. Jibouri).

21 On this subject, refer to: Qutbuddin, T. (2012) "The sermons of 'Alī Ibn Abī Ṭāleb: at the confluence of the core Islamic teachings of the Qur'an and the oral, nature-based cultural ethos of seventh century Arabia". *Anuario de Estudios Medievales*, 42 (1): 201–28.

22 Djebli, M. "Nahdj al-Balāgha". *Encyclopaedia of Islam, Second edition*. Edited by: P. Bearman, Th. Bianquis, C.E. Bosworth, E. van Donzel, and W.P. Heinrichs. Brill online, 2014 [Accessed 20.02.2014].

23 Ṭabāṭabā'ī (1980, p. 9). Muḥammad Mahdī Shams al-Dīn investigated the issue of its sources, and explained that al-Raḍī only included in the book, sayings and writings by 'Alī which he deemed of significant literary value, and he (Shams al-Dīn) wished that more of 'Alī's sayings were included in the book to give further insight into the Imam's thought (Shams al-Dīn, Muḥammad Mahdī (1972) *Dirāsāt fī nahj al-balāgha*. 2nd edn. Beirut: Dār al-Zahrā', pp. 18 and 46).

24 Roald, A.S. (1998) "Feminist reinterpretation of Islamic sources: Muslim feminist theology in the light of the Christian tradition of feminist thought". In Ask, K. and Tjomsland, M. (eds) *Women and Islamization: contemporary dimensions of discourse on gender relations*. Oxford International Publishers, p. 27.

25 Wadud, A. (2006) *Inside the gender Jihad: women's reform in Islam*. Oxford: Oneworld Publications, p. 7.

26 For example, some legal issues normally favoured by women such as the unreserved permissibility of birth control and the conditional permissibility of abortion, are explicitly available in the *ḥadīth* (Kulaynī, 1388h, vol. 5, p. 504).

27 For example: Mubarak, H. (2004) "Breaking the interpretive monopoly: a re-examination of verse 4:34". *Hawwa*, 2: 276, where she notes the irony of feminists rejecting the *ḥadīth* despite its utmost usefulness in the most problematic verse in the Qur'an, and Mahmoud, M. (2006) "To beat or not to beat: on the exegetical dilemmas over Qur'an 4:34". *Journal of the American Oriental Society*, 126: 537–50.

28 Raḍī (n.d.c, vol. 4, p. 53). Also note that while the word used here (*sharr*) means evil, similar words to this have more positive meanings, such as *sharar* meaning a spark of fire, and *sharir* meaning riverside or seaside (Lane, n.d.).

29 Raḍī (n.d.c, vol. 4, p. 52), "The best traits of women are those which are the worst traits of men, namely: vanity, cowardice and miserliness. Thus, since the woman is vain, she will not allow anyone access to herself; since she is miserly, she will preserve her own property and the property of her husband; and since she is weak-hearted, she will be frightened with everything that befalls/is presented to her."

30 Subaytī, Yūsuf 'Alī (2006) *Nahj al-balāghah: fī dā'irat al-tashkīk?!* Beirut: Dār al-Hādī, pp. 188–9.

31 Faḍlallāh, Muḥammad Ḥusayn (1998) *Dunyā al-mar'a*. Beirut: Dār al-Malak, pp. 40–1.
32 al-Ṭūsī, Muḥammad Ibn Ḥasan (1409h) *al-Tibyān fī tafsīr al-Qur'ān*. 10 volumes. Qum: Maktab al-I'lām al-Islāmī, vol. 10, p. 24.
33 al-Ṭabāṭabā'ī, Muḥammad Ḥusayn (1402h) *al-Mīzān fī tafsīr al-Qur'ān*. 20 volumes. Qum: Mu'assasat al-Nashr al-Islāmī, vol. 15, pp. 288–9.
34 Ṭabāṭabā'ī (1402h, vol. 13, pp. 318–19).
35 Raḍī (n.d.c, vol. 3, pp. 73–4) and Raḍī (n.d.c, vol. 4, pp. 16–17).
36 Raḍī (n.d.c, vol. 4, pp. 31–2).
37 al-Majlisī, Muḥammad Bāqir (1403h) *Biḥār al-anwār*. Beirut: Mu'assasat al-Wafā', vol. 70, p. 241. The translation of "*lillāhi darru*" is from Lane (n.d.): *d-r-r*.
38 The description of traditions as aphoristic due to the problematic lack of context is borrowed from Rahman, F. (1965) *Islamic methodology in history*. Pakistan: Central Institute of Islamic Research, p. 76.
39 Ricoeur, P. (1981) *Hermeneutics and the human sciences: essays on language, action and interpretation*. Cambridge: Cambridge University Press, p. 174.
40 Raḍī (n.d.c, vol. 1, p. 129). This particular version of the tradition is graded "*mursal*", and therefore not entirely reliable (Shams al-Dīn, Muḥammad Mahdī (1995) *Ahliyyat al-mar'a li tawallī al-sulṭa*. Beirut: al-Mu'assasa al-Duwaliyya li al-Dirāsat wa al-Nashr, p. 101). A simplified version of the first part, particularly women as deficient in faith and intellect (*nāqiṣāt 'aql wa dīn*) is reported by al-Bukhārī, Muḥammad Ibn Ismā'īl (1401h) *al-Ṣaḥīḥ*. 8 volumes. Beirut: Dār al-Fikr, vol. 1, p. 78, and vol. 2, p. 126, where the occasion is recorded as the holiday (*'īd*) of either *Fiṭr* or *Aḍḥa*. This helped some to speculate that the Prophet was merely joking. Khaled Abou El Fadl sensibly rejected this opinion as implausible in Abou El Fadl, Kh. (2003) *Speaking in God's name: Islamic law, authority and women*. Oxford: Oneworld, p. 229.
41 Hitti, P.K. (1970) *History of the Arabs*. 10th edn. London: Macmillan, pp. 179–80.
42 Bukhārī (1401h, vol. 5, p. 136, and vol. 8, p. 97). The *sanad* of the tradition (*Mā aflaḥa qawmun wallū amrahum imra'a*) and the time it appeared are analysed thoroughly in: Mernissi, F. (1991) *The veil and the male elite: a feminist interpretation of women's rights in Islam*. Reading, MA: Addison-Wesley. Translated by M. J. Lakeland (1991).
43 Shams al-Dīn (1995, p. 102).
44 Shams al-Dīn (1995, p. 103).
45 Shams al-Dīn (1995, p. 103).
46 Also [4: 124], [9: 72], [16: 97], [24: 12], [33: 58, 73], [40: 40], [47: 19], [48: 5], [57: 12], [71: 28], [85: 10].
47 Ibn Hishām, 'Abd al-Malik (1383h) *Sīrat al-Nabī*. 4 volumes. Cairo: Maktabat Muḥammad 'Alī Ṣabīḥ, vol. 3, p. 789.
48 Faḍlallāh, Muḥammad Ḥusayn (2005) *Ta'ammulāt Islāmiyya ḥawl al-mar'a*. Beirut: Dār al-Malāk, p. 43.
49 Kulaynī (1388h, vol. 5, p. 514).
50 Kulaynī (1388h, vol. 5, pp. 508–9). Similarly, some traditions report that women are not allowed to fast voluntarily except with their husbands' consent, nor are they allowed to perform the pilgrimage on someone's behalf even if it were from their own money, except with their husband's consent (Kulaynī, 1388h, vol. 4, p. 151, vol. 5, p. 516).
51 Refer to: Abou El Fadl (2003, pp. 213–14 and pp. 218–22).
52 Nimr, R. (1996) "Women in Islamic law". In Yamani, M. (ed.) *Feminism and Islam: legal and literary perspectives*. London: Ithaca, p. 100. Wadud-Muhsin, A. (1994) *Qur'an and woman*. Kuala Lumpur: Penerbit Fajar Bakti, p. 87.
53 Kulaynī (1388h, vol. 7, p. 85).

54 Faḍlallāh (1998, p. 42). Nimr has made a similar observation on the Islamic system of inheritance in general in Nimr (1996, p. 100). This point of view as expressed in the *ḥadīth* of al-Ṣādiq does not take into account the economic realities of modern life where many women are also breadwinners. The *ijtihād* regarding this is a strictly legal issue and therefore outside the scope of this discussion.
55 The second part of the verse, following the "and", is borrowed from Pickthall because Arberry's translation, "when the time of altercation comes, is not to be seen", is not accurate in the context.
56 Ṭabāṭabā'ī (1402h, vol. 18, pp. 90–1).
57 Ṭabāṭabā'ī (1402h, vol. 18, pp. 89–90).
58 Ṭūsī (1409h, vol. 9, pp. 189–90).
59 Ṭabāṭabā'ī (1402h, vol. 18, p. 90).
60 al-Qummī, 'Alī Ibn Ibrāhīm (1404h) *Tafsīr al-Qur'ān*. 3rd edn. 2 volumes. Qum: Mu'assasat Dār al-Kitāb, vol. 2, pp. 282–3. al-Ḥuwayzī, 'Abd 'Alī Ibn Jumu'a al-'Arūsī (1412h) *Nūr al-thaqalayn*. 4th edn. 5 volumes. Qum: Mu'assasat Isma'ilyān, vol. 4, p. 595.
61 This is the opinion of Shams al-Dīn (1995, p. 74) and Faḍlallāh (2005, pp. 17–20), who both understand this verse to be primarily about women's nurture rather than nature, even though they do not observe that it is grammatically masculine and therefore they do not extend this potential condition to males.
62 Raḍī (n.d.c, vol. 4, p. 47).
63 Kulaynī (1388h, vol. 4, p. 306).
64 Four witnesses are needed in cases of adultery [24: 4, 6, 13], two just witnesses are needed to observe a dying person's will [5: 106], and the same for divorce [65: 2], and two judges who are just are needed to settle hunting trespasses [5: 95]. In none of these is the gender of the witness or judge mentioned. Moreover, the incident when Imam 'Alī and Fāṭima went to the caliph demanding Fadak to be returned to Fāṭima is relevant here. It is reported that they took with them Umm Ayman to witness, along with 'Alī. Their testimony was refused on the grounds that 'Ali is Fāṭima's husband and would naturally have inclined to her, and that the word of Umm Ayman alone was not enough. Shī'ī jurisprudence considers Imam 'Ali the most knowledgeable of the law, and his rulings are binding. Therefore, had he considered the word of one woman inadmissible, he would not have gone to the caliph with that set-up.
65 Ḥuwayzī (1412h, vol. 1, p. 300).
66 Abou El Fadl (2003, pp. 157–8). Contextualising the verse is also the opinion of Fazlur Rahman in Wadud (1994, p. 85).
67 al-Khū'ī, Abū al-Qāsim Ibn 'Alī Akbar (1413h) *Mu'jam rijāl al-ḥadīth*. 5th edn. 24 volumes. Qum: Lajnat Taḥqīq Turāth al-Shaykh al-A'ẓam, vol. 24; this volume is dedicated in its entirety to female transmitters of *ḥadīth* (*muḥaddithāt*). For a contemporary study on the *muḥaddithāt*, refer to: Naeeni, N. Gh. (2011) *Shi'ah women transmitters of hadith: a collection of biographies of the women who transmitted traditions*. Qum: Ansarian. Translated by G. Babst.
68 Shams al-Dīn (1995, pp. 117–23).
69 Sachedina, A. (2000) "Woman, half-the-man? The crisis of male epistemology in Islamic jurisprudence". In Daftary, F. (ed.) *Intellectual traditions in Islam*. London: I.B. Tauris, p. 172.
70 An authentic tradition reports almost identical words attributed to the Prophet (Kulaynī, 1388h, vol. 5, pp. 516–17). Some traditions contextualise this, either explaining it to be concerning women's modesty so that the man does not allow them to go out excessively or to wear thin clothes, or that women must not be obeyed when they intercede (wrongly) for the benefit of their relatives.
71 Subaytī (2006, pp. 226–7).
72 Shams al-Dīn (1995, pp. 103–4), where he considers the *sanad* authentic.

73 Faḍlallāh (1998, pp. 43–4), based on the tradition in Ibn Abī al-Ḥadīd, al-Mu'tazilī, Izz al-Dīn Ibn Hibatallāh (n.d.) *Sharḥ nahj al-balāghah*. 20 volumes. Cairo: Dār Ihyā' al-Kutub al-'Arabiyya, vol. 20, p. 314.
74 For example, his consulting Umm Salama at the Ḥudaybiyya when some Muslims were not obeying him (Ziyāda, Asmā' Aḥmad Muḥammad (2001) *Dawr al-mar'a al-siyāsī fī 'ahd al-nabī wa al-khulafā' al-rashidīn: wa bihā taḥqīq tārīkhī wa fiqhī wa tashrī'ī li fahm dawr al-sayyidah 'Ā'isha fī aḥdāth al-fitna*. Cairo: Dār al-Salām, p. 249).
75 Kulaynī (1388h, vol. 5, pp. 517–18).
76 *Tafsīr* and *fiqh* literature are replete with this argument, for a typical case which seems airtight through its use of the Qur'an and traditions, refer to: al-Ṭahrānī, Muḥammad al-Ḥusayn al-Ḥasanī (1993) *Qaḍā' wa jihād wa ḥukūmat al-mar'a: risāla badī'a*. Beirut: Dār al-Maḥabba al-Baydā'.
77 Shams al-Dīn (1995, p. 106).
78 Āmulī, Javādī (1994) *al-Mar'a fī al-'irfān*. Beirut: Dar al-Tayyār al-Jadīd, pp. 51–4.
79 Āmulī (1994, pp. 55–9).
80 Āmulī (1994, pp. 59–63).
81 Āmulī (1994, p. 68).
82 McMillan, C. (1982) *Women, reason and nature: some philosophical problems with feminism*. Oxford: Basil Blackwell, p. 28. Faḍlallāh makes a similar point, that heightened emotions in women do not necessarily denote lesser intellect (Faḍlallāh, 1998, p. 42).
83 Kulaynī (1388h, vol. 1, p. 21).
84 Kulaynī (1388h, vol. 2, pp. 300–5).
85 Subaytī (2006, p. 212).
86 Kulaynī (1388h, vol. 7, p. 265).
87 Fiorenza, E.S. (1993) *Discipleship of equals: a critical feminist ecclesialogy of liberation*. London: SCM, p. 205.
88 Faḍlallāh (1998, p. 42).
89 Raḍī (n.d.c, vol. 3, pp. 56–7). This version is graded "*mursal*" and therefore not binding, and other versions are weak (*ḍa'īf*) (Shams al-Dīn, 1995, p. 96).
90 It is not known whether this was 'Alī's will to al-Ḥasan, an Imam, or Muḥammad Ibn al-Ḥanafiyya, not an Imam.
91 Subaytī (2006, pp. 209–10).
92 Majlisī (1403h, vol. 100, p. 253).
93 Shams al-Dīn (1995, pp. 94–7). This is the opinion of the majority of the tradition's interpreters.
94 Shams al-Dīn (1995, p. 97). For his views on the extent of women's modest dress, refer to: Shams al-Dīn (1994).
95 Refer to Kulaynī (1388h, vol. 5, pp. 337–8) and Ṣadūq (1404ha, vol. 4, p. 392).
96 These are consulting her father about her marriage if she were a virgin (previously unmarried), and allowing her husband sexual access if she were married (Shams al-Dīn, 1995, pp. 97–8).
97 For some insight into his thought and influence, refer to: Farzaneh, M.M. (2008) "The political thought of Ayatullah Murtaza Mutahhari: an Iranian theoretician of the Islamic state". *International Journal of Middle East Studies*, 40 (4): 689–90. Lafraie, N. (2009) *Revolutionary ideology and Islamic militancy: the Iranian revolution and interpretations of the Qur'an*. London: Taurus Academic Studies.
98 Muṭahharī, Morteza (1987) *Mas'alat al-ḥijāb*. Beirut: al-Dār al-Islāmiyya, pp. 154–7.
99 This is normally understood to have been erased by the later stoning verse [24: 2]. However, people who reject such understanding of *naskh*, argue that imprisonment is for indecency whereas stoning is for proven adultery (Abou El Fadl, Kh. (2001) *Conference of the books: the search for beauty in Islam*. Lanham: University Press of America, pp. 172–3).

100 Muṭahharī (1987, p. 157).
101 Kulaynī (1388h, vol. 1, p. 31), this has been interpreted to mean that acquiring knowledge requires continuous meetings with those who have knowledge and posing questions (Māzandarānī, Muḥammad Ṣāliḥ (2000) *Sharḥ uṣūl al-kāfī*. 12 volumes. Beirut: Dār Iḥyā' al-Turāth al-'Arabī, vol. 2, pp. 18–19).
102 Elshtain, J.B. (1981) *Public man, private woman*. Oxford: Robertson, p. 318.
103 Ṣadūq (1404ha, vol. 3, p. 556). For the meaning of *qahrumān*, refer to: Ibn Manẓūr (1405h, vol. 12, p. 496).
104 Shams al-Dīn, Muḥammad Mahdī (1996b) *Ḥuqūq al-zawjiyya*. Beirut: al-Mu'assasa al-Duwaliyya li al-Dirāsāt wa al-Nashr, p. 114, and Shams al-Dīn (1995, p. 88).
105 For an overview of the topic of women's work and the effects of industrialisation, refer to: Ruether, R.R. (1975) "Home and work: women's roles and the transformation of values". *Theological Studies*. December 1975, pp. 647–59. Available from: www.ts.mu.edu/readers/content/pdf/36/36.4/36.4.4.pdf [Accessed 20.02.2014].
106 Raḍī (n.d.c, vol. 4, p. 34). Kulaynī's version of this tradition in *al-Kāfī* is graded weak (*ḍa'īf*) and therefore unreliable (Shams al-Dīn, 1996b, pp. 53–4). A similar tradition is attributed to the Prophet in Sunnī sources (Ziyāda, 2001, pp. 218–19).
107 Lane (n.d.): *b-'-l*.
108 For example: Kulaynī (1388h, vol. 5, p. 327).
109 This phrase from Pickthall is closer to the Arabic than Arberry's "to their couches".
110 For some summaries of the traditional exegeses point of view on this verse as well as modern feminist efforts towards a more egalitarian understanding, refer to: Wadud (1994, pp. 66–78). Stowasser, B. (1998) "Gender issues and contemporary Qur'an interpretation". In Haddad, Y.Y. and Esposito, J.L. (eds) *Islam, gender, and social change*. New York: Oxford University Press, pp. 30–44. Shaikh, S. (1997) "Exegetical violence: nushuz in Qur'anic gender ideology". *Journal for Islamic Studies*, 17: 49–73. Faruqi, M.J. (2000) "Women's self-identity in the Qur'an and Islamic law". In Webb, G. (ed.) *Windows of faith: Muslim women scholar-activists in North America*. New York: Syracuse University Press, pp. 77–101. Mubarak (2004, pp. 261–89). Rispler-Chaim, V. (1992) "Nusuz between medieval and contemporary Islamic law: the human rights aspect". *Arabica*, 39: 315–27. Mahmoud (2006, pp. 537–50). Scott, R.M. (2009) "A contextual approach to women's rights in the Qur'an: readings of 4:34". *The Muslim World*, 99: 60–85. Ali, K. *Muslim sexual ethics: understanding a difficult verse, Qur'an 4:34*. Available from: www.brandeis.edu/projects/fse/muslim/mus-essays/mus-ess-diffverse.html [Accessed 18.07.2011]. Ibrahim, N. and Abdalla, M. (2010) "A critical examination of Qur'an 4:34 and its relevance to intimate partner violence in Muslim families". *Journal of Muslim Mental Health*, 5: 327–49. For a radical reinterpretation of the verse, well worth reading, refer to: Abou el-Fadl (2001, pp. 167–88).
111 Hibri, A. (1982) *Women and Islam*. Oxford: Pergamon, p. 218.
112 Faḍlallāh, Muḥammad Ḥusayn (1986) *Min waḥy al-Qur'ān*. Beirut: Dār al-Zahrā', vol. 7, pp. 154–5.
113 Ṭūsī (1409h, vol. 3, pp. 188–91), al-Ṭabrisī, Faḍl Ibn Ḥasan (1415h) *Majma' al-Bayān*. 10 volumes. Beirut: Mu'assasat al-A'lamī (1415h, vol. 3, pp. 77–80), and Ṭabāṭabā'ī (1402h, vol. 4, pp. 343–52), and all understand the retribution as sequential.
114 For example: Mubarak (2004, p. 273). Riīspler-Chaim (1992).
115 This is the opinion of the earliest exegetes, and is the predominant view of classical jurists, that *nushūz* is primarily the wife leaving the marital bed. For example: Qummī (1404h, vol. 1, p. 137). For Shams al-Dīn, cohabitation and sexual gratification as a unit, is the only duty the wife has towards her husband (Shams al-Dīn, 1996b, pp. 28–42 and 65–6). However, the *ḥadīth* describes women's

abstinence as *makrūh*, not as *nushūz* (Kulaynī, 1388h, vol. 5, pp. 508–9). Rispler-Chaim (1992) finds that this has been the main definition of *nushūz*, and that the list of what constitutes *nushūz* is growing in the modern period.

116 *Ḥijjat al-wadā'*. Abou el-Fadl (2001, pp. 167–88), where he makes the direct link between *nushūz* and *fāḥisha mubīna* based on the Prophet's statements in his final sermon. For the opinions of classical and modern jurists who generally limit *nushūz*, refer to: Shams al-Dīn (1996b, pp. 28–42). For the history of the legal debates on the subject, refer to Rispler-Chaim (1992, pp. 315–27).

117 Mahmoud (2006, pp. 537–50).

118 Ṭabāṭabā'ī (1402h, vol. 4, pp. 349–51).

119 Shaikh (1997, p. 72). Also: Ṭūsī (1409h, vol. 3, pp. 188–91), Ṭabrisī (1415h, vol. 3, pp. 77–80), and Ṭabāṭabā'ī (1402h, vol. 4, pp. 343–52).

120 Ali (n.d.).

121 Hibri (1982, p. 218).

122 Lane (n.d.): *ṭ-w-'*. The Qur'an contrasts the term "willingly" (*ṭaw'an*) with "unwillingly" (*karhan*) [9: 53 and 41: 11].

123 Faḍlallāh, Mahdī (1987) *al-Ijtihād wa al-manṭiq al-fiqhī fi al-Islām*. Beirut: Dār al-Talī'a, pp. 153–4. Moreover, they do not discuss the problem that if a wife is supposed to obey her husband in everything except that which is wrong, then it follows that she is already capable of making informed decisions, therefore what is the point of her obedience to her husband, when it is readily admitted that he may err and that she should correct him?

124 Shams al-Dīn (1996b, p. 97).

125 Shams al-Dīn (1996b, pp. 53–4).

126 Kulaynī (1388h, vol. 5, p. 9).

127 Faḍlallāh (2005, pp. 88–9).

128 In one tradition, the best of women is described as one who is "honoured among her kin and abased with her husband" (Kulaynī, 1388h, vol. 5, pp. 324–6). In another one, the Prophet allegedly said, "If anyone was required to prostrate to another human being, it would be the wife to her husband" (Kulaynī, 1388h, vol. 5, pp. 507–8).

129 al-'Āmilī, al-Ḥurr, Muḥammad Ibn al-Ḥasan (1414h) *Wasā'il al-Shī'a*. 30 volumes. Qum: Mu'assasat Ahl al-Bayt, vol. 20, p. 172.

130 Shams al-Dīn (1996b, pp. 119–21).

131 Kulaynī (1388h, vol. 5, p. 507).

132 Kulaynī (1388h, vol. 5, pp. 328–9).

133 Abou El Fadl (2003, pp. 87 and 231–2).

134 Kulaynī (1388h, vol. 5, p. 88).

135 Kulaynī (1388h, vol. 6, p. 6).

136 Wadud (1994, pp. 90–1).

137 For a discussion on this, refer to: Shams al-Dīn (1996b, pp. 82–5). Moreover, the degree (*daraja*) men have over women in [2: 228] has often been understood as a degree of forgiveness on the men's part (Shams al-Dīn, 1996b, pp. 106–7 and pp. 156–61). Also in: Mubarak (2004, p. 276). Kindness to the wife as the man's *iḥsān* that is prescribed by the Qur'an, is also discussed in the *ḥadīth* (Kulaynī, 1388h, vol. 5, pp. 510–12). Note the similarity between man's *iḥsān* to his wife, and the women's *ḥusn* discussed here.

138 Faḍlallāh (1998, p. 60).

139 Subhani, J. (1984) *The message*. Tehran: Be'that Foundation, pp. 432–4, where he places this *ḥadīth* in connection with Nusayba bint Ka'b, and right before he describes her bravery at the battle of Uḥud, hence he says that "it is indisputable that *jihād* is unlawful for women in Islam". Then he presents Nusayba as a lawful exception without further comment.

140 Ziyāda (2001, pp. 220–2).

141 Kulaynī (1388h, vol. 5, p. 320).
142 Kualynī (1388h, vol. 5, pp. 320–1).
143 Kualynī (1388h, vol. 5, p. 321).
144 Kualynī (1388h, vol. 5, p. 321).
145 Kualynī (1388h, vol. 515).
146 Ṣadūq (1404ha, vol. 3, p. 385).
147 Dakake, M.M. (2007) *The charismatic community: Shi'ite identity in early Islam*. New York: State University of New York Press, p. 227, where for example he considered the adultery of a poor and thirsty woman a legitimate *mut'a* contract and the wage she received as her *mahr*. Abou El Fadl (2001, pp. 181–2 and 187), that 'Ali prohibited beating the wife even if it were in response to an assault of defamation or cursing, and that he actually punished men who committed physical violence against their wives.
148 Dakake (2007, p. 227).

Conclusion

Many of the female personalities of the Qur'an and *sunna* may be seen to be in diametric opposition to what *ḥadīths* demand and expect of women. Most of these women, if not all, acted completely independently of men in general and their husbands in particular. This applies to the negative and positive models; the wives of Noah and Lot, as well as the wife of Pharaoh. Mary had no husband. Hagar managed to conjure the blessed water into the desert when her husband left her, and due to her own active pursuit. The mother of Moses' husband had no mention in the story. The queen of Sheba was her own mistress and ruled over men. Khadīja served her husband's cause out of choice, before and after his mission, and she is portrayed as having had the upper hand financially and socially; indeed Muhammad is said to have felt insecure in Mecca without her. Even Fāṭima, the prototype daughter, wife, and mother in fact acted on her own, and on her husband's behalf, even while he was available to take charge. Zaynab also acted independently, and her husband is not heard of much, even though she is said to have been married. There are some exceptions to this, such as Lot's daughters, the Prophet's wives, and the *ḥūr* of paradise who are portrayed as obedient to the father or husband. It has been argued that the very variety of personalities presented in the authoritative sources, the very difficulty to group them into a single entity, is in itself empowering because it acknowledges women's humanity. The variety gives women reading the texts ample personalities to be inspired by and emulate. This is unlike the *ḥadīth* which tends to either subjugate or elevate women as a group, and attempts to project a monolithic personality on women.

Therefore, women are not normally defined by men, as traditions would have us believe, but the authoritative texts of Qur'an and *sunna* tend to describe individual women in terms of a human *nafs* on its journey. Decisions taken by women independently were the ones deemed worthy of comment by the Qur'an and *sunna*. While Eve remained a silent partner to Adam, even though a partner, it is the voices of women like Moses' mother, Āsiyā, Bilqīs, even Zulaykha, as well as Fāṭima and Zaynab, that are heard. Where the *ḥadīth* teaches that women are fragile and therefore must not be given any responsibility, the female personalities of the Qur'an and *sunna* carry their own vicegerency as their responsibility. They are often also responsible for their children who are chosen to become prophets or Imams. Far from advocating comfort, the authoritative narrative literature implies that hardship causes growth, as with Hagar and Zaynab whose extreme suffering coupled with perseverance helped change history positively, as far as Muslims are concerned.

It has been argued that despite the androcentric language of the Qur'anic text, and while acknowledging the patriarchy of the Islamic social structure, when looking at women outside of the legal sphere, one finds gynocentric elements in the Qur'an and *sunna* narratives. Femininity and things normally associated with it are sometimes extolled. The womb is described in the opening verse of *Sūrat al-Nisā'*, in addition to its literal sense, as a mysterious entity which warrants reverence and causes God to honour whoever honours it. This, along with the intellect, has been linked to the concept of human beings' vicegerency on earth. Mary's trustful receptivity is her greatest strength to the extent that as a young girl, she inspires God's prophet Zechariah by her example. Even the social scandal associated with her miracle tells of the world's injustice towards truthfulness. Fāṭima plays a similar role to Mary in her matriarchal status, although she is more dependent than Mary on a male figure. She assures the continuity of the Prophet's scripture, and is often herself seen as the source of the Imams' knowledge and light. Furthermore, the emphasis on Fāṭima's feelings as authoritative criteria for what is right and wrong strangely portrays the often despised women's emotions as something to be taken rather seriously and revered as a sign of God's feelings. Of course, these examples are specific to these women, but they still do break from much of the prevalent contempt towards women's biological functions and feelings. With the other, less exceptional, personalities, the Qur'an and *sunna* also bring women's experiences to the forefront. There are the jealous wives and the desperate and victims among those, the women worrying about their children's physical and spiritual safety like Moses' and Mary's mothers, the emotional attachment of breastfeeding, the pain of labour and social scandal. There is the uncontrollable passion towards such a beautiful man like the women of Egypt felt, and the more composed attraction to the strong and trustworthy man, like Moses' bride disclosed. There is the intelligent queen who is both calculating in politics, and trusting in divine signs. There are also the ungrateful women who mock their good husbands and prophets, as the wives of Noah and Lot, and there is the wife subject to a tyrannical husband who is in any case lower than herself in intelligence and righteousness, like Āsiyā. The women of Karbalā' who did not get killed but saw their fathers, brothers, husbands and children get killed nevertheless are also given space for empathy within the tradition.

The Qur'an quite clearly includes women within the expression *ahl al-bayt*, the assembly around truth, as it did with Sara, Mary's mother, and others. Tradition also includes non-impeccable women within this holy group. Therefore, in addition to the revered Fāṭima as among the *ahl al-bayt* of Muhammad,

Zaynab is unanimously portrayed by the religious authorities as having had the spirit of *ahl al-bayt*, even if she did not, in their view, attain the status of impeccability as such.

The theme of *jihād al-nafs* unites these women, thereby portraying them as human beings, and the gendered themes in their description help bring women's experience to the centre. The universally human and the specifically feminine overlap without much difficulty in the Qur'an and *sunna*, as perfectly formulated in verses [66: 10–12] where two women are made as examples for the infidels and two are examples for the faithful.

Sometimes traditions and exegesis, but not the Qur'an, try to limit these women's human experiences. Zulaykha's passion and guile is incorrectly read as a feminine example, but the similar behaviour of men in her story was not seen as gendered. Mary is not considered a prophet despite apparent evidence to the contrary, simply because she is a woman. The impeccable Fāṭima, some traditions insist, did not experience menstruation or any kind of post-natal blood, thereby denying her a main element of her femininity. There is an attempt to restrict women to men's projected image of them as passionate; coupled with an attempt to remove women from the capacity for knowledge and spirituality. This has its beginnings in the story of Eve, when she is seen in traditions not as a person and vicegerent in her own right, but as a wife; a *zawj* but not a *nafs*, a follower who has zeal towards nothing other than her husband, and who had no knowledge planted in her like Adam, but was given it as a dowry.

Yet, it is the theme of *jihād al-nafs* that has been found recurrent in the depiction of the personalities. The coupling of the two sub-categories of spiritual motherhood and earthly *jihād* is important. That is because, as it was explicitly concurred with in some traditions, active involvement in the world and with fellow human beings opens the possibilities for a person's growth, including religious growth. This was also the underlying situation in most or all of the stories of these women. The theme of spiritual motherhood, a status reached through difficult *jihād*, highlights the relevance of feminine characteristics in spirituality; and it portrays the womb and childbirth not as a burden that constricts women's lives and makes them dependent subjects, but as the best contribution to human civilisation, akin to the contributions of prophets, if and only if, the mother herself was of the calibre of Moses' mother, Mary, Khadīja, or Fāṭima. It is the narrative traditions' salient understanding of motherhood not as a self-sacrificing and mundane job, but ultimately as one that is concerned with nothing short of the woman reaching her highest personal potential and coming close to impeccability. Such a change in the position of the mother would eventually cause change to the position of the father/husband and his priorities. It has been proposed that:

> The symbolic positioning of the mother is the linchpin for both the perpetuation and the destruction of patriarchal values. When the maternal position shifts, the patriarchal order is subverted from within. This means

> that those with a vested interest in the perpetuation of patriarchy, whether theologians or psychoanalysts, must expend considerable energy on making sure that the mother remains in the place assigned to her.[1]

If one were to look into Islamic law for equality between men and women, this may be hard to find, with preference belonging to the man. However, if one looks into the narrative literature, the stories provided in the authentic sources, one finds a praise of the feminine. A case in point are the two verses [4: 34] and [3: 36]. While the first is explicit about male superiority, it speaks of *al-rijāl* and *al-nisā'*, that is, adult men and women and the more particular context of the verse is the marital relationship. The verse also puts two conditions on the man's authority. However, in [3: 36], though preference for the female is implicit, it may be easily inferred from the sentence structure and Qur'anic context of the verse. Moreover, it expresses preference for *al-untha* over *al-dhakar*, that is, the female sex over the male at their basic level. Therefore, it is perhaps not a question of who the Qur'an prefers, but where to look for the answer. Differences have to be acknowledged, away from the suppositions of liberal feminism, but these have to be reread by women interpreters; and the scholarship in this pursuit ought to be honest and meticulous. The difference between the two sexes, the relativity of their excellence, and their single goal of actively progressing towards God may be seen in the verse, "Do not covet that whereby God in bounty has preferred one of you above another. To the men a share from what they have earned, and to the women a share from what they have earned. And ask God of His bounty; God knows everything" [4: 32].

Note

1 Beattie, T. (2002) *God's mother, Eve's advocate.* London: Continuum, p. 108.

Bibliography

Arabic sources

'Abd al-Raḥmān, 'A'isha (1967 [1986]) *Nisā' al-nabī*. Beirut: Dār al-Kitāb al-'Arabī.

Abū Mikhnaf, Lūṭ Ibn Yaḥyā (1398h) *Maqtal al-Ḥusayn*. Qum: al-Maktaba al-'Iilmiyya.

Al-'Āmilī, Muḥammad Ibn al-Ḥasan al-Ḥurr (1414h) *Wasā'il al-Shī'a*. 30 volumes. Qum: Mu'assasat Ahl al-Bayt.

Al-'Āmilī, Ja'far Murtaḍā (1997) *Ma'sāt al-Zahrā'*. Beirut: Dār al-Sīrah. Also available from: www.shiaweb.org/books/maasat_alzahraa_1/ and http://www.shiaweb.org/books/maasat_alzahraa_2/ [Accessed 18.07.2011].

Āmulī, Javādī (1994) *al-Mar'a fi al-'Irfān*. Beirut: Dār al-Tayyār al-Jadīd.

Al-'Ayyāshī, Muḥammad Ibn Mas'ūd (n.d.) *Tafsīr al-Qur'ān*. 2 volumes. Tehran: al-Maktaba al-'Ilmiyya al-Islāmiyya.

Bint Muḥammad Ibn Fahd al-Rashīd, N. (1427h) *Shakhsiyyat al-Mara fi al-Qasas al-Qur'ānī: Dirāsa Adabiyya Taḥlīliyya*. Dammam: Dār Ibn al-Jawzī.

Al-Bukhārī, Muḥammad Ibn Ismā'īl (1401h) *al-Ṣaḥīḥ*. 8 volumes. Beirut: Dār al-Fikr.

Faḍlallāh, Mahdī (1987) *al-Ijtihād wa al-Manṭiq al-Fiqhī fi al-Islām*. Beirut: Dār al-Ṭalī'a.

Faḍlallāh, Muḥammad Ḥusayn (1421h) *al-Zahrā' al-Qudwa*. Also available from: http://arabic. bayynat.org.lb/books/alzahraa_index.htm [Accessed December 2013].

——(1986) *Min Waḥy al-Qur'ān*. Beirut: Dār al-Zahrā'.

——(1998) *Dunyā al-Mar'a*. Beirut: Dār al-Malak.

——(2005) *Ta'ammulāt Islāmiyya Ḥawl al-Mar'a*. Beirut: Dār al-Malak.

Al-Fayrūz Ābādī, Muḥammad Ibn Ya'qūb (n.d.) *al-Qāmūs al-Muḥīṭ*. 4 volumes. Cairo: Muḥammad 'Abd al-Ḥamīd.

Al-Ḥākim, Muḥammad Ibn 'Abdallāh al-Nīsabūrī (1406h) *al-Mustadrak 'ala al-Ṣaḥī ḥayn*. 4 volumes. Beirut: Dār al Ma'rifa.

Al-Ḥusaynī, 'Alī Ibn Mūsā Ibn Ṭawūs (1417h) *al-Luhūf fī Qatla al-Ṭufūf*. Tehran: Mehr.

Al-Ḥuwayzī, 'Abd 'Alī Ibn Jumu'a al-'Arūsī (1412h) *Nūr al-Thaqalayn*. 4th edn. 5 volumes. Qum: Mu'assasat Ismā'īlyān.

Ibn Abī al-Ḥadīd al-Mu'tazilī, 'Izz al-Dīn Ibn Hibatallāh (n.d.) *Sharḥ Nahj al-Balāghah*. 20 volumes. Cairo: Dār Iḥyā' al-Kutub al-'Arabiyya.

Ibn 'Aqīl, Bahā' al-Dīn al-Hamdānī (n.d.) *Sharḥ Ibn 'Aqīl li Alfiyyat Ibn Mālik*. 2 volumes.

Ibn 'Arabī, Muḥammad Ibn 'Alī (n.d.) *Tafsīr al-Qur'ān*. Also available from: www.altafsir.com/Tafasir.asp?tMadhNo=3&tTafsirNo=33&tSoraNo=4&tAyahNo=1&tDisplay=yes&UserProfile=0 [Accessed 18.07.2011].

Ibn Ḥanbal, Aḥmad (n.d.) *Musnad*. 6 volumes. Beirut: Dār Ṣāder.
Ibn Hishām, 'Abd al-Malik (1383h) *Sīrat al-Nabī*. 4 volumes. Cairo: Maktabat Muḥammad 'Alī Ṣāabiḥ.
Ibn Manẓūr, Muḥammad Ibn Mukarram (1405h) *Lisān al-'Arab*. 15 volumes. Qum: Nashr Adab al-Ḥawza.
Ibn Sa'd, Muḥammad (n.d.) *al-Ṭabaqāt al-Kubrā*. 8 volumes. Beirut: Dār Ṣāder.
Ibn Ṭayfūr, Ibn Abū Ṭāhir (n.d.) *Balāghāt al-Nisā'*. Qum: Baṣīratī.
Al-Isfahānī, Abū al-Faraj (1385h) *Maqātil al-Ṭālibiyyīn*. Qum: Dār al-Kitāb.
Al-Isfahānī, al-Ḥusayn Ibn Mufaḍḍal al-Rāghib (1404h) *al-Mufradāt fī Gharīb al-Qur'ān*. Tehran: Daftar Nashr al-Kitāb.
Jawād, Ibrāhīm Muḥammad (2005) *al-Sayyida Zaynab: Thawra lā Tahda' wa Dam'a lā Tarqa'*. Beirut: Dār al-Maḥajja al-Bayḍā'.
Al-Kāshānī, Muḥsin Fayḍ (1416h) *al-Ṣāfī fī Tafsīr Kalām Allāh al-Wāfī*. 2nd edn. 5 volumes. Tehran: Maktabat al-Ṣadr.
Khalafallāh, Muḥammad Aḥmad (1999) *al-Fann al-Qaṣaṣī fi al-Qur'ān al-Karīm*. 4th edn. Beirut: Sīna li al-Nashr.
Al-Khaṭīb, 'Abd al-Karīm (1964) *al-Qaṣaṣ al-Qur'ānī fī Manṭūqihī wa Mafhūmihī*. Cairo: Maṭba'at al-Sunna al-Muḥammadiyya.
Al-Khū'ī, Abū al-Qāsim Ibn 'Alī Akbar (1413h) *Mu'jam Rijāl al-Ḥadīth*. 5th edn. 24 volumes. Qum: Lajnat Taḥqīq Turāth al-Shaykh al-A'ẓam.
Al-Khumaynī, Rūḥullāh (n.d.) *Makānat al-Mar'a fī Fikr al-Imm al-Khumaynī*. Damascus: Iranian Embassy.
Al-Kūfī, Furāt (1410h) *Tafsīr al-Qur'ān*. Tehran: al-Tābi'a li-Wizārat al-Thaqāfa wa al-Irshād.
Al-Kulaynī, Muḥammad Ibn Ya'qūb (1388h) *al-Kāfī*. 3rd edn. 8 volumes. Tehran: Dār al-Kutub al-Islāmiyya.
Al-Majlisī, Muḥammad Bāqir (1403h) *Biḥāar al-Anwār*. 110 volumes. Beirut: Mu'assasat al-Wafā'.
Al-Mārandī, Abū al-Ḥasan. (1328h) *Majma' al-Nūurayn*. Qum: Mu'assasat Taḥqīqāt wa Nashr Ma'ārif Ahl al-Bayt.
Al-Mazandarānī, Muḥammad Ṣāliḥ (2000) *Sharḥ Uṣūl al-Kāfī*. 12 volumes. Beirut: Dār Iḥyā' al-Turāth al-'Arabī.
Al-Mufīd, Muḥammad Ibn al-Nu'mān (1403h) *al-Amālī*. Qum: Jāmi'at al-Mudarrisīn fi al-Ḥawza.
——(1413h) *al-Irshād*. 2 volumes. Beirut: Dār al-Mufīd.
Mughniyya, Muḥammad Jawād (1992) *Ma' Baṭalat Karbalā': Zaynab Bint Amīr al-Mu'minīn*. 5th edn. Beirut: Dār al-Ṭalī'a and Dār al-Jawād.
Murtaḍāa, Ja'far (1995) *al-Ṣaḥīḥ min Sīrat al-Nabī al-A'ẓam*. 4th edn. 11 volumes. Beirut: Dār al-Hādī.
Mūsā, Faraḥ (1997) *al-Anbiyā' wa al-Mutrafūn fi al-Qur'n*. Beirut: Dār al-Hādī.
Muslim, Ibn al-Hajjāj (n.d.) *al-Ṣaḥīḥ*. 8 volumes. Beirut: Dār al-Fikr.
Muṭahharī, Morteza (1987) *Mas'alat al-Ḥijāb*. Beirut: al-Dār al-Islāmiyya.
Al-Nīsabūrī, 'Alī Ibn Aḥmad al-Wāḥidī (1388h) *Asbāb Nuzūl al-Āyāt*. Cairo: Mu'assasat al-Ḥalabī & Co.
Al-Qayyūmī, Jawād (1373h) *Saḥīfat al-Zahraā'*. Qum: Daftar Intishārat Islāmī.
Al-Qazwini, Muḥammad Kāẓim (1414h, 2nd edn) *Fāṭima al-Zahrā': min al-Mahd ila al-Laḥd*. Qum: Bassīratī.
——(1991) *Fāṭima al-Zahrā': min al-Mahd ila al-Laḥd*. Beirut: Mu'assasat al-Nūr.

Al-Qummī, 'Alī Ibn Ibrāhīm (1404h) *Tafsīr al-Qur'ān*. 3rd edn. 2 volumes. Qum: Mu'assasat Dār al-Kitāb.
Al-Raḍī, Muḥammad Ibn al-Ḥusayn al-Sharīf (n.d.a) *al-Majāzāt al-Nabawiyya*. Qum: Baṣīratī.
——(n.d.b) *Ḥaqā'iq al-Ta'wīl fī Mutashābah al-Tanzīl*. Beirut: Dār al-Muhājir.
——(n.d.c) *Nahj al-Balāgha*. 4 volumes. Beirut: Dār al-Ma'rifa.
Al-Ṣadūq, Muḥammad Ibn 'Alī Ibn Bābawayh (1379h) *Ma'ānī al-Akhbār*. Qum: Intishārat Islāmī.
——(1386h) *'Ilal al-Sharā'i'*. 2 volumes. Najaf: al-Maktaba al-Ḥaydariyya.
——(1404ha) *Man la Yaḥḍuruhū al-Faqīh*. 2nd edn. 4 volumes. Qum: Jāmi'at al-Mudarrisīn.
——(1404hb) *'Uyūn Akhbār al-Riḍā*. 2 volumes. Beirut: Mu'assasat al-A'lamī li al-Maṭbū'āt.
——(1417h) *al-Amālī*. Qum: Mu'assasat al-Ba'tha.
Shams al-Dīn, Muḥammad Mahdī (1972) *Dirāsāt fī Nahj al-Balāgha*. 2nd edn. Beirut: Dār al-Zahrā'.
——(1981) *Anṣāar al-Ḥusayn*. 2nd edn. al-Dār al-Islāmiyya.
——(1994) *al-Sitr wa al-Naẓar*. 2nd edn. Beirut: al-Mu'assasa al-Duwaliyya li al-Dirāsāt wa al-Nashr.
——(1995) *Ahliyyat al-Mar'a li Tawallī al-Sulṭa*. Beirut: al-Mu'assasa al-Duwaliyya li al-Dirāsāt wa al-Nashr.
——(1996a) *Ḥaqq al-'Amal li al-Mar'a*. Beirut: al-Mu'assasa al-Duwaliyya li al-Dirāsāt wa al-Nashr.
——(1996b) *Ḥuqūq al-Zawjiyya*. Beirut: al-Mu'assasa al-Duwaliyya li al-Dirāst wa al-Nashr.
Al-Shīrāzī, Ḥasan (2000) *Kalimat al-Sayyida Zaynab wa Rubaybāt al-Risāla*. Beirut: Dār al-Qāri'.
Subaytī, Yūsuf 'Alī (2006) *Nahj al-Balāghah: fī Dā'irat al-Tashkīk?!* Beirut: Dār al-Hādī.
Al-Ṭabarī, Muḥammad Ibn Jarīr (1879) *Tārīkh al-'Umam wa al-Mulūk*. 8 volumes. Beirut: Mu'assasat al-A'lamī.
Al-Ṭabrisī, Aḥmad Ibn 'Alī (1386h) *al-Iḥtijāj*. 2 volumes. Najaf: Dār al-Nu'mān.
Al-Ṭabrisī, al-Faḍl Ibn al-Ḥasan (1415h) *Majma' al-Bayān*. 10 volumes. Beirut: Mu'assasat al-A'lamī.
——(1418h) *Jawāmi' al-Jāmi'*. Qum: Mu'assasat al-Nashr al-Islāmī.
Al-Ṭabāṭabā'ī, Muḥammad Ḥusayn (1402h) *al-Mīzān fī Tafsīr al-Qur'ān*. 20 volumes. Qum: Mu'assasat al-Nashr al-Islāmī.
Al-Ṭahrānī, Muḥammad al-Ḥusayn al-Ḥasanī (1993) *Qaḍā' wa Jihād wa Ḥukūmat al-Mar'a: Risāla Badī'a*. Beirut: Dār al-Maḥabba al-Bayḍā'.
Al-Ṭūsī, Muḥammad Ibn Ḥasan (1390ha) *al-Istibṣṣār*. 4th edn. 4 volumes. Tehran: Dār al-Kutub al-Islāmiyya.
——(1390hb) *Tahdhīb al-aAḥkām*. 10 volumes. Tehran: Dār al-Kutub al-Islāmiyya.
——(1409h) *al-Tibyān fī Tafsīr al-Qur'ān*. 10 volumes. Qum: Maktab al-I'lām al-Islāmī.
——(1411h) *al-Ghayba*. Qum: Mu'assasat al-Ma'ārif al-Islāmiyya.
——(1414h) *al-Amālī*. Qum: Dār al-Thaqāfa.
Al-Ya'qūbī, Aḥmad Ibn Ishḥāq (n.d.) *Tārīkh*. 2 volumes. Beirut: Dār Ṣāder.
Ziyāda, Asmā' Aḥmad Muḥammad (2001) *Dawr al-Mar'a al-Siyāsī fī 'Ahd al-Nabī wa al-Khulafā' al-Rāshidīn: wa bihā Taḥqīq Tārīkhī wa Fiqhī wa Tashrī'ī li Fahm Dawr al-Sayyidah 'Ā'isha fī Aḥdāth al-Fitna*. Cairo: Dār al-Salām.

English sources

Abdel Haleem, M. (1999) *Understanding the Qur'an: themes and style*. London: Tauris.

Abou El Fadl, Kh. (2001) *Conference of the books: the search for beauty in Islam*. Lanham: University Press of America.

——(2003) *Speaking in God's name: Islamic law, authority and women*. Oxford: Oneworld.

Abu Lughud, L. (2002) "Do Muslim women really need saving? Anthropological reflections on cultural relativism and its others". *American Anthropologist*, 104 (3): 783–90.

Abugideiri, H. (2001) "Hagar: a historical model for 'gender jihad'". In Haddad, Y.Y. and Esposito, J.L. (eds) *Daughters of Abraham: feminist thought in Judaism, Christianity, and Islam*. Gainesville: University Press of Florida.

Achena, M. "Fayd-i Kashani". *Encyclopaedia of Islam, second edition*. Edited by P. Bearman, Th. Bianquis, C.E. Bosworth, E. Van Donzel, and W.P. Heinrichs. Brill online, 2014 [Accessed 20.02.2014].

Afshar, H. (1982) "Khomeini's teachings and their implications for women". *Feminist Review*, 12: 59–72.

——(1998) *Islam and feminisms: an Iranian case-study*. Basingstoke: Macmillan.

Aghaie, K.S. (2004) *Martyrs of Karbala: Shi'i symbols and rituals in modern Iran*. Seattle: University of Washington Press.

Ahmad, A. (2010) *Qur'anic concepts of human psyche* [online]. Available from: www.biblioislam.net/en/ELibrary/FullText.aspx?tblid=3&id=44 [Accessed 18.07.2011].

Ahmed, L. (1992) *Women and gender in Islam: historical roots of a modern debate*. New Haven and London: Yale University Press.

Ali, K. (2003) "'A beautiful example?' The Prophet Muhammad (pbuh) as a model for Muslim husbands". *In Critical Islamic Reflections Conference*. Yale University. Available from: www.yale.edu/cir/2003/alipaper.doc [Accessed 20.02.2014].

——(2006) *Sexual ethics and Islam: feminist reflections on Qur'an, hadith, and jurisprudence*. Oxford: Oneworld.

——(n.d.) *Muslim sexual ethics: understanding a difficult verse, Qur'an 4:34*. Available from: www.brandeis.edu/projects/fse/muslim/mus-essays/mus-ess-diffverse.html [Accessed 18.07.2011].

Al-Rikabi, J. (2012) "Baqir al-Sadr and the Islamic state: a theory for Islamic democracy". *Journal of Shi'a Islamic Studies*, 5 (3): 249–75.

Amir-Moezzi, M.A. (1994) *The divine guide in early Shi'ism*. New York: State University of New York Press.

——"'Alī b. Ibrāhīm al-Qummī". *Encyclopaedia of Islam, THREE*. Edited by Gudrun Kramer, Denis Matringe, John Nawas and Everett Rowson. Brill online, 2014 [Accessed 20.02.2014].

——"al-Ṭūsī". *Encyclopaedia of Islam, second edition*. Edited by P. Bearman, Th. Bianquis, C.E. Bosworth, E. van Donzel, and W.P. Heinrichs. Brill online, 2014 [Accessed 20.02.2014].

'Arafat, W. (1958) "Early critics of the authenticity of the poetry of the sira". *Bulletin of the School of Oriental and African Studies*, 21: 453–63.

Arberry, J. (1955) *The Koran interpreted*. London: Allen & Unwin.

Ayati, I. (1991) *A probe into the history of Ashura*. London: al-Khoei Foundation.

Ayoub, M.M. (1978) *Redemptive suffering in Islam: a study of the devotional aspects of 'Ashura' in Twelver Shi'ism*. The Hague: Mouton.

——(1988) "The speaking Qur'an and the silent Qur'an: a study of the principles and development of Imami Shi'i tafsir". In Rippin, A. (ed.) *Approaches to the history of the interpretation of the Qur'an*. Oxford: Clarendon Press.

——(2003) *The crisis of Muslim history: religion and politics in early Islam*. Oxford: Oneworld.

Azami, M.M. (1992) *Studies in early hadith literature*. Indianapolis: American Trust Publications.

Badran, M. (2002) "Islamic feminism: what's in a name?" *al-Ahram Weekly* [online]. 17–23 January. Available from: http://weekly.ahram.org.eg/2002/569/cu1.htm [Accessed 20.02.2014].

Bakhtiar, L. (1996) *Shariati on Shariati and the Muslim woman*. Chicago: ABC International Group.

Barazangi, N.H. (2004) *Woman's identity and the Qur'an: a new reading*. Florida: University Press of Florida.

Barlas, A. (2002) *Believing women in Islam: unreading patriarchal interpretations of the Qur'an*. Austin: University of Texas Press.

Beattie, T. (2002) *God's mother, Eve's advocate*. London: Continuum.

Bernhardt, F. (2011) "The legitimacy of party politics and the authority of the 'ulama' in Iraq's Shi'a Islamist movement: the example of the Islamic Da'wah Party (1957–88)". *Journal of Shi'a Islamic Studies*, 4 (2): 163–82.

Bird, P. (1974) "Images of women in the old testament". In Ruether, R.R. (ed.) *Religion and sexism: images of woman in the Jewish and Christian traditions*. New York: Simon & Schuster.

Bouhdiba, A. (1998) *Sexuality in Islam*. London: Saqi Books.

Bronner, L.L. (1994) *From Eve to Esther: Rabbinic reconstructions of Biblical women*. Louisville: Westminster John Knox Press.

Brown, D.W. (1996) *Rethinking tradition in modern Islamic thought*. Cambridge: Cambridge University Press.

Buckley, T. and Gottlieb, A. (eds) (1988) *Blood magic: the anthropology of menstruation*. California: University of California Press.

Calder, N. (1986) "The *sa'y* and the *jabin*: some notes on Qur'an 37: 102–3". *Journal of Semitic Studies*, 31: 17–26.

Cantor, A. (1983) "The Lilith question". In Heschel, S. (ed.) *On being a Jewish feminist: a reader*. New York: Schocken Books.

Clohessy, C. (2009) *Fatima, daughter of Muhammad*. Piscataway, NJ: Gorgias Press.

Cragg, K. (2001) *Muhammad in the Qur'an: the task and the text*. London: Melisende.

Dakake, M.M. (2007) *The charismatic community: Shi'ite identity in early Islam*. New York: State University of New York Press.

Daly, M. (1975) *The church and the second sex*. New York: Harper & Row.

Deeb, L.Z. (2005) "From mourning to activism: Sayyedeh Zaynab, Lebanese Shi'i women, and the transformation of Ashura". In Aghaie, K.S. (ed.) *The women of Karbala: ritual performance and symbolic discourse in modern Shi'i Islam*. Austin: University of Texas Press.

Denny, F.M. (1993) "Islam: Qur'an and hadith". In Denny, F.M. and Taylor, R.L. (eds) *The Holy Book in comparative perspective*. Columbia: University of South Carolina Press.

Djebli, M. "Nahdj al-Balāgha". *Encyclopaedia of Islam, second edition*. Edited by P. Bearman, Th. Bianquis, C.E. Bosworth, E. van Donzel, and W.P. Heinrichs. Brill online, 2014 [Accessed 20.02.2014].

Donner, F.M. (1998) *Narratives of Islamic origins: the beginnings of Islamic historical writing*. Princeton: The Darwin Press.

Doorn-Harder, P.V. (2006) *Women shaping Islam: Indonesian women reading the Qur'an*. Urbana and Chicago: University of Illinois Press.

Dutton, Y. (1999) *The origins of Islamic law: the Qur'an, the muwatta' and madinan 'amal*. Richmond: Curzon.

——(n.d.) *Ibn Warraq's "Origins of the Koran": a critical analysis* [online]. Available from: www.bismikaallahuma.org/archives/2005/ ibn-warraqs-origins-of-the-koran-a-critical-analysis/ [Accessed 20.02.2014].

Eliash, J. (1969) "The Ithna 'ashari-Shi'i juristic theory of political and legal authority". *Studia Islamica*, 29: 17–30.

Elshtain, J.B. (1981) *Public man, private woman*. Oxford: Robertson.

Fadlallah, M.H. (2002) *The infallible Fatimah: a role model for men and women*. Beirut: Dar al-Malak.

Faruqi, M.J. (2000) "Women's self-identity in the Qur'an and Islamic law". In Webb, G. (ed.) *Windows of faith: Muslim women scholar-activists in North America*. New York: Syracuse University Press.

Farzaneh, M.M. (2008) "The political thought of Ayatullah Murtaza Mutahhari: an Iranian theoretician of the Islamic state". *International Journal of Middle East Studies*, 40 (4): 689–90.

Fierro, M. (2002) "Women as prophets in Islam". In Marin, M. and Deguilhem, R. (eds) *Writing the feminine: women in Arab sources*. New York: I.B. Tauris.

Fiorenza, E.S. (1990) *Bread not stone: the challenge of feminist Biblical interpretation*. Edinburgh: T& t Clark.

——(1993) *Discipleship of equals: a critical feminist ecclesialogy of liberation*. London: SCM.

Graham, W.A. (1977) *Divine word and prophetic word in early Islam*. The Hague: Mouton Publishers.

Guillaume, A. (1954) "The biography of the Prophet in recent research". *Islamic Quarterly*, I: 5–11.

Haddad, Y.Y. and Smith, J.I. (1989) "The Virgin Mary in Islamic tradition and commentary". *The Muslim World*, 79 (3–4): 161–87.

Hamdar, A. (2009) "Jihad of words: gender and contemporary Karbala narratives". In Tate, A. (ed.) *Yearbook of English Studies*, 39 (1–2): 84–100. Special Issue on Literature and Religion.

Hassan, R. (n.d.) *Equal before Allah? Woman-man equality in the Islamic tradition* [online]. Available from: www.wluml.org/node/253 [Accessed 20.02.2014].

Heidel, A. (1963) *The Babylonian genesis: the story of creation*. Chicago: Chicago University Press.

Helie-Lucas, M.-A. (1990) "Women, nationalism and religion in the Algerian liberation struggle". In Badran, M. and Cooke, M. (eds) *Opening the gates: a century of Arab feminist writing*. Bloomington: Indiana University Press.

Hibri, A. (1982) *Women and Islam*. Oxford: Pergamon.

Hitti, P.K. (1970) *History of the Arabs*. 10th edn. London: Macmillan.

Hodgson, M. (1955) "How did the early Shi'a become sectarian?" *Journal of the American Oriental Society*, 75 (1): 1–13.

Husseini, R. (2008) "Women, work, and political participation in Lebanese Shi'a contemporary thought: the writings of Ayatollahs Fadlallah and Shams al-din". *Comparative Studies of South Asia, Africa and the Middle East*, 28 (2): 273–82.

Ibrahim, N. and Abdalla, M. (2010) "A critical examination of Qur'an 4:34 and its relevance to intimate partner violence in Muslim families". *Journal of Muslim Mental Health*, 5: 327–49.

Jafri, S.H.M. (1979) *Origins and early development of Shi'a Islam*. London: Longman.

Jawad, H. (2003) "Muslim feminism: a case study of Amina Wadud's Qur'an and woman". *Islamic Studies*, 42 (1): 107–25.

Jawad, H. (2009) "Islamic spirituality and the feminine dimension". In Howie, G. and Jobling, J. (eds) *Women and the divine: touching transcendence*. New York: Palgrave Macmillan.

Jensen, J.M. (1991) *Promise to the land: essays on rural women*. Albuquerque: University of New Mexico Press.

Johns, A.J. (1981) "Joseph in the Qur'an: dramatic dialogue, human emotion and prophetic wisdom". *Islamic Quarterly*, 7: 29–55.

Jomier, J. (2001) "The divine name 'al-Rahman' in the Qur'an". In Rippin, A. (ed.) *The Qur'an: style and contents*. Aldershot: Ashgate.

Juynboll, G.H.A. (1987) "Some new ideas on the development of sunna as a technical term in early Islam". *Jerusalem Studies in Arabic and Islam*, 10: 97–118.

Kahf, M. (2000) "Braiding the stories: women's eloquence in the early Islamic era". In Webb, G. (ed.) *Windows of faith: Muslim scholar-activist in North America*. New York: Syracuse University Press.

Kandiyoti, D. (1991) "Islam and patriarchy: a comparative perspective". In Keddie, N.R. and Baron, B. (eds) *Women in Middle Eastern history: shifting boundaries in sex and gender*. New Haven and London: Yale University Press.

Kashani-Sabet, F. (2005) "Who is Fatima? Gender, culture, and representation in Islam". *Journal of Middle East Women's Studies*, 1 (2): 1–24.

Keeler, A. (2006) *Sufi hermeneutics: the Qur'an commentary of Rashid al-Din Maybudi*. Oxford: Oxford University Press in association with the Institute of Isma'ili Studies.

Kister, M.J. (1965) "God will never disgrace thee: the interpretation of an early hadith". *Journal of the Royal Asiatic Society of Great Britain and Ireland*, pp. 27–32.

——(1997) *Concepts and ideas at the dawn of Islam*. Aldershot: Ashgate.

Kohlberg, E. "al-Ṭabrisī". *Encyclopaedia of Islam, second edition*. Edited by P. Bearman, Th. Bianquis, C.E. Bosworth, E. van Donzel, and W.P. Heinrichs. Brill online, 2014 [Accessed 20.02.2014].

——(1987) "al-Usul al-arba'umi'a". *Jerusalem Studies in Arabic and Islam*, 10: 128–66.

Lafraie, N. (2009) *Revolutionary ideology and Islamic militancy: the Iranian revolution and interpretations of the Qur'an*. London: Taurus Academic Studies.

Lane, E.W. (n.d.) *Arabic-English lexicon* [online]. Available from: www.studyquran.co.uk/PRLonline.htm [Accessed 20.02.2014].

Lassner, J. (1993) *Demonizing the Queen of Sheba: boundaries of gender and culture in postbiblical Judaism and medieval Islam*. Chicago: The University of Chicago Press.

Lawson, B.T. (1993) "Akhbari Shi'i approaches to *tafsir*". In Hawting, G. and Shareef, A.-K.A. (eds) *Approaches to the Qur'an*. London: Routledge.

Lawson, T. (2007) "The authority of the feminine and Fatima's place in an early work by the bab". *Online Journal of Baha'i Studies*, 1: 137–70.

Leacock, E. (1981) *Myths of male dominance: collected articles on women cross-culturally*. New York: Monthly Review Press.

Lewis, B. "al-'Ayyashī", *Encyclopaedia of Islam, second edition*. Edited by P. Bearman, Th. Bianquis, C.E. Bosworth, E. Van Donzel, and W.P. Heinrichs. Brill online, 2014 [Accessed 20.02.2014].

Lings, M. (1994) *Muhammad: his life based on the earliest sources.* 5th edn. Lahore: Suhail Academy.

Lloyd, G. (1990) "Augustine and Aquinas". In Loades, A. (ed.) *Feminist theology: a reader.* London: SPCK.

London, S. (n.d.) "The future of feminism: an interview with Christina Hoff Summers". Available from: www.scottlondon.com/interviews/sommers.html [Accessed 20.02.2014].

Lybarger, L.D. (2000) "Gender and prophetic authority in the Qur'anic story of Maryam: a literary approach". *The Journal of Religion*, 80 (2): 240–70.

Madelung, W. "al-Kulaynī (or al-Kulīnī), Abū Dja'far Muḥammad". *Encyclopaedia of Islam, second edition.* Edited by P. Bearman, Th. Bianquis, C.E. Bosworth, E. van Donzel, and W.P. Heinrichs. Brill online, 2014 [Accessed 20.02.2014].

——(1998) *The succession to Muhammad.* Cambridge: Cambridge University Press.

Mahmoud, M. (2006) "To beat or not to beat: on the exegetical dilemmas over Qur'an 4:34". *Journal of the American Oriental Society*, 126: 537–50.

Mayer, A.E. (1999) *Islam and human rights: tradition and politics.* 3rd edn. Boulder: University of Pennsylvania Westview Press.

McAuliffe, J.D. (1981) "Chosen of all women: Mary and Fatima in Qur'anic exegesis". *Islamic Quarterly*, 7: 19–28.

McLaughlin, E.C. (1974) "Equality of souls, inequality of sexes: woman in medieval theology". In Ruether, R.R. (ed.) *Religion and sexism: images of women in the Jewish and Christian traditions.* New York: Simon & Schuster.

McMillan, C. (1982) *Women, reason and nature: some philosophical problems with feminism.* Oxford: Basil Blackwell.

Merguerian, G.K. and Najmabadi, A. (1997) "Zulaykha and Yusuf: whose 'best story'?" *International Journal of Middle East Studies*, 29 (4): 485–508.

Mernissi, F. (1991) *The veil and the male elite: a feminist interpretation of women's rights in Islam.* Reading, MA: Addison-Wesley. Translated by M. J. Lakeland.

——(1993) *The forgotten queens of Islam.* Cambridge: Polity Press.

Mir, M. (1998) Book reviews. *Journal of Islamic Studies*, 9 (1): 63–4.

——(2007) "The queen of Sheba's conversion in Q. 27:44: a problem examined". *Journal of Qur'anic Studies*, 9 (2): 43–56.

Mir-Hosseini, Z. (1996) "Stretching the limits: a feminist reading of the Shari'a in post-Khomeini Iran". In Yamani, M. (ed.) *Feminism and Islam: legal and literary perspectives.* London: Ithaca.

——(2000) *Islam and gender: the religious debate in contemporary Iran.* London and New York: I.B. Tauris.

——(2006) "Muslim women's quest for equality: between Islamic law and feminism". *Critical Inquiry*, 32: 629–45.

Mirza, Q. (2000) "Islamic feminism and the exemplary past". In Richardson, J. and Sandland, R. (eds) *Feminist perspectives on law and theory.* London: Cavendish.

——(2002) "Islamic feminism, possibilities and limitations". In Strawson, J. (ed.) *Law after Ground Zero.* London: Cavendish.

Modarressi, H. (2003) *Tradition and survival: a bibliographical survey of early Shi'ite literature – Volume 1.* Oxford: Oneworld.

Moghadam, V.M. (2002) "Islamic feminism and its discontents: towards a resolution of the debate". *Journal of Women in Culture and Society*, 27 (4): 1135–71.

Moghissi, H. (1999) *Feminism and Islamic fundamentalism: the limits of post-modern analysis.* London: Zed Books.

Momen, M. (1985) *An introduction to Shi'i Islam*. New Haven: Yale University Press.
Motzki, H. (2000) "The biography of Muhammad: the issue of the sources". *Journal of Law and Religion*, 15 (1/2): 627–32.
Mubarak, H. (2004) "Breaking the interpretive monopoly: a re-examination of verse 4:34". *Hawwa*, 2: 261–89.
Murata, S. (1992) *The Tao of Islam: a sourcebook on gender relationships in Islamic thought*. Albany: State University of New York Press.
Naeeni, N. (2011) *Shi'ah women transmitters of hadith: a collection of biographies of the women who transmitted traditions*. Qum: Ansarian. Translated by G. Babst.
Naguib, S. (2010) "Horizons and limitations of Muslim feminist hermeneutics: reflections on the menstruation verse". In Anderson, P.S. (ed.) *New topics in feminist philosophy of religion, feminist philosophy collection*. Dordrecht: Springer Press.
Najmabadi, A. (1998) "Feminism in an Islamic republic: years of hardship, years of growth". *In* Haddad, Y.Y. and Esposito, J.L. (eds.) *Islam, gender, and social change*. New York: Oxford University Press.
——(1999) "Reading and enjoying 'wiles of women' stories as a feminist". *Iranian Studies*, 32 (2): 203–22.
Newman, A.J. (2000) *The formative period of Twelver Shi'ism: hadith as discourse between Qum and Baghdad*. London: Routledge.
——(2006) *Safavid Iran: rebirth of a Persian empire*. London: I.B. Tauris.
——(2013) *Twelver Shi'ism: unity and diversity in the life of Islam, 632 to 1722*. Edinburgh: Edinburgh University Press.
Nimr, R. (1996) "Women in Islamic law". In Yamani, M. (ed.) *Feminism and Islam: legal and literary perspectives*. London: Ithaca.
Pauliny, J. (1998) "Some remarks on the *qisas al-anbiya'* works in Arabic literature". In Rippin, A. (ed.) *The Qur'an: formative interpretation*. Aldershot: Ashgate Variorum.
Pelly, L. (1879) *The miracle play of Hasan and Husain*. London: W.H. Allen.
Peterson, E.L. (1964) *'Ali and Mu'awiya in early Arabic tradition*. Copenhagen: Ejnar Munksgaard.
Pickthall, M.M. (2002) *The meaning of the glorious Qur'an: text and explanatory translation*. Maryland: Amana Publications. Revised edition.
Pinault, D. (1998) "Zaynab bint 'Ali and the place of the women of the households of the first imams in Shi'ite devotional literature". In Hambly, G.R.G. (ed.) *Women in the medieval Islamic world: power, patronage, and piety*. Basingstoke: Macmillan.
Qutbuddin, T. (2012) "The sermons of 'Alī ibn Abī Ṭāleb: at the confluence of the core Islamic teachings of the Qur'an and the oral, nature-based cultural ethos of seventh century Arabia". *Anuario de Estudios Medievales*, 42 (1): 201–28.
Radi, Sh. (1996) *Peak of eloquence*. 7th edn. New York: Tahrike Tarsile Qur'an. Translated by Y.T. Jibouri.
Rahman, F. (1965) *Islamic methodology in history*. Pakistan: Central Institute of Islamic Research.
Reynolds, G.S. (2007) "The Qur'anic Sarah as prototype of Mary". In Thomas, D.R. (ed.) *The Bible in Arab Christianity*. Leiden: Brill.
Ricoeur, P. (1981) *Hermeneutics and the human sciences: essays on language, action and interpretation*. Cambridge: Cambridge University Press.
Rippin, A. (1988) "The function of 'Asbab al-Nuzul' in Qur'anic exegesis". *Bulletin of the School of Oriental and African Studies*, 51 (1): 1–20.
——(1996) "The commerce of eschatology". In Wild, S. (ed.) *The Qur'an as text*. Leiden: Brill.

——(1997) "Book review: eye of the beholder: the life of Muhammad as viewed by the early Muslims. A textual analysis". *Journal of the American Oriental Society*, 117 (4): 768–70.

Rispler-Chaim, V. (1992) "Nusuz between medieval and contemporary Islamic law: the human rights aspect". *Arabica*, 39: 315–27.

Roald, A.S. (1998) "Feminist reinterpretation of Islamic sources: Muslim feminist theology in the light of the Christian tradition of feminist thought". In Ask, K. and Tjomsland, M. (eds) *Women and Islamization: contemporary dimensions of discourse on gender relations*. Oxford: Berg.

Robinson, N. (1996) *Discovering the Qur'an: a contemporary approach to a veiled text*. London: SCM Press.

——(2001) "Jesus and Mary in the Qur'an: some neglected affinities". In Rippin, A. (ed.) *The Qur'an: style and contents*. Aldershot: Ashgate.

Rosiny, S. (2001) "The tragedy of Fatima al-Zahra': in the debate of two Shiite theologians in Lebanon". In Brunner, R. and Ende, W. (eds) *The Twelver Shi'a in modern times: religious culture & political culture*. Leiden: Brill.

Rubin, U. (1995) *The eye of the beholder: the life of Muhammad as viewed by the early Muslims: a textual analysis*. Princeton: Darwin Press.

Ruether, R.R. (1975) "Home and work: women's roles and the transformation of values". *Theological Studies*. December 1975, pp. 647–59. Available from: www.ts.mu.edu/readers/content/pdf/36/36.4/36.4.4.pdf [Accessed 20.02.2014].

——(1989) *Sexism and God-talk: towards a feminist theology*. London: SCM Press Ltd.

Sabbah, F.A. (1984) *Woman in the Muslim unconscious*. New York: Pergamon Press. Translated by M.J. Lakeland.

Sachedina, A. (2000) "Woman, half-the-man? The crisis of male epistemology in Islamic jurisprudence". In Daftary, F. (ed.) *Intellectual traditions in Islam*. London: I.B. Tauris.

al-Sadr, M.B. (1989) *Our philosophy*. 2nd edn. Iran: Ansariyan Publications. Edited and translated by Sh.C. Inati.

——(1991) *Trends of history in the Qur'an*. London: al-Khoei Foundation.

——(2010) *The Islamic economic doctrine: a comparative study*. 2nd edn. MECI Ltd. Edited and translated by K.J. Shubber.

Sands, K.Z. (2006) *Sufi commentaries on the Qur'an in classical Islam*. Oxon: Routledge.

Sankari, J. (2005) *Fadlallah: the making of a radical Shi'ite leader*. London: Saqi.

Schimmel, A. (1997) *My soul is a woman: the feminine in Islam*. New York: Continuum.

Schleifer, A. (1998) *Mary, the blessed virgin of Islam*. Louisville: Islamic Texts Society.

Scott, R.M. (2009) "A contextual approach to women's rights in the Qur'an: readings of 4:34". *The Muslim World*, 99: 60–85.

Sells, M. (1999) *Approaching the Qur'an: the early revelations*. 2nd edn. Oregon: White Cloud Press.

Shaikh, S. (1997) "Exegetical violence: *nushuz* in Qur'anic gender ideology". *Journal for Islamic Studies*, 17: 49–73.

Shams al-Din, M.M. (n.d.) *The revolution of Imam al-Husayn: its impact on the consciousness of Muslim society*. [online] Available from: www.al-islam.org/revolution-imam-al-husayn-shaykh-muhammad-mahdi-shams-ad-din-al-amili [Accessed 20.02.2014].

Sharify-Funk, M. (2008) *Encountering the transnational: women, Islam and the politics of interpretation*. Aldershot: Ashgate.

Smith, J.I. and Haddad, Y.Y. (1982) "Eve: Islamic image of woman". In al-Hibri, A. (ed.) *Women and Islam*. Oxford: Pergamon.

Sonbol, A. (2001) "Rethinking women and Islam". In Haddad, Y.Y. and Esposito, J.L. (eds) *Daughters of Abraham: feminist thought in Judaism, Christianity, and Islam*. Florida: University Press of Florida.

Spellberg, D.A. (1991) "Political action and public example: 'A'isha and the battle of the camel". In Keddie, N.R. and Baron, B. (eds) *Women in Middle Eastern history: shifting boundaries in sex and gender*. New Haven and London: Yale University Press.

——(1994) *Politics, gender, and the Islamic past: the legacy of 'A'isha bint Abi Bakr*. New York: Columbia University Press.

——(1996) "Writing the unwritten life of the Islamic Eve: menstruation and the demonization of motherhood". *International Journal of Middle East Studies*, 28 (3): 305–24.

Stanley, A. (1995) *Mothers and daughters of invention: notes for a revised history of technology*. New Brunswick: Rutgers University Press.

Stanton, E.C. and the Revising Committee (1974) *The woman's Bible*. Seattle: Coalition Task Force on Women and Religion.

Stowasser, B. (1994) *Women in the Qur'an, traditions, and interpretation*. New York: Oxford University Press.

——(1996) "Women and citizenship in the Qur'an". In Sonbol, A. (ed.) *Women, the family, and divorce laws in Islamic history*. New York: Syracuse University Press.

——(1997) "The *hijab*: how a curtain became an institution and a cultural symbol". In Asfaruddin, A. and Mathias Zahniser, A.H. (eds) *Humanism, culture and language in the Near East: essays in honor of Georg Krotkoff*. Winona Lake: Eisenbrauns.

——(1998) "Gender issues and contemporary Qur'an interpretation". In Haddad, Y.Y. and Esposito, J.L. (eds) *Islam, gender, and social change*. New York: Oxford University Press.

——(2009) "The women's *bay'a* in Qur'an and *sira*". *The Muslim World*, 99 (1): 86–101.

Subhani, J. (1984) *The message*. Tehran: Be'that Foundation.

Sufi, A. (2002) *The way of Muhammad*. London: Madinah Press.

Surty, M.I.H. (1986) "Reflections on the Qur'anic concept of paradise". *The Islamic Quarterly*, 30: 179–88.

Tabataba'i, M.H. (1979) *Shi'ite Islam*. 2nd edn. New York: State University of New York Press. Edited and translated by Seyyed Hossein Nasr.

——(1980) *A Shi'ite anthology*. London: Muhammadi Trust of Great Britain & Northern Ireland. Translated by William C. Chittick, with an Introduction by Seyyed Hossein Nasr.

——(1987) *The Qur'an in Islam: its impact and influence on the life of Muslims*. London: Zahra. Edited and translated by Seyyed Hossein Nasr.

Thurlkill, M.F. (2007) *Chosen among women: Mary and Fatima in medieval Christianity and Shi'ite Islam*. Indiana: University of Notre Dame Press.

Tottoli, R. (2006) "Narrative literature". In Rippin, A. (ed.) *The Blackwell companion to the Qur'an*. Malden, MA and Oxford: Blackwell.

Varisco, D.M. (2005) *Islam obscured: the rhetoric of anthropological representation*. New York: Palgrave Macmillan.

Waddy, C. (1980) *Women in Muslim history*. London: Longman.

Wadud-Muhsin, A. (1994) *Qur'an and woman*. Kuala Lumpur: Penerbit Fajar Bakti.

Wadud, A. (2006) *Inside the gender Jihad: women's reform in Islam*. Oxford: Oneworld Publications.

"Women feed the world" (n.d.) [online]. Available from: www.fao.org/docrep/ x0262e/ x0262e16.htm [Accessed 20.02.2014].
Yusuf-Hanson, H. (n.d.) *Men and women in Islam* [online audio]. Available from: www. youtube.com/watch?v=BhEirLTl8ig [Accessed 20.02.2014].
Zaatari, Z. (2006) "The culture of motherhood: an avenue for women's civil participation in south Lebanon". *Journal of Middle East Women's Studies*, 2 (1): 33–64.

Index

Abraham: and Bilqīs (Queen of Sheba), compared 71–72; family of 79; Hagar (wife) 47, 48–51; Sarah (wife) 47–49, 50–51, 78, 79, 92
Abū Bakr 120–21, 122, 123, 125–26
Adam *see* Eve, creation of
agriculture/land, women's connection to 28, 29
ahl al-bayt 1, 5–6, 48, 79, 106–7, 182–83; *see also* Fāṭima *al-Zahrā*; Khadīja *al-Kubrā* Zaynab al-'Aqīla
Āmulī, Javādī 162–63
anger 33–34
Āsiyā, Pharaoh's wife 63–64, 65–66, 92
'Ā'isha, Prophet's wife 6, 84, 157–58
Al-'Ayyāshī, Muḥammad Ibn Mas'ūd 16–17, 18, 23

bay'at al-nisā (pledge of allegience) 87–88, 89
betrayal, wives of Noah and Lot 46
Bilqīs *see* Queen of Sheba (Bilqīs)
birth: of illegitimate child 87; "the male is not as the female" 73–74, 83, 91; Mary's annunciation and parturition 75–77
breastfeeding/suckling 61, 62–63

compassion 28, 160, 163; and vicegerency 32, 35–36; and womb 33, 35
conversion of Queen of Sheba (Bilqīs) 66–68
creation story *see* Eve, creation of
"crookedness" of women 27–28
"culture of motherhood" 127

disbelievers 68; wives of Noah and Lot 46–47
divorce 84; and *ẓihār* 88

emotions: anger 33–34; intellect vs. 162–63; jealousy 48, 84–85; *see also* compassion
equality/inequality 6–7, 184; Adam and Eve 24–25, 33; "the male is not as the female" 73–74, 83, 91; *see also ḥadīth*; marriage
"equity feminism" 2
Eve, creation of 15–16, 155; in *ḥadīth* 22–29; human duality in Qur'an and exegesis 16–22; reassessment of symbols 32–36; universal meanings 29–32
evil, women as 56–60, 155–57, 162

Fadak estate, dispossession of Fāṭima 120–21
Faḍlallāh, Muḥammad Ḥusayn 112, 127–28, 158–59, 164–65, 168
faith, deficiency of 157–59, 163–65
Fāṭima *al-Zahrā* 108–28, 136–37; among *ahl al-bayt* 109–14; daughter *see* Zaynab *al-'Aqīla*; death and burial 125–26; dispossessed of Fadak estate 120–21; *jihād* 119–28; and Mary 115, 116, 118–19, 137; names and traits 114–19; Prophet's succession declaration and death 119–20, 122–23; in Qur'an 109–10; as role model 127–28; son *see* Ḥusayn; speech (and politics) 121–28; in *sunna* 111–14
feminist perspectives 1–7
financial independence 108
financial *jihād* 108, 137
fortune, lack of 159–60, 164
"Fourteen Impeccables" 108

Ghadīr Khum, Prophet's succession declaration at 119–20
guile 52–54

ḥadīth 152–55, 172–73; creation of Eve in 22–29; definition 152; and Qur'an 8, 10, 152; research approach 9–10; and *sunna* 152–53, 171; woman's *jihād* towards husband 167–71; women as deficient in faith, fortune, and intellect 157–65; women as evil and necessary 155–57; women as flowers to be secluded 165–67; women-friendly traditions 171–72
Ḥafṣa, Prophet's wife 84
Hagar, Abraham's wife 47, 48–51, 167
ḥijāb (seclusion) 86
Al-Ḥuwayzī, 'Abd 'Alī Ibn Jumu'a al-'Arūsī 8–9, 17, 64
human duality, creation of 16–22
al-Ḥūr al-'Īn (women of paradise) 89–91, 93, 108
Ḥusayn 108; and Jesus 119; and Zaynab *al-'Aqīla* 128, 129, 131, 132–33, 134, 136

Ibn 'Arabī, Muḥammad Ibn 'Ali 34–35
Ibn Isḥāq 87–88, 120
Imam al Bāqir 8, 17, 23, 77
Imam al-Kāẓim 68
Imam al-Riḍa 8, 59, 112
Imam al-Ṣadiq 23–24, 28–29, 33, 68, 74, 77; deficiencies of women 160, 161; Fāṭima as source of light 112–13; *ḥadī th* 153; Zaynab's *jihād* 134–35
Imam 'Alī 7, 26, 32, 34, 64; deficiencies of women 157–58, 161, 165; evil 155, 156; *ḥadīth* 153; Zaynab's *jihād* 134
Imam Zayn al-'Ābindīn 86–87
Imams: and Fāṭima *al-Zahrā* 112–14, 128; knowledge of 112–13; purity of 117
imprecation, supplication and 109–10
inheritance 120–21, 122–23, 124, 126, 159–60
intellect 160–62; emotion vs. 162–63; and Islamic law 163–65; and seclusion 165
Islam, feminist perspectives on 1–7
Islamic law 2–3, 4; and spiritual equality 6–7; women's deficiencies and 161–62, 163–65

jealousy 48, 84–85
Jesus: and Ḥusayn 119; and Muhammad 83, 110; in Qur'an 80–82
jihād 64; financial 108, 137; towards husband 167–71
jihād al-nafs 20, 44–45, 67, 88–89, 106, 158, 183–84
Joseph *see* Zulaykha and Joseph

al-Kāfī (book of Shī'a traditions) 22–23
Al-Kāshānī, Muḥsin Fayḍ 26–27, 75, 82
Karbalā', battle and aftermath 129–33, 134–36
Khadīja *al-Kubrā*, Prophet's wife 107–8, 136, 137, 167
Al-Khumaynī, Rūḥullāh 82, 127
Khawla bint Khuwaylid 88–89
kinship 18–19, 33–34, 35; "verse of the relatives" 110
knowledge: Fāṭima *al-Zahrā* 111–12, 113; men and women 161; mother of Moses 62; and vicegerency 29–33, 35, 36
Al-Kulaynī, Muḥammad Ibn Ya'qūb 9

land/agriculture, women's connection to 28, 29
Lot and Noah, wives of 45–47, 92

Al-Majlisī, Muḥammad Bāqir 25
Al-Maybūdī, Rashīd al Dīn 55–56
"the male is not as the female" 73–74, 83, 91
marriage 167–71; of Adam and Eve 23–24; women's zeal towards men 28–29
Mary 72–83, 91–92, 93; annunciation and parturition 75–77; and Fāṭima *al-Zahrā* 115, 116, 118–19, 137; "the male is not as the female" 73–74, 83, 91; messengers, prophets, and "muḥaddathūn" 77–78; and Pharaoh's wife (Āsiyā) 63; prophethood 77–83; in Qur'an 78–81; *rizq* (provision/bounty) 74–75
mate (*zawj*) 18, 21, 22, 25, 29, 36
menstruation: Fāṭima *al-Zahrā* 115–16, 117–18; laughter and 47–48; religious rituals and 73, 158–59, 164
minhā 20–21, 36
misogyny, *ḥadīth* literature 27, 154, 157–58
modesty: bride of Moses 65; Muslim women 89
Moses, women in life of 60–66; bride 64–66; mother 61–63, 66, 91; Pharaoh's wife (Āsiyā) 63–64, 65–66, 92

mothers 183–84; of believers 84–87; "culture of motherhood" 127; of Moses 61–63, 66, 91; and political role 127
Mughniyya, Muḥammad Jawād 132
Muhammad *see* Prophet Muhammad
Muṣḥaf Fāṭima 112
Muṭahharī, Morteza 166

nafs (soul) 3, 17, 22, 36, 44–45; Adam and Eve 24–25; *jihād al-nafs* 20, 44–45, 67, 88–89, 106, 158, 183–84; *nafs wāḥida* 19–20; that incites to evil 56–60
Nahj al-Balāgha 153, 154
narratives of the prophets (*Qiṣaṣ al-Anbiyā'*) 43, 44
Noah and Lot, wives of 45–47, 92

obedience (to Prophet and husbands) 45, 87–89, 169–71

paradise, women of (*al-Ḥūr al-'n* and *khayrātun ḥisān*) 89–91, 93, 108
Pharaoh: and Queen of Sheba (Bilqīs), compared 72; wife of (Āsiyā) 63–64, 65–66, 92
pilgrimage rite 49–51
pledge of allegience (*bay'at al-nisā'*) 87–88, 89
politics: Fāṭima *al-Zahrā* 121–28; Queen of Sheba (Bilqīs) 70–72
polygamy 86
Prophet Muhammad 83, 92–93; *al-Mujādila* 88–89; 'Ā'isha (wife) 6, 84, 157–58; daughter *see* Fāṭima *al-Zahrā*; Ḥafṣa (wife) 84; and Jesus 83, 110; Khadīja *al-Kubrā* (wife) 107–8, 136, 137, 167; mothers of believers 84–87; pledge of allegience (*bay'at al-nisā'*) 87–88, 89; purity of 117; succession declaration and death 119–20, 122–23; Zaynab bint Jaḥsh (wife) 85–86
prophets: Mary 77–83; narratives of the (*Qiṣaṣ al-Anbiyā*) 43, 44; Noah and Lot, wives of 45–47, 92
provision/bounty (*rizq*) 74–75
purification: Mary's election and 74, 78–79; "verse of purification" 109, 130
purity of Prophet and Imams 117

Qiṣaṣ al-Anbiyā' (narratives of the prophets) 43, 44
Al-Qummī, 'Ali Ibn Ibrāhīm 8, 17, 18, 90
Queen of Sheba (Bilqīs) 66–72, 92; conversion 66–68; politics 70–72; throne, symbol of 69–70
Qur'an: female personalities 43–45, 91–93 (*see also named women*); and *ḥadīth* 152, 153, 154, 155–57; research approach 8–9, 10; and *sunna* 8, 105, 171, 181–82
Qutb, Sayyid 52

research approach 7–11
rib metaphor 27–28
rib story *see* Eve, creation of
righteousness, rewards for 110
rizq (provision/bounty) 74–75
role reversal 133

Al-Ṣadr, Muḥammad Bāqir 125
Al-Ṣadūq, Muḥammad Ibn 'Ali Bābawayh 9, 25
Sarah, Abraham's wife 47–49, 50–51, 78, 79, 92
sa'y and *zamzam* (pilgrimage rite) 49–51
seclusion 165–67; *hijāb* 86
sexuality: Adam and Eve 24, 26; *see also* Zulaykha and Joseph
Shams al-Dīn, M.M. 4, 7, 157–58, 161, 165, 166, 169–70
Sharī'atī, 'Alī 127
Shī'ī traditions/scholars 7, 8–9, 22–25, 107; creation debate 20–21; and Sunni Islam 6, 117, 118–19, 153; *see also* Fāṭima *al-Zahrā*; *sunna*
Solomon *see* Queen of Sheba (Bilqīs)
soul *see nafs*
spiritual equality 6–7
suckling/breastfeeding 61, 62–63
Sufism 3, 51, 54, 55–56; Jesus 82; Mary 76
sunna: definition 105; female personalities 105–7, 136–37 (*see also named women*); and *ḥadīth* 152–53, 171; and Qur'an 8, 105, 171, 181–82; research approach 9
supplication and imprecation 109–10
Sūrat al Qadr 81
Sūrat al-Anbiyā' 80
Sūrat l-'Imrān 72, 73, 75
Sūrat al-Naml 66
Sūrat al-Nisā' 16, 18, 32, 36
Sūrat al-Nūr 54
Sūrat al-Qaṣaṣ 61
Sūrat al-Taḥrīm 45, 63, 84, 93
Sūrat Maryam 72, 75–76, 79–80

Sūrat Ṭā Hā 65
Sūrat Yūsuf 51, 54

Al-Ṭabāṭabā'ī, Muḥammad Ḥusayn 9, 17–18, 19–20, 21, 30, 31, 34; Āsiyā (Pharaoh's wife) 63–64; childbirth 87; honouring of wives 168–69; Jesus 82; knowledge of Prophet 110; Mary 73, 74, 75, 77–78, 79, 80, 115; mother of Moses 62; *Nahj al-Balāgha* 153; obedience to the Prophet 45, 87; paradise 89; Queen of Sheba (Bilqīs) 68; Sarah 78; wiles of women 52–53; Zulaykha and Joseph 52–53, 55–56, 57–58, 59
Al-Ṭabrisī, al-Faḍl Ibn Ḥasan 8, 20
Al-Ṭusī, Muḥammad Ibn Ḥasan 8, 17, 18–19, 45, 52, 60; Mary 79, 115; Queen of Sheba (Bilqīs) 68
testimony/witnesses 161–62, 164
throne, symbol of 69–70
"Throne of God", interpretations of 34–35

veiling 165, 166
vicegerency 29–33, 35, 36
virginity 118

war, attitude of Queen of Sheba (Bilqīs) to 71
War of the Camel 157–58
wife-beating 168–69
wiles of women 51–54
witnesses/testimony 161–62, 164
wombs: and God 17, 18–19, 35; symbolism 32, 33–36
work: women's 64, 167; women's connection to agriculture/land 28, 29

zamzam and *sa'y* (pilgrimage rite) 49–51
zawj (mate) 18, 21, 22, 25, 29, 36
zawjahā 21–22
Zaynab *al-'Aqīla* 128–36, 137, 167; battle of Karbalā' and aftermath 129–33, 134–36; historical background 128–29; legacies 133–36; mother *see* Fāṭima *al-Zahrā*
Zaynab bint Jaḥsh, Muhammad's marriage to 85–86
ẓihār, divorce and 88
Zulaykha and Joseph 51–60, 92; lover and beloved 54–56; soul that incites to evil 56–60; wiles of women 51–54

Printed in Great Britain
by Amazon

54454772R00122